CW01379145

THE PLACE, ROLE AND FUNCTION OF WOMEN

IN THE CHURCH
IN THE HOME
IN THE WORKPLACE
IN SOCIETY AND
IN THE WORLD AT LARGE

BIBLICAL PRINCIPLES AND IMPERATIVES

by
Rev. Prof. Dr. Robert H. Creane

Professor of Systematic Theology
Urban Divinity Ministries

Urban Divinity Unit UK Limited
Affiliated to Canada Christian College and School of Graduate Theological Studies
11-13 Oughton Road, Highgate, Birmingham, U.K.

"Study to show thyself approved unto God,
a workman that needeth
not to be ashamed,
rightly dividing
the Word of
truth",
(2 Tim. 2 v.15)

Urban Divinity Ministries Publications
P.O. Box 55, 57 Parkmore, Townland of Balteagh, Craigavon,
County Armagh, BT64 2AE

in association with
The Bible Christian Mission
and
RHC Consultancy Services

Scripture quotations are from the

Authorised Version of the Bible
(King James)

and

The Scottish Metrical Psalms

First published 2009
by
Urban Divinity Ministries Publications

ISBN -13: 978-0-9561911-0-6

Urban Divinity Ministries
Covenant School of Theology UDU Ireland

To

My wife, Rhoda,

With deep gratitude

For the love, family, home, and friendship

The Lord in His providence

Has graced us to share

SECOND NEWTOWNHAMILTON PRESBYTERIAN CHURCH

COUNTY ARMAGH

WHERE REV. PROF. DR. R. H. AND MRS. CREANE WERE MARRIED

REV. PROF. DR. R.H. AND MRS. CREANE
WEDDING PHOTOGRAPH, 14TH APRIL 1965

"For the Lord thy God hath blessed thee in all the works of thy hand: He knoweth thy walking through this great wilderness: these forty years the Lord thy God hath been with thee; thou hast lacked nothing", (Deut. 2 v.7)

Rev. Prof. Dr. R.H. and Mrs. Creane

Forty Years later!!

2005

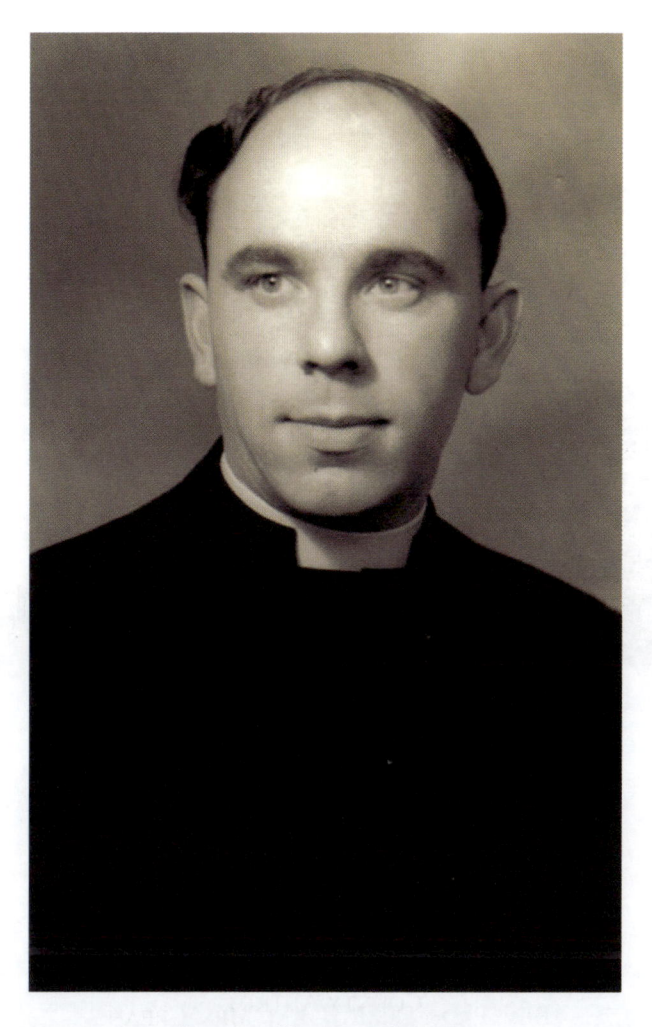

ROBERT HAROLD CREANE

A licentiate of the Southern Presbytery, when he was ordained to the office of the Gospel Ministry and installed pastor of Dervock Reformed Presbyterian Congregation, Co. Antrim, at a special meeting on 21ST OCTOBER 1964

DERVOCK REFORMED PRESBYTERIAN CHURCH
(COVENANTER)

COUNTY ANTRIM

WHERE REV. PROF. DR. R. H. CREANE WAS MINISTER

CONTENTS

	Page Number
Prologue	19
Acknowledgements	24
Foreword One by The Right Rev. Dr. J. S. Carson	29
Foreword Two by Rev. Dr. S. J. Millar	31
Foreword Three by Rev. Dr. Wm. J. Malcolmson	34
Commendation by Dr. M. W. J. Phelan	37
Preface by Rev. G. Thomas	40
Introduction	42
Chapter One **The Scripture cannot be broken**	50
The Claims of Scripture	51
The Infallible Truth	52
The Divine Order, Equality and Male Headship	54
Man not at liberty to alter the Divine Word	66
Solemn Warning and Sanction	67
Liberalism and Ecumenism causing Havoc and Destruction	69
The Only Basis of Belief and Practice	71
God is not the author of Confusion	72
Upholding Biblical Authority	75
Chapter Two **The Basic Principle of Headship**	82
Creation Order and Leadership	87
New Testament Distinctions in Roles	90
The Devices of Feminism	92
Damaging Effects of Radical Feminism	95
The Subtle Strategy of the Enemy	98

Chapter Three   101
Male and Female in the Image of God

     The Image of God defaced   103

     The Image of God renewed and restored   108

     The Weaker Vessel   112

     Heirs Together of the Grace of Life   114

     Choosing a Marriage Partner   116

     Man made to Serve   119

Chapter Four   123
An Helpmeet for the Man

     A Suitable Companion   125

     Marriage Instituted by God   128

     A Union of Body, Soul and Spirit   133

     Christian Morality and the Purpose of Sex   134

     Marriage Honourable and the Bed Undefiled   141

     The Sacredness of Marriage and Sex   144

     The Secret of a Happy Marriage   150

     Sacrificial Love endures   153

     Three Forms of Love: Eros, Phileo, and Agape   155

Chapter Five   160
Headship, Head Covering and Dress

     Honour and Dignity   162

     Head Covering a Scriptural Requirement   165

     Liberty and Biblical Obligations   168

     The Christian Woman and Modern Feminism   171

     Modesty, Humility and Godly Fear   172

     Distinctive Femininity   174

     Unisex an abomination   176

     The Meaning of "kephale" – "head"   179

Chapter Six   182
Women in the Church

    The Offices of the Church   184

    Presbyters   187

    Deacons   190

    The Importance of proper Church Structures   193

    Let the Women learn   197

    Women keep silence in Church   202

    Women and Ordination.   208

    Different Functions   217

    Scripture prohibits certain Roles by Women   221

    Scripture prohibits Women as Deacons   225

    The Place of Women in the Church   228

    The Labour of Women in the Gospel   231

    Submission, Teaching and Authority   234

    Adornment, Meekness and a Quiet Spirit   241

    The Design and Role of Women   245

    The Divine Pattern for the Church   249

    The Great Commission   253

Chapter Seven   257
Leadership and Responsibility in the Church

    The Glory of the Visible Church   259

    The Qualifications required of Leaders   262

    The Responsibilities to be Undertaken   272

    Shared Leadership: Elders and Deacons   273

    Restoring Leadership to its Rightful Place   275

Chapter Eight   279
Women in the Home

    Praise of the Virtuous Woman   281

    Childbearing and Motherhood   283

    Home-making, Love and Friendship   288

Duties and Responsibilities of Wife and Mother	292
Discipline, Relationships and Contentment	296
Building on a Firm Foundation	300
Family the Basic Unit of Society	305
Real Love is Giving	310
The Evils of Society	319
God's Design for the Home	320

Chapter Nine 324
The Single Woman

The Challenge of Singleness	326
Happiness in Singleness	330
Homemaking par Excellence	332
Godliness and Zeal	335

Chapter Ten 339
Women in the Workplace

Social Engineering weakens the Family	340
Peculiar Circumstances may arise	344
Invaluable Contribution to Society	352
Promotion of Women in the Workplace	354
Diligence, Integrity and Attitude	357
Perseverance and the Humble Spirit	360
Witnessing as Salt and Light	361

Chapter Eleven 364
Women in the World

Biblical Instructions to Various Groups	366
The Aged Men	367
The Aged Women	369
The Young Women	372
The Young Men	375
Servants	377

Chapter Twelve 380
Women of Conviction, Faith and Truth

    Going from Strength to Strength   382

    The Perspicuity of the Scriptures   388

    True Prosperity   389

    Sins that are Offensive before God   390

    The Final Court of Appeal   392

    Successful Living   394

    The Virtues Women should Possess   395

    The Testings Women should Expect   399

    God's Universal Dominion and Plan   407

    Truth and Righteousness   415

Conclusion 419

Epilogue 427

Appendix One 436

    Worship
     Psalms and Hymns and Spiritual Songs unaccompanied

Appendix Two 445

    Fairview Reformed Presbyterian Church

Appendix Three 448

    The Bible Christian Mission

Appendix Four 458

    Urban Divinity Ministries

Appendix Five 469

    Brief Personal Profile on Rev. Prof. Dr. R. H. Creane with interview, by Rev. Dr. Wm. J. Malcolmson

What They Say . . . . . Reviews

    Dr. S. J. McCammick   481
    Rev. Canon B. T. Blacoe   483

Rev. S. Barnes	485
Pastor V. Maxwell	486
Rev. W. W. Porter	487
Pastor J. Hughes	488
Dr. A. R. Passmore	489
Rev. T. Boyle	490
Rev. F. F. Greenfield	491

Four Closing Scripts

Rev. Prof. Dr. C. L. Ryan	492
Rev. Dr. S. N. Morgan	493
James A. Dickson	495
Maurice Grant	498

Scripture Index

Old Testament	500
New Testament	510

Word Index	529
Bibliography	549
Other Published Works by the Author	564
Other Theses and Dissertations by the Author	565
Miscellanea	567-576

PROLOGUE

I humbly and reverently acknowledge, as an undeserving sinner, my thankfulness and praise to Almighty God:

(1) For His "goodness and mercy" (Psalm 23 v.6) extended towards me through sovereign grace in calling me savingly unto Himself through Christ by His Word and Spirit in salvation, and to be a minister of the Gospel, a preacher of the Word and Bible lecturer "according to the gift of the grace of God given unto me by the effectual working of His power. Unto me, who am less than the least of all saints, is this grace given, that I should preach among the Gentiles the unsearchable riches of Christ", (Eph. 3 v.7-8);

(2) For His enabling power and grace, in the face of much opposition in the battle for truth and righteousness, to remain steadfast in the service of Christ, the King and Head of His Church, in various spheres of ministry, wherever in Providence one's lot has been cast. "And God is able to make all grace abound toward you; that ye, always having all sufficiency in all things, may abound to every good work", (2 Cor. 9 v.8); and

(3) For His sustaining grace and guidance as a servant of the Lord, a servant of the Word, and a servant of the people of Christ, to continue with fervency and perseverance in the enormous task, yet most rewarding with rich fellowship, of providing theological education and Bible training to students world-wide, with the unceasing burden of a lecturer's heart and a teacher's desire to uphold, maintain, and defend the truth of God's inspired and inerrant Word, and by the help and power of the Holy Spirit, proclaiming a proper relationship between sound doctrine and sincere heavenly zeal in evangelism.

> "The Lord is the portion of mine inheritance and of my cup: Thou maintainest my lot. The lines are fallen unto me in pleasant places; yea, I have a goodly heritage", (Psalm 16 v.5-6).

I am very conscious of feebleness and weakness, yet in dependence on Divine grace, greatly exercised in heart to remain steadfast and faithful to the Word of God in the most noble and illustrious service of the Lord day by day. Out of love and devotion to the Saviour, and with deepest conviction being fully persuaded by the guiding Hand of Providence, it is my earnest hope, desire, and prayer, to persevere and "press toward the mark for the prize" (Phil. 3 v.14) in active Christian work and labour for the Master, God-willing, while health and strength permit during the remaining days of my earthly pilgrimage and sojourn. While deeply acknowledging my utter unworthiness and inadequacy, I nevertheless fully realise the clear call of God upon my life over many years to a Bible-teaching ministry, and praise the Lord for His grace, help, and enabling power to guard zealously and righteously an authentic and uncompromising witness for:

(1) a fully inspired, inerrant, and infallible Bible, originally given as the Word of God in the Old and New Testaments, and that its teaching and authority are absolute and final as the sole and all-sufficient rule in all matters of faith and practice, providentially preserved by God and able to make men and women, boys and girls, wise unto salvation, through faith in the Lord Jesus Christ: "Thou hast magnified Thy Word above all Thy name", (Psalm 138 v.2);

(2) the belief and persuasion that the accuracy and trustworthiness of the Authorised Version of the Bible is technically as well as spiritually superior to all other translations and is the best and most faithful translation to be found in the English language based on the Hebrew Masoretic Text as the textual basis of the Old Testament,

and the Greek Textus Receptus as the text which underlies the New Testament; that there should be no compromise with corrupted and inferior versions of the Bible which deny the central doctrines and cardinal truths of the Christian Faith; and that the importance of preserving the use and purity of Holy Scripture is vital to the true worship of God, not only in this generation but also for those to come: "Seek ye out of the Book of the Lord, and read", (Isaiah 34 v.16);

(3) the perpetual obligation and due observance of the Christian Sabbath and the means of grace: "I was in the Spirit on the Lord's Day" (Rev. 1 v.10) . . . . . "Not forsaking the assembling of ourselves together, as the manner of some is" (Heb. 10 v.25);

(4) the raising of a strong voice against the evils and compromise of Church and State on all matters of doctrine and practice that are contrary to sound Biblical teaching and at variance with The Scripture: "To the law and to the testimony: if they speak not according to this Word, it is because there is no light in them", (Isaiah 8 v.20);

(5) the promotion of expository, evangelical preaching of the Word of God, the true well-being of men, and earnestly proclaiming the present great and urgent need of reformation and revival in both Church and Nation: "My people are destroyed for lack of knowledge", (Hosea 4 v.6);

(6) the purity of worship, doctrine, form of Church government, and discipline that are founded upon and agreeable to The Scripture: "He that hath My commandments, and keepeth them, he it is that loveth

Me" (John 14 v.21) . . . . . "Hold fast the form of sound words" (2 Tim. 1 v.13); and

(7) the glory of God, our sole aim, by standing firm for Biblical Truth upholding the principles of New Testament Christianity with loyalty, courage, and wholehearted devotion to the Lord Jesus Christ, the only King and Head of the Church: "But grow in grace, and in the knowledge of our Lord and Saviour Jesus Christ" (2 Peter 3 v.18) . . . . . "to Him be glory and dominion for ever and ever. Amen" (Rev. 1 v.6).

I clearly state unashamedly and without apology that the ground upon which I stand is the Word of God. The Scripture of the Old and New Testaments, commonly called the Bible, is the only infallible rule to direct us how we may glorify and enjoy Him. By showing a deep reverence for the Holy Bible, this book is presented and committed to the Providence and Grace of Him Whose "name is called The Word of God", (Rev. 19 v.13).

נָבִיא אָקִים לָהֶם מִקֶּרֶב אֲחֵיהֶם כָּמוֹךָ וְנָתַתִּי דְבָרַי בְּפִיו וְדִבֶּר אֲלֵיהֶם אֵת כָּל־אֲשֶׁר אֲצַוֶּנּוּ׃

Hebrew text of Deuteronomy 18 v.18

"I will raise them up a Prophet from among their brethren, like unto thee, and will put My words in His mouth; and He shall speak unto them all that I shall command Him".

"Ότι ἐγὼ ἐξ ἐμαυτοῦ οὐκ ἐλάλησα· ἀλλ' ὁ πέμψας με πατήρ, αὐτός μοι ἐντολὴν δέδωκε, τί εἴπω καὶ τί λαλήσω.

Greek text of John 12 v.49

"For I have not spoken of Myself; but the Father which sent Me, He gave Me a commandment, what I should say, and what I should speak".

Ἃ καὶ λαλοῦμεν, οὐκ ἐν διδακτοῖς ἀνθρωπίνης σοφίας λόγοις, ἀλλ' ἐν διδακτοῖς Πνεύματος, πνευματικοῖς πνευματικὰ συγκρίνοντες.

Greek text of 1 Corinthians 2 v.13

"Which things also we speak, not in the words which man's wisdom teacheth, but which the Holy Ghost teacheth; comparing spiritual things with spiritual".

Robert H Creane

Principal
Covenant School of Theology
Urban Divinity Unit
Ireland

ACKNOWLEDGEMENTS

As I began writing this book, my wife and I had just celebrated our 40th wedding anniversary. All the members of our immediate families arranged to come together for a Special Dinner Evening at the Slieve Donard Hotel, Newcastle (where we had our wedding reception), to give thanks to the Lord and to celebrate, and they presented us with flight and hotel vouchers to return to Nice for a holiday where we spent our honeymoon. Together we have been involved in service for the Master for over four decades and we continue to grow in grace, love and knowledge of Him in the midst of weakness and struggles. Jesus Christ is the King and Head of His Church, and we acknowledge we are still learning that "His grace is sufficient" and His "strength is made perfect in weakness", (2 Cor. 12 v.9). "And God is able to make all grace abound toward you; that ye, always having all sufficiency in all things, may abound to every good work", (2 Cor. 9 v.8).

Realising the deep value of the loyal support of a true help meet of over forty years, I am grateful for the wholehearted love and encouragement of my wife, Rhoda, and that of my family in my calling to engage in theological and pastoral ministry. We humbly acknowledge God's goodness and mercy, and by His grace pray that together we might yet be long blessed in this world in the Lord's service with all the blessings of that everlasting Covenant which is ordered in all things and sure, (2 Sam. 23 v.5). We are thankful that in the Lord all the members throughout our extended family are made partakers of the redemption purchased by Christ, being united to Him by the power of the Holy Spirit "unto salvation to everyone that believeth" (Rom. 1 v.16), and enjoying the privileges of "the sons of God" (1 John 3 v.1).

I was greatly privileged in the providence of God to be born into and brought up in the fellowship of a Christian home. Having come to faith in Christ as a young teenager "by hearing the Word of God" (Rom. 10 v.17), I soon became involved in work, witness and mission for the Lord, and eventually finding my true vocation in preaching, lecturing and teaching --- "Holding forth the Word of life", (Phil. 2 v.16). I praise God for believing parents, the good example and early training in formative years, for household salvation, and in thanksgiving rejoice along with my four brothers and two sisters, together with our spouses, children and grandchildren, who have come to know the Lord, gladly serving Him, and are enabled by the grace of God, even in the midst of trials and suffering, to testify to the saving and keeping power of our souls "to Him in well doing, as unto a faithful Creator", (1 Peter 4 v.19).

I express my most sincere and profound gratitude to Mr. and Mrs. G. Kenny (George and Helen) for their particular expertise and professionalism, which has proved invaluable in the production of this book. Between them they typed the complete text and made valuable comments regarding accuracy, presentation, and layout thereof. I greatly appreciate their help, friendship and encouragement throughout the entire project. Any weaknesses, errors, shortcomings, and defects that remain are entirely my responsibility. I am deeply indebted to George and Helen for the excellence of their work and the kindly patience with me during the typing and re-typing of the manuscript of an ever-growing volume. As on previous occasions it is always a pleasure to assign such an undertaking to them knowing that due care and practical attention would be given throughout.

I appreciate the opportunity to acknowledge and pay a word of tribute to Rev. J. Stafford Carson, who for a number of years was the Academic Dean and Associate Professor of Practical Theology at Westminster Theological Seminary, Philadelphia, USA, before coming to minister in First Portadown Presbyterian Church in 2005. I am grateful to him for writing a Foreword. His masterful exposition of Scripture is a blessing to many and gives great encouragement of how Christians can speak by life and lip of the grace of God in Christ to a generation that has largely rejected the teaching of Scripture and which has little or no place for the claims of Bible Truth. He passionately urges his flock that in order to be effective witnesses to Christ in our day and age, we will have to go back to the Bible and learn to present our faith as the Word of God directs: "Teach me Thy way, O Lord, and lead me in a plain path . . . . . Wait on the Lord: be of good courage, and He shall strengthen thine heart", (Psalm 27 v.11 and 14). As a faithful expositor and teacher of the Word, his godly influence infuses action in the service of Christ, and his vigorous leadership is a model for ministry in the Christian Church.

I also warmly welcome and value the fellowship and contribution by way of a Foreword from the pen of Rev. Dr. S. James Millar, Sovereign Grace Fellowship, Cairnbulg, Aberdeen. He is a well-seasoned Scottish stalwart with a deep passion and prayerful heart for careful Biblical exposition. In a day of superficial discipleship, and of ailing and dying Churches, I humbly acknowledge his sober and practical perspective on the vital theme of this book which give much encouragement to the believer who knows how to withstand the enemy and what spiritual weapons to take up against him. We must defeat him by "taking the shield of faith . . . . . the helmet of salvation, and the Sword of the Spirit, which is the Word of God" (Eph. 6 v.16-17), through lives that bear fruit and spread the truth to the glory of God. Every true believer is a vessel snatched from the power of the devil, "a brand plucked out of the fire" (Zech. 3 v.2), whom Satan wants back "that he may sift you as wheat" (Luke 22 v.31). The genuine Christian is in a fierce spiritual battle and we should not underestimate an enemy who is cunning and deceitful in drawing us away from following the Word of God. Dr. Millar expresses deep concern about how the ecumenical, feminist, and other movements have had a profound effect upon our society, which frequently undermine the authority of Scripture in the arguments they use, albeit falsely, to support their claims. He strongly points out that the challenges facing women in today's world must be met with the guidance and teaching of the Holy Bible. The true Christian woman who desires to obey and honour God, can confidently assert that the feminine virtues described in Titus 2 and other Scriptures, have transformed her life. That being so, she will witness and appeal to countless other women to live for God and allow the Biblical principles help obtain a comprehensive grasp of their essential disciplines, specific roles, and distinctive functions, in the Church, in the Home, in the Workplace, in Society, and in the World at large.

I would furthermore record my sincere gratitude to Rev. Dr. Wm. J. Malcolmson for reading the manuscript, writing a Foreword and also the brief profile and interview at the end of the book. His encouragement and guidance is unbounded, and I greatly appreciate his inspiration and unwavering support as a friend and colleague throughout many years. I have drawn heavily on his expertise and knowledge, and that of others, which has proved to be of enormous help and assistance in the development of this book with helpful comments and practical suggestions in the field of

Biblical hermeneutics and interpretation, so that the meaning of Scripture is truly and accurately apprehended and applied. He deeply shares my Scriptural convictions and Reformation principles, and I warmly welcome his cordial enthusiasm for the need of such a treatise, so that the ordinary student, if led at all into long-continued and successful searching of the Scriptures, must become interested in the practical work of exposition. I wish to thank Dr. Malcolmson most profoundly, for challenging my thinking about the Biblical text while at the same time encouraging me to minister and teach in response to Divine authority in accordance with the Word of God. Students and other colleagues and friends have also challenged and exercised my mind, and they receive my humble gratitude.

It was a very moving and humbling experience to receive warmest greetings, heartfelt encouragement and words of undeserving commendation from Dr. M. W. J. Phelan. As an accomplished writer and Biblical scholar it is always uplifting and a joy to read his works. In his writings he not only deepens our understanding of the Truth of Scripture but also enhances our ability to impart the message of the Christian Faith to a world so desperately in need of it. As a firm believer in Christ and a strong advocate that the Words of Scripture are true and its message powerful, he fervently upholds the fact that the Bible conveys the infallible promise of God, its Author, which will not return unto Him void, but will certainly accomplish His intended purpose (Isaiah 55 v.11). All who have benefited in particular from reading his book, entitled, 'The Inspiration of the Pentateuch', are deeply grateful for his clear exhortation, valuable exposition, and sound exegeses of the Biblical text as Divinely given, ever bearing in mind that God's Word is inerrant and infallible, and as such is the only authority in all matters of faith and practice.

It is always an enormous privilege to share mutual understanding and enjoy sweet fellowship in the glorious Gospel of our Lord and Saviour Jesus Christ with so many friends and fellow-labourers in Christ's Vineyard. With a common desire and zeal to hold fast the purity of the Word of God, it is a blessed thing to encourage each other in the Lord (1 Sam. 30 v.6). As servants of Christ we are called upon to be faithful in declaring "all the counsel of God" (Acts 20 v.27), and to maintain our vigilance "in the midst of a crooked and perverse nation" (Phil. 2 v.15) in defending the Doctrines of Grace to the glory of God. Among the stalwarts, I am most grateful for the warm encouragement and loyal support of Dr. S. Barnes, Canon B. T.

Blacoe, Dr. T. Boyle, Dr. F. F. Greenfield, Dr. J. Hughes, Dr. S. J. McCammick, Dr. V. Maxwell, Dr. A. Passmore, and Dr. W. W. Porter. The real poignancy of such benefit and fellowship is the reassuring confidence and advice not to rest any conclusions on the thoughts and opinions of great theologians, eminent though they may be, but always be careful to "be fully persuaded" (Rom. 14 v.5) by The Scripture alone. 'Sola Scriptura' was the great watchword of the Reformers, Covenanters, Puritans, Martyrs and Heroes of the Faith down through the centuries --- and the Church today needs to get back to a full appreciation of the revelation, inspiration, inerrancy, authority, sufficiency and truth of the Word of God. "For all the promises of God in Christ are yea, and in Him Amen", (2 Cor. 1 v.20).

As the book has finally taken shape, I want to thank Rev. Geoff Thomas for writing the Preface, and also Rev. Prof. Dr. C. L. Ryan, Rev. Dr. S. N. Morgan, James A. Dickson and Maurice Grant for their Closing Scripts. I am indebted to these distinguished friends and owe them a word of sincere gratitude for their keen interest in the subjects here dealt with, which has greatly encouraged me to present them in this form to the best of my ability. As a teacher of Biblical studies, it is gratifying to mark the eagerness with which people await the publication of this book. One can have no greater reward than to see others, even with divergent interests, fired with enthusiasm to uphold, maintain and defend the Divine inspiration and inerrancy of Holy Scripture as the sole authority and only infallible rule in all matters of faith and life. "Thy Word is truth", (John 17 v.17).

And last, but by no means least, my warm and sincere thanks to Mr. Stephen Gregory, B.A., M.A., Librarian, at the Union Theological College, Belfast, for all his help in securing proper bibliographical information and providing invaluable assistance in the final days.

The book may be helpful and useful for individual benefit and group discussion, and in His providence, my prayer is that God will be pleased to use it to His glory.

Robert H. Creane

FOREWORD ONE

Matters of religion and faith need to be stated as clearly as possible, and in the modern debate with regards to the role of men and women in the Church and society we need say clearly what our foundations are, and the implications of building our beliefs and practices on those foundations. Orthodox Christians believe that our doctrinal convictions should not be based upon human wisdom. The Christian faith in its entirety ought to be based upon God's own self-revelation rather than the conflicting opinions of men or their untrustworthy speculations. In 1 Cor. 2 v.5, the Apostle Paul expresses what it is that should control and guide the beliefs of the Christians in Corinth. In 1 Cor. 2 v.4 he says, "And my speech and my preaching was not with enticing words of man's wisdom, but in demonstration of the Spirit and of power". Why is Paul making that point? Verse 5 says: "That your faith should not stand in the wisdom of men, but in the power of God".

Paul puts the power of God on one side, and the wisdom of men on the other. And not only is the power of God and the wisdom of men in two different categories, he says, but "Your faith should not stand in the wisdom of men". You should never build your faith on human wisdom, he says.

In the matter of the roles of men and women, we are facing a situation where human speculation and human wisdom are being pitted against the plain words of Scripture.

One New Testament professor at an evangelical seminary surveyed all the scholarly articles that had been written about the New Testament passages that dealt with the role of men and women. And he noted that it was only in 1969 that a progressive, revisionist view of passages such as 1 Timothy 2 began to appear in the literature of the academy. But in the period since 1969, there has been a whole flood of articles trying to revise and re-interpret the traditional view of those passages which speak about male headship. He concludes that the rise in the progressive interpretation of these passages followed the women's movement of the 1960s and "is indebted significantly, and at times possibly culpably, to the prevailing social climate rather than to the Biblical text".

This work by Rev. Prof. Dr. R. H. Creane challenges that prevailing social climate. It reflects a Biblical perspective on this important discussion and shows that when it comes to our beliefs and practices with regard to the roles of men and women in Church and in society we ought to be guided by God speaking plainly in Scripture rather than by the mood and tone of the age in which we live. Dr. Creane discusses a number of areas where our understanding of the original intention of the Creator has been challenged and needs to be reviewed so that our thinking and behaviour are brought into line with the clear teaching of the Bible. Those who are interested in pursuing this discussion from a Biblical basis will be interested to read this wide-ranging review of the current debate, and will be encouraged by it to base their beliefs and practices not "in the wisdom of men, but in the power of God", (1 Cor. 2 v.5).

J. Stafford Carson

Moderator of the General Assembly 2009-2010
First Presbyterian Church (Edenderry)
Portadown
Co. Armagh

FIRST PORTADOWN PRESBYTERIAN CHURCH

FOREWORD TWO

It was a great privilege to read Rev. Prof. Dr. Creane's manuscript with the request to comment on the exegeses of it, and I am greatly honoured to be invited to write a Foreword to it. Over a number of years our fellowship and friendship have grown, and I have come to understand the commitment that the author has concerning the full council of God's Word, and appreciate his strong walk of faith by which he proclaims the glorious Truths of Holy Scripture.

The title may be one that raises a few eyebrows, but this book clearly demonstrates a most needful work that is long overdue in the Christian Church. The contents of each chapter are broken down into clearly defined headings, which make for both an easy reading and understanding of his treatise. We are left in no doubt as to the true nature of the downfall of the Church in our society today, and I would like to see this book reach the Christian best seller list.

The Church at large urgently needs to be solemnly reminded of the sovereign authority of God's Word. This is a book of instruction that is true to the Bible. The questions that the author poses and answers are those that the Church shuns in this day of political correctness so as to accommodate and pander to the ecumenical, feminist, and other 'religious' movements by sitting in the mire of her own choosing. The earnest desire that Prof. Creane has for the Church to return in obedience to the inspired and inerrant Word of God cannot be overstressed or echoed sufficiently.

The Church of the 21st century seems to take for itself an authority that she does not find in Scripture, thus the altering of the text of Holy Scripture to suit her own purposes, the downplaying of the need of the New Birth and salvation by faith alone in Christ alone, and thereby holding communions which she calls inter-faith. This robs God of His sovereign Personage as revealed in the Lordship of Jesus Christ and makes the Church appear more authoritative than the Scriptures. Prof.

Creane rightly states that with the spirit of apathy and indifference prevailing at the present time throughout Church and State, and in that "the doctrines of men" (Matt. 15 v.9) now supersede the teaching of Holy Scripture, there is strong delusion throughout the land. The teaching of the Word of God is today largely despised, greatly rejected, and even wholly abandoned concerning the Place, Role and Function of Women within the structure of a Christian Church and society.

Most emphatically, the author does not advocate discrimination against women, but clearly demonstrates to the Church her error in the way that she now promotes the woman's function often above Scriptural authority. The need for women in the Church is not questioned; in fact he upholds and honours their position in the correct light of Scripture. The place of women is just as important as men in the Church, but it must be honourable to God and not dishonour His name or disobey His Word.

The text on the title page that has been chosen, Psalm 127 v.1, illustrates the deep thought and prayerful study that have gone into this dissertation, for it is true that man cannot build the House of God. Even the Temple of Solomon when finished could not be called the House of God until His Shikina Glory came down and filled it. Therefore we labour in vain when we attempt to build the Church of God that is not in accordance with His Divine Word, plan and ordinance. This book teaches us that we must build according to the commands of Scripture alone.

The Church today in her deliberate action of putting women before Scriptural authority has encouraged the world at large to do likewise all the more. With the voice of the Church keeping silence, the world now holds no respect for her, and furthermore turns its back upon the Creator and even disputes His being.

We are indebted to the author and thank him for a very inspiring work, and pray that the Lord will use it to bring again a light into a dark world. May the God of our salvation, bless all who read this book. To Him be the glory.

"Teach me Thy way, O Lord, and lead me in a plain path", (Psalm 27 v.11).

S. James Millar

Chairman
The Scottish Reformation Society
Beth-Uel
Lambhillock
Auchnagatt
Aberdeenshire

BALLIOL COLLEGE, OXFORD,
of which JOHN WYCLIFFE (1324 - 1384), a leading
theologian, was elected MASTER in 1360

Wycliffe became known as 'THE MORNING STAR OF THE REFORMATION', graduated with a Doctor of Divinity degree in 1372, and in 1378 authored the book, 'THE TRUTH OF HOLY SCRIPTURE'. He died of a stroke in 1384, and in 1428, forty-two years later, his bones were dug up and burnt to ashes and cast into the River Swift.

FOREWORD THREE

I am both privileged and honoured to have been requested to write a foreword to this book on "The Place, Role and Function of Women: in the Church, in the Home, in the Workplace, in Society, and in the World at large . . . . . Biblical Principles and Imperatives".

The author is to be congratulated sincerely in dealing with matters of vital importance concerning the Christian Churches, the State, and the individual. This particular work is very instructive. It is most illuminating and invaluable, and has been greatly needed for a long time because of the rapid falling away of standards of numerous Churches in doctrine and worship which ultimately has led to the lowering of spiritual standards and an absence of moral principles in the nation. Spiritual declension, moral decadence, barrenness, and corruption are widespread around us today.

This book is written in a most able and scholarly fashion which firmly emphasises the Biblical teaching on this vast and complex subject, with a fervent call for a return to the truths of the Bible. It is patently clear. It is openly disturbing. It is penetratingly challenging, and reveals a deep conviction in the author's heart and mind for the glory of God and for reformation and revival in the Churches.

Scriptural Truth is presented with great accuracy and there is an earnest faithfulness of exegeses of the Biblical text calling Christian people and Churches unto obedience to the Word of God in all matters of faith and life. Unfortunately many today have almost lost their identity as a people of God, and the need for repentance is therefore great.

Rev. Prof. Dr. Creane has demonstrated in these pages the source of his Christian strength in Pastoral Ministry and Practical Theology, and has given us a lively and fitting book which is both lucid and easily readable. The format, structure, and content thereof are based upon a sound Biblical Theology and not upon the passing ideas and shallow philosophies of men.

This book will greatly humble and rightly disturb the reader who comes to it with an honest and open mind. It is a clarion call for obedience to the Word of God in every area of our lives. It calls those Churches who have disobeyed and neglected The Scripture, (1) to honour, magnify, and glorify the Lord, (2) to obey the Great Commission of Matthew 28 v.19-20, (3) to return to the teaching of the great doctrines of grace, (4) to urge the people of God to "walk worthy of the vocation wherewith" they have been called (Eph.4 v.1), and (5) to persevere to the end: "This is the victory that overcometh the world, even our faith", (1 John 5 v.4).

In seeking to be diligent and faithful to the Divine revelation of inspired Scripture, this book expresses a Biblical Theology that is imminently exegetical, systematic, historical, and practical. It challenges the Government of the day to bring in laws that are founded upon the Word of God rather than popular opinion contrary to the Bible. It calls for Christian people to "read, mark, learn, and inwardly digest the Word of God, to lay it up in their hearts, and to practice it daily in their lives".

Another important feature of this book is that Scripture references are printed in full in the words of the Authorised King James Version of the Bible, which still remains far and away the best translation of the Scriptures in the English language.

The book firmly exposes the Spiritual apathy, the indifference to the things of God, and the growing complacency towards false teachers, which abound in Christian circles and Churches throughout Western Christendom. This book is not written for mere pleasure or comfort. It is inspiring and nourishing, and compels the honest reader to turn to God in repentance and follow Him in the way of truth and righteousness.

If we are all prepared to take heed and follow the Biblical directions of this book, there will inevitably follow a vital transformation and glorious reformation that is sorely needed, which in turn will lead to the joy and blessing of revival in true religion that is honouring to Christ the King and Head of the Church.

I highly commend this book to the Christian public and trust in the providence of God it will command a wide readership and pray that the commands of Scripture will be obeyed and put into practice by the Lord's people everywhere. We thank the author for so courageously challenging "the spirit of this godless age" in calling the Church, the State, and the individual to "return again" (Jer. 3 v.1) to the Lord, and to live according to His ways, to the glory of God.

"Turn us, O God of our salvation, and cause Thine anger toward us to cease. Wilt Thou not revive us again: that Thy people may rejoice in Thee? Shew us Thy mercy, O Lord, and grant us Thy salvation", (Psalm 85 v.4, 6-7).

Wm. J. Malcolmson

Congregational Reformed Church
Cregagh
Belfast

CONTEMPORARY MURAL TESTIMONY
TO THE LEGACY OF CROMWELL

COMMENDATION

In this excellent book, 'The Place, Role and Function of Women', the author has brought before readers a truly exhaustive study of the rôle of women that is characterised by fidelity to Scripture and real scholarship. This work is bound to be extremely controversial however, and will certainly upset, if not alarm, Liberal Theologians and their followers. This is because the author's analysis of his subject is based exclusively upon the eternal Truth of the Scriptures, while the agenda of Feminism and Gender-Studies, as with Liberalism generally, is built upon the wisdom of this world, which is utterly antagonistic to the Word of God.

This controversy must not be avoided however, it must be addressed head-on, with boldness and determination, so that contemporary society generally, and believers in particular, may discern its key issues with the utmost clarity. That objective has certainly been achieved by Prof. Creane. For the most part, true Christians are keenly aware of the assaults made upon the Word of God by proponents of biologic, geologic, and cosmic evolution; by those who advocate the views of cynical Source Criticism; and by the adherents of Post-Modernism. But Prof. Creane has highlighted another area that is every bit as vital, and which contains spiritual dangers which are just as deadly. In fact, it may even be the case that these dangers are more sinister simply because they relate to a field of study that frequently is regarded as being less critical than these other issues, yet it is unquestionably of fundamental importance. The subjects dealt with by the author impinge directly upon every Christian individual, family, Church, and organisation; no believer may remain aloof from the subject.

The Rev. Prof. Dr. has rendered ordinary believers an incalculable service by his forthright presentation of the facts in a manner which is particularly easy to read, and which is so marked by his graciousness as to prevent the possibility of any charge of misogyny. However, there is another aspect to the author's work, which is more important still. This book has the potential to make a key contribution to the current debate on Feminism within a Christian context, and even to make a significant impact upon the future direction and 'shape' of this debate. By basing his arguments unequivocally upon the teaching of Scripture, a light has been cast upon the rôle of women which is especially searching, and which highlights conspicuously the manner in which the arguments have moved away from the solid rock of Divine Revelation, and have strayed into the quick-sands of Political-Correctness, and worldly wisdom; the "way that seemeth right" to man (Prov. 14 v.12, 16 v.25). Herein lies the value of this work, and the value of the controversy that inevitably it will generate. We are presented with the awful contrast between the easy and well-trodden Broad Way that leadeth to destruction, and the Narrow Way, through the Strait Gate which leadeth unto Life. A radical change of direction is required, and urgently.

I was especially pleased to find an entire Chapter given over to the difficult subject of single women. This situation often brings real heartache to many people, and the author is certainly right to draw our attention to the matter. That he has done so in such a sensitive manner is something for which I, at least, am truly grateful.

For me, the result of having perused this magnificent work has been twofold. Firstly, the respect I feel for my brother in Christ whom I have known for a number of years has been increased by this exposure to the breadth and depth of his grasp of this essential subject. Secondly, my understanding of the key fact that submission to Christ and to the Word of God, is the only way that as individuals we may find, happiness, meaning, purpose and peace has been reinforced enormously.

It is especially satisfying that a book that is so stimulating, should simultaneously emphasise and enhance the Glory of Christ and exalt the Scriptures.

Michael W. J. Phelan

Baptist Church
Brighton
East Sussex

THE OLD TOWN SQUARE, PRAGUE,
with memorial of JOHN HUSS (1373 - 1415), a Czech
Reformer and 'FORERUNNER OF THE REFORMATION'

In 1396 Huss graduated with a Master of Arts degree at the University of Prague, of which he was appointed its RECTOR, and later with a Bachelor of Divinity degree in 1404. He become a national leader of reform against the evils and corruption in the Church during the Great Schism when Europe was divided between three rival popes. It was the Council of Constance in 1414, to which he was invited and promised safe conduct, which brought the Schism to an end. But he was thereupon swiftly put on trial, imprisoned, found guilty of heresy, and refusing to recant and renounce his faith, he was sent to be burned at the the stake on 6th July 1415.

PREFACE

It is a privilege to recommend this book by the Rev. Prof. Dr. Creane. In these days of apathy, indifference and barrenness in Christian practice and witness, there is a passionate call in these pages for a return to the paths of truth and righteousness according to the teaching of the Word of God. "Stand ye in the ways, and see, and ask for the old paths, where is the good way, and walk therein, and ye shall find rest for your souls", (Jer. 6 v.16).

Will this book be taken seriously by the evangelical church? The easiest response is to make every reference to women in the Bible culturally relative and so irrelevant and unbinding on family and church life today. Then what glares of anger and pitying scorn confront those who challenge this prevalent common interpretation by daring to ask the question, "But what does the Word of God say about the role of women and the glorious calling of motherhood?" Can one ignore the Divine order of woman being created by man, from man and for man's help? Man and woman are both equal in creative dignity, native sinfulness and redemptive privilege, but man and woman are different from each other. Each are enabled by grace to glorify God in his and her own way. This is the Divine pattern of the Creator for all His creatures, and this is what this fine exhaustive study of *The Place, Role and Function of Women* sets out before us; it is noteworthy for its comprehensiveness.

This further work from the author's pen is much needed and deserving of not only serious consideration, but more importantly, as a warning and guide to the Lord's people for a firm application of the Truths of Scripture in every matter of faith and practice --- "being fervent in the spirit" to speak and to teach "diligently the things of the Lord", (Acts 18 v.25). In a day of spiritual declension, levity and compromise, this book will be "as a beacon upon the top of the mountain, and as an ensign on an hill", (Isaiah 30 v.17).

In every generation, the devil has used his agents to oppose certain doctrines and truths of the Word of God which have come under severe attack, not only by those outside in the world, but alas also by many inside the Church. Over the last four or five decades, "The place, role and function of women, in the Church, in the home, in the workplace, in society, and in the world at large" has become a particular focus of intense criticism. The controversial seeds of this modern attack were sown by the so-called Enlightenment and theological liberalism of the late nineteenth century period. The humanistic philosophies, ideology, and propaganda of the 'radical feminist' Liberation Movement became more vocal during the 1960's, the devastating effects of which are being felt today.

The Christian Church must continue to resist all such attacks. This book, therefore, is most timely and significant, and is focused on a pivotal subject providing the Biblical authority and teaching on a series of vital issues to assist a new generation of Christians to stand firm in upholding, maintaining, and defending the truth of Holy Scripture. "The Lord our God will we serve, and His voice will we obey", (Joshua 24 v.24).

Our appreciation is due to Prof. Creane for a clear and forthright presentation of the message of Scripture in this marvellous volume. He tackles the most important questions confronting today's Church in its engagement with truth. In a meek, yet courageous fashion, he directs readers to many of the principles and imperatives of the Bible. Complete obedience to and confidence in the inerrant and infallible Word of God is essential to the very life and vitality of the Christian Church. This book is deserving of the attention of every evangelical believer. What this book teaches will be the best friend of a husband and wife, and of every Gospel Church.

"Buy the truth, and sell it not; also wisdom, and instruction, and understanding", (Prov. 23 v.23).

Geoff Thomas

Alfred Place Baptist Church
Aberystwyth
Wales

INTRODUCTION

This is a very complex subject, but as we examine The Scripture, we shall obtain a clearer grasp of what the Bible teaches about it.

Many women today are being brainwashed and encouraged to think they can command the world, and have 'career' success and family fulfilment at the same time. By what standard or yardstick is 'success' thus measured? Every woman is vested with dignity and honour as she has been made in the image of God. Every woman can find true fulfilment when she understands, enjoys and fulfils her creation design by Divine order. Christian women who desire to be all that God intends them to be, will strive to live under Scripture's authority. They will want to follow positive Biblical teaching on womanhood, including such issues as marriage, sex, motherhood, singleness, and a Scriptural perspective on their place, role and function in the Church, in the home, in the workplace, in society, and in the world at large.

In approaching any subject bearing on Divine Truth, we need the help of the Holy Spirit in coming to a clear understanding of what the Word of God says and teaches. So we must prayerfully seek the help of heaven as we proceed on matters of such profound gravity and importance.

"And judgment is turned away backward, and justice standeth afar off: for truth is fallen in the street, and equity cannot enter. Yea, truth faileth; and he that departeth from evil maketh himself a prey: and the Lord saw it, and it displeased Him that there was no judgment", (Isaiah 59 v.14-15). These words sound amazingly apt today. The battle for truth is intensifying on all fronts, and none more fiercely as concerning the role of women in society and in the Church. It seems that truth on this matter is being called into question on every level --- Biblically, historically, and of course the daily 'twists' that are put upon contemporary religion and events by the spin of various liberal theologians and the media.

In his book, 'The Christian Mind', Harry Blamires asks the question, Where did it all go wrong? His survey and detailed analyses of the sad state of the Church and the low morality of the nation are very telling and revealing. He concludes: "there is no longer a Christian mind . . . . . the Christian mind has succumbed to the secular drift with a degree of weakness and nervelessness unmatched in Christian history". Today, as never before, secular thinking and ideas pervade every area of life, and the Church has fallen foul to adopting the standards of the world, thus surrendering Divine revelation in Scripture as the inspired and inerrant touchstone of truth: "tossed to and fro, and carried about with every wind of doctrine, by the sleight of men, and cunning craftiness, whereby they lie in wait to deceive", (Eph. 4 v.14). For us, the whole Bible, and the Bible only, is the infallible rule of faith and behaviour for all mankind. "For this cause also thank we God without ceasing, because, when ye received the Word of God which ye heard of us, ye received it not as the word of men, but as it is in truth, the Word of God, which effectually worketh also in you that believe", (1 Thess. 2 v.13).

Over the past thirty or forty years especially, the debate concerning the role of women has reached massive proportions. 'Feminist' philosophy and notions have penetrated almost every area of our society and made large inroads into the Church. I am greatly surprised and very perplexed that many evangelical Churches, colleges, and seminaries have abandoned Biblical Truths which they have held from their inception.

The Scripture passages which clearly teach the proper roles of men and women have been re-interpreted, watered down, even ignored or abandoned altogether. The Church generally, once the bastion of the Truth of God, is falling fast and foul to the whims, wishes and march of so-called Women's Liberation.

The enormous efforts to overthrow authority and to cast aside the design of God for men and women, is the work of Satan, the archenemy of the Lord Jehovah. The devil uses willing sinful human agents to attain his goals. This evil controversy with dire consequences for the Church is so tragic and dangerous. Multitudes are being deceived by the lies of the Enemy of souls, "insomuch that, if it were possible, they shall deceive the very elect", (Matt. 24 v.24). The Bible emphatically declares that God has specific roles with distinctive functions for men and women in the Church, in the home, in the workplace, in society and in the world at large.

In the absence of expository preaching in many Churches today, what the Bible has to say on the role of women is gravely overlooked and often deemed irrelevant. The art of explaining and applying the text of Holy Scripture in context, largely, no longer prevails throughout much of Christendom. Preaching that has no theological and doctrinal depth and content cannot deliver truth with such passion as to persuade men and women to listen, believe, and obey the Word. To bring a real sense of God to the listener's attention is the true aim of preaching, with the fervent conviction that He makes His presence known when His Word is preached with clarity and convicting force in the power of the Holy Spirit.

The only solution to the spiritual malaise and the sad state of the Church at large, the lethargy concerning the things of God among the people, the moral decay in society, and the impotency of Christians in witness and evangelism, is a fresh outpouring of the Spirit of God in reformation and revival. Evangelicals today are facing a cultural push not only to accept all Protestants and Roman Catholics, regardless of their personal beliefs and practices, as true Christians, but also to embrace Jews, Muslims, and other non-Christians as brothers and sisters. The exclusivity of the Gospel is becoming more and more unpopular, and Evangelicals are faced with the choice of embracing either tolerance or truth. If we really believe what the Bible says, we should have no fear about the consequences. We must step out with faith and courage in obedience to the Lord's commands.

"The Lord is good, a strong hold in the day of trouble; and He knoweth them that trust in Him", (Nahum 1 v.7).

"But thanks be to God, which giveth us the victory through our Lord Jesus Christ. Therefore, my beloved brethren, be ye stedfast, unmoveable, always abounding in the work of the Lord, forasmuch as ye know that your labour is not in vain in the Lord", (1 Cor. 15 v.57-58).

Without a doubt, one of the most difficult and perplexing debates for the Church during the past four decades, and especially today, is in regard to 'the role of women', as we have witnessed more and more denominations ordaining them into the diaconate, the eldership, and the ministry. The vital question, therefore, which we must inquire into, is this: Does the Word of God allow women to become deacons, elders, pastors, and ministers?

Many mistakenly believe because of the worldwide shortage of male candidates for these roles, that the tide of opinion is so strong for the inclusion of women in Church leadership. It is argued that as things stand at the present time, it must surely be right. But is it right? The answer to this question will be determined according to the standards we use to make our decisions in life.

(1) In proclaiming to be the people of God, do we place ourselves wholly and completely and fully under God's Word, allowing The Scripture to govern all our choices and practice?

(2) Or instead, do we seek to sit above Scripture, and judge for ourselves in deciding which parts of the Bible we will or won't accept?

(3) Do we approach matters of faith and conduct according to our own pre-conceived notions, or even those of the world?

(4) Or again, whilst accepting the authority of some of the Word of God, do we believe that other parts of the Bible do not apply to this our day and generation?

Our approach to The Scripture, therefore, determines where we stand on all the issues of life, and for the purpose of this book, I am very conscious of bringing the Word of God to bear upon such an important and weighty subject, namely, "The Place, Role and Function of Women in the Church, in the Home, in the Workplace, in Society and in the World at large", as a "Thus saith the Lord", (Jer. 2 v.2).

Out of a deep personal concern to make doctrine understandable, this book endeavours to show how the Biblical teaching on this all-important subject should dispel the uncertainty surrounding it. The theological understanding of many students on this matter is elementary and sadly in too many instances deficient. Such a simplistic understanding is not confined to laymen either; there are many ministers and pastors who have never grasped the significance, not only of this vital topic, but also many of the basic Biblical truths and Christian doctrines of the faith as well.

Sadly, too, there are many preachers today who attempt to generate spiritual excitement which is quite unrelated to genuine Scriptural knowledge, and alas, contrary to Truth, that will never produce conviction in the mind, confidence in the heart, or stability in character. "My people are destroyed for lack of knowledge", (Hosea 4 v.6). The Bible warns us not to follow "cunningly devised fables", (2 Peter 1 v.16), to "refuse profane and old wives fables", and instead, to exercise ourselves rather "unto godliness", (1 Tim. 4 v.7). God has given us a Book of Truth, the Holy Scriptures, through which we are enlightened, restored, warned, and sanctified: "the people that do know their God shall be strong, and do exploits", (Dan. 11 v.32).

While some doctrines are more important than others, that does not mean some truths can be ignored or forgotten. I am deeply indebted to fellow-workers, colleagues, friends and others for their Christian love, support and encouragement in warmly requesting that I write this book. I trust that Christians at all levels, young and older, especially those who do not have the benefit of sound Bible teaching in their local congregations will profit. This book makes no claim to be exhaustive bearing in mind the wide range of topics discussed. The purpose of this book is to show how these truths relate to the Church of Christ in all ages, with the prayer that all who read these pages might rejoice in the Truth, and be strong in the Lord to take action for Him, to the praise of His name. "For the Word of the Lord is right; and all His works are done in truth", (Psalm 33 v.4).

God's high design and calling for women is outlined in several parts of Scripture, and if followed, His plan results in blessing, unity, and honour for God. May God the Holy Spirit enable us to comprehend the Truth and enlighten our understanding of His Word. May He grant us that conviction of belief and that unquestioning obedience to be firm in the faith, so that we will manifest a godly enthusiasm and a winsome confidence in our daily walk and witness to the glory of God.

In dealing with the complexity and vastness of the subject on hand, the principle aim of this book is to advance in some little measure the Biblical teaching thereon, and to cultivate an obedience of the Word and a joyful spirit among the people of God. It offers practical directions and guides the reader's attention to the storehouse of God's Divine truth in the Holy Bible. By seeking to analyse some broad foundational truths about God's revelation, the claims of Scripture, sin, and marriage, as well as more particular issues such as a woman's responsibilities to Christ, home and husband, I have endeavoured not to shirk from taking up difficult topics concerning submission, headship, and common devices of Satan. In addressing the struggles and problems associated with godly relationships as husband and wife, etc., this book also challenges many of the wrong conceptions and un-Scriptural practices about leadership in the Church today, and urges steadfast trust in God's providential care in all of life's situations by walking in His way.

It is a rewarding Divine call with deep fellowship, and a supreme joy, yet enormous task and burden of heart for me as a minister of Christ and a Bible teacher, in the providence of God to have the opportunity and privilege of preaching, lecturing, instructing, and teaching The Scripture to hungry and thirsty students worldwide; to uphold and promote the ministry of God's Word; to encourage men called of the Lord to preach His Gospel and pastor Churches; to further the proclamation and defence of the doctrines of Free and Sovereign Grace; and to provide training for all who are called to serve God in religious education, missionary work, and in other spheres of Christian work and witness, at home and abroad.

My goal is always to know the will of God in the study and understanding of His Word, and out of that experience to explain to students and researchers; to ministers, elders and deacons; to other workers in Christ's vineyard and to congregations, the meaning of truth in what the Bible teaches. In the words of Nehemiah 8 v.8, which reads: "So they read in the Book in the law of God distinctly, and gave the sense, and caused them to understand the reading". My prayer is that I shall always strive to do likewise, to give the sense of God's Truth, so that my hearers and readers may truly hear the Lord speak through the Scriptures, and in so doing, may obey and respond to Him, and thus bring honour and praise to His great name.

God's dear people need to understand the Mind and Will of God, which demands knowing His Word of Truth: "Study to shew thyself approved unto God, a workman that needeth not to be ashamed, rightly dividing the Word of Truth", (2 Tim. 2 v.15). We need to allow the Word of Christ to dwell in us richly: "Let the Word of Christ dwell in you richly in all wisdom; teaching and admonishing one another in psalms and hymns and spiritual songs, singing with grace in your hearts to the Lord", (Col. 3 v.16). (See Appendix One).

The main thrust of this book is to help to make God's written Word, the living Word, alive and refreshing by explaining and applying The Scripture to the wider Church, so that His revelation may be established upon the earth and bring greater obedience and faithfulness among His people, to the glory of God.

"For the Word of God, and for the testimony of Jesus Christ", (Rev.1 v.9).

"Thou art worthy, O Lord, to receive glory and honour and power: for Thou hast created all things, and for Thy pleasure they are and were created", (Rev.4 v.11).

> "His name for ever shall endure;
>   last like the sun it shall:
> Men shall be bless'd in Him, and bless'd
>   all nations shall Him call.
>
> Now blessed be the Lord our God,
>   the God of Israel,
> For He alone doth wondrous works,
>   in glory that excel.
>
> And blessed be His glorious name
>   to all eternity:
> The whole earth let His glory fill.
>   Amen, so let it be".
>   (Psalm 72 v.17-19)

Robert H. Creane

CHAPTER ONE

THE SCRIPTURE CANNOT BE BROKEN

The Claims of Scripture

The Infallible Truth

The Divine Order, Equality and Male Headship

Man not at liberty to alter the Divine Word

Solemn Warning and Sanction

Liberalism and Ecumenism causing Havoc and Destruction

The Only Basis of Belief and Practice

God is not the author of Confusion

Upholding Biblical Authority

THE SCRIPTURE CANNOT BE BROKEN

Whenever Christ and the Apostles quote The Scripture, they consider all Scripture as the very Word of God, and think of it as the living voice of the great Jehovah and therefore Divinely authoritative. Jesus explicitly declares that "the Scripture cannot be broken", (John 10 v.35), affirming that it is impossible to annul, or withstand, or deny The Scripture. Its authority is final even to its minute details.

In His stinging rebuke to the religious Sadducees, "Ye do err, not knowing the Scriptures", (Matt. 22 v.29), the very thing which Jesus points out is that their error comes precisely because they have not followed the Scriptures. Those who build and establish their doctrine and practice solely on The Scripture do not err. The authority of Scripture is unquestionable, so that when tempted by the devil Christ needed no other weapon than His final Word: "It is written", (Matt. 4 v.4,7,10; Luke 4 v.4,8).

Christ's last words before His Ascension are most arresting. They contained a stern rebuke to the disciples because they had not understood that all things which were written in the entire Scriptures "must be fulfilled", (Luke 24 v.44). "For verily I say unto you", says Jesus, "Till heaven and earth pass, one jot or one tittle shall in no wise pass from the law, till all be fulfilled", (Matt. 5 v.18). Paul stoutly asserts that what the Apostles preached and taught was "in truth, the Word of God", (1 Thess. 2 v.13), which must be believed and practiced with a tenacity that knows no wavering --- the Bible in all its parts is the Word of God.

The Claims of Scripture

"For ever, O Lord, Thy Word is settled in heaven", (Psalm 119 v.89).

"The Holy Scriptures of the Old and New Testaments are the Word of God, the only rule of faith and obedience", (Larger Catechism No.3).

Before proceeding to develop the subject on hand, it is incumbent upon us to confirm what The Scripture has to say about itself. In 2 Timothy 3 v.16-17, we read, "All Scripture is given by inspiration of God, and is profitable for doctrine, for reproof, for correction, for instruction in righteousness: That the man of God may be perfect, throughly furnished unto all good works".

Notice the "all" --- "all Scripture" is inspired, whether we like what it says or not. "All Scripture is given by inspiration of God", and therefore is His Word.

The Bible is Divine revelation, which we may depend upon as infallibly true. It instructs us in that which is true, reproves us for that which is amiss, and directs us in that which is good. The Scripture is the perfect rule of faith and practice. If we consult The Scripture, which is inspired, inerrant and infallible, and follow its directions, we shall be made men and women of God.

"Thy Word is true", (Psalm 119 v.160).

The Infallible Truth

The Westminster Confession of Faith fervently asserts that, "The authority of the Holy Scripture, for which it ought to be believed and obeyed, dependeth not upon the testimony of any man or Church, but wholly upon God, (Who is Truth itself), the Author thereof; and therefore it is to be received because it is the Word of God, --- yet, notwithstanding our full persuasion and assurance of the infallible Truth, and Divine authority thereof, is from the inward work of the Holy Spirit, bearing witness by and with the Word in our hearts", (Chap. 1, Sec. 4-5).

We must always adhere to the Truth, and submit to it, by putting ourselves under the authority and teaching of God's Holy Word, and allow it to mould and shape our lives in all matters of faith and obedience. We can expect the happy end of our faith only when we continue in the faith, and are so far "grounded and settled" in it, as not to be moved from it, (Col. 1 v.23).

Again, the Westminster Confession of Faith makes it perfectly plain and clearly states that, "The Supreme Judge, by which all controversies of religion are to be determined, and all decrees of councils . . . . . and doctrines of men . . . . . are to be examined, and in whose sentence we are to rest, can be no other but the Holy Spirit speaking in The Scripture", (Chap. 1, Sec. 10).

Those therefore who deny the Scriptures, either have not conversed with The Scriptures, or do not believe them, or do not take the true meaning of them. Ignorance of The Scripture is a tool which the devil greatly employs to bring abundance of mischief to the Truth and injury to the Church. "Ye do err, not knowing the Scriptures, nor the power of God", (Matt. 22 v.29), says Christ. The Sadducees in that story had succeeded only in putting their own ignorance on display for everyone in the Temple to see and hear. "Planao", from which "do err" is translated from the Greek, means to go astray, wander off, or deceive. In its original form given here it means to lead oneself off course or to stray from the truth. There are two reasons for this, "not knowing the Scriptures" and not understanding "the power of God".

In view of the controversy surrounding the role of women in the Church today, it is imperative to get back to the Bible with humble obedience, steadfast commitment and fervent prayer, resolving by God's grace to uphold, maintain and defend the Biblical principles of faith and practice which "are built upon the foundation of the apostles and prophets, Jesus Christ Himself being the chief corner stone", (Eph. 2 v.20).

The Bible is the eternal Word of God. The whole Bible is given by inspiration of God to man, and is as such the absolute, supreme, authoritative, infallible, and unchangeable Standard of faith and practice for all mankind in every generation, in all matters, at all times.

Although the storms of criticism continue to rage heavily against the authority of God's Holy Word, it must be firmly asserted that the humble believer's confidence in it is justifiable and substantiated. This Sacred Volume, the Bible, is, and always will be, the Book of God. "The foundation of God standeth sure", (2 Tim. 2 v.19).

The Divine Order, Equality and Male Headship

The 'feminist' movement in recent years has mounted a massive assault in the ongoing controversy on the Divine order of being. Christians who are truly concerned with the fundamental question of headship and of the proper relationship between men and women in the home, in the Church, and in society, will want to uphold the Biblical teaching on sexual identity, vocation, and roles. In western Christendom today there is the increasing tendency to oppose any unique leadership role of the man in the family and in the Church. Sadly much of the modern teaching within many Churches does not reflect the pattern of Biblical truth. The blurring of God-given sexual distinctions is the master-ploy of Satan to distort the teaching of Scripture, and ultimately to harm and damage the family and the Church.

It is imperative, therefore, at the present time to set forth the Biblical view of the relationship between men and women, and to encourage the true understanding and practice of their God-given roles. To that end it is most vital that our convictions and beliefs are firmly rooted and founded upon the Word of God, and thus discover more and more the true nature of Biblical manhood and womanhood. Allowing Scripture to challenge and govern our faith and conduct will determine the factors we employ to measure fitness for leadership according to the Divine standard. Male and female roles are complementary, not interchangeable, and the Bible is our only source of finding the true understanding of God's will for manhood and womanhood in the home and in the Church.

While recognising our own abiding sinfulness and fallibility, believers humbly acknowledge that the whole Bible is given by inspiration of God, and is as such the only infallible rule of faith and practice for all mankind. Right from the beginning of Scripture, all the patriarchs, prophets, and apostles, were very conscious of bringing the Word of God to the people as a "Thus saith the Lord", and "received it not as the word of men, but as it is in truth, the Word of God, which effectually worketh also in you that believe", (1 Thess. 2 v.13).

In the opening chapters of the Bible, in the Book of Genesis, it is clearly taught that Adam and Eve were created in God's image, equal before God as persons, and distinct in their manhood and womanhood. These distinctions in the masculine and feminine roles are ordained by God as part of the Creation order. The headship of the man in marriage was established by God before the Fall, and was not as a result of sin. The Fall introduced distortions into the relationship between men and women. In the home the husband's loving, humble headship tended to be corroded and replaced by domination, and the wife's intelligent, willing submission tended to be blighted and replaced by usurpation. In the Church, sin has driven men to a worldly love of power with an absence of spiritual responsibility, and has caused women in their haughtiness and pride to resist limitations on their role and neglect the use of their gifts in appropriate ministries.

It is important to acknowledge the first thing the Scriptures tell us about human beings . . . . . they were created "male and female", and that both men and women were created "in the image of God", (Gen. 1 v.27). From the very beginning, the Bible clearly states that man is not superior to woman, and woman is not inferior to man. Both are of equal value and dignity before God, but they were created to fulfil different roles. Before the Fall, God has established a distinct leadership role, male headship, for the husband in marriage.

In the Creation order the following are among the Biblical evidences of this headship principle:-

(1) Male headship in marriage is first seen in the order that men and women were created. Adam was created first, and Eve was created second. "And the Lord God formed man of the dust of the ground, and breathed into his nostrils the breath of life; and man became a living soul", (Gen. 2 v.7). "And the rib, which the Lord God had taken from man, made He a woman, and brought her unto the man. And Adam said, this is now bone of my bones, and flesh of my flesh: she shall be called Woman, because she was taken out of man", (Gen. 2 v.22-23). The order of Creation is not a minor detail, but an important Biblical precedent and principle. This is very evident when the Apostle Paul refers to the fact that "Adam was first formed, then Eve", (1 Tim.2 v.13), as a reason for men and women having different roles in the life of the New Testament Church.

(2) "Why did God not create Adam and Eve simultaneously from the same lump of clay?" asks the Rev. J. S. Carson in a special conference paper given on 'The Principle of Biblical Headship', "Would that not have established their equality of personhood more clearly? The answer is that He had already established that beyond all doubt in Genesis 1 v.27 where it says that both were created in His image. Now God wants to say something more (in Gen. 2) about the relationship between man and woman. And what He wants to say is that when it comes to their differing responsibilities there is a 'firstness' of responsibility that falls to the man. This is not an issue of superior value. That issue has been settled in Gen. 1 v.27. It is a matter of a sinless man, in childlike dependence on God, being given a special role or responsibility. God makes him the initial half of the pair

to say something about his responsibility in initiating and leading. God makes him lead the way into being in order to say something about his responsibility of leadership".

(3) It was Adam, not Eve, who had a special role in representing the human race. Even though Eve sinned before Adam (Gen. 3 v.6), the Scriptures tell us: "For as in Adam all die, even so in Christ shall all be made alive", (1 Cor. 15 v.22). Adam alone represented the human race because of the particular leadership role God placed upon him, a role Eve did not share.

(4) Not only was Adam created before his wife, Eve, he was given the responsibility of naming her: "She shall be called Woman, because she was taken out of man", (Gen. 2 v.23). The naming activities in Genesis 1-2 is given to Adam who has authority over those things as detailed in the Genesis narrative.

(5) The naming of the human race by God is recorded in Genesis 5 v.1-2: "This is the book of the generations of Adam. In the day that God created man, in the likeness of God made He him; male and female created He them; and blessed them, and called their name Adam, in the day when they were created". When God chose to name the human race, He chose a distinctively male term to indicate male leadership.

(6) It was Adam whom God called to account after he and Eve sinned. "And the Lord God called unto Adam, and said unto him, where art thou?", (Gen. 3 v.9). Why did God not summon both Adam and Eve to account together? It was because, as the God-appointed head, Adam bore the primary responsibility to lead their marriage partnership in a God-glorifying direction. This demonstrated that Adam, as leader, had the primary

accountability for his family, even though the serpent spoke first to Eve and Eve sinned first, (Gen. 3 v.1 and 6).

(7) Eve was created by God as a "helpmeet" for Adam, (Gen.2 v.18). "Helper" here does not mean someone who is inferior, but someone "fit for him", meaning "a help corresponding to him" that is "equal and adequate to himself".

(8) The woman alone, out of all the creatures, was "suitable for him". Eve alone was Adam's equal, his companion and helper. The man was not created to help the woman, but the reverse. He is to love his wife by accepting the primary responsibility in the marriage partnership, and she is to love her husband by supporting in that godly undertaking.

(9) In relationship to each other Adam bears responsibility for leadership and headship over Eve. "This is the way God meant it before there was any sin in the world", writes Rev. J. S. Carson in his paper on 'The Principle of Biblical Headship', "sinless man, full of love, in his tender, strong, moral leadership in relation to woman; and sinless woman, full of love, in her joyful, responsive support for man leadership. No belittling of the man, no grovelling from the woman. Two intelligent, humble, God-centred beings living out, in beautiful harmony, their unique and different responsibilities".

(10) The assault by Satan on our first parents came in the form of a question: "Yea, hath God said, ye shall not eat of every tree of the garden? (Gen. 3 v.1), was designed to cast doubt on the veracity of God's Word by attacking and undermining the Creation order. God created Adam first. God gave Adam the moral commandment in the Garden of Eden first. God held Adam responsible and

accountable for disobedience first. Satan had lured Adam and Eve into a role reversal by the sin of "unbelief" and "rebellion" at the Fall.

(11) As a result of the Fall sin brought conflict into Adam and Eve's relationship by creating a distortion of the roles God set for the sexes. It did not create new roles, it made the current ones more difficult to fulfil.

(12) "Unto the woman He (God) said, I will greatly multiply thy sorrow and thy conception; in sorrow thou shalt bring forth children; and thy desire shall be to thy husband, and he shall rule over thee", (Gen. 3 v.16). God's decree here is two-fold. First, as a mother, the woman will suffer in relation to her children. She will still be able to bear children. But now she will suffer in childbirth. This is God's severity for her sin. The new element in her experience, is not childbirth, but the pain of childbirth. Second, as a wife, the woman will suffer conflict in relation to her husband, in her desire to usurp his headship.

(13) In Genesis 4 v.7, the same Hebrew Word, "teshuqah", translated "desire" as in Gen. 3 v.16, is found: "Sin lieth at the door. And unto thee shall be his (its) desire, and thou shalt rule over him". In both texts the meaning strongly implies a "desire to conquer or rule over", not sexual desire, but leadership over the man. It is clear from these verses that part of the curse of sin was pain and conflict in the relationship between husband and wife, and this distortion in the relationship must be overcome.

(14) The Good News of the first promise of the Gospel in Gen. 3 v.15 is that when Jesus came, He came to bring restoration. In Col. 3 v.18-19 the Apostle Paul is

giving an explanation of Gen. 3 v.16: "Wives, submit yourselves unto your own husbands, as it is fit in the Lord. Husbands, love your wives, and be not bitter against them". In both the Old and New Testaments it is clear that God's design for marriage was for the wife to be subject to her husband, and for the husband to love his wife and lead her in the way Adam and Eve related to each other before the Fall.

(15) The marriage relationship prior to the Fall (Gen. 2 v.24), and the "great mystery" that Paul refers to in Eph. 5 v.31-32, are to be understood that from the beginning, God designed marriage to show how Jesus relates to the Church, His Bride. That is why the Apostle writes: "For the husband is the head of the wife, even as Christ is the Head of the Church", (Eph. 5 v.23). There is a leadership or headship role that belongs to Christ that the Church does not have. From the beginning this is the same with marriage. God created within marriage a leadership or headship that belongs to the husband that the wife does not have.

(16) In the Trinity, the One Divine Being, there are equality, differences, and unity among the Father, Son, and Holy Spirit. It goes without saying that, when we speak of the Trinity of God, we refer to a trinity in unity, and to a unity that is trinal. So too in marriage there is equality, differences, and unity that reflect the relationships within the Trinity. "But I would have you know, that the Head of every man is Christ; and the head of the woman is the man; and the Head of Christ is God", (1 Cor. 11 v.3).

(17) Adam had a responsibility to lead in a way that was pleasing to God, and Eve had a responsibility to be submissive to and supportive, a "helpmeet", of Adam in his leadership role.

(18) It is the husband who bears the primary responsibility of protecting and providing for his family, and this even involves a willingness to lay down his life for his wife as implied in Eph. 5 v.25.

(19) The idea of headship and submission has always existed, for it is part of God's eternal decree. When Paul writes in 1 Cor. 11 v.3, "But I would have you know, that the head of every man is Christ; and the head of the woman is the man; and the Head of Christ is God", he demonstrates how important these roles are in marriage. Headship and submission are noble virtues. Just as the relationships between the Father, Son, and Holy Spirit are good and fair, so too is the relationship between a man and a woman that God established in marriage.

(20) God's created order for marriage is beautiful, and by following His pattern honours both men and women by encouraging each to exercise their gifts as they were created to use them. "They shall be one flesh", (Gen. 2 v.24), is a beautiful expression of unity, as husband and wife are attracted to the parts of each other that are most different. Marriage is a wonderful expression of love between one man and one woman as ordained by God to reflect the equality, difference, and unity of such a relationship.

(21) Heterosexual fidelity is the Scriptural pattern in marriage. Man is not to put asunder what God has united, nor is man to join in any other form of 'union' which the Bible clearly states is sinful.

(22) Those who wish to destroy sexual distinctions will harass and persecute Christians who defend Creational structures. As we affirm male-female distinctions and

live out a "one man - one woman for life" marriage in the context of the Church, Christ's Bride, we embody God's glory and declare His truth to the world as we live morally and in harmony with His will.

(23) The Christian woman should rejoice in her femininity, honour her husband, and as a true "helpmeet", actively submit to him and seek to bring everything within her domain under his "headship" in accordance with the Word of God.

(24) Biblical headship and submission undergird each other, and when God brought the first woman to the first man, He not only provided Adam with a suitable helper and companion, He established marriage as the first and most basic of all human institutions. Today, marriage is under great attack, and when marriage falls, all other institutions --- home, family, Churches, schools, hospitals, businesses, and governments --- will inevitably fall too.

(25) The Divine pattern of headship and submission is ignored at our peril, and the strategy of the devil is to undermine and abolish the roles which God in His wisdom gave to the man and to the woman. Christ has come to redeem us from the curse of sin, and society needs Christian husbands and Christian wives who are committed to Christ, obey His Word, and practice it in their lives. "Nevertheless let every one of you in particular so love his wife even as himself; and the wife see that she reverence her husband", (Eph. 5 v.33).

(26) Marriage exists for God's glory. The Bible tells us explicitly that God created marriage in order that by marriage we might understand the most important of spiritual relationships. Jesus Christ is portrayed in the

Bible as the Great Bridegroom and Husband of the Church. That is why we who believe in Him are portrayed as His Bride. "Wives, submit yourselves unto your own husbands, as unto the Lord. For the husband is the head of the wife, even as Christ is the Head of the Church: and He is the Saviour of the body. Therefore, as the Church is subject unto Christ, so let the wives be to their own husbands in every thing. Husbands, love your wives, even as Christ also loved the Church, and gave Himself for it", (Eph. 5 v.22-25).

God's all-wise design is that men and women are equal in value, but different in roles. Writing in her book, 'Does Christianity Squash Women?', Rebecca Jones states, "Being a woman may seem complicated, but it is also simple. Being a real woman is believing and acting on the truth that we (women) have been set aside for a special job by Jesus Christ our Creator and Saviour . . . . . When we accept God's authority to define and use us, we discover what it means to be a woman".

The Bible clearly manifests the equally high value and dignity which it attaches to the roles of both men and women. Throughout both the Old and New Testaments male headship, not only in the family, but also in the Church, is affirmed. In the home, Christian husbands should forsake harsh and selfish leadership, and grow in love and care for their wives and families. Christian wives should forsake resistance to their husband's authority and grow in willing, joyful, submission to their husband's leadership as true helpmeets. In the Church, redemption in Christ gives men and women an equal share in the blessings of that "everlasting covenant, ordered in all things, and sure", (2 Sam. 23 v.5). Yet, nevertheless, the governing and teaching roles within the Church are reserved to men only. In both men and women a heartfelt sense of call to serve the Lord should never be used to set aside Scriptural standards and Biblical criteria for particular ministries, namely, that of the eldership and the diaconate, which are appointed to men only as will be explained more fully later in the book. (1 Cor. 11, 1 Cor. 14, 1 Tim. 2).

With a proper understanding then of the early chapters of Genesis, we see that both male-female equality and male headship were instituted by God at Creation and remain permanent, beneficent aspects of human existence. Men and women are equal in the sense that they bear God's image equally. In marriage, of one man and one woman, the man bears the primary responsibility to lead the partnership in a God-glorifying manner. Under God, a wife must not compete for that primary responsibility. By God's decree this is the husband's responsibility and he is accountable before the Lord as head of the home. The true outcome of male headship is female fulfilment, not a denial of female rights. The proper Biblical understanding of male headship sadly has largely been lost as 'feminist ideals' have been aggressively pursued throughout society, and consequently under these conditions, sexual exploitation, confusion, and perversity have exploded at an alarming rate. Male 'domination' on the one hand and 'feminism' on the other are the twin evils attacking and corrupting the Biblical teaching on sexuality at this very time, with the result that God's creation is vandalised and human misery multiplied.

All who love the Lord, follow His Word, obey His commands, seek His glory, feel for people, and cherish the proper use and gift of sexuality, cannot but be appalled at the enormities being committed as rape, prostitution, cohabitation, homosexualism, lesbianism, pornography, fornication, and adultery are the supreme expression of human depravity. But if the roles of men and women are properly defined from Holy Scripture and duly adhered to and practised as godly male headship and willing submission, then the supreme result of true nobility, genuine fulfilment, and constant joy will be rightly manifested and enjoyed.

After God created man and woman, we read in Gen. 1 v.31 that He "saw everything that He had made, and, behold, it was very good". The way God created man and woman, each one in His own image, each one equal in status, and each one with differing roles, God said was "very good". A marriage exercising the God-designed relationship is the marriage relationship that God called "very good". The beautiful expressions of love "cleave unto his wife" and "they shall be one flesh" are expressed not only in a physical union, but also an emotional and spiritual union as well. This is God's design for marriage when we understand His purpose for us as we live according to His Word.

It is sincerely hoped that this book will prove helpful and useful to all who are looking for a summary of the Bible teaching on the issues raised herein, and by grace are seeking to understand more deeply what the Scriptures say about men and women and about their similarities and differences as created by God in His eternal and unchangeable wisdom. Controversy is often difficult and overwhelming even to the point of losing our joy and tempers with those who disagree with us. In such a situation we should remember the New Testament exhortation of serving the Lord without bitterness, but rather with graciousness and gentleness that reflect a spirit of humility in the hope that God will lead disobedient believers to repentance out of their sin and falsehood into the knowledge of the truth. "And the servant of the Lord must not strive; but be gentle unto all men, apt to teach, patient, In meekness instructing those that oppose themselves; if God peradventure will give them repentance to the acknowledging of the truth; And that they may recover themselves out of the snare of the devil, who are taken captive by him at his will", (2 Tim. 2 v.24-26).

God is gracious and faithful, "Who will not suffer you to be tempted above that ye are able" (1 Cor. 10 v.13), for He "knoweth how to deliver the godly out of temptations" (2 Peter 2 v.9), and even promises His unfaithful, dishonourable vessels that "if we confess our sins, He is faithful and just to forgive us our sins, and to cleanse us from all unrighteousness" (1 John 1 v.9).

God has clearly defined the place, role and function of women and what He wants them to do. He has given them the gifts, the power, and the love necessary for their task, and He promises to establish the work of their hands. (Psalm 90 v.17). Christian women owe it to the Lord to follow His design in their lives, rather than seeking honour from the voice of the world. "Being confident of this very thing, that He which hath begun a good work in you will perform it until the day of Jesus Christ", (Phil. 1 v.6).

All the righteous desires of a Christian woman's heart are truly met in the Lord's service by understanding the richness and beauty of God's clear, unambiguous, and unchanging design for women from the days of Creation throughout all generations. Being in the image of God as are their husbands and thus equal to them, they have the God-given responsibility to respect and submit to their husbands and to serve as their "helpers" in managing the home and nurturing the next generation.

May God give us grace to uphold the Biblical teaching about marriage and the family; to understand the place, role and function of women in the Church, the home, the workplace, society, and in the world at large. Those who refuse God's design bring scandal on the Gospel. Take heed, therefore, "that the Word of God be not blasphemed", (Titus 2 v.5).

Man not at liberty to alter the Divine Word

We are not at liberty in seeking to alter the teaching and meaning of the Bible to suit our own agenda. "Ye shall not add unto the Word which I command you, neither shall ye diminish ought from it, that ye may keep the commandments of the Lord your God which I command you", (Deut. 4 v.2). "What thing soever I command you, observe to do it: thou shalt not add thereto, nor diminish from it", (Deut. 12 v.32).

It is of the utmost importance that the Lord's people be thoroughly rooted and grounded in the great doctrine of the plenary inspiration of Holy Scripture, and be wholly convinced that the whole Bible is the very Word of God. Since all aspects of Christian teaching is derived from the Bible, and rests upon it alone for its authority, this doctrine concerning the inspiration, inerrancy, and infallibility of the Word of God, is the mother and guardian of all truth.

Sadly, in our day and generation, it has to be said, that the Bible is greatly neglected, even in many of our Churches. May God awaken us to the reality of the great truths and teaching of the Word of God, and give us a new reformation and revival in these sad days of declining Christianity, perversity and apostasy.

In an age of shallow thinking we pray that the sovereign Lord will yet again raise up in providence a people who by the enabling power of the Holy Spirit will hold forth the grand old teaching of the Sacred Volume, and by Divine grace humbly bow before an omnipotent and merciful God as He is revealed to us in an infallible Bible.

Solemn Warning and Sanction

In the Book of the Revelation, a most solemn warning and sanction is declared, condemning all who should dare to corrupt or change the Word of God, either by adding to it or taking from it.

"For I testify unto every man that heareth the words of the prophecy of this Book, if any man shall add unto these things, God shall add unto him the plagues that are written in this Book: And if any man shall take away from the words of the Book of this prophecy, God shall take away his part out of the book of life, and out of the holy city, and from the things which are written in this Book", (Rev.22 v.18-19).

Here in these solemn verses we have a dire threat to those who assume an indifferent and unbelieving attitude toward the contents of Holy Writ. The Bible can indeed be so augmented and can be so abridged that the light of the Word is bedimmed, deliberately corrupted and denied. The warning in this passage is straightly aimed against the wilful distortion of the message of the greatest of all books, The Bible. The speaker is Christ Himself, and anyone who dares to corrupt and change the Word of God shows himself not to be a genuine believer.

He that adds to the Word of God draws down upon himself all the plagues written in this Book, and he who takes away anything from it cuts himself off from all the promises and privileges of it. This sanction is like a flaming sword, to guard the canon and veracity of The Scripture from profane and deceitful hands. God has set such a fence around the whole Bible, assuring us that it is a Book of the most sacred nature, Divine authority, and of final and last importance.

The blessing pronounced in Rev.1 v.3, is to encourage us to study the Bible. It is not sufficient to read and hear The Scriptures, but we must keep the things that are written therein, we must keep them in our minds, in our affections, and in our practices, and we shall be blessed. The proper way to use the Bible as the Shorter Catechism teaches is that "we must attend thereunto with diligence, preparation, and prayer, receive it with faith and love, lay it up in our hearts, and practise it in our lives", (S.C. No.90). "Blessed is he that readeth, and they that hear the words of this prophecy, and keep those things which are written therein", (Rev. 1 v.3). In these words a blessing is promised to the devout, obedient believer of the Word and in the application of Rev. 22 v.18-19, a curse is denounced against those who add to, or take anything away from the Word of God. Now what is said in these startling verses does not apply to the imperfect understanding of believers. We realise clearly our own feebleness in understanding perfectly all that is implied in this prophecy --- The Bible.

Liberalism and Ecumenism causing Havoc and Destruction

The main factors attributed to the death and ruin of the Church by liberalism, are, first and foremost, the destruction and replacement of the Bible's authority. In order to make Christianity more saleable and mission enterprise become easier, the liberals aim at undermining the inspiration, inerrancy, and authenticity of the Bible with a complete disregard to the supernatural origin and Divine preservation of Holy Scripture. In the liberal Church the key factor substituting the Bible is the authority of the synod, the episcopacy, the assembly, the theological colleges, or some other constituted ecclesiastical forum.

Having thus destroyed the main foundation and only basis of faith and obedience, the liberals then set about the reformulation of Christian truth, thus creating much confusion and uncertainty in the Protestant camp with regard to what to believe and how to behave. The resulting consequences include the undermining of preaching, weakening of faith, shallow spiritual life, drifting away from Reformation principles, and a falling away from systematic Bible reading. Furthermore, there is the constant aim to reject, substitute, or revise the Confessions of Faith and other ancient Historic Creeds of the Christian Church, to which they now only pay lip service and are not regarded any longer as the norm, claiming that the Biblical stipulations thereof are not authoritative, and therefore, do not apply today. So by the cunning use of words, the door is now open, among other things, to admit women to the ministry, the eldership, and the diaconate.

By skilfully employing a storehouse of devices, many well-meaning Christians are totally misled by the new theological concepts which carry a completely different meaning and content, and thus the liberals continue to proceed largely unchallenged. This declension always works from the top downwards under the label of Church scholarship through the various theological institutions and seminaries.

Liberalism, ecumenism and pluralism go hand in hand with the emphasis on unity rather than Bible truth and Scripture teaching, resulting in the fact that Christian mission now takes on a new meaning whenever the Biblical foundations are removed. Today, there is a marked indifference towards systematic theology, and the doctrines of grace are largely ignored. Because of spiritual infancy and lack of proper Biblical knowledge, today's Christians fall into the trap of blindly following the so-called modernism of 'persuasive' leaders.

In many places the Church has now become a social institution, and the fulfilment of the mandate received from Christ is greatly neglected and spurned. Such Churches emphasise unity and tolerance at the expense of truth. Luther once said, "Cursed be that love and unity for whose sake the Word of God must be put at stake".

Giving up on the exclusiveness of the Gospel of Christ with no Church discipline, --- the rejection of the absolute authority of Holy Scripture, defective Bible translations, the relegation of Protestant Creeds, abandonment of subordinate standards, admission of women as ministers/elders/deacons, the creation of a so-called broad Church, deceitfulness in doctrine, damnable heresies, religious trappings of professionalism, accommodation of unbiblical practices, patterns of relationships other than traditional marriage, lack of proper female dress and headwear, malpractice and maladministration, etc., --- are some of the symptoms of an ailing Church which demonstrates how lightly and tenuous is the official commitment of many Churches today to the teaching and authority of the Word of God. Because of such spiritual adultery, idolatry, and conformity to the world, "the showers" of blessing "have been withholden", (Jer. 3 v.3).

We need to repent of our sin, waywardness, worldliness, and unfaithfulness, and pray that in His mercy "the Spirit of the Lord shall lift up a standard", (Isaiah 59 v.19), against the enemy. May we commit ourselves and the Cause of Christ to our sovereign Lord Who searches the heart and judges righteously, (1 Peter 2 v.23; Rev. 2 v.23). "And thou, Solomon my son, know thou the God of thy father, and serve Him with a perfect heart and a willing mind: for the Lord searcheth all hearts, and understandeth all the imaginations of the thoughts: if thou seek Him, He will be found of thee; but if thou forsake Him, He will cast thee off for ever", (1 Chron. 28 v.9).

The Only Basis of Belief and Practice

The God of heaven and earth is the God of truth; He cannot lie. What He says to us in His Word is absolutely right and true. Whenever there is a dispute between the ideas of men and the Word of God, we must say, "Let God be true, but every man a liar; as it is written, That Thou mightest be justified in Thy sayings, and mightest overcome when Thou art judged", (Rom. 3 v.4), ... "when Thou judgest", (Psalm 51 v.4). The general sentiment here is the vindication of the righteousness of God. "The Lord is righteous in all His ways, and holy in all His works", (Psalm 145 v.17). Man cannot presume to quarrel with God for "the Word of the Lord endureth for ever", (1 Peter 1 v.25).

So our views on the subject of 'the role of women' must be shaped by the Word of God. Only then will they be correct and God-glorifying. In considering the role of women, it is therefore imperative to ask the question, namely, What are the Biblical principles that govern and determine the issues before us in this treatise?

Unless these principles are adopted and applied in society, in the home, and in the Church, no one can remedy the confusion which prevails about the role of women. Much of this confusion has been caused by 'feminist' activists, some of whom 'profess' to be 'Christians', and even 'theologians'. "To the law and to the testimony: if they speak not according to this Word, it is because there is no light in them", (Isaiah 8 v.20).

"For the prophecy came not in old time by the will of man: but holy men of God spake as they were moved by the Holy Ghost", (2 Peter 1 v.21). They were holy men of God employed to pen that Book which we receive as the Word of God. They were moved by the Holy Ghost in what they delivered as the mind and will of God. He is the Supreme Agent, the holy men are but the instruments. The Holy Ghost inspired and dictated to them the words they were to deliver of the mind of God, engaging them to write what He had put in their mouths, so that the very words of The Scripture proceeded from God Himself.

The entire Bible, from Genesis 1 v.1 to Revelation 22 v.21, is the very Word of God. It is authoritative, complete, perfect, and holy; and "the infallible rule of interpretation of Scripture is The Scripture itself", (WCF Chapt. 1 Sec. 9). It is a Book to be reverenced, believed, and obeyed. The Bible is the Word of God, let us therefore study and use it reverently and prayerfully, preach it faithfully, hear it believingly, submit to it willingly, and obey it implicitly, to the glory of God.

God is not the author of Confusion

In First Cor. 14 v.33-34 we read, "For God is not the author of confusion, but of peace, as in all the Churches of the saints. Let your women keep silence in the Churches: for it is not permitted unto them to speak; but they are commanded to be under obedience, as also saith the Law".

The instruction, edification and comfort of the Divine Word, is that for which God instituted the ministry, so that confusion might be avoided by upholding the principles of Scripture. The honour of God requires that every thing should be managed so as not to transgress the teaching of the Bible. Other Churches are not to be our rule and guide, and the scant regard they show for God's infallible Word in matters of faith and practice, should restrain us from breaking His

Law. "Let all things be done unto edifying . . . . . decently and in order", (1 Cor. 14 v.26 and 40).

Our worship of God should always reflect the character and nature of God. He is the God of peace and harmony, not of strife and confusion. God cannot be honoured where there is disobedience, disharmony and confusion. Chaos and discord in a Church meeting is certain proof that the Spirit of God is not present, much less in control. Where His Spirit rules by His Word there is always peace and blessing.

"Who is a wise man and endued with knowledge among you? Let him shew out of a good conversation his works with meekness of wisdom. But if ye have bitter envying and strife in your hearts, glory not, and lie not against the truth. This wisdom descendeth not from above, but is earthly, sensual, and devilish. For where envying and strife is, there is confusion and every evil work. But the wisdom that is from above is first pure, then peaceable, gentle, and easy to be entreated, full of mercy and good fruits, without partiality, and without hypocrisy. And the fruit of righteousness is sown in peace of them that make peace", (James 3 v.13-18).

True wisdom is God's gift through His Word. It is not gained by conversing or arguing with men, nor by the knowledge of the world, as some think and speak. True wisdom will go on to sow the fruits of righteousness in peace. True Christian religion will not admit anything that is contrary to The Scripture, but holds to the absolute authority of the Bible in every matter of faith and conduct.

As we note the last words of David, "the sweet psalmist of Israel", (2 Sam. 23 v.1), we would do well to heed, take to heart, and emulate. In the closing chapters of Second Samuel, he is enthusiastic about what God has done for him in His everlasting covenant and in providing salvation. Out of thankfulness he praises Him for His grace and many blessings: "The Lord is my rock, and my fortress, and my deliverer; The God of my rock; in Him will I trust: He is my shield, and the horn of my salvation, my high tower, and my refuge, my Saviour; Thou savest me from violence. I will call on the Lord, Who is worthy to be praised: so shall I be saved from mine enemies . . . . . God is my strength and power, and He maketh my way perfect", (2 Sam. 22 v.2-4, 33). See also Psalm 18.

Deep gratitude in the heart will find its way to the lip "because the love of God is shed abroad in our hearts by the Holy Ghost which is given unto us" (Rom. 5 v.5). So it is in the heavenly world, for there we are told the redeemed Church gives expression to its grateful love in songs of praise and adoration. The foundation of all joy in God is found in a Holy Ghost conviction of His personal interest in the individual believing man, who has a deep sense of intimate relationship to the Almighty Father through Christ as the object of His saving grace and providential care. Paul's gratitude was never deeper than when he speaks of the Saviour Who "loved" him, "and gave Himself for" him, (Gal. 2 v.20). True Christians with a passion for souls are never at rest unless they can persuade others to partake of the same blessedness. The Psalmist would enjoin upon us an urgency of resolution to seek God's help to faithfully serve Him by magnifying the Lord and encouraging all around us to taste God's goodness and blessedness which come from trusting in Him. "O taste and see that the Lord is good: blessed is the man that trusteth in Him", (Psalm 34 v.8).

An unshaken confidence that God is our God in a personal and direct sense, is the only foundation and resting place of the soul and satisfaction of the spirit, without which no obedience to God or service for Christ can ever be rendered. "As workers together with Him", (2 Cor. 6 v.1), we acknowledge the many blessings and token's of God's favour upon our lives. We, therefore, cannot but burst forth into songs of thanksgiving, which, although addressed to our sovereign Lord, are doubtless intended also to be a testimony to our fellow-man. "For He established a testimony in Jacob, and appointed a law in Israel, which He commanded our fathers, that they should make them known to their children: That the generation to come might know them, even the children which should be born; who should arise and declare them to their children: That they might set their hope in God, and not forget the works of God, but keep His commandments", (Psalm 78 v.5-7). The Church was not to be a thing of one age in a bygone day, but is to be kept up from one generation to another.

Upholding Biblical Authority

An examination of many of the old Creeds and Confessions of Faith of the majority of the major evangelical Churches of the world, testify to the tremendous influence that they have exerted upon past centuries in expressing their unswerving loyalty to the Bible and the doctrines of grace.

>   The Apostles' Creed 2nd - 4th Cent.
>   The Nicene Creed 325
>   The Athanasian Creed 373
>   The Chalcedonian Creed 451
>   The Scotch Confession 1560
>   The Belgic Confession of Faith 1561
>   The Thirty-Nine Articles of the Church of England 1562
>   The Heidelberg Catechism 1563
>   The Helvetic Confession 1564
>   The Canons of the Synod of Dort 1619
>   The Westminister Confession of Faith 1646
>   The Savoy Declaration 1658
>   The Baptist Confession of Faith 1689

The leading Fathers of Church history held firmly to the belief that the Bible is the very Word of God, that it is God's unique revelation, without error, and is all-sufficient in every way for our salvation. God not only has spoken through the Holy Scriptures to mankind, but has communicated to us a trustworthy and authoritative message. Throughout all ages, the Bible has stood, as J. M. Boice describes "as a rock of refuge for God's people". In his book, 'Standing on the Rock', Boice rightly affirms that "the Word of God remains like a rock in the midst of raging storms, treacherous offshore currents, and nearly invisible quicksands. It is good it does, because only the one who builds on this rock will truly stand forever . . . . . The authority of Scripture is a key issue for the Christian Church in this and every age. Those who profess faith in Jesus Christ as Lord and Saviour are called to show the reality of their discipleship by humbly and faithfully obeying God's written Word. To stray from Scripture in faith or conduct is disloyalty to our Master. Recognition of the total truth and trustworthiness of Holy Scripture is essential to a full grasp and adequate confession of its authority".

The Bible is the only infallible rule and guide of faith and practice. The Holy Scriptures cannot contradict themselves. There are no inconsistencies in the Word of God. While admitting the importance of studying the writings of the Early Fathers, and the works of the Reformers, Covenanters, Puritans and other divines, this writer holds that the pious, dutiful, diligent, and accurate study of the Sacred Text, is the appointed means of obtaining a wise and practical understanding of the Truth, both as it regards the character and work of God and the duty and hopes of man.

The author readily acknowledges that in the preparation of this manuscript, he has gained a deepened conviction of the truth, the unity, and the authority of the Scriptures, and prayerfully desires that all who read this book will enter upon a sincere and sympathetic study of the Sacred Volume, the Bible, and thus be drawn closer to God and nearer to one another, and be stimulated to live in the "unity of the Spirit in the bond of peace", (Eph. 4 v.3), and "in the way of righteousness", (Prov. 12 v.28), awaiting the Masters Return to reward all who have laboured in His Spirit and on His side according to His Word: "and then shall every man have praise of God", (1 Cor. 4 v.5).

From beginning to end, Scripture proclaims its Divine inspiration. The patriarchs, prophets, Christ Himself, and the apostles fully confirmed this truth without any reservation. The Bible is "the Word of Life" (Phil. 2 v.16), and as such regenerates the sinner. It gives light to the world (Phil. 2 v.15), and works effectually in those who believe (1 Thess. 2 v.13), for it is Spirit and life. Martin Luther, crushed by the burden of his sin and exhausted from his useless mortification, crawled on his knees up Pilate's fabulous staircase at Rome. One simple word from Scripture suddenly seized him with superhuman power: "The righteous shall live by faith", (Rom. 1 v.17). That word sufficed: the Reformation came into existence, giving to mankind the Bible, the Saviour, the liberty of the children of God, and assurance of eternal life.

The Bible is the Book for all men. It is God's written Word to such as receive by faith its testimony of life and power. "And my speech and my preaching was not with enticing words of man's wisdom, but in demonstration of the Spirit and of power: That your faith should not stand in the wisdom of men, but in the power of God", (1 Cor. 2 v.4-5). Scripture is vested with Divine authority, which no other power could either bestow or take away that quality. The French writer, J. H. Merle d' Aubigné, in his book, 'The Authority of God', points out: "The Divine authority of the Scriptures and their inspiration are two distinct, but inseparable, truths. The authority of the Scriptures proceeds from their inspiration, and their inspiration establishes their authority; just as the tempering of the metal produces the steel, and the steel results from the tempering. If the authority of the Scriptures falls, their inspiration falls; if, on the contrary, it be the inspiration that is taken from us, the authority likewise vanishes away. The Scripture without inspiration is a canon from which the charge has been removed".

The unconditional return to the sovereign authority of Scripture was the great objective of the Reformers. We would do well to take their motto and make it ours today: "Scripture alone and the whole of Scripture". "Then said Jesus to those Jews which believed on Him, If ye continue in My Word, then are ye My disciples indeed; and ye shall know the truth, and the truth shall make you free", (John 8 v.31-32). The rediscovery of this great principle set believers free from all the usurpations, superstitions, encroachments, and impoverishments of false teaching and corrupt doctrines of men. "Be not carried about with divers and strange doctrines. For it is a good thing that the heart be established with grace", (Heb. 13 v.9). The sad fact, today, is that the Written Word of God in many areas is suffering from serious neglect. Many Churches throughout our nation are losing sight of its authority, power, and efficacy. This manifests itself in various ways: -

(1) The Public reading of the Word of God is denied its prominence in worship.

(2) Trustworthy translations of the Scriptures are exchanged and replaced for corrupted and 'inferior' versions.

(3) The expository preaching of the Bible and solid Biblical ministry are giving place to topical addresses, drama, and various forms of entertainment.

(4) Vast portions of the Bible are scorned, ridiculed, unread, and even unknown.

It is no longer considered sufficient or fashionable to quote verses of Scripture in defence of truth or refutation of error. Rather than expounding truth from Scripture, so-called 'sermons' today are based and supplemented by the words of philosophers, commentators, or theologians. The most urgent need in the Christian Church is a renewal of true preaching. The aim of this book is to encourage the practical usefulness and study of the Bible, and hence it steers away from any theoretical or abstract treatment of the subject on hand.

Those who compromise the faith may object to dogmatic assertions. Apology for convictions is never in order and every preacher should believe passionately and strongly in the trustworthiness of the Word of God. All who are privileged to preach the Gospel surely ought to guard zealously and righteously an authentic and uncompromising witness for a fully inspired, inerrant, and infallible Bible. The teaching and authority of the inspired Word are absolute and final as the sole and all-sufficient rule and guide in all matters of faith and practice, providentially preserved by God and able to make men wise unto salvation, through faith which is in Christ Jesus.

In the Epistles, Paul reminds Timothy that the Church is "the pillar and ground of the truth", (1 Tim.3 v.15). She is not a social organisation, not a business institution, not a political society, not a sporting club, not a cultural association, but "the pillar and ground of the truth", (1 Tim.3 v.15). The Apostle urges Timothy to "Preach the Word; be instant in season, out of season; reprove, rebuke, exhort with all longsuffering and doctrine", (2 Tim. 4 v.2).

When Jesus dwelt on earth amongst men, He read the Scriptures as is evident from Luke 4 v.16, where it is described as being His customary engagement: "And He came to Nazareth, where He had been brought up: and, as His custom was, He went into the synagogue on the Sabbath Day, and stood up for to read". His knowledge of that Word was intimate and entire, but still He read it in its written form and made it His "meditation all the day", (Psalm 119 v.97). He exhorted His hearers to the same godly exercise, repeatedly asking the rhetorical question: -

> "Did ye never read in the Scriptures?", (Matt. 21 v. 42).
> "Is it not written?", (Mark 11 v.17).
> "Have ye not read in the Book of Moses?", (Mark 12 v.26).
> "What is written in the Law?", (Luke 10 v.26).
> "How readest thou?", (Luke 10 v.26).
> "What is this then that is written?", (Luke 20 v.17).
> "Is it not written in your Law?", (John 10 v.34).

Most directly of all, He gives this simple yet timeless three-word challenge :- "Search the Scriptures", (John 5 v.39).

The Lord Jesus Christ came to magnify the Law, and make it honourable", (Isaiah 42 v.21), and He confirmed this aspect of His work, when he said, "To this end was I born, and for this cause came I into the world, that I should bear witness unto the truth. Every one that is of the truth heareth My voice", (John 18 v.37). He demonstrated the veracity of the Scripture, and its power to bring life, light, and understanding. "He preached the Word", (Mark 2 v.2) unto the multitudes, and in the company of His disciples we are told: "And beginning at Moses and all the prophets, He expounded unto them in all the Scriptures the things concerning Himself", (Luke 24 v.27).

Perhaps most notably of all, when confronted by the devil, three times His choice of defence was a declaration of the Word of God (Matt. 4 v.4, 7, and 10): -

(1) "It is written, Man shall not live by bread alone, but by every Word that proceedeth out of the mouth of God", (Cf. Deut. 8 v.3).

(2) "It is written again, Thou shalt not tempt the Lord thy God", (Cf. Deut. 6 v.16).

(3) "It is written, Thou shalt worship the Lord thy God, and Him only shalt thou serve", (Cf. Exod. 20 v.3, Deut. 10 v.20).

The power of the Scriptures is undiminished with age, and still today they prove "quick, and powerful, and sharper than any two-edged sword, piercing even to the dividing asunder of soul and spirit, and of the joints and marrow, and is a discerner of the thoughts and intents of the heart", (Heb. 4 v.12). They of course demand proper handling and rigorous application. The Bible speaks for itself. Christ did not come to destroy, but glorify, verify, and exemplify its every word. It constitutes the lively oracles of God (Acts 7 v.38), His Word which liveth and abideth for ever (1 Peter 1 v.23), magnified above all His name (Psalm 138 v.2), which cannot pass away (Luke 21 v.33). "For ever, O Lord, Thy Word is settled in heaven", (Psalm 119 v.89).

For all believers the Bible truly is "the Sword of the Spirit" (Eph. 6 v.17), sharp, two-edged, which they may wield against the enemy. May our prayer be that the Holy Spirit will affirm in our hearts the conviction of the inerrancy of Holy Scripture, and give to us a clear understanding of its infallible truth and authority in every matter of faith and truth.

In order to uphold the glory of God, such a vital and central doctrine as the Authority of Scripture commands the earnest believer to seek and proclaim only that which is Biblically based and rests alone upon a sure and solid Scriptural foundation. "We are persuaded", writes J. M. Boice, "that to deny it is to set aside the witness of Jesus Christ and of the Holy Spirit and to refuse that submission to the claims of God's own Word which marks true Christian faith. We see it as our timely duty to make this affirmation in the face of current lapses from truth of inerrancy among our fellow Christians and misunderstanding of this doctrine in the world at large".

May God enable and strengthen all who read the inspired Volume by His Holy Spirit to behold and practice the testimony of Scripture by bringing all thoughts, deeds, traditions, and habits into true subjection to the Divine Word. May it be that God will enable many to be workmen "that needeth not to be ashamed, rightly dividing the Word of truth" (2 Tim. 2 v.15), as they further study and meditate on 'The Place, Role and Function of Women, in the Church, in the Home, in the Workplace, in Society, and in the World at large'. This book makes no claim to completeness or pretence to systematic treatment of the vast array of issues of this entire subject. As we contemplate the Biblical principles and imperatives involved, may we experience the blessing of the Lord and seek His wisdom and guidance in comprehending more fully the truth of the Bible. To God be the glory.

CHAPTER TWO

THE BASIC PRINCIPLE OF HEADSHIP

Creation Order and Leadership

New Testament Distinctions in Roles

The Devices of Feminism

Damaging Effects of Radical Feminism

The Subtle Strategy of the Enemy

THE BASIC PRINCIPLE OF HEADSHIP

God is a God of order, peace, righteousness, and justice. The basic principle undergirding the role of women in society and in the Church, is that God has appointed a certain order between the man and the woman. This we find in First Cor. 11 v.3, "But I would have you know, that the head of every man is Christ; and the head of the woman is the man; and the head of Christ is God". This fundamental rule must be our constant benchmark in exploring and defining the role of women in society and in the Church.

There is no doubt that the role of women has become a battleground in society during the last several decades. The 'feminist' movement has escalated to a place of imbalance in society that threatens the future. The efforts of the enemy today in secular society has now worked its way into the Church by adopting the world's standards and conforming to the spirit of the age. So much so that some Church leaders have gone as far as to teach principles that attempt to redefine and even alter Biblical truths to accommodate contemporary thinking and practice in the world. To do that, they advocate that certain parts of the Word of God are not applicable to today's Church. By placing man as the judge over God's Word, Satan in all his subtlety is strenuously endeavouring to upset the Divine order in any way he can, and one foundational way is by perverting the male and the female roles and relationships.

We need to "keep the ordinances", "the traditions", Greek word "paradoseis", which means "that which is passed along by teaching". The same word occurs in 2 Thess. 2 v.15, "Therefore, brethren, stand fast, and hold the traditions which ye have been taught, whether by word, or our own epistle (example)". We must hold firmly to Divine truth which was fervently put right and defended by the apostolic teaching of the New Testament Churches, especially at Corinth, Crete, Thessalonica and Ephesus.

The principle of subordination and authority pervades the entire universe. The Apostle Paul shows that women's subordination to man is but a reflection of that greater general truth. "The head of every man is Christ; and the head of the women is the man; and the head of Christ is God", (1 Cor. 11 v.3). If Christ had not submitted to the will of God, redemption for mankind would have been impossible, and we would forever be doomed, lost and dammed. If individual human beings do not submit to Christ as Saviour and Lord, they are still doomed, lost and dammed, because they reject God's gracious provision. And if women do not submit to men, then the family and society as a whole are disrupted and destroyed. Both on the Divine and human scale, subordination and authority are fundamental principles in God's order and plan for mankind.

It should be noted here that the Apostle Paul gives three ways in which headship is manifested.

(1) "The head of every man is Christ". He is uniquely the Head of the Church as its Saviour and Lord, (Col. 1 v. 18). He has redeemed and bought it with His own blood, (1 Peter 1 v.18-19). In His Divine authority Christ is Head of every human being, believer and non-believer: "All power is given unto Me in heaven and in earth", (Matt. 28 v.18). Most of mankind has never acknowledged or accepted Christ's authority: "Thou has put all things in subjection under His feet", (Heb. 2 v.8), and one day every knee will bow, "of things in heaven, and things in earth, and things under the earth", and every tongue will "confess that Jesus Christ is Lord, to the glory of God the Father", (Phil. 2. v. 10-11).

Those who willingly submit to Christ's authority constitute the Church, and those who rebel against Him constitute the world. In the patience and forbearance of God the rebellious continue, but one day they will acknowledge His ultimate control for evermore.

(2) "The head of the women is the man". This principle applies to all men and all women, even beyond the family to all aspects of society. That is the basic order of creation: "For the man is not of the women; but the women of the man. Neither was the man created for the women; but the women for the man", (1 Cor. 11 v.8-9). That is the way God planned and created mankind. It is the way He has made us. God established the principle of male authority and female subordination for the purpose of order and complementation, not on the basis of any inherent superiority of males. Elders and deacons are to be chosen from among the most spiritual men of the congregation, but there may be other men in the Church who are even more spiritual. Yet, for the very reason that they are spiritual, those who are not in positions of leadership will submit to those who are.

(3) "And the head of Christ is God". Jesus made it perfectly clear that He submitted to, and to do, the Fathers will: "My meat is to do the will of Him that sent Me, and to finish His work", (John 4 v.34). In His role as Saviour and Redeemer, He lovingly subjected Himself completely to His Father's will as an act of humble obedience in fulfilling the Divine purpose.

In these three examples Paul inseparately ties the three aspects of the principle of subordination together. As Christ is submissive to the Father and Christians are to be submissive to Christ, women are to be submissive to men. In each of these cases love is the predominate factor, not tyranny. The Father sent Christ out of love to redeem the world. The Son submitted to the Father out of love that He died for the Church. The Church submits to Him in love, and men should exercise their authority in love, not tyranny. They do not have authority because of greater worth or greater ability, but simply because of God's design and loving will. Women respond in loving submission as they are designed to do, "if they continue in faith and charity and holiness with sobriety", (1 Tim. 2 v.15).

The Bible emphatically tells us as the Shorter Catechism stoutly affirms, "There are three Persons in the Godhead, the Father, the Son, and the Holy Ghost; and these three are one God, the same in substance, equal in power and glory", (S.C. No.6). They are equal, but Christ submitted Himself to the Father in all things. In His mediatorial character and glorified humanity He is at the head of humanity.

As God is the head of Christ, and Christ is the head of the entire humankind, so the man is the head of the two sexes, not indeed with such absolute dominion as Christ, but a headship, and the woman should be in subjection and not assume or usurp the man's place. This is the situation in which God has placed her, and for that reason, she should not do anything that looks like an attempt at changing places. Women are not prohibited from praying and speaking forth the Word of God. The Corinthian women were reprehended and reprimanded for the manner and place in which they were doing it, (1 Cor. 14).

If Christ had intended women to be in leadership He would have chosen them and could easily have appointed six men and six women as His apostles. In Christ's ministry and that of the Apostolic Church, women were not called, commissioned, or initiated into any such role, either as elders or deacons, ministers or pastors. In Rom. 16 v.1 mention is made of "Phebe our sister" in grace, and she seems to be a person of quality and high standing. She had business to perform which called her to Rome. Paul recommends her as a friend and servant in acts of charity and hospitality. Every Christian should be a servant of the Lord in ministries of mercy, evangelism, and of helping others.

The Bible teaching on headship is nowhere more plain than in such passages as First Corinthians 11 and Ephesians 5. These speak of man having authority over the woman as Christ has authority over man, and God over Christ. This does not mean that man is more important than the woman. She is not a second-class person, but as a sign of submission in obedience to the authority of God's Word, she should have her head covered in public worship. We shall deal with this aspect of head covering more fully later.

Creation Order and Leadership

From the beginning of the Old Testament we see the role of men and women being revealed. Both man and woman were created in the image of God, and it is to be noted that they are both radically different from the animals God had created. Scripture determines that men and women are equal in value, potential and destiny.

However in Genesis 2 the chapter mentions some clear differences and distinctions between the first man and woman. They were made differently, Adam from the dust of the ground, and Eve from a rib of Adam. "For the man is not of the woman; but the woman of the man. Neither was the man created for the woman; but the woman for the man", (1 Cor. 11 v.8-9). They were made for different purposes, and at different times.

The Bible is quite clear: God made the first man "of the dust of the ground", (Gen 2 v.7, Child's Catechism No.3), then later, "caused a deep sleep to fall upon Adam, and he slept: and He took one of his ribs, and closed up the flesh instead thereof; And the rib, which the Lord God had taken from man, made He a woman, and brought her unto the man", (Gen. 2 v.21-22). All this occurred because the Lord had said, "It is not good that the man should be alone; I will make him an help meet for him", (Gen. 2 v.18). Notice, God did not give Adam a woman to be boss over him. Nor was the woman given to nag him or be a hindrance to him, which often, is the sad situation today, but the woman was one given to Adam, to "help" him. Woman was made as "an helpmeet" for man, which does not make her position inferior to that of man, simply different.

"Wives, submit yourselves unto your own husbands, as unto the Lord", (Eph. 5 v.22). The husband is to love his wife, "and the wife see that she reverence her husband", (Eph. 5 v.25 and 33). If Eve had not eaten the forbidden fruit, and tempted her husband to eat it, she would never have complained of her subjection. Those wives who despise God's Word and disobey their husbands violate a Divine law. Adam's sin brought death upon the whole human race. Eve's sin brought particular judgment upon her own sex, pain in childbirth and submission to male leadership. In Gen. 3 v.16 we read of God's punishment upon Eve and all women since the Fall because of her sin in the Garden of Eden. God said unto the woman, "I will greatly multiply thy sorrow and thy conception; in sorrow thou shalt bring forth children; and thy desire shall be to thy husband, and he shall rule over thee".

As we look at leadership in the Church, there are certain qualities God requires of elders and deacons. "Take heed unto yourselves, and to all the flock, over the which the Holy Ghost hath made you overseers, to feed the Church of God, which He hath purchased with His own blood", (Acts 20 v.28). An elder "must be blameless, as the steward of God; not selfwilled, not soon angry, not given to wine, no striker, not given to filthy lucre; But a lover of hospitality, a lover of good men, sober, just, holy, temperate; Holding fast the faithful Word as he hath been taught, that he may be able by sound doctrine both to exhort and to convince the gainsayers", (Titus 1 v.7-9).

The words "overseer", "presbyter", "elder" and "bishop" are interchangeable in Scripture. The New Testament envisages an identifiable, distinctive group of 'men' whose sphere of authority and ministry is of a spiritual nature. The plurality of elders is a check on self-will and dictatorship, and protects against the introduction of false doctrine. Their unity in the truth should be an example for the "flock" to imitate.

In the Hebrew Old Testament the word for elder is "zagen", and in the Greek New Testament it is the word "presbyteros". The "elders of the people" or "elders of Israel" are frequently associated with Moses' leadership. (Exod. 4 v.29, 17 v.5, 24 v.1, Numb. 11 v.16). They were prominent during the Monarchy (1 Sam. 8 v.4, 2 Sam. 3 v.17, 1 Kings 21 v.8), the Exile (Jer. 29 v.1, Ezek. 20 v.1), and after the Return (Ezra 5 v.9-11, 6 v.7). They were also associated with Moses and Aaron in conveying the Word of God to the people (Exod. 3 v.16-18). The Sanhedrin is regarded as having been set up by Moses in his appointment of the seventy elders (Numb. 11 v.16- 30).

"Elders" or "presbyters" appear early in the life of the New Testament Church and they are associated with James in the government of the local Church at Jerusalem after the manner of the synagogue (Acts 11 v.30, 21 v.18). With the Apostles they share in the wider government of the church (Acts 15 v.2,6,23; 16 v.4).

An apostle can be a presbyter (1 Peter 5 v.1). The presbyters whom Paul addressed at Ephesus (Acts 20 v.17-35) and those addressed in 1 Peter and Titus have a decisive place in Church life. They share in the ministry of Christ toward the flock (Acts 20 v.28, Eph. 4 v.11, 1 Peter 5 v.1-4).

In the Gentile Churches the name "episkopos" is used as a substitute for "presbyteros" with identical meaning. In Acts 20 v.17,28 and Titus 1 v.5-9 the words are interchangeable. In 1 Tim. 5 v.17 teaching as well as oversight is regarded as a function of the presbyter, and thus the office and qualifications of those holding it developed as the New Testament clearly indicates.

The Biblical guidelines must be followed in the appointment of elders and deacons. The process of leadership, elders and deacons, is begun by the Spirit of God. "This is a true saying, if a man desire the office of a bishop, he desireth a good work", (1 Tim. 3 v.1). Only the one who has learned to serve is qualified to lead. After much prayer, study of the Word of God, and experience in life and service does a true elder emerge. He is recognised and respected as worthy of the office in whom the congregation can have confidence.

Ideally, an elder, or deacon, should be a married man with a disciplined and respected family. The elder's wife is to be supportive and submissive, an example in good works and words. "Even so must their wives be grave, not slanderers, sober, faithful in all things", (1 Tim. 3 v.11). A leader is one who knows the way, shows the way, and goes the way. He cannot lead where he does not go, and cannot teach what he does not know.

The glory of God and the blessing of His people are the objectives, self-interest has no place. For the first time in the appointment of deacons the laying on of hands is mentioned in Acts 6. The rule of 1 Cor. 14 v.34, "Let your women keep silence in the Churches", is positive, explicit, universal. It is simple, clear, plain, authoritative. The meaning cannot be mistaken, it refers to all acts of preaching, teaching, and asking of questions in the public worship and administration of the Church, "For it is a shame for women to speak in the Church", (1 Cor. 14 v.35). The Greek word translated "shame" means disgraceful, unbecoming, indecorous, indecent, unseemly.

New Testament Distinctions in Roles

The Lord Jesus Christ placed a high value on women during His earthly ministry. He said, "He Who made them at the beginning made them male and female", (Matt. 19 v.4). In other words, both men and women were created in the image of God. He does not look down on women. Take for example the woman of Samaria (John 4), the widow of Nain (Luke 7), and others, it is worthy to note that He afforded women a spiritual and covenant status equal to that of men. Not only did He minister to women, He also received a certain ministry from women. What is more, women were last at the Cross, and first at the Tomb.

However, the New Testament clearly shows there are distinctions in the roles that males and females fill. This is clearly observed in Jesus' selection of men only to be His Apostles. Many so-called Biblical 'feminists' would argue against this, claiming that culture today is different from the early days of the Church which of course is a mere truism.

In the selection of the seven deacons as recorded in Acts 6 v.1-8, again men only were chosen to take care of the material needs and temporal affairs of the Church: "Men of honest report, full of the Holy Ghost and wisdom", that is, those who are fitted to such a trust, and whom you can confide in. By prayer and the laying on of hands gave them authority to execute that office, so that the Apostles were free to give themselves continually to prayer and to the ministry of the Word of life.

Likewise, throughout the New Testament, the selection of elders in the Early Church, men only were called and chosen. The qualifications for Christian leaders to this office are given in detail in such passages as 1 Timothy 3 and Titus 1.

"This is a true saying, if a man desire the office of a bishop, he desireth a good work. A bishop then must be blameless, the husband of one wife, vigilant, sober, of good behaviour, given to hospitality, apt to teach; Not given to wine, no striker, not greedy of filthy lucre; but patient, not a brawler, not covetous; One that ruleth well his own house, having his children in subjection with all gravity; For if a man know not how to rule his own house, how shall he take care of the Church of God? Not a novice, lest being lifted up with pride he fall into the condemnation of the devil. Moreover he must have a good report of them which are without; lest he fall into reproach and the snare of the devil. Likewise must the deacons be grave, not double tongued, not given to much wine, not greedy of filthy lucre; Holding the mystery of the faith in a pure conscience. And let these also first be proved; then let them use the office of a deacon, being found blameless. Even so must their wives be grave, not slanderous, sober, faithful in all things. Let the deacons be the husbands of one wife, ruling their children and their own houses well. For they that have used the office of a deacon well purchase to themselves a good degree, and great boldness in the faith, which is in Christ Jesus", (1 Tim. 3 v.1-13).

"For this cause left I thee in Crete, that thou shouldest set in order the things that are wanting, and ordain elders in every city, as I had appointed thee: If any be blameless, the husband of one wife, having faithful children not accused of riot or unruly. For a bishop must be blameless, as the steward of God; not self willed, not soon angry, not given to wine, no striker, not given to filthy lucre; But a lover of hospitality, a lover of good men, sober, just, holy, temperate; Holding fast the faithful Word as he hath been taught, that he may be able by sound doctrine both to exhort and to convince the gainsayers", (Titus 1 v.5-9).

By Divine appointment this is a work of the greatest importance. The office of "elder", as noted earlier, is sometimes referred to in Scripture as "overseer", "presbyter", or "bishop", whose business is the spiritual care and charge of the Churches, to feed and govern them, and perform all pastoral work and duty in and towards them. "Holding fast the faithful Word as he hath been taught, that he may be able by sound doctrine both to exhort and to convince the gainsayers", (Titus 1 v.9).

The Devices of Feminism

Fifty years or so ago, the role of women in society was a subject seldom aired, let alone discussed at Church synods, assemblies, or conferences. In other words, the Bible's teaching on the role of women was still largely accepted by society.

But there was a tremendous shift in thinking when the 'feminist' movement got under way in a somewhat more militant fashion in the 1960's. The 1960's were times of change in both culture and Church. In the goal for ecumenical unity, doctrine was being decried and belief in Biblical truth minimized, if not lost. The country and the world are becoming increasingly irreligious. Man in his intellectual pride is rejecting the Word of God.

At present we are living in a time when many women are not satisfied with their lot in life. Many have found no real happiness or joy in being wives, mothers, and homemakers. They want freedom, liberation and equality with men, so much so that some have united to form a vocal minority called the Women's Liberation Movement.

It would seem that few of these so-called modern women really know what the women's role in life is logically and Scripturally. The Bible, they say, is an out-dated Book for most people today. True indeed, the average woman never reads it, for if she did, her God-given role in life would be known and practised. The non-Christian woman, like the non-Christian man, rarely, if ever, reads the Bible and even when they do they lack the enabling of the Holy Spirit to give them true understanding of it.

Herein lies the root of all the 'feminist' woman's problems, they, that is the 'feminist' lobby, are ignorant of the teachings of the Word of God. The Scriptures clearly teach us that all mankind "have sinned, and come short of the glory of God", (Rom. 3 v.23). The Bible tells us that unregenerate souls are "dead in trespasses and sins", (Eph. 2 v.2). The natural man is destitute of the principles and powers of spiritual life, cut off from God, and walking "according to the course of this world" (Eph. 2 v.2) in "the bondage of corruption" (Rom. 8 v.21) and sin as the slave of Satan: "Having the understanding darkened, being alienated from the life of God through the ignorance that is in them, because of the blindness of their heart", (Eph. 4 v.18). The trouble about men and women in sin is that they are being carried along in rebellion against God, governed and controlled by the world, the flesh, and the devil. There is only one answer, one remedy, to this calamitous condition, and that is deliverance from sin through Christ Who "hath once suffered from sins, the Just for the unjust, that He might bring us to God", (1 Peter 3 v.18). Every converted sinner is a saved sinner, delivered from sin and the wrath of God's judgment to come. They are brought into a state of salvation, into the kingdom of God, and have a right given them by grace to eternal joy and happiness. The grace that saves them is the free, unmerited favour and undeserved goodness of God. He saves them through faith in Christ Jesus. "For by grace are ye saved through faith; and that not of yourselves: it is the gift of God: Not of works, lest any man should boast", (Eph. 2 v.8-9). The God Who saves us is the God Who keeps us. Nothing less than the power of God can redeem us from the curse of sin. We who are Christians are delivered from the plight and penalty of sin solely because of His wondrous grace and love. Sin, therefore, as the Bible teaches, is lawlessness: "sin is the transgression of the Law", (1 John 3 v.4). It is lack of conformity to the Law of God, and because of this, it is no wonder then that women today are complaining, murmuring, grumbling, and upset over a situation they do not have any spiritual discernment about.

"The classical definition of feminism", as Sharon James states in her helpful book, 'God's Design for Women', "would be a wish for equal opportunities and an end of legal discrimination against women, we surely all sympathize with feminism in the broadest sense, that of calling for women to have political, economic and social rights. The first stage of feminist agitation took place from the late eighteenth to the early twentieth century (sometimes referred to as 'liberal' feminism). Whether as a result of wider societal change, or as a result of this agitation (or both), women were eventually granted the vote, property rights, access to education and to the professions".

"Second-wave feminism", she goes on to write, "was very different. A small number of thinkers aimed, in effect, to liberate women from their womanhood. The very things that were of central importance for so many (marriage, motherhood, homemaking) were derided as being fit only for those who were mentally subnormal or emotionally weak. These ideas could not have insulted women more. Those who propagated them were often academics, who had a deep compassion for the plight of the majority of women. They argued that those who devoted themselves to their families were ignorant and deceived. All would be solved if they were re-educated by going to consciousness-raising classes (in the 1960's) or a Woman's Studies Course (in the 1980's)". Sharon James rightly argues that adoption of these ideas led only to misery and frustration. Far from being liberated by modern 'feminism', women have been betrayed.

Damaging Effects of Radical Feminism

The effect of the permissive sixties, the era marked by 'Women's Lib', when the popular notion that equality means sameness took root, the idea that there is any essential difference between the sexes has been defined by some academics as heresy. The 'feminist' movement now took on a very different role and meaning, which augured omens for the future, certainly not for good, but evil.

During that revolutionary period, as Sharon James highlights in her book, 'God's Design for Women', "the traditional family came under vicious attack. Radical 'feminists' said that marriage was an outdated institution which kept women imprisoned at home doing menial things like looking after children. Women would only be free if they were independent, if they could sleep with whom they wanted, and if they had the right to raise children on their own".

Such philosophy led to a serious fragmentation and transformation of traditional family values and structures. Society has been adversely influenced by these 'feminist' assumptions. These changes have resulted in a massive explosion of babies being born outside of marriage, and also that men, in their role as husbands and fathers, are considered no longer necessary for the job of raising children. The dictate and drive to get women 'out' of the house by inferring that being a housewife is terribly demeaning, is reflected in the free-fall of morality and justice throughout the entire nation. This immoral situation is greatly aided, abetted and encouraged by government legislation while penalising marriage by its tax and welfare systems to accommodate 'equal rights' for single mothers, cohabitation, gay partners, homosexuals, lesbians, and others.

Marriage nowadays is largely abandoned, and the idea that a woman may find her chief role in life as a wife and mother has been discredited almost beyond repair. "Radical Feminists", as Sharon James again points out, "reject all gender distinctions as sexist, others argued that women are the superior sex, but all united to mock the notion that God created male and female with distinctive characteristics for distinctive callings". There is no God, and there are no rules, some may claim, but as Sharon James emphasises, "It is increasingly common today to demand the freedom to define our own sexuality and our own sexual orientation, whether male or female heterosexual, male or female homosexual, male or female bisexual". However fashionable all this may appear to be as being a matter of choice, runs completely counter to the plain teaching of the Word of God. The Bible tells us that when God created man, male and female, He designed marriage as a Divine institution to unite one male with one female. "Wherefore they are no more twain, but one flesh. What therefore God hath joined together, let not man put asunder", (Matt. 19 v.6).

The devil is at work to overthrow the Divine order, and while Satan is constantly undermining the God-given distinctions between male and female, nevertheless manhood and womanhood will always be part of our humanity in God's good creation. The enemy's strategy is to manipulate, destroy and deny the differences of gender, but as Christians we must ever uphold and affirm the Biblical truth that "male and female created He them", (Gen. 1 v.27).

The union between one man and one woman in marriage is the most intimate that can be, a sacred thing that must not be violated. God Himself has joined them together. He has not only, as Creator, fitted them to be comforts and helpmates for each other, but He has, in wisdom and goodness, appointed them to live together in love until death parts them. Marriage is not an invention of men, but a Divine institution, and therefore is to be religiously observed, and the more so, because it is a figure of the mystical, inseparable union between Christ and His Church, often referred to in Scripture as His bride. "But from the beginning of creation God made them male and female. For this cause shall a man leave his father and mother, and cleave to his wife; And they twain shall be one flesh: so then they are no more twain, but one flesh. What therefore God hath joined together, let not man put asunder", (Mark 10 v.6-9).

Radical 'feminism' has been at the forefront in public debate and policy over the past four decades, the effects and consequences of which have been devastating in society as a whole, and sadly its corruption has crept into the life of the Church as well. It has skilfully, forcefully and persuasively advanced the idea and promoted the notion that women must be liberated from marriage. Radical 'feminists', furthermore, insist that women must be released and liberated from motherhood, from housekeeping, from staying at home, from family life, from having children, and even from their femininity. Their greatest push, of course, is to be liberated and freed from men, and especially from the religion and truths of the Bible.

God's law, order and appointment are completely disregarded and totally annulled by the modern 'feminist' movement. The Bible establishes God's order, and God's appointment, that Adam is the father of the entire human race; the man is the head of the woman and of the family; Abraham is the father of the faithful; and the genealogy of the Messiah from Abraham is reckoned through the male line.

In Genesis, chapters 1-3, the principle of headship is laid, which has to do with leadership and direction, not domination and suppression.

It has nothing to do with superiority and power, or inferiority and physical weakness, but has everything to do with the proper orderly functioning of a family, society, or nation. God created man, male and female, with distinctive qualities for distinctive roles.

It is not at all surprising when God's holy law is crudely and rudely challenged, openly called into question, and blatantly opposed and rejected by radical 'feminists', that dark clouds of sexual immorality and promiscuity may be seen in society which greatly corrupt and blight the nation. We must also observe, and be vigilant, that the devil, by using such enemies of God, and enemies of the Scriptures, as his willing tools, is himself the attacker. Night and day he goes about seeking whom he may ensnare to their eternal ruin. We are warned in Scripture to "be sober, be vigilant; because your adversary the devil, as a roaring lion, walketh about, seeking whom he may devour: whom resist stedfast in the faith . . . . . knowing that . . . . . the God of all grace . . . . . make you perfect, stablish, strengthen, settle you. To Him be glory and dominion for ever and ever", (1 Peter 5 v.8-11).

Satan's objective is to eradicate the creation order and distinctions between male and female; the creation ordinance of marriage as a natural relationship of life; and the creation institution and Divine pattern for the family. We are to be "followers of God", (Eph. 5 v.1), ever seeking to carry out our responsibilities and obligations according to the pattern God has revealed in His Word.

The Subtle Strategy of The Enemy

More serious is the fact that Christian family values and standards are under constant attack with the object of eliminating the teaching of the Bible from society. The radical 'feminist' agenda of 'liberating' women is aimed at bringing an end to the traditional family. The divisive strategy and destructive subtlety of the devil are being implemented in three stages:-

(1) The removal of privileges from the traditional family;

(2) Alternative family patterns would be given greater support; and

(3) History would be re-written with an all-out attack launched against the traditional Christian family unit.

For a number of decades now these strategies are being successfully employed throughout the Western world. Chastity, morality and modesty are ridiculed with the result that today two generations have been cheated by this evil philosophy. The results have been catastrophic. Women, in fact, are the victims, not the victors, in this battle of the sexes waged by radical 'feminists'. Rather than being liberated, they are being betrayed and exploited.

It is most needful, therefore, for us to be clear about God's purpose for women. In today's society it is absolutely necessary to set forth afresh the basic standards and Biblical truths concerning the 'role of women', in order that the Church might rejoice more greatly in the truth, be strong in the Lord, and take action for Him. May God give us firm convictions to stand solidly upon the teaching of Holy Scripture, and that the Bible's authority is absolute and final in all matters of faith and life.

Let us, then, remind ourselves that in the Scriptures, God has given to His Church, His Testimony. Being inspired, infallible, inerrant, complete, and invariable, the Bible contains the authoritative revelation of His Mind and Will to mankind. "For He established a testimony in Jacob, and appointed a law in Israel, which He commanded our fathers, that they should make them known to their children: That the generation to come might know them, even the children which should be born; who should arise and declare them to their children", (Psalm 78 v.5-6).

As we acknowledge the sole Headship of the Lord Jesus Christ and His exclusive right to rule as King and Head over His Church, we must realise that no human interpretation can ever be regarded as final. The infallible rule of interpretation of Scripture is the Scripture itself. "Knowing this first, that no prophesy of The Scripture is of any private interpretation", (2 Peter 1 v.20). The Church is under obligation to be guided in all her doings by His Word alone. It is her solemn duty to uphold, maintain and defend a witness that is not at variance with the truth of Scripture. Some Churches have so far degenerated from the witness of God's Word as to become citadels of error and synagogues of Satan. Nevertheless, God will never leave Himself without a true witness, and there shall always be a Church on earth to worship God according to the Scriptures. "His name shall endure forever: His name shall be continued as long as the sun: and men shall be blessed in Him: all nations shall call Him blessed", (Psalm 72 v.17).

As we, therefore, pursue the subject before us from a Biblical perspective, we shall consider several principles governing the role of women in society and in the Church. We will now examine in a little more depth and detail some of these principles, then proceed, among other things, to show the Scriptural requirements and qualifications of leadership, and the Divine command to restore eldership to its rightful place in the Church.

CHAPTER THREE

MALE AND FEMALE IN THE IMAGE OF GOD

The Image of God defaced

The Image of God renewed and restored

The Weaker Vessel

Heirs Together of the Grace of Life

Choosing a Marriage Partner

Man made to Serve

MALE AND FEMALE IN THE IMAGE OF GOD

When God created mankind, He made them "male and female". "So God created man in His own image, in the image of God created He him; male and female created He them", (Gen. 1 v.27).

Here right at creation we have the very important principle, that morally and spiritually, there was a wonderful sameness between the male and the female. Both were created in the image of God, in perfect knowledge, perfect righteousness, and perfect holiness. There is no hint here of superiority or inferiority. Men and women enjoy equality of personhood, dignity, and worth.

In making man, God had a wonderful purpose as we discover what it means to be made in God's image. The Westminster Shorter Catechism brings Biblical facts together when it states, "God created man, male and female, after His own image, in knowledge, righteousness, and holiness, with dominion over the creatures", (No.10).

We read in Prov.19 v.2, "that the soul be without knowledge, it is not good". God gave Adam a true understanding of the world in which he lived, and what he knew about God, about himself, and about the creation was accurate. We know this to be true from Paul's statement to the Colossians, "And we have put on the new man, which is renewed in knowledge after the image of Him that created him", (Col. 3 v.10). From this we learn that knowledge must have been an original gift of God. We are told that God walked with Adam in the Garden, and no doubt that was a time of fellowship and instruction and communion together.

Not only was man made in the image of God in knowledge, but also in righteousness and holiness. Paul speaks of "the new man, which after God is created in righteousness and true holiness", (Eph. 4 v.24), which confirms that these also must have been original attributes of man as God made him. When God made Adam, He made him holy, just, good, and true. Adam was not only a rational being, he was also made a moral being.

Furthermore, man was created, male and female, in the image of God to have dominion, for God said unto them, "Be fruitful, and multiply, and replenish the earth, and subdue it: and have dominion over . . . . . every living thing that moveth upon the earth", (Gen. 1 v.28). When God created man, He did so for a definite purpose, which is "to glorify God and to enjoy Him for ever", (W.S.C. No.1). This of course means to recognise God's sovereignty over all things, and to worship Him, love Him, and to serve Him faithfully. It means to accept His Word, His instructions, and His commands without hesitation, question or complaint; and to utilize fully the gifts, talents, and resources He has given, in such a way that His name is hallowed, His Kingdom extended, and His will done on earth.

Adam knew the dignity of work and the satisfaction of accomplishment. To do the will of God is always purposeful, satisfying, and fulfilling because that is the reason we are made. Man is a wonderful being because he is made by God, like God, and for God.

The Image of God defaced

Of course, through the Fall in the Garden of Eden by the entrance of sin into the world, man lost his innocence and his relationship with the Creator --- that communion and fellowship with God was broken. Sin has now defaced that part of the image of God in a certain way, for James 3 v.9 says, that all "are made after the similitude of God".

The Bible teaches us that sin entered the world as the result of the transgression of Adam and Eve in paradise. The first sin was occasioned by the temptation of Satan in the form of a serpent who sowed in man's heart the seeds of distrust and disbelief.

The first sin consisted in man's eating of the tree of the knowledge of good and evil. This eating was sinful simply because God had forbidden it. It clearly showed that man was not willing to subject his will unconditionally to the will of God. In the mind and intellect it revealed itself as unbelief and pride, in the will as the desire to be like God, and in the affections as an unholy satisfaction in eating of the forbidden fruit. As a result, man lost the image of God in the restricted sense, became estranged from God, guilty and utterly corrupt, and fell under the curse and sway of death. "Wherefore, as by one man sin entered into the world, and death by sin; and so death passed upon all men, for that all have sinned", (Rom. 5 v.12). We further read in Rom. 6 v.23, "For the wages of sin is death; but the gift of God is eternal life through Jesus Christ our Lord".

The only way to restore spiritual health and be reconciled to God is to face the problem of sin. Forgiveness and cleansing from sin come only when we acknowledge our true sinful condition before a holy God. The Psalmist, David, said, "I acknowledge my sin unto Thee, and mine iniquity have I not hid. I said, I will confess my transgressions unto the Lord; and Thou forgavest the iniquity of my sin", (Psalm 32 v.5).

We must understand how sin has affected us, otherwise a weak and superficial view of sin inevitably leads to a weak view of salvation. Sin is a serious matter, it is terrible, tragic. We have noted above that man was made in the image of God as a rational, moral, and purposive being. Here we are dealing with the whole man, his mind, his emotions or desires, and his will. Sin has affected the whole man. Hence, the Scriptural doctrine known as the Total Depravity of Mankind.

If sin has only partially affected man, as the modernists argue, there is some possibility that man can have some part in his salvation. This is the devil's lie, and is the major difference between the teaching of Arminianism and that of the Bible for which the Reformers, Covenanters, Puritans, Heroes and Martyrs of the Faith consistently contended (Jude v.3). It has tremendous consequences, either our salvation is in the hands of God or it is in the hands of man himself. "Salvation belongeth unto the Lord: Thy blessing is upon Thy people", (Psalm 3 v.8), declares the Psalmist.

When our first parents fell from the estate wherein they were created, they lost their original attributes of true knowledge, righteousness and holiness. They no longer desired to do what was right and holy, but rather became prejudiced against righteousness and holiness, in rebellion against God.

Adam was to be a good steward of all that God had entrusted to him. Instead he chose to do his own thing, with the consequence that all mankind fell with him in his first transgression. "For all have sinned, and come short of the glory of God", (Rom. 3 v.23). As descendants of Adam we are guilty of sin, lack original righteousness, and are corrupted in our whole nature. Because we are corrupt, we commit actual transgressions, which affects our minds, our morals, our manners and behaviour. Sin has affected our thinking, our character, and our will. It has had total effect. We are utterly lost in sin and need to be saved by the sovereign grace of God. Salvation can only be effected by the power of the Holy Spirit, through the blood shed on Calvary of the Everlasting Lamb, the Lord Jesus Christ, Who gave Himself a sacrifice for the sins of His people upon the Cross, as our Substitute, "that He might bring us to God", (1 Peter 3 v.18).

In order to receive the gift of God's salvation, there must be an inward transformation and renewal "in the spirit of your mind", (Eph. 4 v.23); there must be reconciliation to God through Christ: "For God hath made Him to be sin for us, Who knew no sin; that we might be made the righteousness of God in Him", (2 Cor. 5 v.21); and there must be restoration to the purpose for which God made us.

The work of Christ as our Prophet, Priest, and King, has secured for us our eternal redemption. God says, "This is My beloved Son, in Whom I am well pleased; hear ye Him", (Matt. 17 v.5). He is our great Advocate, Who "is able also to save them to the uttermost that come unto God by Him, seeing He ever liveth to make intercession for them", (Heb. 7 v.25).

How wonderful to know the assurance that "sin shall not have dominion over you: for ye are not under the law, but under grace", (Rom. 6 v.14). Jesus said, "I am the way (priest), and the truth (prophet), and the life (king): no man cometh unto the Father, but by Me", (John 14 v.6). We need not only revelation, reconciliation, and restoration, but also a renewed mind, renewed desires, and a renewed will. We need the Word of God to give us information, and we need the Spirit of God to give us the illumination if we are to come to faith in God. "But without faith it is impossible to please Him: for he that cometh to God must believe that He is, and that He is a rewarder of them that diligently seek Him", (Heb. 11 v.6).

The only way to have a clear conscience before God, is to confess and forsake our sin, and take our burdens to Calvary. It is the Spirit of God Who enlightens our minds to bring us to faith, and He convicts our conscience to bring us to repentance. With so much spurious and superficial Christianity around us in these days, the Scriptures warn us to "give diligence to make your calling and election sure", (2 Peter 1 v.10).

"No man can come to Me, except the Father which hath sent Me draw him", says Christ in John 6 v.44. We need to be effectually called, and for our calling to be effectual, the Holy Spirit must enlighten the mind, convict the conscience, and renew the will. "Effectual calling is the work of God's Spirit, whereby, convincing us of our sin and misery, enlightening our minds in the knowledge of Christ, and renewing our wills, He doth persuade and enable us to embrace Jesus Christ, freely offered to us in the Gospel", (W.S.C. No.31).

It is the Holy Spirit Who enlightens the mind to bring us to faith in Christ, He convicts the conscience to bring us to repentance from sin unto life, and He renews the will to bring us to obedience of His holy

Truth. Jesus said, "He that hath My commandments, and keepeth them, he it is that loveth Me . . . . . If any man love Me, he will keep My words", (John 14 v.21 and 23).

We do not stand still in the Christian life, it is never static. We "grow in grace, and in the knowledge of our Lord and Saviour Jesus Christ", (2 Peter 3 v.18). When we discover from the Word of God what He wants us to be and to do, and we do it, then we have found the wonderful discovery and purpose for which God has made us. The benefits and blessings of redemption are those set forth in such Biblical terms as life, faith, repentance, justification, adoption, sanctification, together with assurance of God's love, increase of grace, pardon and forgiveness of sin, peace of conscience, joy in the Holy Ghost, perseverance and the hope of eternal glory in heaven. God's great plan and purpose in giving us these benefits is that we might be like Him as we obey His Word. This is God's work in the whole man to make him whole. "And we know that all things work together for good to them that love God, to them who are the called according to His purpose. For whom He did foreknow, He also did predestinate to be conformed to the image of His Son, that He might be the firstborn among many brethren. Moreover whom He did predestinate, them He also called: and whom He called, them He also justified: and whom He justified, them He also glorified", (Rom. 8 v.28-30). "We are more than conquerors" through Christ Who loved us; and nothing "shall be able to separate us from the love of God, which is in Christ Jesus our Lord", (Rom. 8 v.37 and 39). May it be our prayer day by day to know what the Psalmist David knew: "He restoreth my soul: He leadeth me in the paths of righteousness for His name's sake", (Psalm 23 v.3).

The short Twenty Third is often referred to as the "Pearl of the Psalms", which speaks of the Shepherd and the Sheep, the Guide and the Traveller, and the Host and the Guest. The sheep are a purchased possession, God's own redeemed people. The travellers are making progress as pilgrims on the Homeward journey, and the guests are those who have arrived at the Home of many mansions. Poor indeed is that soul that cannot say, "yea, though I walk through the valley of the shadow of death, I will fear no evil; for Thou art with me; Thy rod and Thy staff they comfort me", (Psalm 23 v.4) . . . . . for the grave is not the end, but the passage way that leads to endless light and life, into the glory and beauty of "the House of the Lord", where the believer will "dwell for ever", (Psalm 23 v.6) . . . . . in heaven. Beyond the night of death, lies the perfect day. Beyond the valley of the shadow, lie the plains of peace, the Homeland, Glory itself, the Father's House, not made with hands, but eternal in the heavens.

The Image of God renewed and restored

It has been rightly said that every sermon should contain the three Rs --- ruin by sin in Adam, redemption by the shedding of blood in the substitutionary nature of the atonement of Christ, and regeneration by the quickening power of the Holy Spirit. We rejoice in the Gospel of the Lord Jesus Christ, "and have no confidence in the flesh", (Phil. 3 v.3). It is the glorious message of God to guilty hell-deserving sinners, as all of us are by nature --- that to His own glory God justly saves His people from their sins through Christ's redeeming blood. "For all have sinned, and come short of the glory of God; Being justified freely by His grace through the redemption that is in Christ Jesus: Whom God hath set forth to be a propitiation through faith in His blood, to declare His righteousness for the remission of sins that are past, through the forbearance of God; To declare, I say, at this time His righteousness: that He might be just, and the justifier of him which believeth in Jesus", (Rom. 3 v.23-26).

The Apostle John in the Book of Revelation writes of Christ Who "loved us, and washed us from our sins in His own blood, And hath made us kings and priests unto God and His Father; to Him be glory and dominion for ever and ever", (Rev.1 v.5-6). The Gospel of Jesus Christ declares that He came to save sinners. "I am not come to call the righteous, but sinners to repentance", said Jesus, (Matt. 9 v.13).

If all men are not guilty, or if they can work up their own righteousness and salvation, there was no need for Christ to come in the flesh to establish a righteousness for sinners and then die to bestow it on them. "And the Word was made flesh, and dwelt among us, and we beheld His glory, the glory as of the only begotten of the Father, full of grace and truth", (John 1 v.14).

But all men are totally depraved, "sold under sin" (Rom. 7 v.14), that is, every part of them is affected by sin and thus they stand guilty before God and unable to save themselves, and cannot entertain any righteous notion or perform any righteous action toward heaven. "We are all as an unclean thing, and all our righteousnesses are as filthy rags; and we all do fade as a leaf; and our iniquities, like the wind, have taken us away. And there is none that calleth upon Thy name, that stirreth up himself to take hold of Thee: for Thou hast hid Thy face from us, and hast consumed us, because of our iniquities. But now, O Lord, Thou art our Father; we are the clay, and Thou our Potter; and we all are the work of Thy hand", (Isaiah 64 v.6-8). The Apostle Paul writing to the Romans declared, "They are all under sin; There is none righteous, no, not one. There is none that understandeth, there is none that seeketh after God. They are all gone out of the way, they are together become unprofitable; there is none that doeth good, no, not one", (Rom. 3 v.9-12).

To preach a 'gospel' that denies total ruin by the Fall of man in the Garden of Eden, is to deny the message of the Lord Jesus Christ altogether. "But if we walk in the light, as He is in the light, we have fellowship one with another, and the blood of Jesus Christ His Son cleanseth us from all sin. If we say that we have no sin, we deceive ourselves, and the truth is not in us. If we confess our sins, He is faithful and just to forgive us our sins, and to cleanse us from all unrighteousness. If we say that we have not sinned, we make Him a liar, and His Word is not in us", (1 John 1 v.7-10).

The Gospel of the Lord Jesus Christ declares that His priestly work was absolutely successful. "I have glorified Thee on the earth", says

Christ, "I have finished the work which Thou gavest Me to do. And now, O Father, glorify Thou Me with Thine own Self with the glory which I had with Thee before the world was", (John 17 v.4-5). Writing to the Hebrews, Paul clearly states, "For by one offering He hath perfected for ever them that are sanctified. Wherefore the Holy Ghost also is a witness to us: for after that He had said before, This is the covenant that I will make with them after those days, saith the Lord, I will put My laws into their hearts, and in their minds will I write them; And their sins and iniquities will I remember no more", (Heb. 10 v.14-17).

Christ died, not to make salvation 'possible' for all sinners, but to make complete atonement for the sins of all His elect covenant people. "Wherefore in all things it behoved Him to be made like unto His brethren, that He might be a merciful and faithful High Priest in things pertaining to God, to make reconciliation for the sins of the people", (Heb. 2 v.17). "But Christ being come an High Priest of good things to come, by a greater and more perfect tabernacle, not made with hands, that is to say, not of this building; Neither by the blood of goats and calves, but by His own blood He entered in once into the holy place, having obtained eternal redemption for us", (Heb. 9 v.11-12). Those for whom He died shall most certainly be saved. "All that the Father giveth Me shall come to Me; and him that cometh to Me I will in no wise cast out", (John 6 v.37). "For by grace are ye saved through faith; and that not of yourselves: it is the gift of God: Not of works, lest any man should boast", (Eph. 2 v.8-9).

To preach a 'gospel' that denies the effectual and particular redeeming work of Jesus Christ, is again to deny the Gospel of Christ altogether. Paul warns the Galatians when he says, "I marvel that ye are so soon removed from Him that called you into the grace of Christ unto another gospel: which is not another; but there be some that trouble you, and would pervert the Gospel of Christ. But though we, or an angel from heaven, preach any other gospel unto you than that which we have preached unto you, let him be accursed. As we said before, so say I now again, if any man preach any other gospel unto you than that ye have received, let him be accursed. For do I now persuade men, or God? Or do I speak to please men? For if I yet pleased men, I should not be the servant of Christ", (Gal. 1 v.6-10).

What a glorious message we have, for the Gospel of the Lord Jesus Christ also declares that those He died to justify, will, in due time, be irresistibly called and saved through the preaching of the Everlasting Gospel. "For whom He did foreknow, He also did predestinate to be conformed to the image of His Son, that He might be the firstborn among many brethren. Moreover whom He did predestinate, them He also called: and whom He called, them He also justified: and whom He justified, them He also glorified", (Rom. 8 v.29-30). "For we preach not ourselves, but Christ Jesus the Lord; and ourselves your servants for Jesus sake. For God, Who commanded the light to shine out of darkness, hath shined in our hearts, to give the light of the knowledge of the glory of God in the face of Jesus Christ", (2 Cor. 4 v.5-6).

This is most certainly not reformation and education of the old sinful nature, but rather the saving power and revelation of the glory of Christ within us. "Howbeit when He, the Spirit of Truth, is come, He will guide you into all Truth", (John 16 v.13). "I am crucified with Christ: nevertheless I live; yet not I, but Christ liveth in me; and the life which I now live in the flesh I live by the faith of the Son of God, Who loved me, and gave Himself for me", (Gal. 2 v.20). "But God, Who is rich in mercy, for His great love wherewith He loved us, Even when we were dead in sins, hath quickened us together with Christ, by grace ye are saved", (Eph. 2 v.4-5). This is the regenerating work of God the Holy Spirit, making sinners new creatures in Christ Jesus, and implanting within them a new sinless nature after the image of God. "Except a man be born of water and of the Spirit, he cannot enter into the Kingdom of God. That which is born of the flesh is flesh; and that which is born of the Spirit is spirit. Marvel not that I said unto thee", says Jesus, "Ye must be born again", (John 3 v.5-7). "Therefore if any man be in Christ, he is a new creature: old things are passed away; behold, all things are become new", (2 Cor. 5 v.17).

"Put on the new man which after God is created in righteousness and true holiness. Wherefore putting away lying, speak every man truth with his neighbour: for we are members one of another", (Eph. 4 v.24-25).

As believers open their hearts to God in His Word and prayer, the Holy Spirit will enable them to flee from sin and temptation, and guide them to live godly lives in Christ Jesus. The great need today is to promote Biblical teaching that will serve to correct the all too common pseudo-spirituality of our time. With a clear mind, a warm heart, and an obedient will, we are commanded to serve God with the whole person, which is our reasonable service. Christians today stand in urgent need of sound Scriptural teaching --- which humbles man, strengthens faith, and glorifies God.

"I beseech you therefore, brethren, by the mercies of God, that ye present your bodies a living sacrifice, holy, acceptable unto God, which is your reasonable service. And be not conformed to this world: but be ye transformed by the renewing of your mind, that ye may prove what is that good, and acceptable, and perfect, will of God", (Rom. 12 v.1-2).

This book is written to restore believers to a lost heritage of Christian observance and obedience to Biblical standards, for Scripture alone is the final, infallible authority in all matters of faith and conduct. "Teach me Thy way, O Lord, and lead me in a plain path", (Psalm 27 v11).

The Weaker Vessel

In addressing the subject of the weaker vessel, we will notice in Gen. 1 v.27, that there is a basic difference between man and woman: "Male and female created He them". They are different physically and biologically. Physically, the man is stronger; while the woman, as The Scripture say, is "the weaker vessel", and as such is to be honoured. "Likewise, ye husbands, dwell with them according to knowledge, giving honour unto the wife, as unto the weaker vessel, and as heirs together of the grace of life; that your prayers be not hindered", (1 Peter 3 v.7).

Husbands are here exhorted as to their domestic responsibilities. As to the order in the home, man is answerable to God for all that goes on in his house, and in regard to harmony there is a mutual consideration to "submit yourselves one to another in the fear of God", (Eph. 5 v.21).

The husbands are to "dwell with" their wives as the Greek word "sunoikeo" quite literally means "house together", or "make a home together" in every aspect of a shared home-life. The implications of this are far-reaching, pointing back to the primal union of leading in the loving, and in the leaving, and in the cleaving, (Gen. 2 v.24; Eph. 5 v.25-33). The continuing exercise of home-making is to be "according to knowledge", not only in the physical, but also in the bringing together of their separate gifts and attributes to provide one harmonious contribution to the home and family.

Generally speaking, men by nature are usually physically larger and stronger than women. Their strength and physic were designed for the protection and welfare of women. In previous generations it was comparatively quite safe for women to travel alone, but alas today that is no longer the norm. The relative physical weakness of women is to be helped by the relative physical strength of men, which seems to be the obvious meaning of the reference in 1 Peter 3 v.7, as quoted above. But nowadays with the false notion that 'equality means sameness', women do not need men to protect them, chivalry and gallantry have largely disappeared, and the concept of due respect and courtesy no longer prevail. God designed men and women with differences precisely so that we would need each other, and enjoy that mutual support, comfort and help, which sadly is so distorted as to be almost unrecognisable: "That every one of you should know how to possess his vessel in sanctification and honour", (1 Thess. 4 v.4).

Husbands are to lead lovingly for the benefit of the family as a whole. In a Christian marriage the wife entrusts herself to her husband, knowing that he loves her, and will leap into action if she is in danger. He will want her to be the best woman she can be in terms of natural gifts, of a loving relationship, and of spiritual development: "Submitting yourselves one to another in the fear of God", (Eph. 5 v.21).

Some commentators point out that this reference to the wife as "the weaker vessel", (1 Peter 3 v.7), reflects a measure of physical and emotional vulnerability. The Christian husband will understand that need, assuring her of his love and respect --- honouring her as a fellow Christian, a fellow heir, "heirs together", and honouring her as a woman, a "weaker vessel", (1 Peter 3 v.7).

Heirs Together of the Grace of Life

It is true that First Peter 3 v.7 speaks of believing husbands and wives who are "heirs together of the grace of life". While the verse contains the principle that the woman, as "the weaker vessel", is not on that account to be despised by the man, but rather honoured. The main idea here in the word "honour" is respect.

In recognising, as believers, a mutual inheritance "as heirs together of the grace of life", there is a relationship by grace which shall never pass away. Prayer is the cohesive power that binds a home together, and the importance of a well-balanced life in following the Divine order must be maintained in all aspects and areas of living. In the midst of a world that dishonours and disobeys God, the Christian couple can, not only know, but also display the true meaning of being together. Having a sense of the high privilege of being heirs of the life of Christ, they are to live in a loving unity, not allowing discord to mar the relationship and hinder their fellowship together with the Lord. God's Word is our guide to glorify and enjoy Him. "And let the peace of God rule in your hearts, to the which also ye are called in one body; and be ye thankful", (Col. 3 v.15).

Man is so constituted as to lead, and God has invested him with the leadership role. The woman, on the other hand, is to be under the leadership of the man, who is to protect her, provide for her, and respect her. Man himself, however, needed a helper, and the helpmeet given him by God was the woman. John Calvin makes the comment that the words in Gen. 1 v.27, "Male and female created He them", are of the same force as --- "the man himself, that is, by himself, or alone, was incomplete".

In finding intimacy, passion and peace in marriage, three simple commands in Scripture sum up the Biblical teaching on being a good wife, --- help him, honour him, and love him. Adam was unable of himself to fulfil the creation mandate alone. He lacked a companion 'of the same kind' as himself, one who would be a friend, one who could strengthen and support him. God created "an help meet for him", (Gen. 2 v.18). The Apostle Paul writes in 1 Cor. 11 v.9, "Neither was the man created for the woman; but the woman for the man". This is not pointing to weakness or inferiority of the woman, but rather a calling to provide support, companionship and assistance to the man. The ideal wife of Prov. 31 v.12 brings her husband "good, not evil", and he has confidence in her.

A good wife brings honour and glory to her husband. Showing him respect and submission is not mindless or degraded, but Biblical subordination is willingly saying 'yes' to the husband's calling to give leadership. By so doing she affirms the calling God has given to her husband as leader in the relationship. Her primary calling is to love and nurture her husband and children, and enable them to be what God wants them to be. When we see submission as the Christian wife's response to her husband, it becomes positive and attractive --- accepted not rejected, respected not despised.

True love involves an act of the will, understanding, patience, kindness and longsuffering. The love of marriage is exclusive and faithful, designed to unite husband and wife into a 'one flesh' relationship: "they shall be one flesh", (Gen. 2 v.24). It is incredible that some in the history of the Church have demeaned sexual love when a whole Book in the Bible celebrates it. In the Song of Solomon love is described as constant, self-giving, enduring, protective, and stronger than death. The word used for love, "agape", in the Scriptures has the meaning of passionate sexual love, loyalty and friendship, including the relationship between God and His people. There is nothing Christian about neglecting erotic love in marriage, the Bible indicates that a wife should enjoy and express enjoyment, and assure her husband that he is giving her pleasure. "Let the husband render unto the wife due benevolence: and likewise also the wife unto her husband. The wife hath not power of her own body, but the husband: and likewise also the husband hath not power of his own body, but the wife. Defraud ye not one the other, except it be with consent for a time, that ye may give yourselves to fasting and prayer; and come together again, that Satan tempt you not for your incontinency", (1 Cor. 7 v.3-5). The mutuality of Christian marriage is shown by the intense ecstasy of sex in the Song of Solomon where both lover and beloved, man and wife, freely and unashamedly initiate love.

God's design for marriage is perfect, and as we devote ourselves to helping, honouring and loving of one the other, the more wonderfully, He will empower us to be the husbands and wives He wants us to be. "Whoso findeth a wife findeth a good thing, and obtaineth favour of the Lord", (Prov. 18 v.22).

Choosing a Marriage Partner

Apart from salvation in Christ, marriage is one of the most important questions anyone will ever think about. It is therefore vital to consider the Scriptural teaching on the subject. Many Christians ignore and wilfully neglect the instructions of the Word of God on such an important matter. Any attempt to compromise the teaching of the Bible is bound to have unhappy consequences. "For them that honour Me", says the Lord, "I will honour, and they that despise Me shall be lightly esteemed", (1 Sam. 2 v.30).

In First Corinthians 6 and 7, the Apostle Paul reminds us of some very basic guidelines and Christian teaching. Our primary qualification for a suitable marriage partner is to marry "only in the Lord", (1 Cor. 7 v.39). This is the most basic rule for Christian marriage. Sadly many Christians object and turn aside from guidance that is clear and straightforward. "Thus saith the Lord, Stand in the ways, and see, and ask for the old paths, where is the good way and walk therein, and ye shall find rest for your souls", (Jer. 6 v.16).

Marriage to an unbeliever is clearly forbidden in Scripture, and is a potential recipe for disaster. It will undoubtedly hinder the spiritual life and growth of the believer. The husband should be a suitable partner for his wife, and the wife should be a suitable helpmeet for her husband. "And the Lord God said, It is not good that the man should be alone; I will make him an help meet for him", (Gen. 2 v.18). Only the union of two believers can achieve the aims of Christian marriage. It is a relationship that is intended to grow and develop over the years. Together they achieve that pattern of marital love and fulfilment which Paul emphasises and describes in Eph. 5 v. 22-23: "Wives, submit yourselves unto your own husbands, as unto the Lord. For the husband is the head of the wife, even as Christ is the head of the Church: and He is the Saviour of the body".

When both partners are believers seeking to live up to their marriage vows and responsibilities, they help each other. There is simply no way that such a commitment can be kept by a couple that are not united in the Lord. If God's order is broken there is no way that the partnership can fulfil the purpose of Christian marriage, or raise and bring up children as God intends when parents are pulling in different directions. "Can two walk together, except they be agreed?" (Amos 3 v.3).

Another aim of Christian marriage is the witness of a Christian home in the world, and the potential for good whenever husband and wife seek by the grace of God to live and honour Him in all their relationships. For the good of the believer God forbids such folly as marriage to an unbeliever, and He gives every Christian the opportunity of responding to His love by keeping His commandments.

The Apostle Paul teaches us that our whole life should be controlled and governed by the principle that "Whether therefore ye eat, or drink, or whatsoever ye do, do all to the glory of God", (1 Cor. 10 v.31). Christian marriage is for life: "For this cause shall a man leave father and mother, and shall cleave to his wife: and they twain shall be one flesh. Wherefore they are no more twain, but one flesh. What therefore God hath joined together, let not man put asunder", (Matt. 19 v.5-6).

No Christian can please God in his marriage unless there is a sincere commitment to a life-long union and relationship of faithful wedlock. Jesus told His disciples, "If ye love Me, keep My commandments . . . . . he that hath My commandments, and keepeth them, he it is that loveth me . . . . . if any man love Me, he will keep My words . . . . . he that loveth Me not keepeth not My sayings", (John 14 v.15,21,23-24). The real evidence of a believer's love for the Saviour is obedience to His teaching. "For this is the love of God, that we keep His commandments: and His commandments are not grievous", (1 John 5 v.3).

Do not err in seeking a marriage partner, the Scripture firmly warns. We are to trust God, and "seek first the Kingdom of God and His righteousness", and all other "things shall be added unto you", (Matt. 6 v.33). Our whole lives must be seen to be controlled by our passion and concern for the glory of God. In 1 Peter 3 v.1-7, the duties of husbands and wives are enjoined upon us, and we should aim to be men and women of prayer, delighting to walk closely with God in all His ways. To do so we must continually read and study His holy Word, and be clothed in the beauty of a "meek and quiet spirit", (1 Peter 3 v.4), to do those things that please God --- "that your prayers be not hindered", (1 Peter 3 v.7).

"Trust in the Lord with all thine heart; and lean not unto thine own understanding. In all thy ways acknowledge Him, and He shall direct thy paths. Be not wise in thine own eyes: fear the Lord, and depart from evil", (Prov. 3 v.5-7).

Man made to Serve

Man is made by God, to love and serve Him. Created in God's image, man has distorted it by his sin at the Fall. The sin problem can only be dealt with through the Gospel of Jesus Christ, Who provides the forgiveness, freedom and renewal that man needs, in order to be reconciled to God. "Therefore if any man be in Christ, he is a new creature: old things are passed away; behold, all things are become new. And all things are of God, Who hath reconciled us to Himself by Jesus Christ, and hath given to us the ministry of reconciliation; To wit, that God was in Christ, reconciling the world unto Himself, not imputing their trespasses unto them. And hath committed unto us the word of reconciliation. Now then we are ambassadors for Christ, as though God did beseech you by us: we pray you in Christ's stead, be ye reconciled to God. For He hath made Him to be sin for us, Who knew no sin; that we might be made the righteousness of God in Him", (2 Cor. 5 v.17-21).

We need the light of Truth. The Psalmist described God's Word as "a lamp unto my feet, and a light unto my path", (Psalm 119 v.105). He also said, "The entrance of Thy words giveth light; it giveth understanding unto the simple", (Psalm 119 v.130).

When the Word of God penetrates our hearts and minds by the illuminating power of the Holy Spirit, we are enabled to see things in a true and proper perspective on life. We cannot live without the Word of God. Jesus Himself said, "Man shall not live by bread alone, but by every word that proceedeth out of the mouth of God", (Matt. 4 v.4). The Word of Christ is very true, and it is a very serious matter to ignore the "light", distort it, modify it, or adjust it. We read in Psalm 119 v.160, "Thy Word is true from the beginning: and every one of Thy righteous judgements endureth for ever".

We are not to hide the Word of God "and put it under a bushel", (Matt. 5 v.15), when we disagree with what it says, or dislike what it reveals. We must accept what it says, and practice what it preaches. That is what the Christian life is about, we are to "walk in the light", (1 John 1 v.7), and our lives are to be conformed to the will of God as revealed in the Scriptures. "Ye are the salt of the earth: but if the salt have lost his savour, wherewith shall it be salted? It is thenceforth good for nothing, but to be cast out, and to be trodden under foot of men. Ye are the light of the world. A city that is set on a hill cannot be hid. Neither do men light a candle, and put it under a bushel, but on a candlestick; and it giveth light unto all that are in the house. Let your light so shine before men that they may see your good works and glorify your Father which is in heaven", (Matt. 5 v.13-16).

We need the Word of God to give us information, guidance and wisdom. We need the Spirit of God to give us illumination and enlightenment to walk in the light of His Word. "But without faith it is impossible to please Him: for he that cometh to God must believe that He is, and that He is a rewarder of them that diligently seek Him", (Heb. 11 v.6). With so much superficial Christianity around at the present time, we thank God that He "hath given unto us all things that pertain unto life and godliness", (1 Peter 1 v.3). Because of the "exceeding great and precious promises" and privileges, (1 Peter 1 v.4), we should give diligent attention to making a worthy response in spiritual growth that "ye shall neither be barren nor unfruitful in the knowledge of our Lord Jesus Christ . . . . . Wherefore the rather, brethren, give diligence to make your calling and election sure", (1 Peter 1 v.8,10).

Growth in the Christian life is the prominent point of the teaching in Peter's Epistles. He seems to sum up what he would most anxiously impress in the closing words, "But grow in grace, and in the knowledge of our Lord and Saviour Jesus Christ. To Him be glory both now and for ever", (2 Peter 3 v.18). Every saved man cherishes the assurance that he was called of God, and led to make choice of God. There are two factors here in human redemption, the moving of Divine grace towards us, and the response of our hearts to it. True assurance comes out of growth in godly character and in practical godly living. One grace is added to another and develops into higher Christian diligence and determination to press on and work as faithful servants to obtain the Master's approval now, and His joy hereafter.

Sadly, many professing Christians, instead of searching the Scriptures to determine what the Lord requires, seek man's opinions and are often motivated by the fashions and practice of society. To understand the teaching of God's Word, to be obedient to God's will, to grow in grace and the knowledge of Jesus Christ, to be holy and righteous, we must search "the Scriptures daily", (Acts 17 v.11), with readiness of mind to receive His truth and walk in His way. "Study to shew thyself approved unto God, a workman that needeth not to be ashamed, rightly dividing the Word of truth", (2 Tim. 2 v.15). When we discover from the Scriptures what God wants us to be and to do, and we do it, then we have found the purpose for which God made us as we noted earlier. As we truly discover His Divine will as revealed to us in the Scriptures, will the real meaning and significance of living dawn upon us, so that we shall be compelled to glorify Him all the more in every aspect of life, whether in the Church, in the home, in the workplace, in society, or in the world at large.

The true understanding and application of God's Word will transform lives, homes, society, and the world. "Where there is no vision, the people perish: but he that keepeth the law, happy is he",

(Prov. 29 v.18). As a people of God we must beware of the sin of disobedience, for it is the parent of all corruption, compromise and darkness, the chief cause in the falling of Biblical standards and dishonour to His name. We must therefore seek Him in penitence and prayer, and be encouraged in doing so by the exceeding great and precious promises which He has given to us. "Thou hast given a banner to them that fear Thee, that it may be displayed because of the truth", (Psalm 60 v.4).

In the conflict God's people are called upon to fight for Truth, "that it may be displayed". Going into battle with the watchword, "The Lord of hosts is with us; the God of Jacob is our refuge", (Psalm 46 v.11), we are confident in that the issue is certain victory: "So shall My Word be that goeth forth out of My mouth: it shall not return unto Me void, but it shall accomplish that which I please, and it shall prosper in the thing whereto I sent it", (Isaiah 55 v.11). The men and women to do the work and fight the battles of the Lord, His righteous cause, must be godly disciples who fear and serve Him according to the Scriptures. "Woe to them that are at ease in Zion", (Amos 6 v.1). "Blessed is the man that trusteth in the Lord, and whose hope the Lord is", (Jer. 17 v.7).

CHAPTER FOUR

AN HELPMEET FOR THE MAN

A Suitable Companion

Marriage Instituted by God

A Union of Body, Soul and Spirit

Christian Morality and the Purpose of Sex

Marriage Honourable and the Bed Undefiled

The Sacredness of Marriage and Sex

The Secret of a Happy Marriage

Sacrificial Love endures

Three Forms of Love: Eros, Phileo, and Agape

AN HELPMEET FOR THE MAN

In Genesis, right at the beginning, we have the record of how the woman was created and given to the man as his wife: "An help meet for him", (Gen. 2 v.18), "ezer kenegdo" (Hebrew) meaning, "a help as his counterpart", that is, an aid suitable and supplementary to him, a delicate and beautiful designation of a wife (Gen. 2 v.18-20), which exactly expresses her relation.

"And the Lord God said, It is not good that the man should be alone; I will make him an help meet for him. And out of the ground the Lord God formed every beast of the field, and every fowl of the air; and brought them unto Adam to see what he would call them: and whatsoever Adam called every living creature, that was the name thereof. And Adam gave names to all cattle, and to the fowl of the air, and to every beast of the field; but for Adam there was not found an help meet for him. And the Lord caused a deep sleep to fall upon Adam, and he slept: and He took one of his ribs, and closed up the flesh instead thereof; And the rib, which the Lord God had taken from man, made He a woman, and brought her unto the man. And Adam said, This is now bone of my bones, and flesh of my flesh: she shall be called Woman, because she was taken out of Man. Therefore shall a man leave his father and his mother, and shall cleave unto his wife: and they shall be one flesh. And they were both naked, the man and his wife, and were not ashamed", (Gen. 2 v.18-25).

This is a very striking passage of Scripture in which we have the phrase "an help meet for him", which really means "corresponding to him". The woman was brought to the man in order that she might be an intelligent companion, a helpmeet in the struggles of life, and that she might receive his love, protection and care. A wife is the helper of her husband, not his guide, not his ruler, and not his slave. She is to be a meet and fit wife, for man was not made for a solitary, but for a sociable life, and to commune with God.

"The Lord God caused a deep sleep to fall upon Adam", to take from him the sense of pain, which the taking out of his rib would involve, and that the Divine Providence might be the more apparent in providing a helpmeet for him. The rib was taken not from his head or foot, to manifest that the place of the wife was to be neither above nor below her husband. It was taken from near his heart, to indicate the true affection with which man must regard his wife. And because this part of the body is covered with arms, it denotes the protection the wife should receive. The rib was taken from that part of the body of man without deforming it.

Man's first sight of woman was one of admiration, gratitude, and love. He that marrieth in the Lord recognises that God hath allowed but one wife to one man. True marriage is of God's making, of woman's consenting, and of man's reception. Marriage as a Divine institution is an emblem of the spiritual union between Christ and His Church, the Bride. In true marriage, the man and the woman "cleave" together, as one flesh in mutual love, and such cleaving must be sincere, reciprocal, and without end.

A Suitable Companion

In the above passage it clearly states, "And the Lord God said, It is not good that man should be alone; I will make him an help meet (or a help suitable) for him", (Gen. 2 v.18). Out of this pronouncement comes the creation of one who is to be Adam's wife and companion.

The passage continues at v.21, "And the Lord God caused a deep sleep to fall upon Adam and he slept: and he took one of his ribs, and closed up the flesh instead thereof; And the rib, which the Lord God had taken from man, made He a woman, and brought her unto the man. And Adam said, This is now bone of my bones, and flesh of my flesh: she shall be called Woman, because she was taken out of man", (Gen. 2 v.21-23).

In his commentary, Matthew Henry makes this pithy statement about the creation of the woman: "The woman was made of a rib out of the side of Adam; not made out of his head to rule over him, nor out of his feet to be trampled upon by him, but out of his side to be equal with him, under his arm to be protected by him, and near to his heart to be loved by him".

From the above verses we learn that the woman was made "for" man, she was made "from" man, and she was given "to" man --- the greatest of all God's gifts. In verse 23, we find that she was named "by" man. On the basis of this created order, and the New Testament instructions, for the relationship of a man and woman within marriage and the function of a man and woman within the Church, are constructed.

The first part of the story of God's creation of woman is the preparation of Adam for Eve's arrival. Adam had been made in God's image. God needed to show Adam that in all the created order, with all its variety and beauty, there was still at this time no creature suited to be his companion. Adam's first lesson was to learn to appreciate his wife. Out of the vast array of animals "there was not found an help meet for him", (Gen. 2 v.20). Animals have no spirits and so could not commune with Adam on the spiritual level. If he were to have a companion, the companion would have to be specially created by God and in the image of God, as he was. So Adam was prepared for Eve, and Eve was now to be prepared for Adam. She was to be made for him as his ideal counterpart in this world.

Eve was made "for" the man, as a "helper" suitable for him. In this, among other things, we see her unique position in life. This fact incenses today's radical 'feminists', and sometimes other women too. To speak of woman being made for man, even more to speak of her need to be obedient to the man in marriage, etc., seems to such persons to reek of rank prejudice, inequality, and injustice.

Are men and women equal? We need to understand what we are talking about here. There are important ways in which men and women are equal.

(1) They were both created in the image of God, which makes the woman a fit companion for the man.

(2) They were both placed under the moral command of God, and thus given moral responsibility.

(3) They were both guilty of disobeying the command of God, and were therefore judged by God for their disobedience.

(4) Men and women are alike objects of God's grace in Jesus Christ.

Social status, nationality, and sexuality are all irrelevant to our qualifications for being members of Christ's body. Beyond these items, equality has no relevance. The subordinate relationship of wife to husband is found in Genesis, not after the Fall but before it, as earlier indicated. No woman is obliged to accept a proposal of marriage, but if she does, and if she is a Christian woman, she must know that the pattern of her relationship to the man is found in Genesis 2, where God said that he would make a "helper suitable for" Adam. If she cannot be a helper to her man or does not want to be, the woman should not marry him.

In the story of Robert Moffat, the gardener lad from Scotland who became a missionary, it is recorded that "on 27th December 1819, Robert Moffat and Mary Smith were married in Cape Town, and proceeded from there to their new home in Lattakoo. For over fifty years, in storm and sunshine, they were truly one in heart and mind, and together served the Lord Who had saved them and called them to be His witnesses in Africa. What a blessing it is for a servant of Christ to get a true helpmeet, and a hindrance to be yoked for life to one who has little heart for the Master's service".

Marriage Instituted by God

It is clearly observed from Genesis 2, that God brought the newly-created woman to the man, and gave her to him as his wife. So marriage was appointed and established by God Himself. Matthew Henry rightly says again, "Marriage is honourable, but this surely was the most honourable marriage that ever was, in which God Himself had all along an immediate hand. Marriages (they say) are made in heaven. We are sure this one was, because the man, the woman, the match, were all God's own work. He, by His power, made them both, and now, by His ordinance, made them one". The Bible stresses throughout that marriage is to be honoured.

At creation, God made man, male and female, and before the Fall, ordained marriage as a natural relationship of life. This relation of marriage is in a general way represented by several Hebrew words, the most distinctive of which are several forms of "chathan" (Hebrew), meaning "to give in marriage"; and the Greek equivalent word is "gamoz", which means, "a wedding". The institution of marriage was ordained by God, as man, an intellectual and spiritual being, needed a companion – "it is not good that the man should be alone", (Gen. 2 v.18).

It was absolutely necessary, not only for his comfort and happiness, but still more for the perfection of the Divine work, that God should have a "help meet for him", or as the words more perfectly mean "the exact counterpart of himself" --- a being capable of viewing and reflecting his thoughts and affections. No sooner was the formation of woman effected, than Adam recognised in that act the will of the Creator as to man's social condition, and immediately enunciated the important statement, to which his posterity might refer as the charter of marriage in all succeeding ages. "Therefore shall a man leave his father and his mother, and shall cleave unto his wife: and they shall be one flesh", (Gen. 2 v.24).

From these words, in the above verse, coupled with the circumstances attendant on the formation of the first woman, we may confidently conclude the following principles:-

(1) The unity of man and wife, as implied in her being formed out of man, and as expressed in the words "one flesh"; (Gen. 2 v.18,22 and 24, Matt. 19 v.4-5);

(2) The indissolubleness of the marriage bond, except on the strongest grounds as in the case of adultery or of wilful, causeless, and irremediable desertion: (1 Cor. 7 v.39, Rom. 7 v.2-3, Matt. 19 v.3,6 and 9, Matt. 5 v.31-32, 1 Cor. 7 v.15);

(3) Monogamy, as the original law of marriage, resulting from there having been but one original couple, as is forcibly expressed in the subsequent reference to this passage by our Lord in Matt. 19 v.5, "they twain"; and by Paul in 1 Cor. 6 v.16, "for two", saith Christ, "shall be one flesh";

(4) The social equality of man and wife, as implied in the Hebrew terms "ish" and "ishshah", the one being the exact correlative of the other, as well as in the words "help meet for him"; (Gen. 2 v.18);

(5) The subordination of the wife to the husband, consequent upon her subsequent formation; (1 Cor. 11 v.8-9, 1 Tim. 2 v.13);

(6) The respective duties of man and wife, as implied in the words "help meet for him"; (Gen. 2 v.18); and,

(7) Marriage, as ordained by God, is for the mutual help and benefit of husband and wife, the legitimate procreation of mankind, the increase and building up of the Church with a

holy seed, and for the promotion and regulation of morality and religion; (Mal. 2 v.15, 1 Cor. 2 v.7).

The introduction of sin into the world at the Fall modified to a certain extent the mutual relations of man and wife. As the blame of seduction to sin lay on the woman, the condition of subordination was turned into subjection, and it was said to her of her husband, "he shall rule over thee", (Gen. 3 v.16). See also: 1 Cor. 14 v.34, Eph. 5 v.22-23. She is not "to usurp authority over the man", (1 Tim. 2 v.12).

The evil effects of the Fall were soon apparent in the corrupt usages of marriage. The unity of the bond was impaired by polygamy, which appears to have originated among the Cainites. "And Lamech took unto him two wives: the name of the one was Adah, and the name of the other Zillah", (Gen. 4 v.19). And its purity was deteriorated by the promiscuous behaviour of the Sethites with the Cainites, in the days preceding the Flood. Indeed, such corruption which rendered the Flood necessary is directly traced to mixed marriages.

"And it came to pass, when men began to multiply on the face of the earth, and daughters were born unto them, That the sons of God saw the daughters of men that they were fair; and they took them wives of all which they chose. And the Lord said, My Spirit shall not always strive with man, for that he also is flesh: yet his days shall be an hundred and twenty years. There were giants in the earth in those days; and also after that, when the sons of God came in unto the daughters of men, and they bare children to them, the same became mighty men which were of old, men of renown. And God saw that the wickedness of man was great in the earth, and that every imagination of the thoughts of his heart was only evil continually. And it repented the Lord that He had made man on the earth, and it grieved Him at His heart. And the Lord said, I will destroy man whom I have created from the face of the earth; both man, and beast, and the creeping thing, and the fowls of the air; for it repenteth Me that I have made them. But Noah found grace in the eyes of the Lord", (Gen. 6 v.1-8).

The expression of Divine authority, is to be regarded as comprehending that principle of His people in all ages, that here they ought not to walk in the counsel of the ungodly, nor stand in the way of sinners. "Blessed is the man that walketh not in the counsel of the ungodly, nor standeth in the way of sinners, nor sitteth in the seat of the scornful. But his delight is in the law of the Lord; and in His law doth he mediate day and night", (Psalm 1 v.1-2). Christians are to marry "only in the Lord", they being united to the Lord Jesus Christ by the Divine Spirit, and possessing an interest in the redeeming blessings He has purchased on their behalf. They are to marry only on Christian principles, and, of course, only such as are thus also "in the Lord" – believer with believer, and with none else. "The wife is bound by the law as long as her husband liveth; but if her husband be dead, she is at liberty to be married to whom she will; only in the Lord", (1 Cor. 7 v.39).

At this point, we refer, albeit briefly to the question of celibacy with proper consideration. Shortly before the Christian era a change took place in the views entertained on the question of marriage as affecting the spiritual and intellectual parts of man's nature. Throughout the Old Testament period marriage was regarded as the indispensable duty of every man, nor was it surmised that there existed in it any drawback to the attainment of the highest degree of holiness.

In the interval that elapsed between the Old and New Testament periods, a spirit of asceticism had been evolved. Such practice often involved rigorous self-discipline and austerity by the imposition of abstinence in marriage and retiring into solitude to exercise themselves in meditation and prayer by celibacy, fasting and toil, by which perfection and virtue may be attained.

The Essenes were the first to propound any doubts as to the propriety of marriage, and some of them avoided it altogether. Other groups adopted similar views, thence they passed into the Christian Church, and finally developing into the system of monachism with all the confinement that monasticism contains. The philosophical tenets on which the prohibition of marriage was based are generally condemned in Colossians 2 v.16-23, and specifically in 1 Timothy 4 v.1-3.

"Let no man therefore judge you in meat, or in drink, or in respect of an holyday, or of the new moon, or of the Sabbath days: Which are a shadow of things to come; but the body is of Christ. Let no man beguile you of your reward in a voluntary humility and worshipping of angels, intruding into those things which he hath not seen, vainly puffed up by his fleshly mind, And not holding the Head, from which all the body by joints and bands having nourishment ministered, and knit together, increaseth with the increase of God. Wherefore if ye be dead with Christ from the rudiments of the world, why, as though living in the world, are ye subject to ordinances. Touch not; taste not; handle not; Which all are to perish with the using; after the commandments and doctrines of men? Which things have indeed a shew of wisdom in will worship, and humility, and neglecting of the body; not in any honour to the satisfying of the flesh", (Col. 2 v.16-23).

"Now the Spirit speaketh expressly, that in the latter times some shall depart from the faith, giving heed to seducing spirits, and doctrines of devils; Speaking lies in hypocrisy; having their conscience seared with a hot iron; Forbidding to marry, and commanding to abstain from meats, which God hath created to be received with thanksgiving of them which believe and know the truth", (1 Tim. 4 v.1-3).

The general propriety of marriage is enforced on numerous occasions in Scripture. Abstinence from it is commended only in cases where it is rendered expedient by the call of duty "for the kingdom of heaven's sake", (Matt. 19 v.12). In the Apostolic Church, re-marriage after the death of one of the parties, was not prohibited. "The wife is bound by the law as long as her husband liveth; but if her husband be dead, she is at liberty to be married to whom she will; only in the Lord",

(1 Cor. 7 v.39). Among the list of qualifications regarding elders and deacons it is plainly stated that "A bishop then must be blameless, the husband of one wife . . . . . Let the deacons be the husbands of one wife", (1 Tim. 3 v.2 and 12), never neglecting the duty of "holding the mystery of the faith in a pure conscience", (1 Tim. 3 v.9).

The sanctity of marriage is acknowledged and preserved by the fact that at creation, the wife occupied a position of subordination, being a part of man, yet, as she became the cause of his sin, God ordained it as part of her punishment that the wife should be in subjection to the will of her husband, and that he should "rule over her", (Gen. 3 v.16).

In the English language, several words are used to describe marriage, e.g., matrimony, wedlock, covenant, the union of one man and one woman which contains in itself an inseparable life-intercourse. The marriage bond is beautifully expressed in those words contained in the first Book of the Bible, "Therefore shall a man leave his father and his mother, and shall cleave unto his wife: and they shall be one flesh", (Gen. 2 v.24).

Marriage is conceived of as a union so close that it separates a man from the union of the family, two persons cleave to one another denoting in the original Hebrew Bible, "to be glued to", "to stick to", and the result is that they become "one flesh", they unite their bodies, souls and spirits together, which gives true, spiritual, and heart communion to the wedded pair --- "which God hath created to be received with thanksgiving of them which believe and know the truth" (1 Tim. 4 v.3).

A Union of Body, Soul and Spirit

There is something very poignant about the creation of woman. She is not to be man's servant, but rather a helpmeet, a companion, because of their essential similarity and union. Husband and wife are to be one on each level of their being. As man and woman were created a trinity of body, soul, and spirit, then they are to be united on each of these levels in marriage. A union of body is a sexual union. This is important, for if a physical union does not or cannot take place, then the marriage is not a true marriage. If the relationship is based on nothing but sex and physical attraction, it is a marriage of body with body alone, and is weak and headed for trouble with nothing more to sustain it.

A better marriage is one that is also a union of soul with soul, involving the characteristics with the functioning of the mind. This embraces the couple sharing a common interest in the same things, establishing a meeting of minds both intellectually and emotionally. This is something that needs to be worked at and built up which of itself does not come naturally. It is vital, that both, by the grace of God, increasingly accept totally each other, and under God, seek the highest standards by cultivating the interests and aspirations of both spouses as they honour the Lord together.

A true union must also be a marriage of spirit with spirit, and this means that both the husband and wife must be Christians. If you are a Christian, you must marry another Christian or not marry at all, otherwise much unhappiness will ensue and an absence of the blessing of God because of disobedience. In obeying God make sure your future partner becomes a Christian before engagement. If the other person is not a Christian, then on the authority of God's Word, he or she is not the husband or wife for you. The Bible strictly says, "Be ye not unequally yoked together with unbelievers: for what fellowship hath righteousness with unrighteousness? And what communion hath light with darkness?", (2 Cor. 6 v.14).

Christian Morality and the Purpose of Sex

"To every thing there is a season, and a time to every purpose under heaven: A time to be born, and a time to die; a time to plant, and a time to pluck up that which is planted; A time to kill, and a time to heal; a time to break down, and a time to build up; A time to weep, and a time to laugh; a time to mourn, and a time to dance; A time to cast away stones, and a time to gather stones together; a time to embrace, and a time to refrain from embracing", (Eccles. 3 v.1-5).

Christian morality is totally different from the standards commonly advocated in today's society. The main conflict with current ideas, fashions and practice go back to the question of authority, of absolutes, and of fixed standards. For our good God has commanded His people in every age, and in the context of their culture, to live the Christian life according to the Rule of His Holy Word, the Scriptures. Sex is a God-given power for our human welfare. We thank God for it, and we should discipline ourselves to use it in the way He directs, knowing that that is best, that is, within marriage.

Any attempt to enforce legalism only serves to squeeze out love, for love is the primary Christian virtue. Love between the sexes is a highly vulnerable thing and its shield and breastplate is the moral law of God. Those who advocate 'freedom' by adopting so-called 'fashionable' trends are no criterion whatsoever of what is right. The practical consequences of the so-called 'new' behavioural patterns cause wreckage and havoc to society, and the claims made for the 'new morality' are deeply false and extremely dangerous.

As Christians we believe that Christian morality is best by yielding obedience to God's commands. We need the power of God to follow the right path, and men and women owe it to one another to help each other to observe the highest standards as laid down in the Word of God. "Godliness is profitable unto all things, having promise of the life that now is, and of that which is to come", (1 Tim. 4 v.8).

In Ephesians 5 and First Timothy 4, the Apostle Paul sets out an exalted and laudatory view of marriage which is quite unmistakable as explained elsewhere in this book. He emphasises that there is real danger of misusing God's gifts. In referring to First Corinthians 7, he is addressing in particular, unmarried men, widows, the married, unmarried women, and young people, by setting out some guidelines and practical considerations in regard to marriage.

We must respect and never resent the Bible's instructions, and if we are truly spiritually minded we shall not be like those who wilt and grumble, but rather our delight will be to please God at all costs. From a Biblical point of view we are to establish what is lawful within marriage, and what is unlawful without it. Pre-marital intercourse is what the Bible calls "fornication", and extra marital sex is "adultery". "Know ye not that the unrighteous shall not inherit the kingdom of God? Be not deceived: neither fornicators, nor idolaters, nor adulterers, nor effeminate, nor abusers of themselves with mankind, Nor thieves, nor covetous, nor drunkards, nor revilers, nor extortioners, shall inherit the kingdom of God", (1 Cor. 6 v.9-10). "Now the body is not for fornication, but for the Lord", (1 Cor. 6 v.13). "Flee fornication. Every sin that a man doeth is without the body; but he that committeth fornication sinneth against his own body. What? Know ye not that your body is the temple of the Holy Ghost which is in you, which ye have of God, and ye are not your own? For ye are bought with a price: therefore glorify God in your body, and in your spirit, which are God's", (1 Cor. 6 v.18-20).

"Thou shalt not commit adultery", (Exod. 20 v.14). The purport of this commandment is, that as God desires chastity and purity, we ought to guard against all uncleanness and defilement. The thing expressly forbidden here is adultery, and its every form of lust and filthiness must be greatly abhorred. In the Divine plan and order, man was created not to lead a life of solitude, but enjoy a helpmeet provided for him by the institution of marriage, which was prescribed not for the first pair alone, but for all posterity. It is evident from Scripture that any mode of cohabitation different from marriage as ordained by God, is cursed in His sight. The right of sexual relations with a spouse is permitted only when one man and one woman are joined together in marriage, entered into under God's authority, which, under His blessing can be strong and happy where the sacredness of the marriage bond is held in honour. Let us beware, therefore, of yielding to indulgence, seeing that the curse of God lies on every man and woman cohabiting without marriage.

"Now the works of the flesh are manifest, which are these; Adultery, fornication, uncleanness, lasciviousness . . . . and such like: of which I tell you before, as I have also told you in time past, that they which do such things shall not inherit the kingdom of God", (Gal. 5 v.19-21).

"For this is the will of God, even your sanctification, that ye should abstain from fornication: that every one of you should know how to possess his vessel in sanctification and honour", (1 Thess. 4 v.3-4).

It is easy to read rather hurriedly through such passages as those warning against fornication and adultery, and also other things less easily definable, but detailed in the same contexts, such as, "lasciviousness", "all uncleanness", "inordinate affection", and "evil concupiscence". When we come across good advice as in 2 Timothy 2 v.22: "Flee also youthful lusts: but follow righteousness, faith, charity, peace, with them that call on the Lord out of a pure heart" --- we often do not pause to apply it to ourselves. It is important, therefore, to distinguish between the prevailing glossy magazines and low standards of society, and the lofty morals of the Word of God in all these matters.

According to the Bible the primary purpose of sex is companionship and friendship. Eve was created because "it is not good that the man should be alone", (Gen. 2 v.18), and she was to be a helpmeet for him. The "one flesh" of marriage refers and embraces all aspects of life, and the main emphasises in New Testament teaching on marriage is on love, and Christ's relationship to His Church is compared to the relationship of husband and wife.

"Wives, submit yourselves unto your own husbands, as unto the Lord. For the husband is the head of the wife, even as Christ is the head of the Church: and He is the Saviour of the body. Therefore as the Church is subject unto Christ, so let the wives be to their own husbands in every thing. Husbands, love your wives, even as Christ also loved the Church, and gave Himself for it; That He might sanctify and cleanse it with the washing of water by the Word, That He might present it to Himself a glorious Church, not having spot, or wrinkle, or any such thing; but that it should be holy and without blemish. So ought men to love their wives as their own bodies. He that loveth his wife loveth himself. For no man ever yet hated his own flesh; but nourisheth and cherisheth it, even as the Lord the Church: For we are members of His body, of His flesh, and of His bones. For this cause shall a man leave his father and mother, and shall be joined unto his wife, and they two shall be one flesh. This is a great mystery: but I speak concerning Christ and the Church. Nevertheless let every one of you in particular so love his wife even as himself; and the wife see that she reverence her husband", (Eph. 5 v.22-33).

Such companionship is the most important element in marriage. Sex makes it possible and so gives us the greatest of all kinds of human friendship.

The second purpose of sex in the Bible is the bearing of children and the establishment of the family. Man and wife are held together by sexual attraction and by the physical side of sex in a way that would otherwise be impossible. Deep and stable sexual love is a magnificent gift of God. "Children are an heritage of the Lord: and the fruit of the womb is His reward", (Psalm 127 v.3). This must be seen primarily as a human and a spiritual responsibility and blessing. The family is a far greater thing than merely perpetuating the race. The modern cult of sex turns out in fact to be but a 'worship' of only one aspect of sex. To purpose sexual intercourse outside the relationship of entire commitment to live in love and care for one another, which is possible only in marriage, is prostitution.

The Biblical principle of purity is emphasised by Sharon James in her book, 'God's Design for Women'. She points out that "the Biblical standard is very simple: no sex outside of marriage. If a married person engages in sexual intimacy with anyone but their marriage partner, that is adultery. If a single person engages in sexual intimacy, that is fornication. The purpose of sex is two-fold: the procreation of children (Gen. 1 v.28), and the bonding or making one flesh of a married couple (Gen. 2 v.18,23-24) . . . . . God's design, one man for one woman for life, is the route to true happiness . . . . . For sexual intimacy is designed by God as the means by which a married couple express their unique commitment and covenant faithfulness. The fact that they cannot share that intimacy with anyone else underlines the exclusive nature of their union. Sexual intimacy within this covenant framework is portrayed in the Bible as beautiful, exciting, passionate, enjoyable and tender. The Song of Songs is an uninhibited celebration of erotic love. The lovers express unembarrassed enjoyment of each other's bodies; they vie with each other in finding new ways of communicating the delight they find in each other".

The Christian then should not be ashamed of sex. But the Scriptures warn, "That whosoever looketh on a woman to lust after her hath committed adultery with her already in his heart", (Matt. 5 v.28). The fact that we find the opposite sex attractive is not in itself sinful. But as fallen creatures, the effect of our sinfulness is that we tend to misuse sex, and thus our unwarranted pleasure-seeking temptation becomes an occasion of evil thoughts and wrong desires. "Unto the pure all things are pure: but unto them that are defiled and unbelieving is nothing pure; but even their mind and conscience is defiled. They profess that they know God; but in works they deny Him, being abominable, and disobedient, and unto every good work reprobate", (Titus 1 v.15-16).

The stern warning of our Lord in Matthew 5 v.27-30, is today given no attention or heed whatsoever. "Ye have heard that it was said by them of old time, Thou shalt not commit adultery: But I say unto you that whosoever looketh on a woman to lust after her hath committed adultery with her already in his heart. And if thy right eye offend thee, pluck it out, and cast it from thee: for it is profitable for thee that one of thy members should perish, and not that thy whole body should be cast into hell. And if thy right hand offend thee, cut it off, and cast it from thee: for it is profitable for thee that one of thy members should perish, and not that thy whole body should be cast into hell", (Matt. 5 v.27-30). The characteristic result of the Fall is to make an idol of something good, and how easily human thoughts can become sensual, selfish and impure. To allow the physical to dominate our thinking or our relationship, we have got things in a quite false perspective. True love is not merely an emotion or excitement, it is a practical concern for the other's good. Failure of constant mutual love, care and friendship one for the other contributes to instability in marriage.

The devil is having a field-day by the promotion of the 'new morality' throughout modern society, with the result that flirtation and all kinds of sexual experimentation are so acceptable in many circles. Such practices injures and warps the true attitude of sex and corrodes the capacity truly to love. To act against God's plan and the teaching of the Bible is completely wrong and sinful. Because of our sinful nature we must realise that at every stage of life, we need discipline and especially so with such powerful forces of evil all around us. The call of Scripture is to "be sober, be vigilant; because your adversary the devil, as a roaring lion, walketh about, seeking whom he may devour: whom resist stedfast in the faith, knowing that the same afflictions are accomplished in your brethren that are in the world. But the God of all grace, Who hath called us unto His eternal glory by Christ Jesus, after that ye have suffered a while, make you perfect, stablish, strengthen, settle you. To Him be glory and dominion for ever and ever. Amen", (1 Peter 5 v.8-11).

We discipline a child whom we love for his good, so that ultimately he may get more out of life and enjoy its riches more fully to the praise of God. The Apostle Paul compares the Christian life to an athletic contest, and stresses the need for continuous discipline if we are to obtain the prize. "Know ye not that they which run in a race run all, but one receiveth the prize? So run, that ye may obtain. And every man that striveth for the mastery is temperate in all things. Now they do it to obtain a corruptible crown; but we an incorruptible", (1 Cor. 9 v.24-25).

In Genesis 39, we have the story of Joseph, how he met the seductions of an immoral woman, and with everything against him except God, chose slander and imprisonment rather than lose his honour and live with an unhappy conscience. "Favour is deceitful, and beauty is vain: but a woman that feareth the Lord, she shall be praised", (Prov. 31 v.30). Joseph resisted his master's wife's temptation and refused to lie with her, exclaiming, "how then can I do this great wickedness, and sin against God?", (Gen. 39 v.9). He was very wise in taking all reasonable precautions, refusing not only to give way to her, but also to listen to her, or even to be with her. The best place to win the battle for chastity is due to the habit of living a disciplined life that does not hesitate to honour God. "If any man serve Me, let him follow Me; and where I am, there shall also my servant be: if any man serve Me, him will My Father honour", (John 12 v.26).

Marriage is Honourable and the Bed Undefiled

What a sad reflection on society today to note that marriage is under attack as never before. Divorce used to be a rare thing but now almost half the marriages in the United Kingdom end in divorce. A recent survey revealed that only three percent of couples are virgins when they marry.

It is argued by many, rejecting God's law, that if they try out living together before getting married by co-habiting, then marriages are more likely to be successful. This is utter nonsense, as statistics clearly show. If people treat the marriage bed so lightly that they are prepared to live together before getting married, is it any wonder that, when they 'feel' the desire, they will indulge in adultery after marriage?

God meant the union between a husband and wife to be for life. Those who marry promise to be loving, faithful and dutiful to one another through troubles, poverty or ill-health "till death us do part". How much heartbreak and how many disturbed and delinquent children are the product of immoral parents? Millions in today's world are dying of AIDS, but if God's pattern were followed there would have been no epidemic, and even now this terrible disease could be quickly brought under control.

The first few chapters of Genesis are foundational to all the rest of Scripture. Genesis 1 gives a general account of the origin of man who is made in the image of God, male and female, and given dominion over the whole world. Chapter 2 describes that creation in more detail. There is no contradiction between the two accounts.

God formed Adam from "the dust of the ground, and breathed into his nostrils the breath of life; and man became a living soul", (Gen. 2 v.7). There are two parts to man. He has the body like the animals and a soul like God. "But for Adam there was not found any help meet for him", (Gen. 2 v.20), a suitable partner. God saw that it was good for Adam to have a wife. Marriage is best for most people. Some may have the gift of singleness and not need to marry, but they still need the company of their fellowman.

The creation account is fascinating. "God caused a deep sleep to fall upon Adam", (Gen. 2 v.21), and then performed an operation on him. He removed a rib, and then closed up and healed the wound. Around that rib He built the woman, very like the man and yet distinctive and complementary. He brought her to Adam and it was love at first sight. The first woman was born from a man and ever after, every man is born from a woman.

God performed the first marriage. He took Adam and Eve and joined them in wedlock. Since then, God is present and active in every marriage, for Jesus says, "They twain shall be one flesh: so then they are no more twain, but one flesh. What therefore God hath joined together, let not man put asunder", (Mark 10 v.8-9).

The Scriptures assure us that "Marriage is honourable in all, and the bed undefiled: but whoremongers and adulterers God will judge", (Heb. 13 v.4). There are certain requirements in marriage. It involves a separation, for "a man shall leave his father and mother", (Gen. 2 v.24). This is vital. Parents must be careful not to come between the married couple. Scripture makes plain that while children should continue to honour and lovingly care for their parents, their first responsibility now is to their spouses.

Then, there is to be a "cleaving" to their spouses. This involves a deep and growing love, a faithfulness that will let no one else come in between or break the "one flesh" bond, and a dutifulness which involves the individual in serving his wife, or serving her husband, to the best of their ability. Our Lord said, "It is more blessed to give than to receive", (Acts 20 v.35), and that is true in marriage too.

Marriage is between one man and one woman. In today's world the homosexual and lesbian lobbies for 'gay marriage', ask the question, why should two people of the same sex who love each other be prevented from getting married? But even apart from Scripture, the basic definition of marriage which has evolved through the centuries, is that it is a legal union of two adults of the opposite sex who are unrelated to each other. Society in the past has had good reasons for defining marriage in that way. The civil law now of this land, legalises polygamy, incest, bestiality, and gay marriage.

Scripture describes the evils of homosexuality, lesbianism, etc., as "vile affections" to which God gave up the wicked. "Wherefore God also gave them up to uncleanness through the lusts of their own hearts, to dishonour their own bodies between themselves: Who changed the truth of God into a lie, and worshipped and served the creature more than the Creator, Who is blessed for ever. Amen. For this cause God gave them up unto vile affections: for even their women did change the natural use into that which is against nature: And likewise also the men, leaving the natural use of the woman, burned in their lust one toward another; men with men working that which is unseemly, and receiving in themselves that recompense of their error which was meet", (Rom. 1 v.24-27).

To these things the Corinthian Christians have turned their back from which they have been washed by the Blood of Christ. "Know ye not that the unrighteous shall not inherit the Kingdom of God? Be not deceived: neither fornicators, nor idolaters, nor adulterers, nor effeminate, nor abusers of themselves with mankind, Nor thieves, nor covetous, nor drunkards, nor revilers, nor extortioners, shall inherit the Kingdom of God. And such were some of you: but ye are washed, but ye are sanctified, but ye are justified in the name of the Lord Jesus, and by the Spirit of our God", (1 Cor. 6 v.9-11).

The Sacredness of Marriage and Sex

Marriage is a solemn and sacred pact and in all the powers of mind, body, and spirit, will find opportunity for full expression. It is a covenant ratified by God, between one man and one woman, which binds them together in true love so long as life shall last. When a man and a woman are married, there comes into play, perfectly naturally and normally, that which we call sex. Sex is natural, normal, good, sweet, clean, a God-given function of the body. By it, of course, we join with God in His pro-creative and progressive purpose.

Sex is sacred, and must be seen in its true light, not in the vulgarity and smuttiness as slung at it by the world. The happily married couple need to get it clear in both their minds that sex is natural and any wrong thoughts about it ought to be removed. Sex is an act in which both partners should find equal satisfaction and have real consciousness of the sacred significance of the act. The physical side of married life is a true expression of love, and if there is any failure here there is likelihood of failure in all other aspects of married life.

Get this right and life is set on a good foundation: "and they shall be one flesh", (Gen. 2 v.24). It is good advice to talk about it to each other as each gets to know each other's thoughts, emotions, hopes, and desires.

In providence, God has graciously drawn both husband and wife together in mutual love, so therefore thank Him for His guidance and goodness, and seek His grace and help day by day. Only then will one's faith and love for each other grow stronger, which will enable them to trust each other in God's care and belong to Him. By so doing they will live out before the world a true Christian married life, so that their marriage will be a blessing.

Sex relations and intercourse outside of marriage are completely and utterly wrong. It is a vile thing to enter upon sex relations without any pretence of either affection or respect, which is mere prostitution to gratify a physical appetite which brings disgust and self-contempt. It appears in the present age that 'free' love abounds throughout society. Such practice is wrong in the eyes of God, and being only temporary, does not lead to any permanent relationship. Such experiences always do damage to the personality and leads to suffering. The man loves it, the woman loves it, but not enough to go on to marriage. They want to treat sex lightly as an occasional vivid pleasure. This leads to further sex desires and experiences, and they harden themselves by concealing a very fierce anger for the real love which life has denied them and ultimately leads to nothing.

In true sex experience, a man has communion with his dear wife in spirit and in mind, as well as in body. It is only when the experience is a complete one like that, that it is also perfectly joyful and beautiful, and leaves nothing but harmony behind it. Total respect and loyalty must go with the activity of the body, otherwise the finest harmonies are upset and coarsened.

To deny and deprive one the other of the completeness of this most blessed of human relationships, is a failure for Christian husbands and wives to submit sexually to the authority of their spouses, and brings dishonour to God because it dishonours marriage. "The wife hath not power of her own body, but the husband: and likewise also the husband hath not power of his own body, but the wife. Defraud ye not one the other, except it be with consent for a time, that ye may give yourselves to fasting and prayer; and come together again, that Satan tempt you not for your incontinency", (1 Cor. 7 v.4-5).

Spouses mutual authority over each other's bodies is continuous, it lasts throughout marriage. A Christian's body is his own, but in the marital realm it also belongs to the marriage partner. Sexual expression within marriage is not an option or an extra. It is certainly not just a necessary thing in which spiritual Christians engage only to procreate children. It is far more than a physical act. God created it to be the expression and experience of love on the deepest human level and to be a beautiful and powerful bond between husband and wife.

God intends for marriages to be permanent, and for sexual relationships within it to be permanent. His original plan for marriage did not allow for divorce or for celibacy. Christians are not to forsake their spouses (1 Cor. 7 v.12-17), and they are not to sexually deprive spouses, whether believing or unbelieving. "Defraud ye not one the other", (1 Cor. 7 v.5), is an emphatic command, and sexual relations between a husband and wife are God-ordained. The only exception for abstinence from sex is both mutual and temporary: "except it be with consent for a time, that ye may give yourselves to fasting and prayer", (1 Cor. 7 v.5).

To abstain from sexual activity for a short while, is by mutual agreement for a specific period of time, and for a specific purpose, that of fasting and prayer. But when such an urgent period of prayer is past, normal marital relationships are to resume. Husbands and wives are to "come together again", (1 Cor. 7 v.5). The reason for their coming together again is explicit: "that Satan tempt you not for your incontinency", (1 Cor. 7 v.5). When the time of concentrated prayer is over, and as a guard against falling into temptation, sexual relations are to resume immediately. Sexual abstinence is never to be used as a pretence for spiritual superiority, or as a means of intimidating or manipulating one's spouse. Physical love is to be a normal and regular experience shared by both marriage partners alike, as a gift from God.

When sex and love in marriage enters with you into the inner chamber of life, that lovely place where love has its full expression, you feel your whole body and self unified and you are a better person and more adequate to life. Anything short of that, any poor, superficial, half-sincere and incomplete sex experience, fails entirely to produce these results and creates disharmony.

True marriage then in its moral and spiritual essence, is when a man and a woman in love have given themselves to each other completely and for always. They owe it to God, to themselves, and to society to register this before the world. In setting up home together they are making a permanent spiritual, social, and civil arrangement, having given all to each other without reserve. Sex experience, when it is the true thing, is a most intense pleasure whenever such intimacy is fully spontaneous as the culmination of their true and sincere love for each other.

Christian practice embraces all our duties and responsibilities not only to God, to our fellow-men, to ourselves, but also in this context especially between husband and wife: "that in all things He might have the pre-eminence", (Col. 1 v.18). God created man, male and female, and the institution of marriage was ordained by God, whereby one man and one woman solemnly vow to live together in mutual love and fidelity. They promise and covenant together in holy wedlock to be loving, faithful, and dutiful unto each other, until God shall separate them by death. As a token of that covenant, rings are given and received as a sign that they take each other, to have and to hold from the wedding day forward, for better, for worse, for richer, for poorer, in sickness and in health, to love and to cherish till death do them part, with the prayer that God will bless, preserve and keep them as they live together as husband and wife in peace and harmony.

The Greek word "agape" in First Corinthians 13, does not mean "charity" only in the sense of giving to the needy. It means "love", and this chapter is itself the best definition of "agape". "Love suffereth long and is kind; love envieth not; love vaunteth not itself, is not puffed up, Doth not behave itself unseemly, seeketh not her own, is not easily provoked, thinketh no evil; Rejoiceth not in iniquity, but rejoiceth in the truth; Beareth all things, believeth all things, endureth all things. And now abideth faith, hope, love, these three; but the greatest of these is love", (1 Cor. 13 v.4-7,13).

The three greatest spiritual virtues are: faith, hope, and love. Love is the greatest of these, not only because it is eternal, but because, even in this temporal life, where we now live, love is supreme. It will outlast all other virtues, because it is inherently greater by being the most God-like. God does not have faith or hope, but "God is love", (1 John 4 v.8).

There is a very striking verse in Malachi 2 v.14, with this statement: "She is thy companion, and the wife of thy covenant". The people were being reproved for breaking the tenderest ties of humanity by unlawful divorce in putting away their lawful wives in order to marry strange women. The unity of marriage faithfully kept is in harmony with God's will, and when violated is pernicious to society. Marriage is sacred, a solemn contract and a life-long covenant to be dissolved only by death. The Bible teaches the permanence of the marriage bond. Paul Tournier makes the comment, "Immaturity in one or other partner due to maternal or paternal fixation is the commonest cause of marriage breakdown". Marriage means total commitment of the one to the other, not the mother and daughter discussing and criticising the son-in-law and husband, or vice versa.

Christian believing parties should marry "only in the Lord", (1 Cor. 7 v.39). It is a "great evil, to transgress against our God in marrying strange wives", (Neh. 13 v.27), or to marry someone "near of kin to him, to uncover their nakedness", (Lev. 18 v.6). Leviticus 18 warns of unlawful marriages and abominations, clearly stating in v.6, "None of you shall approach to any that is near of kin to him". The Westminster Confession of Faith emphatically declares that "Marriage ought not to be within the degrees of consanguinity or affinity forbidden in the Word of God, nor can such incestuous marriages ever be made lawful by any law of man", (Chapt. 24 para.4). Co-habiting, lesbianism and homosexuality are roundly condemned in Scripture: "For this cause God gave them up unto vile affections: for even their women did change the natural use into that which is against nature: And likewise also the men, leaving the natural use of the woman, burned in their lust one toward another; men with men working that which is unseemly, and receiving in themselves that recompense of their error which was meet", (Rom. 1 v.26-27). The moral validity of marriage is a contract for life between one man and one woman, and is dissolved only by death. "What therefore God hath joined together, let not man put asunder", (Matt. 19 v.6).

It may not always be the will of God for a person to marry, but it is lawful for all kinds of people to do so. "Marriage is honourable in all, and the bed undefiled: but whoremongers and adulterers God will judge", (Heb. 13 v.4). The marriage laws of the State should not contravene the laws of Holy Scripture which God has ordained that man should obey and conform to them.

Sadly, the marriage vows are greatly ignored and disregarded by so many in society in our day. Unfaithfulness and infidelity are widely rampant, and defilement of the marriage bond by having sexual relations with a third party. Adultery is one of the sins specifically forbidden in the Ten Commandments, and is contrary to the whole concept of Christian marriage. In marriage we leave our parents and we cling to each other as husband and wife. We become one flesh with our spouse. There is no room for anyone else. We are bound together by God. We sin if we allow another person to interfere in our marriage relationship.

The marriage vows and promises are to hold until death us do part. They do not become invalid by 'falling out of love', or if our circumstances change. Breaking the marriage bond is not the way that God planned things. The marriage covenant is broken only when one of the parties to it dies. This is the original plan of God. As sad as it is, there will come a time when our spouse will die. Until that time we are to be one flesh, we are to love, cherish, honour, submit and comfort. No circumstance other than death is to break this bond. No one is to interfere in that union, and we, as husband and wife, are not to allow our sin to ruin it.

Men and women who take the places God has assigned to them may expect that reward of virtue, that blessing of God, a love which does not wither when hair turns white or vanishes, and when bodily passions pass away. The Word of God very clearly states: "The wife is bound by the law as long as her husband liveth; but if her husband be dead, she is at liberty to be married to whom she will; only in the Lord", (1 Cor. 7 v.39). Death breaks the union and a person is free to marry again should he or she wish . . . . . "only in the Lord". "Nevertheless let every one of you in particular so love his wife even as himself; and the wife see that she reverence her husband", (Eph. 5 v.33).

The Secret of a Happy Marriage

In the Song of Solomon, Chapter 8 v.7, we read, "Many waters cannot quench love, neither can the floods drown it: if a man would give all the substance of his house for love, it would utterly be contemned". Of the three great events in the average human existence --- birth, marriage, and death --- the central one, marriage, is the only one in which men and women have a choice. The choice of a life partner in marriage is exceedingly important.

God's will as revealed to us in the Scriptures is that the Christian should marry only someone who is also a Christian---"in the Lord". To marry an unbeliever is called the "unequal yoke". "Be ye not unequally yoked together with unbelievers: for what fellowship hath righteousness with unrighteousness? and what communion hath light with darkness? And what concord hath Christ with Belial? Or what part hath he that believeth with an infidel? And what agreement hath the temple of God with idols? For ye are the temple of the living God; as God hath said, I will dwell in them, and walk in them; and I will be their God, and they shall be My people", (2 Cor. 6 v.14-16).

It is of absolute necessity to ascertain, before any friendship is made, which in all likelihood might lead to love, courtship, and eventually marriage, that such a companion is a genuine believer in the Lord Jesus Christ. In Proverbs 31 v.10-31 we very plainly observe that there are also other essential factors to be taken into consideration when choosing a wife, which we shall summarise, as follows:-

(1) She is to be trustworthy: "the heart of her husband doth safely trust in her", (v.11);

(2) She is to be industrious, not a spendthrift: "worketh willingly with her hands", (v.13); "she looketh well on the ways of her household, and eateth not the bread of idleness", (v.27);

(3) She is to be benevolent, charitable and generous: "She stretcheth out her hand to the poor; yea, she reacheth forth her hands to the needy", (v.20);

(4) She is to be kindhearted: "She openeth her mouth with wisdom; and in her tongue is the law of kindness", (v.26).

Such then is the Biblical description of the woman that would make an excellent wife which will command not only God's smile of approval but also His blessing for the future. Forming such a friendship requires wisdom and prayerful consideration in seeking the Lord's will.

Likewise when choosing a husband, there are a number of factors to be considered that must thoughtfully and prayerfully characterise him:-

   (1)   that he is a man of strict integrity: "He that walketh uprightly, and worketh righteousness, and speaketh the truth in his heart", (Psalm 15 v.2);

   (2)   that he has control and command of his tongue: "He that backbiteth not with his tongue, nor doeth evil to his neighbour, nor taketh up a reproach against his neighbour", (Psalm 15 v.3);

   (3)   that he is a man of his word, his word is his bond: "He that sweareth to his own hurt, and changeth not", (Psalm 15 v.4);

   (4)   that he is magnanimous, honourable and generous: "He that putteth not out his money to usury, nor taketh reward against the innocent", (Psalm 15 v.5).

We are not to expect the traits of character as mentioned above to be found in absolute perfection, in either man or woman, on this side of the land of glory. Husbands and wives are to be "heirs together of the grace of life", (1 Peter 3 v.7), and to ensure mutual happiness, each must courteously and constantly consider the well-being of the other.

As we have already seen, Matthew Henry, the great Bible commentator, writes very well in connection with marriage and the provision of a helpmeet in Genesis 2 v.21-24. He states that "when God created woman, He did not take her out of man's head, to lord it over him; nor out of his feet, to be trampled on by him; but out of his side, to be equal with him; from under his arm, to be protected by him; and from near to his heart, to be loved by him".

Again, another worthy quotation, this time from the gifted pen of Mrs. Heman, shows how a noble Christian wife responds to marriage: "Except the love we pay to heaven, there is none purer, none holier, than that which a virtuous woman feels for him she would cleave through life to. Brother parts from brother, sister from sister, children from their parents, but such a woman from the object of her choice --- never".

May God bless all Christian couples in wedlock, and may:

> "Sweet concord ever ov'r their home preside,
> And mutual love their every action guide;
> May she love him when time has touched his hair,
> And he, when she is old, still think her fair".

Sacrificial Love endures

Nowhere more so in Scripture are the proper roles of husbands and wives described in such detail as in Ephesians 5. These are crucial verses, based on the creation ordinances, which expand greatly on the Christian concept of marriage: Eph 5 v.22-33.

In the heart of this passage, two questions quickly stand out which can be put like this:

(1) Husbands, do you really love your wives enough to die for them?

(2) Wives, do you really love your husbands enough to live with them?

The husband must learn to love his wife as Jesus Christ loves His Church. A wife should so love her husband that she is willing to live for him. She must be willing to give herself completely into being his helper. This involves living for him just as the Church is required to live for Jesus Christ.

Both of these commands are very large requirements that God has laid down and which we must follow. This is the Biblical language that the Women's Liberation movement take exception to, and are extremely opposed to Ephesians 5, which like all other Scripture, is the inspired and inerrant Word of God. Any Christian woman who speaks or argues against the Scriptures is a disgrace, and shows that she has a belligerent attitude and an aggressive spirit against the teaching of Divine Truth. The subordinate role of women in 1 Corinthians 14 and 1 Timothy 2, is not based on the culture of the period in which Paul was writing, but on the most basic factors of all, Creation and The Fall.

"Wives, submit yourselves unto your own husbands, as unto the Lord", (Eph 5 v.22). Certain people have tried to explain this in some other way, to dull the edge, twist it, and even ignore it. There is no option about this command. The wife must obey, not primarily for the benefits of her and her husband will receive, but in order to exhibit the relationship of Jesus Christ to His Church.

The principle of submission runs through all of life, and it pertains to relationships within the Church, as well as within the home. (1 Tim. 2 v.11-15, 1 Cor. 14 v.34-35). The two works of the elder, teaching and ruling, are denied her, which is based on the order of creation and the circumstances involved in the Fall. The key words in First Timothy 3 v.4 to describe successful headship, are the words, "ruleth well", proistemi" (Greek), meaning "to manage", "to preside over", his family.

The husband is to realise and recognise that God has given him a wife to be a "help meet", a helper, (Gen. 2 v.18). She has certain abilities and gifts that God has given her to use to the fullest for the glory of God and the blessing of the home.

The Biblical woman is described as one who learns and performs her role with joy and delight. The husband is responsible to God for the organisation of the home, to oversee and ensure everything runs according to the Divine pattern, and his wife must help him to do so. By God's grace the wife can learn the joys of the truly submissive helper, and the freedom of living within the structure of God's law. "A prudent wife is from the Lord", (Prov. 19 v.14).

Three Forms of Love: Eros, Phileo, and Agape

In Ephesians 5 we have the detailed teaching of the Apostle Paul with regard to Christian marriage, a part of the order of Creation, a part of God's ordinances, of God's decree, of God's will, of what God has stated with regard to this relationship between men and women. This teaching is also emphasised in other portions of Scripture throughout the Bible. The aggressiveness of 'feminism' in distorting the role of wife and mother undermines the place and authority of the husband and father not only in the home but also gravely distorts and warps the minds of the children. Often the unhappy result is of course the growth of crime, violence, and the enormous flood of terrible social problems throughout the country. Through the film industry, soaps, smutty magazines, and other means, these evil influences and wicked attitudes are endemic right across the entire world. With the woman usurping the position of man as head of the home is a denial of the Biblical teaching, a repetition indeed of the old sin of Eve.

There is a crying need that we must get back to God, get back to the revelation He has given us in His authoritative Word, get back to God's plan --- that is, man, and the woman by his side in marriage, complementing him, his "helpmeet" (Gen. 2 v.18), loving one another, revering, respecting, honouring one another, never confusing but rather submitting to the teaching of Scripture, "as unto the Lord", (Eph. 5 v.22). "The husband is the head of the wife" (Eph. 5 v.23), God ordained it so when He made man and woman at the beginning. The New Testament not only confirms this but constantly goes back to that original ordinance of God, which is basic and fundamental to the whole of man's life on earth and his well-being.

In order to understand the true nature of Christian marriage, the Apostle Paul is emphasising the organic, the vital union, the ultimate relationship. The wife is kept, preserved, guarded, shielded, provided and cared for by the husband --- as Christ nourishes and cherishes the Church, so the husband nourishes and cherishes the wife (Eph. 5 v.24). The wife is to the husband what the church is to Christ --- the idea of complement, completeness, "helpmeet" (Gen. 2 v.18). The husband and wife are not separate, "they are no more twain, but one flesh", (Matt. 19 v.6).

Ephesians 5 is quite remarkable in what it tells us about the duties of husbands and wives. "Husbands, love your wives" (v.25) and "wives, submit yourselves" (v.22). In the wife submitting herself love is implicit, so that harmony, peace, and unity are maintained in the marriage relationship, and because the husband loves his wife the leadership will never become a tyranny. "For God hath not given us the spirit of fear; but of power, and of love, and of a sound mind", (2 Tim. 1 v.7).

No husband is entitled or worthy of the name to say that he is the head of the wife unless he loves his wife. He is not carrying out the Scriptural injunction unless he does so. These two things really go together. It is a leadership of love, it is not the idea of a despot or a dictator. The fundamental truth and the controlling idea of the whole matter is: "Husbands, love your wives", (Eph. 5 v.25).

What then is the character, nature, and meaning of the word "love"? What is love? Paul straightly gives us the definition in this very succinct and concise manner: "Husbands, love your wives, even as Christ also loved the Church", (Eph. 5 v.25). The very word the Apostle has used here for "love" is most eloquent in its teaching and in its meaning.

In the Greek language, as used in the days of the New Testament church, there are three words which can be translated by our English word "love".

(1) One of the three words is "eros", which describes the "erotic" love that belongs entirely and exclusively to the husband-wife relationship. For many this kind of love may only be something carnal, selfish, lustful, and of a fleshly desire, which brings out the animal instinct in man. This is what generally passes as wonderful "love" and "romance" in the eyes of the world today, despite the fact that the man may have been unfaithful to his wife, or the wife to her husband. They are both guilty of breaking their vows by desecrating the sanctity of marriage and causing children to suffer.

(2) The second word is "phileo", which means "to be fond of", and comes in as a root in such words as "philanthropic" and "Philadelphia". The classic example of its use in the New Testament is found in John 21 v.15-17. We read in v.15: "So when they had dined, Jesus saith to Simon Peter, Simon, son of Jonas, lovest thou Me more than these? He saith unto Him, Yea, Lord; Thou knowest that I love Thee". The interesting point here is that when Peter answered, "Thou knowest that I love Thee", the word he used was "phileo", "Thou knowest that I am fond of Thee". Jesus, in this conversation, uses the strongest Greek word for "love", "agape", and again asks him the second time in v.16, "Lovest thou Me?" To this Peter replies the second time, "Yea, Lord; Thou knowest that I am fond of Thee". Then we come to v.17 where our Lord does a very interesting thing. Jesus does not use the word "agape" that He had been using twice previously, but now lowers the conception by using the same word that Peter had been using, "phileo". "Simon, son of Jonas, are you really fond

of Me?" This grieved Peter, and in the light of his failure he could but trust himself to the Lord's knowledge and say, "Thou knowest that I am fond of Thee". We would do well to remember and to keep in mind the word translated as "love" may mean "being fond of".

(3) The third word is "agape" which rises to a much higher level. This is the word that is always used in the Bible to express God's love to us: "God so loved the world", (John 3 v.16). This is the very word which is used in Eph. 5 v.25: "Husbands, love your wives", so in that sense, love as God loves. There is nothing higher than this. This is the love, says the Apostle, which husbands should love and show towards their wives. Christians should manifest this kind of love in the way they behave towards each other. "Be filled with the Spirit" (Eph. 5 v.18), so one of the ways a husband behaves towards his wife in the home is this love which is "the fruit of the Spirit" (Gal. 5 v.22).

It is important that we get the whole question of marriage and the marriage relationship into proper perspective. This is not to advocate that the first element, "eros", should not come in at all. That would be quite wrong. We should not regard sex as evil, it is human, it is natural, it is honourable, it is a God-given gift within marriage. The erotic love, "eros", is included and should be present, and as husband and wife it is right that we should feel that mutual attraction one to the other.

The purpose and message of the erotic little Book, The Song of Songs, speaks of the order of Creation and marriage as it ought to be. It describes physical love within that relationship as good, being the will of God, and should be a delight to both partners who become "one flesh" (Matt. 19 v.6). In the Song, the lover pays his beloved the ultimate compliment to her sexual attractiveness. The beloved's impact on her lover was just as great as his on her. Love has its own hallowing touch on all of life. This sexual love in marriage is also expressed and emphasised in Proverbs 5 v.15-19 and 1 Corinthians 7 v.3.

More than that, the husband and wife in true marriage are fond of each other as well, "phileo". In other words they like the companionship of each other which is an important factor of Christian marriage and living in harmony, peace, and unity.

True Christian marriage includes all of these three elements --- "eros", "phileo", and "agape". Christianity elevates marriage, sanctifies it, and gives it a splendour that cannot be equalled outside the teaching of the Bible. Let us then examine ourselves in the light of God's Word. Let us thank the Lord for this true love, love that is of God, the love that is defined in 1 Cor. 13. "Giving thanks always for all things unto God and the Father in the name of our Lord Jesus Christ; Submitting yourselves one to another in the fear of God", (Eph. 5 v.20-21).

CHAPTER FIVE

HEADSHIP, HEAD COVERING AND DRESS

Honour and Dignity

Head Covering a Scriptural Requirement

Liberty and Biblical Obligations

The Christian Woman and Modern Feminism

Modesty, Humility and Godly Fear

Distinctive Femininity

Unisex an Abomination

The Meaning of "Kephale" – "Head"

HEADSHIP, HEAD COVERING AND DRESS

In First Corinthians 11 v.1-16, we see that "the head of the woman is the man", and how she therefore is to have her head covered in public worship.

"Be ye followers of me, even as I also am of Christ. Now I praise you, brethren, that ye remember me in all things, and keep the ordinances, as I delivered them to you. But I would have you know, that the head of every man is Christ; and the head of the woman is the man; and the head of Christ is God. Every man praying or prophesying, having his head covered, dishonoureth his Head. But every woman that prayeth or prophesieth with her head uncovered dishonoureth her head: for that is even all one as if she were shaven. For if the woman be not covered, let her also be shorn: but if it be a shame for a woman to be shorn or shaven, let her be covered. For a man indeed ought not to cover his head, forasmuch as he is the image and glory of God: but the woman is the glory of the man. For the man is not of the woman; but the woman of the man. For this cause ought the woman to have power on her head because of the angels. Nevertheless neither is the man without the woman, neither the woman without the man, in the Lord. For as the woman is of the man, even so is the man also by the woman; but all things of God. Judge in yourselves: is it comely that a woman pray unto God uncovered? Doth not even nature itself teach you, that, if a man have long hair, it is a shame unto him? But if the woman have long hair, it is a glory to her: But if any man seem to be contentious, we have no such custom, neither the Churches of God", (1 Cor. 11 v.1-16).

The Biblical account of the creation of the man and the woman presents us with the following principle: "the woman is for the man". The man has headship over the woman. This is plainly taught in First Cor. 11 v.8-9, "The man is not of the woman; but the woman of the man. Neither was the man created for the woman; but the woman for the man".

The Bible commentator, John Gill, makes the statement that the woman was "to be a companion and associate of the man, both in religious worship and in civil life; and for the procreation and education of children".

Anne Graham, in her book, 'Womanhood Revisited', makes the comment: "God created the woman for the support and companionship of the man, and her acceptance of the man's loving leadership".

"The head of every man is Christ; and the head of every woman is the man", (1 Cor. 11 v.3). This is the situation in which God has placed her, and for that reason, she should not do anything that looks like an attempt at changing places. The woman who prays and worships God in public with her head uncovered dishonours her head, namely, the man. When she appears in the dress of her head she throws off her subjection by wearing trousers, short haircut, no head-wear, etc., which the Scripture says are the signs of indecency. Such behaviour is a desire for superiority which God has conferred on the other sex. The order in which Divine wisdom has placed persons, both male and female, is best and therefore most fitting. To endeavour to destroy the order that God has ordained introduces confusion. The woman should keep to the rank God has chosen for her, and not to dishonour her head; to do so also results in dishonour to God. We must learn to behave in public worship so as to express a reverence for God, and a contentment and satisfaction with the rank in which He has placed us.

Honour and Dignity

The verses in Genesis 2 v.18-25, teach us that the woman was created after the man, out of the man, and for man. Therefore the woman is the glory of the man. First Cor. 11 v.7 says, "A man indeed ought not to cover his head, forasmuch as he is the image and glory of God: but the woman is the glory of the man". This means as most commentators agree, that the woman "is a distinguished ornament of the man" --- "an expression of his honour and dignity", because made out of him, created to help him, and given to be "a crown of honour and glory to him". "The woman is the glory of the man", (1 Cor. 11 v.5).

Another implication of the woman being created after the man, out of the man, for the man, and as the glory of man, is that the man is over the woman --- that he has a certain primacy and leadership role in relation to the woman. This is explicitly stated, "I would have you know, "that the head of every man is Christ; and the head of the woman is the man".

According to First Cor. 11, the Apostle Paul blames the women for the misbehaviour, and endeavours to rectify a number of manifest disorders in the Church at Corinth. The misconduct of their women in public worship must be corrected by asserting the authority of the man, yet so as to remind the husband that both were made for mutual help and comfort, (v.1-16).

The basic problem in the Corinthian Church concerned doctrine, morals, and life-styles. They were claiming to be orthodox, but not pure, and did not live godly lives. Paul praises them for their strengths before he begins to correct their weaknesses and sin, which in this case especially is their misunderstanding of male and female roles and relationships.

In regard to the headcovering, it is best to understand that the Apostle is here referring to activities of worship in public, where a clear testimony is essential. The principle of male headship is not a matter of custom but a matter of God's order and creation, and should never be compromised. God gave man dominion over all the created world, rulership over it, and to care for it according to His Divine plan, and is by that fact the glory of God.

Genesis 3 v.16-17, confirms these roles in a more dramatic way by saying to the woman, "thy desire shall be to thy husband, and he shall rule over thee". To Adam He said, "cursed is the ground for thy sake; in sorrow shalt thou eat of it all the days of thy life".

As far as saving and sanctifying grace is concerned, a woman comes as deeply into communion with God as a man. She is made equally in the image of God, and that image is equally restored through faith in Christ Jesus. She is not intellectually, morally, or spiritually inferior to man. She is unique from him. Her role is to come under the leadership, protection, and care of man, and she is to be "an help meet for him", (Gen. 2 v.30).

In returning to the application of the principle, we read in First Cor. 11 v.10, "For this cause ought the woman to have power on her head because of the angels". The head covering represents the Divine and universal principle of a woman's subordination to man's authority --- the Greek word "exousia" means "rightful power", or "authority". The covered head was the woman's symbol of authority or right to pray and worship, since it demonstrated her submissiveness, (1 Cor. 11 v.4-7).

"Because of the angels": these messengers are God's protectors of His Church, over which they stand in perpetual guard. It is proper for a woman to cover her head as a sign of subordination "because of the angels", in order that these most submissive of all creatures will not be offended by non-submissiveness. Furthermore, the angels were present at creation to be witnesses of God's unique design for man and woman, and would be offended at any violation of that order.

If Satan cannot get men to deny or disregard God's Word, he will try to get them to misinterpret it and carry it to extremes the Lord did not intend. Lest men abuse their authority over women, the Apostle Paul reminds them, "Nevertheless neither is the man without the woman, neither the woman without the man, in the Lord. For as the woman is of the man, even so is the man also by the woman; but all things of God", (1 Cor. 11 v.11-12).

In Christ all believers, male and female, are "in the Lord", and are alike under the Lord. In His work, women are as important as men. Their roles are different in function and relationships, but not in spirituality or importance. Men and women are complementary in every way in life, but particularly in the Lord's work do they function together as Divinely ordered. In many times and places, faithful women have kept the Church alive with little or no support from men. Many mission fields would not exist if it were not for God's elect women. A Church without godly women cannot be a strong and effective Church.

The man's proper authority does not make him independent of women, nor does her proper subordination make her alone dependent. Neither is independent of the other; they are mutually dependent. Women are not to be teachers of men and in the work of the Church, the man is the leader, and the woman is the supporter.

Head Covering a Scriptural Requirement

The radical Women's Liberation movement in society today is sadly behind the times, and in great ignorance of the distinctive characteristics of the Gospel that wherever it has been faithfully preached, it has elevated womanhood from the degradation of heathenism to a place of nobility beside the man. It appears that every flourishing fashion or movement in the 'world' tends to overspill into the Church. To say that headcovering is inconsequential reveals the neglect of spiritual leaders by not teaching what is spiritually and Scripturally correct.

The question thus arises, is headcovering inconsequential or is it indeed a Scriptural tenet, a tradition, or a truth? A cursory reading of First Corinthians 11, readily shows that there were two distinct lessons which deal with the head. The first, is a lesson in headship, and second, a lesson in glory.

In the Divine order of authority, Scripture declares: "that the head of every man is Christ; and the head of the woman is the man; and the head of Christ is God", (1 Cor. 11 v.3). In Ephesians, the headship of Christ is related corporally to the whole body of the Church. In First Corinthians, His headship is related individually to the believer. The man having his head covered (v.4) dishonours Christ. The woman is warned in (v.5) that the uncovered head dishonours 'her figurative head'. The word "dishonour" in the Greek New Testament has the meaning, "to thoroughly put to shame", and in the context of the chapter, it is an implicit denial of the Divine teaching regarding headship, whether intentional or otherwise.

The Holy Spirit now leads Paul to press the issue and to give strong reasons for compliance with this word of instruction. The reason for the uncovered head of the man is stated in verse 7, "forasmuch as he is the image and glory of God". Image is not likeness, but "similitude". "Therewith bless we God, even the Father; and therewith curse we men, which are made after the similitude of God", (James 3 v.9). The Lord Jesus is never spoken of as being in the likeness of God, He is God. "Jesus Christ is Lord", (Phil. 2 v.11).

Man must never cover his head in the exercise of spiritual functions, forasmuch as he represents God as his image. Furthermore, he is the glory of God, and if image is representation, then glory is manifestation. God's authority must be unchallenged, and His glory must not be hid. This is the twofold reason for the uncovered head of the man.

In First Corinthians 11, the woman is not spoken of as the image of man, but as his glory. Here it is not representation but manifestation. The glory of the man must not be manifest in spiritual exercises, therefore that glory must be covered. No glory but God's glory is to be seen in the spiritual realm.

The reason for the woman's covering is also twofold. First, it is a natural one: "For the man is not of the woman; but the woman of the man", (1 Cor. 11 v.8). This verse shows that the man had precedence in the natural realm --- "for Adam was first formed", (1 Tim. 2 v.13). Second, a spiritual reason is given in verse 10: "For this cause ought the woman to have power (a sign of submission to authority) on her head because of the angels". Notice carefully, it is not because of her husband or other men in the congregation, but rather "because of the angels". Why is this? Two further Scriptures will help us to answer this point. We read in Ecclesiastes 5 v.6, "Suffer not thy mouth to cause thy flesh to sin, neither say thou before the angel, that it was an error: wherefore should God be angry at thy voice, and destroy the work of thine hands?" And Ephesians 3 v.10, says "To the intent that now unto the principalities and powers in heavenly places might be known by the Church the manifold wisdom of God". God uses the Church to teach them (principalities and powers) something of His manifold wisdom and Lordship of Christ, the place of the Church, and individual believer.

When a woman comes into Church with her head covered, she shows her submission to Divine headship, and a rebuke to the wicked angels. Their sin is that of rebelling against Divine authority. However, in verse 11, there is the assurance that positionally, "in the Lord", there is no inequality or priority because of sex. "Nevertheless neither is the man without the woman, neither the woman without the man, in the Lord", (1 Cor. 11 v.11).

Notice also here, that for the woman there are two glories involved. "The woman is the glory of the man", (1 Cor. 11 v.7). But she also has a glory of her own: "But if a woman has long hair, it is a glory to her", (1 Cor. 11 v.15). God has given her a natural covering, her long hair, and she must submit her will to the Word of God to cover her own glory, her hair, with another covering when presenting herself in Church to worship God.

There is a solemn responsibility upon all ministers, elders, deacons and members of the congregation to obey God's Word. Leaders are accountable to give the needed instructions, and not shun to declare "all the counsel of God", (Acts 20 v.27), without fear or favour.

Long–haired men are not left out of these verses containing stern words of exhortation and warning: (1 Cor. 11 v.1-16). In this our day, verse 14, is timely, though not always welcome. "Doth not even nature itself teach you, that, if a man have long hair, it is a shame unto him?", (1 Cor. 11 v.14). For a man to have long hair is contrary to the teaching of Scripture, because the Bible specifically states that long hair is a glory only for the woman. The reading of Revelation 9, is very striking, and long hair on men is the badge of rebellion and of the drug cult, and albeit unwittingly, making object lessons for the adversary, the devil, against the standards set out in the Word of God. Because of spiritual infancy, ignorance of Bible truth, and the failure of ministers and elders to teach The Scripture, the Church today is in a sad state of declension and barrenness.

It is therefore not a strange thing, that such a verse, as First Corinthians 11 v.16, should stir up the ire, fire, and anger in some people, as this one does. "But if a man seem to be contentious, we have no such custom, neither the Churches of God", (1 Cor. 11 v.16). This verse speaks of the possibility of contention, and despite the many temptations, Christians are to behave and conduct themselves according to Divine Truth, to the glory of God.

Liberty and Biblical Obligations

In the minds and actions of some there may be the attitude that the subject of woman's headcovering is of very little importance. Are we at liberty to reduce any matter on which God has spoken to such a level? Unimportant? In the inspired Word, that discussion has been preserved for all succeeding generations, and it is, therefore, our solemn obligation and duty to attend, to listen, to obey, and to practice all of God's commands. Failure to manifest such a response and conform to God's Word will affirm that we have imbibed the defying spirit of the modern age and adopted the pattern of the world, being as those who "have cast away the law of the Lord of hosts, and despised the Word of the Holy One of Israel", (Isaiah 5 v.24). From such folly, may God preserve us.

Paul exhorts Timothy, his son in the faith, to "hold fast the form of sound words", (2 Tim. 1 v.13). He charges him to commit the truth "to faithful men, who shall be able to teach others also . . . . . that they strive not about words to no profit, but to the subverting of the hearers", (2 Tim. 2 v.2 and 14). "For the time will come when they will not endure sound doctrine; but after their own lusts shall they heap to themselves teachers, having itching ears; And they shall turn away their ears from the truth, and shall be turned unto fables", (2 Tim. 4 v.3-4). "But evil men and seducers shall wax worse and worse, deceiving, and being deceived", (2 Tim. 3 v.13). What solemn words of warning.

Today, regrettably, we are living in an age when the prevailing attitude, even within the Church, is openly defiant to the Holy Scriptures, when the teaching and authority of the Bible are blatantly disregarded, despised, and rejected.

The passage of Scripture found in First Corinthians 11 v.1-16, is the foundational portion of Divine Truth for the people of God who desire to know the will of the Lord on the matter of headcovering. We must follow the example of Christ, Who is the King and Head of the Church. God's order of authority is very clear in these verses:

(1) the head of Christ is God;

(2) the head of the man is Christ; and

(3) the head of the woman is the man.

Whenever we consider the relationship of the woman to the man, we must understand that there is no essential inequality between the two, but in the Divine order the woman is subordinate to the man in her role and function. This does not mean that she is inferior. God has given to both their respective places, and it is therefore the honour and privilege of both, not only to accept, but to rightfully occupy their respective places as assigned by God, not merely within marriage and the home, but also within the Church.

In worship, it is clear, that the man's head is to be uncovered, and the woman's head is to be covered, for in the spiritual realm, no glory is to be seen but that of Him Who sits upon the everlasting Throne on High. This is not a matter for individual opinion or practice, and the Apostle emphasises quite emphatically that in regard to headcovering, it should be the same in all congregations. "But if any man seem to be contentious, we have no such custom, neither the Churches of God", (1 Cor. 11 v.16). Matthew Henry in his commentary on this passage of Scripture, concludes by stating that "it was the common usage of all the New Testament Churches for women to appear in public assemblies, and join in the public worship, with head covering; and it was manifestly decent that they should do so. Those people must be very contentious indeed who would quarrel with this, or lay it aside".

Today in many of our Churches, the practise of covering the head is ignored by many women, whether consciously or through ignorance of the Biblical teaching on the issue, and sadly their actions are condoned, if not encouraged, by the leaders of those Churches who fail to deliver "all the counsel of God", (Acts 20 v. 27). The submissive heart, willing to please the Lord, will not argue, but rather will have that desire to live in the light of His Word, and will not compromise in rightly obeying the commands of God. The Lord Himself says, "Ye are my friends, if you do whatsoever I command you", (John 15 v.4).

The Christian Woman and Modern Feminism

The Scriptures clearly tell us that a man disgraces his Head if he has something on his own head in worship which is completely wrong; but completely right for a woman. Because of the various movements of women's liberation and 'feminist' campaigns, many women nowadays often take off their head coverings, and cut their hair short, in order to look like men. They attack marriage and the raising of children as unjust restrictions of their rights. They often assert their so-called independence by leaving their husbands and homes, refusing to care for their children, living with other men, demanding jobs traditionally held by men, wearing men's clothing and hairdos, and by discarding all signs of femininity. Such misconduct is downright rebellion against God-ordained principles and is totally wrong. The wearing of immodest or sexually suggestive dress is immoral.

The Christian woman should have her dress and hair length such that distinguishes her from men, and she should cover her head in the public worship of God. The woman's hair is a natural thing, to wear it long is a glory to her; but for a man to have long hair is a token of softness and effeminacy. "Doth not even nature itself teach you, that, if a man have long hair, it is a shame unto him? But if a woman have long hair, it is a glory to her: for her hair is given her for a covering", (1 Cor. 11 v.14-15).

Back in the early Jewish times women guilty of adultery, prostitution and rebellious behaviour, had their hair cut off and often shaven that marked them out as disobedient and sinful. It is astoundingly remarkable that any Christian woman would seek such an identification, and when we see and observe women today, who appear so worldly, profane and contemptuous, as to make the same comparison possible.

In regard to the matter of dress, we note in First Timothy 2 v.9-10, three very important words or phrases which greatly guide us ---

"modest apparel", "sobriety", and "becometh". What are the principles that should guide a woman in her dress, in the use of jewellery, and in her choice of hairstyle, especially when she is coming to the house of God? Are they modest, sober, sensible, becoming, suitable, and in good taste? Women are certainly not to be dowdy in their dress or careless and slovenly in their appearance. On the other hand, they should not give too much thought or spend too much money on these outward things.

Modesty, Humility and Godly Fear

It is interesting to observe in First Timothy 2 v.8, where it says, "I will therefore . . . . .", and in verse 9, goes on to state "In like manner also . . . . .".

"I will therefore that men pray everywhere, lifting up holy hands, without wrath and doubting. In like manner also, that women adorn themselves in modest apparel, with shamefacedness and sobriety; not with broided hair, or gold, or pearls, or costly array; But which becometh women professing godliness with good works", (1 Tim. 2 v.8-10).

The word "will", "boulomia" (Greek), refers to intent, purpose, determination, and command. It carries Divine authority commanding men to pray and women to adorn themselves in a proper manner. The meaning of "adorn", from the Greek word "kosmo", means "to arrange", "put in order", instructing women how they are to prepare themselves for worship. The Greek word "kosmios", translated "modest", means "well ordered" or "well arranged". The word "apparel", refers not only to clothing but also "demeanour" or "attitude". It encompasses a woman's total preparation for worship, involving both attitude of heart and proper adornment on the outside. Indeed her clothing should reflect a heart focused on God, not on the appearance of "self".

The Apostle was concerned that the Ephesian Church be a godly example and testimony to society. For women to call attention to themselves, or dress to lure men is to blaspheme the intent of true worship. In addition they are forbidden to display elaborate "broided hair" styles or expensive jewellery, stressing the importance of women dressing modestly for the worship service.

The Church is the place for worship, not a show. For Christians who parade their glamour are preoccupied with their outward appearance is hypocrisy, and brings discredit upon the Church. A Christian wife should attract attention to her godly character, not her clothing. By her dress and demeanour, she should show her love and devotion to her husband, and demonstrate a humble heart committed to the worship of God.

Such a woman has an attitude of modesty, humility, and godly fear --- "with shamefacedness and sobriety". This denotes a sense of shame of being a distraction or temptation or being dishonourable to God. Instead of doing good, some women cause great problems in the congregation by causing someone to stumble and hinder the worship of God. In themselves, wearing jewellery and nice clothes is not evil, but wearing them for evil or impure motives should have no place in the life of a Christian woman.

In coming to Church the issue is one of sincerity, not as a spectator but a participant. A provocatively dressed woman distracts the service. With the Psalmist we should give prominence to "sing of mercy and judgement: unto Thee, O Lord, will I sing. I will behave myself wisely in a perfect way – I will set no wicked thing before mine eyes", (Psalm 101 v.1-3). Indeed, did not Job make "a covenant with" his eyes (Job 31 v.1), and we likewise should obey God's command to avoid and to "flee" from all forms of "lust" (2 Tim. 2 v.22), which are so often courted by reading books, looking at magazines, or watching television programmes and 'soaps' that we know to be immoral, licentious, and wrong. "For all that is in the world, the lust of the flesh, and the lust of the eyes, and the pride of life, is not of the Father, but is of the world. And the world passeth away, and the lust thereof: but he that doeth the will of God abideth for ever", (1 John 2 v.16-17).

As honourable vessels for the Lord, the Scripture commands us to "follow righteousness, faith, charity, peace, with them that call on the Lord out of a pure heart", (2 Tim. 2 v.22). The Apostle's admonition in his previous letter to Timothy is almost identical: "But thou, O man of God, ... follow after righteousness, godliness, faith, love, patience, meekness. Fight the good fight of faith, lay hold on eternal life, whereunto thou art also called, and hast professed a good profession before many witnesses", (1 Tim. 6 v.11). These are the characteristics of a pure heart which exhibit an honourable vessel for the Lord who continues faithfully to serve and obey Him, sanctified, useful to the Master, and prepared for every good work.

The Biblical charge, therefore, underlines the command that women who profess the Christian religion should be modest, sober, silent, and submissive, as becomes their place. They must be modest in their apparel, avoiding gaudiness, or costliness. Those who profess godliness should, in their dress, as well as in other things, act as becomes their profession of faith. The showing of piety and charity are the best ornaments, which in the sight of God, is of great price. "These things speak, and exhort, and rebuke with all authority. Let no man despise thee", (Titus 2 v.15).

"Who can find a virtuous woman? For her price is far above rubies. The heart of her husband doth safely trust in her, so that he shall have no need of spoil. She will do him good and not evil all the days of her life", (Prov. 31 v.10-12).

Distinctive Femininity

The unique beauty of a Christian woman is gloriously manifest in the distinctive femininity portrayed by her hair, her dress, and her attendance to feminine customs, demonstrating womanly loveliness and submissiveness. There should be no confusion about male and female identities. God has made the sexes distinct --- in roles and relationships. He wants men to be masculine, to be responsibly and lovingly authoritative. He wants women to be feminine, to be responsibly and lovingly submissive.

In almost every Church today there are those who would be inclined "to be contentious", (1 Cor. 11 v.16), and who are not satisfied with God's way, but want to discard or modify it to suit themselves.

Summing up on First Corinthians 11, we note the Biblical pattern is that women are to be submissive to men because of :-

the headship principle (v.3).

the Divine design of male and female (v.7).

the order of creation (v.8).

the role of women (v.9).

the power and token of headcovering (v.10), and

the characteristics of due order and decency (v.13-15).

That is why the Apostle Paul declares, that neither God, nor the faithful people of His Church, will recognise any other principle or follow any other pattern of behaviour. The argument is utterly convincing and the New Testament Churches were firmly committed to these practices. "But if any man seem to be contentious, we have no such custom, neither the Churches of God", (1 Cor. 11 v.16).

A Church may have some women who are better Bible students than any of the men, including the minister. But if those women are obedient to God's order, they will submit to male leadership and will not try to usurp it, simply because that is God's design. A wife may be better educated, better taught in the Scripture, and more spiritually mature than her husband. But because she is spiritual, she will willingly submit to him as head of the family. This is the proper relationship which is specifically described in Ephesians 5 v.22-23, as we shall see later.

In Isaiah 3 v.12, it is interesting to note that the prophet spoke judgement on his generation because they had allowed women to rule over them: "As for My people, children are their oppressors, and women rule over them. O My people, they which lead thee cause thee to err, and destroy the way of thy paths", says the Lord.

Christian women must learn the principles of their religion, learn of Christ, and learn the Scriptures and be built up in their "most holy faith", (Jude v.20), and walk "in the truth", (Jude v.3). They must be silent, submissive, and subject; and not usurp authority.

Unisex an Abomination

Does equality of the sexes in Christ mean unisex which rules out all differences between men and women?

In the Old Testament we read in very clear language: "The woman shall not wear that which pertaineth unto a man, neither shall a man put on a woman's garment: for all that do so are abomination unto the Lord thy God", (Deut. 22 v.5). Unisex clearly is an abomination to God. Women who put on the role of men, and men who put on the role of women, are an abomination to the Lord our God. Men should be men, and women should be women. It is, of course, true, that spiritual privileges come to both men and women alike. But if this means there can be no subordination of women to men, then it follows also that there can be no subordination of men to men, which would contradict all Biblical principles of Church organisation.

The Word of God expressly states that "The woman shall not wear that which pertaineth unto a man, neither shall a man put on a woman's garment: for all that do so are abomination unto the Lord thy God", (Deut. 22 v.5). This is a very clear command, which among other things, is greatly ignored in the teaching of the Church today.

The apparel of sex pertaining to dress appearance is designed to oppose idolatrous practices and to prevent licentious misconduct. The distinction of the sexes is to be held sacred by clothing suitable to each sex. A woman is not permitted by Scripture to put on a man's clothing, nor a man a woman's. Such would be a display of indecent conduct, a distraction of natural distinction, and an abomination to God.

The putting on of the apparel of the one sex by the other is an outrage of ordinary decency, which often leads to hypocrisy and unbecoming levity, and opens the door to an influx of so many evils that all who wear the dress of another sex are pronounced "an abomination unto the Lord", (Deut. 22 v.5). Modesty should be the guard of female virtue and the charm of social life.

In Divine worship the changing of attire is forbidden, a practice that was prevalent in idolatrous worship as the sexes of heathen deities were often confounded, and such worshippers endeavoured to please them by dressing like a particular god. "God created man in his own image, in the image of God created He him; male and female created He them", (Gen. I v.27). "Male and female . . . . .", this natural distinction should be preserved in manners and dress, but is destroyed when women forget their sex and men their decorum. (First Corinthians 11 v.1-19).

The interchange of apparel is "an abomination unto the Lord thy God", (Deut. 22 v.5). Such habits defaces the natural image of God in mankind, opens up the way to arrogance, impudence, licentiousness, and deception. These evils are detestable to God and He has given a standard of dress and life for men and women. Sex is distinguished by nature, by dress, by manners, and by conduct. This is a precept against boldness and effrontery in women, and against fostering softness and effeminacy in men, or of lightness, lasciviousness and petulance in both. It is a precept against all infraction of these laws which God has established at the creation of man, and against all confusion of attire of men and women, in society and in the Church.

The prohibition against a woman wearing the habiliments of a man, and of a man wearing the clothing of a woman can scarcely refer to transvestism as some would maintain. The inclusion of this rule in Deuteronomy, among others, under the proscription of things the Lord detests suggests a serious problem, and as elsewhere in the Bible, Scripture considers the natural differences between male and female to be the Lord's creation, and so should not be disregarded or camouflaged. In the original Hebrew the word "keligeber" means "men's clothing"; and the word "simlat 'issah" means "women's clothing".

The attempt of many to explain away the true meaning of Deuteronomy 22 v.5, is the ploy of Satan under various guises to distort the Truth of the Bible, not only in this portion of God's Word, but in other Scriptures as well. All of God's commands still stand, He never abrogated any part of His Word, and in the main the fervent witness of the true Church of God all down the ages, has stood firm on all of these matters during the past two millennia since the early days of the New Testament Church.

The distinction of the sexes by the apparel is always to be kept up, for the preservation not only of our own and our neighbour's chastity, but also from the temptation of committing uncleanness. The confounding of the dispositions and affairs of the sexes is forbidden. Nature itself teaches that a difference be made between them in their hair (1 Cor. 11 v.14-15), and by the same rule in their clothes (Deut. 22 v.5), which therefore ought not to be confounded, either in ordinary wear, casual or occasional, or otherwise. To befriend what some would call a 'lawful' escape from this, is highly unwarranted practice, and for whatever reason, is justly questionable; and all who wear the dress of another sex are pronounced "an abomination unto the Lord", (Deut. 22 v.5). It is an insult to Him, which says that the offender does not care and is arrogant in regard to God's commands. Even showing the spirit of half-heartedness is thus provoking and insulting to God.

The design of this prohibition was to maintain the sanctity of that distinction of the sexes which was established by the creation of man and woman, and the wiping out of this distinction by the so-called emancipation of women, is unnatural and against the will of God, and therefore an abomination in the sight of the Lord. The symbols of gender difference must be respected and the principle of gender distinction remains. Violations of the creation order and the interchange of clothing was part of pagan religious practice. Women are to dress "in that which is not corruptible, even the ornament of a meek and quiet spirit, which is in the sight of God of great price. For after this manner in the old time the holy women also, who trusted in God, adorned themselves, being in subjection unto their own husbands: Even as Sara obeyed Abraham, calling him lord: whose daughters ye are, as long as ye do well, and are not afraid with any amazement", (1 Peter 3 v.4-6).

The meaning of "kephale" – "head"

Modern 'feminists so-called theologians' argue that the Greek word "kephale", in First Cor. 11 v.3, translated as "head" in the Authorised Version, should be translated "source" or "origin", and therefore does not have in it the idea of authority and leadership. The fact is, as Sharon James notes in an appendix to 'God's Design for Women', that Professor Wayne Grudem, after a deep and extensive study of "kephale", showed convincingly that nowhere is it used in the New Testament, or in other Greek literature, to mean "source" or "origin" when referring to a person. The correct translation is indeed, "The head of the woman is the man".

Another argument of modern 'feminists' against Christian teaching on the headship of man is that this headship did not exist when man was created male and female. Rather it comes, they say, after the Fall and as a result of the Fall. Therefore, as the 'feminists' proclaim, the ideal state for the woman is liberation from dominion by man.

There is clear proof, as we have noted earlier, that the man was given the responsibility of leadership and authority right from the beginning. It was the man who was created first, it was the man who named his new companion and wife, it was to the man that the command was given not to eat of the forbidden fruit of the tree, it was the man who was called to account by God, and it is the man who is presented as the head of the whole human race.

The danger of tampering with Scripture, or any attempt to change the clear meaning of a Bible text, in order to bring it into harmony with secular theology and worldly thinking is reprehensible. We should let the passage stand just as it is and not interfere or meddle with it in any way. "Buy the truth, and sell it not; also wisdom, and instruction, and understanding", (Prov. 23 v.23). "My son, fear thou the Lord and the King: and meddle not with them that are given to change", (Prov. 24 v.21). Truth is that by which all matters of faith and practice must be guided and governed for without truth there is no goodness. "We ought to obey God rather than men", (Acts 5 v.29).

Man's position as "head" is not by merit but by Divine appointment. Biblically, men are delegated leadership roles as God's representatives in the home and in the Church. While some feel this truth denigrates women, few really consider the solemnity of the responsibility associated with this position. "My brethren, be not many masters, knowing that we shall receive the greater condemnation", (James 3 v.1). "Obey them that have the rule over you, and submit yourselves: for they watch for your souls, as they that must give account, that they may do it with joy, and not with grief: for that is unprofitable for you", (Heb. 13 v.17).

Bible teachers and leaders are subject to correction and judgement should they act unworthily "not discerning the Lord's body", (1 Cor. 11 v.29). "But when we are judged, we are chastened of the Lord, that we should not be condemned with the world", (1 Cor. 11 v.32). "Let the prophets speak two or three, and let the other judge", (1 Cor. 14 v.29). Overseers, ministers, elders, deacons, cannot be "lords" over God's people. "The elders which are among you I exhort, who am also an elder, and a witness of the sufferings of Christ, and also a partaker of the glory that shall be revealed: Feed the flock of God which is among you, taking the oversight thereof, not by constraint, but willingly; not for filthy lucre, but of a ready mind; Neither as being lords over God's heritage, but being ensamples of the flock", (1 Peter 5 v.1-3),

Biblical headship is not an issue of equality any more than is the relationship that exists between God the Father and God the Son. First Corinthians 11, reminds us that "the head of Christ is God", yet surely there is no inequality between God the Son and God the Father. When it comes to equality between the sexes, God's perspective is this: "There is neither Jew nor Greek, there is neither bond nor free, there is neither male nor female: for ye are all one in Christ Jesus", (Gal. 3 v.28).

Therefore, the concept of headship does not suggest a gender inequality, but rather that God desires order among His people. "Let all things be done unto edifying . . . . . Let all things be done decently and in order", (1 Cor. 14 v.26 and 40).

CHAPTER SIX

WOMEN IN THE CHURCH

The Offices of the Church

Presbyters

Deacons

The Importance of proper Church Structures

Let the Women learn

Women keep silence in Church

Women and Ordination

Different Functions

Scripture prohibits certain Roles by Women

Scripture prohibits Women as Deacons

The Place of Women in the Church

The Labour of Women in the Gospel

Submission, Teaching and Authority

Adornment, Meekness and a Quiet Spirit

The Design and Role of Women

The Divine Pattern for the Church

The Great Commission

WOMEN IN THE CHURCH

It is clearly commanded in First Cor. 14, v.34, "Let your women keep silence in the Churches".

"For God is not the author of confusion, but of peace, as in all Churches of the saints. Let your women keep silence in the Churches: for it is not permitted unto them to speak; but they are commanded to be under obedience, as also saith the law. And if they will learn any thing, let them ask their husbands at home: for it is a shame for women to speak in the Church", (1 Cor. 14 v.33-35).

In the Greek of this passage there is a startling call here to the Corinthians to awake and be aware of the seductions of sensualism, the heathen society, and the fumes of intellectual pride. The sense and force of the call signifies the manner of the awakening; it is right the Corinthians should rouse themselves from self-delusion: 'Rouse up to soberness in righteous fashion, and cease to sin'. The Apostle Paul is emphasising the fact that the principle of women not speaking in Church services was not local, geographical, or cultural, but universal, "in all Churches of the saints". Women are not to exercise any such ministries.

In God's order for the Church, women should subject themselves, just as the Law also says, (v.34). This principle as taught in the Old Testament from creation onwards, is reaffirmed in the New, and Scripture declares that no women are permitted to speak in Church services. When women usurp man's God-ordained role, they inevitably fall into other unBiblical practices and delusions. Women may be highly gifted teachers and leaders, but those gifts do not constitute the right of authority in the services of the Church. When any part of God's order is ignored or rejected, His Church is weakened and He is dishonoured. It is improper, "aischros" (Greek), "shameful", "disgraceful", for a woman to speak in Church. "It is not permitted unto them to speak", (v.34), and this statement leaves no question as to its meaning.

The Offices of the Church

Before proceeding to elaborate on the theme, 'Women in the Church', we shall consider at this point, the offices of the Church, and while every member of the Church is a prophet, a priest, and a king, it is only ministers, elders, and deacons, men, not women, who represent Christ in its government. Is it not true that few there are in times of doctrinal error, spiritual declension, or other controversy concerning women in the Church, refuse to pray, refuse to seek the will of God, refuse to search the Scriptures, refuse to admonish erring fellow members, and refuse to follow blind leaders --- by insisting that the Church should modernise and conform to popular demand, thus disregarding the teaching of God's Holy Word?

In the absence of Christ's authority and His anointing, the glory of the Christian Church is veiled, and the devil gains the victory. "But ye are a chosen generation, a royal priesthood, an holy nation, a peculiar people; that ye should shew forth the praises of Him Who hath called you out of darkness into His marvellous light: Which in time past were not a people, but are now the people of God: which had not obtained mercy, but now have obtained mercy", (1 Peter 2 v.9-10).

The Church's task is to teach and preach the Word of God. The prophets and apostles of old did not hesitate to preface their message with the unqualified declaration: "Thus saith the Lord", (Jer. 10 v.2). Second Timothy contains the last inspired words penned by the Apostle Paul, who knew that his earthly life was nearing its end. In his final charge, he beseeches Timothy to be faithful in his ministry to the Lord Jesus Christ. "I charge thee therefore before God, and the Lord Jesus Christ, Who shall judge the quick and the dead at His appearing and His kingdom; Preach the Word; be instant in season, out of season; reprove, rebuke, exhort with all longsuffering and doctrine. For the time will come when they will not endure sound doctrine; but after their own lusts shall they heap to themselves teachers, having itching ears; And they shall turn away their ears from the truth, and shall be turned unto fables", (2 Tim. 4 v.1-4).

The Church must not degenerate into a social club, nor go into the entertainment business, or take sides in party politics. The Church's business is to declare "all the counsel of God", (Acts 20 v.27), preaching repentance, good tidings, and the wrath of God --- to "reprove the world of sin, and of righteousness, and of judgment", (John 16 v.8).

There are many Churches and denominations today that pride themselves on being 'well-oiled and smoothly running' ecclesiastical machinery, while in reality and fact they largely or perhaps completely, neglect sound doctrine and Biblical practice. It does not seem to the World Council of Churches and the iniquitous ecumenical movement, that the smallest Church which contends uncompromisingly for the truth once for all delivered to the saints (Jude v.3), is contributing real Biblical service to the Kingdom of God, which is not the case by a globe-encircling federation of Churches that darkens the truth by ambiguous words and corrupt doctrine. In reality the former is a manifestation of the body of Christ, while the latter is not. "O Zion, that bringest good tidings, get thee up into the high mountain; O Jerusalem, that bringest good tidings, left up thy voice with strength; lift it up, be not afraid; say unto the cities of Judah, Behold your God", (Isaiah 40 v.9).

The believing communicant members of the Church choose their own officers, they are governed with their consent by these officers, and they are chosen from among their own number. In this limited sense the Church is a democracy, but not a hierarchy. Yet their ultimate responsibility is not to the congregation but to Christ, the sole King and sovereign Head of His Church, which makes the Church a monarchy. His Law, the Bible, is its only law. The officers, therefore, are not to please men, but Christ, through His Word. It is when the Church departs from this Standard, that problems arise and apostasy creeps in.

Essentially there are two main offices in the Church, that of elder and deacon. The eldership has two divisions, teaching and ruling. The teaching elder, usually the minister or pastor, is both teaching and ruling, representing Christ as preachers of the Word and overseeing the spiritual life of the congregation. "Let the elders that rule well be counted worthy of double honour, especially they who labour in the Word and doctrine", (1 Tim. 5 v.17).

In regard to the various offices the Scripture allows for some overlapping, but not for women to participate or be officers. It is not unusual for ruling elders and deacons to bring the Word of God to the people. Paul enjoined the ruling elders of the Church at Ephesus to "Take heed therefore unto yourselves, and to all the flock, over the which the Holy Ghost hath made you overseers, to feed the Church of God, which He hath purchased with His own blood", (Acts 20 v.28). In chapters 6 and 7 of the Book of the Acts of the Apostles, when the Church at Jerusalem had chosen deacons, seven men, not women, to care for the poor and other material necessities of the Church, one of them, namely Stephen, declared the Word of God.

The central task of the teaching elder, the minister or pastor, is to declare "all the counsel of God", (Acts 20 v.27). It goes without saying that he cannot possibly do this without being, and continuing to be, a diligent student of the Word of God. He will relate his work as ruling elder directly to his work as teaching elder. The most valuable contribution that he can make to the rule of the Church is to inform himself and instruct the other ruling elders concerning the teaching of Holy Scripture on the subject of Church government and management. The supreme responsibility of the Church is to proclaim the Word of God. The minister must not allow himself to lord it over God's heritage or become domineering, pretentious, or pompous in his attitude as an autocrat.

There is also the danger that the minister, the teaching elder, might 'spread himself thin' to do so many things becoming a 'jack of all trades' concerning things that may interest him more than do the spiritual riches of the Word of God. He should ever have an eye to the glory of Christ, Whom he preaches, and count himself out: "Yea doubtless, and I count all things but loss for the excellency of the knowledge of Jesus Christ my Lord: for Whom I have suffered the loss of all things, and do count them but dung, that I may win Christ", (Phil. 3 v.8).

It should be the minister's constant aim that Christ may increase while he himself decreases. "He must increase, but I must decrease", (John 3 v.30). Being a minister or pastor, which means being a servant, he should humbly and passionately serve the Lord Jesus Christ and His Church, ascribing the words of the Apostle Paul to be his very own: "Whose I am, and Whom I serve", (Acts 27 v.23).

Presbyters

An alternative name for ruling elder is "presbyter", something referred to in Scripture as "bishop" or "overseer". The term bishop nowadays is used to denominate someone who stands above other clergymen in authority. But such is not at all the Biblical usage of that term. When Paul arrived at Miletus, he sent to Ephesus and called the presbyters of the Church: "And from Miletus he sent to Ephesus, and called the elders of the Church", (Acts 20 v.17). In his exhortation to them, he charged them to "take heed therefore unto yourselves, and to all the flock, over the which the Holy Ghost hath made you overseers (bishops)", (Acts 20 v.28). It is clear that according to Scripture every presbyter is a bishop, and that is a way of saying that the work of the elder is to oversee the Church.

We have already seen that the minister or pastor, is both a teaching and a ruling elder, and the work of the ruling elder and that of the minister overlap. In exhorting the Ephesian elders to take heed to the "flock", the Apostle evidently thought of the members of the Church as "sheep", and of the elders as "shepherds". The command to "feed" the Church undoubtedly had reference to the Word of God, for it is the only spiritual food that God has provided for His people. Therefore, when the minister or pastor is absent, it is highly proper for a ruling elder to conduct public worship either by reading a sermon or giving his own discourse.

It may be necessary for ruling elders to correct the minister if he fails to lead an exemplary life, or if he is not diligent in his pastoral work. If his preaching is lacking in passion, or not according to the Scriptures, the ruling elders as presbyters should take steps to overcome that defect and not rest until that evil has been remedied. The work of the ruling elder is not only important, momentous, but at times, perhaps, difficult. It is their task to accept or reject applicants for Church membership, and to exercise discipline upon the erring members of the flock. What a responsibility, and such tasks can only be performed with fear and trembling. No man can look into the hearts of men and women, and the applicant who uses pious terminology glibly may be a hypocrite, whereas the applicant who has to be 'prompted' to say anything at all may be a true and sincere child of God. A modernist will vow that he believes in Jesus, and even among self-styled evangelicals there is no perfect unanimity as to what is saving faith. The elders must determine that an applicant honours Christ, not only as Saviour, but also as Lord, in his daily walk and witness.

In regard to discipline, elders dare not claim to be infallible, and many neglect this duty and salve their conscience by referring to the parable of the tares, (Matt. 13), "let both (the wheat and the tares) grow together", (v.30). Scripture clearly teaches most emphatically that Church members who err in either doctrine or conduct in life, must be disciplined. For elders to resort to worldly tactics on the pretext of contumacy by casting out an alleged offender because he refuses to cooperate with the mismanagement and abusive leadership of ecclesiastical courts, is not only a grave mistake, but wrong, while committing the sin of believing themselves to be infallible.

It is important for presbyters in their role as elders to truly attend to the spiritual matters with truth and righteousness, and to leave the material interests and Church finances to the deacons. It must be remembered that the deacons are subject and responsible to the elders. All matters in relation to the oversight of the Church must be carried out in a spiritual way to a spiritual end. And well might any ruling elder exclaim, "And who is sufficient for these things?" (2 Cor. 2 v.16).

It is a great folly to consider a man because he is highly achieved academically, or successful in business, is qualified for any position of responsibility in the Church. Seldom is a humble and relatively poor labouring man elected to the eldership. Yet he may well possess the qualifications for this office in a much higher degree than does the president of a bank or chairman of a board of directors. A prime requisite for the office of elder, teaching or ruling, is godliness, not popularity. "A bishop then must be blameless, and husband of one wife, vigilant, sober, of good behaviour, given to hospitality, apt to teach; Not given to wine, no striker, not greedy of filthy lucre; but patient, not a brawler, not covetous; One that ruleth well his own house, having his children in subjection with all gravity . . . . . Not a novice, lest being lifted up with pride he fall into the condemnation of the devil", (1 Tim. 3 v.2-6). He must be able to hold "fast the faithful Word as he hath been taught, that he may be able by sound doctrine both to exhort and to convince the gainsayers", (Titus 1 v.9).

A most important requisite is that of humility. While the eldership is a high, exalted, and honourable office, only the humble man is fit to hold it. Pride, arrogance, and self-importance in a man will have detrimental and damaging effects, and the position of elder is not for a "novice", "lest being lifted up with pride he fall into the condemnation of the devil", (1 Tim. 3 v.6). In many Church Sessions there is a 'leading elder'. This is unscriptural and almost invariably he is a hindrance to the minister and a detriment to the Church.

In order to maintain proper standards in the Church, it is necessary that the elder is "able by sound doctrine both to exhort and to convince the gainsayers", (Titus 1 v.9). He needs to know his Bible, and he should always be a diligent student of the Word of God. It was for good reason that James said, "If any of you lack wisdom, let him ask of God, that giveth to all men liberally, and upbraideth not; and it shall be given him", (James 1 v.5). This is becoming more and more rare and scarce. Wisdom is indispensable which is the ability to make good and proper use of knowledge, and is manifested in good judgement in dealing with people in the Church. Therefore, The Scripture emphasises that an elder must be "one that ruleth well his own house, having his children in subjection with all gravity; For if a man know not how to rule his own house, how shall he take care of the Church of God. Moreover he must have a good report of them which are without; lest he fall into reproach and the snare of the devil", (1 Tim. 3 v.4-5 and 7). If this is not the case, it is because the underlying cause of failure is paucity and lack of godliness. "The fear of the Lord is the beginning of wisdom: and the knowledge of the holy things is understanding", (Prov. 9 v.10). Godliness is the essence of wisdom.

Deacons

As well as elders in the Church, The Scripture also directs and gives guidance on the matter of deacons. Apart from these, no other office is mentioned in the Bible. Some Churches do not elect and appoint deacons, which is not only neglectful, but also an outright rejection of the teaching of the Word of God. Indeed, for some, not much importance, if any, is attached to the office of deacon. The reason perhaps for this unhealthy attitude is that consideration of the natural in taking care of the poor and material things, as the spiritual aspects of this office, are not deemed to hold high esteem, respect, and honour.

The diaconate was initiated practically at the beginning of the New Testament Church where we have its apostolic origin recorded in Acts 6. When the number of the disciples and followers of Christ was greatly multiplied, it became so onerous that the apostles, busy as they already were with preaching and teaching, did not have the time any longer to discharge and combine the function of deacon. "And in those days, when the number of the disciples was multiplied, there arose a murmuring of the Grecians against the Hebrews, because their widows were neglected in the daily ministration. Then the twelve called the multitude of the disciples unto them, and said, It is not reason that we should leave the Word of God, and serve tables", (Acts 6 v.1-2).

It is clear that the office of deacon concerns the physical, the temporal, the material, the natural. Scripture teaches that the natural was created by God as well as the spiritual, and that as a Divine creation it is entitled to the Christian's high esteem. Before God established the covenant of grace with Abraham, He made the covenant of nature with Noah. Thus He first guaranteed the continuity of the human race, and subsequently the continuity of the Church.

However, it would be quite wrong to think that the deacons of a Church have done their duty when they have gathered from the members of the Church their gifts, offerings, and tithes, and have properly distributed the funds as good stewards. Their duty also extends to the spiritual, for the exercise of charity and attending to the needs of God's "labourer" in the Word, also entails the consoling of the distressed and giving exhortation and encouragement to the servants of Christ coupled with words of comfort and deeds of mercy. The true preparation for work for Christ is the clear sight and deep feeling of the immensity of the field, the consequent pressure of need, and the small supply of labourers. "The labourer is worthy of his hire", (Luke 10 v.7). What the minister of Christ receives for his sustenance is not an alms, the message he brings to the people entitles him to it. The minister of Christ is not to seek for great temporal prosperity, nor from a false modesty to refuse adequate sustenance from those whom he serves in spiritual things. "And we beseech you, brethren, to know them which labour among you, and are over you in the Lord, and admonish you; And to esteem them very highly in love for their work's sake. And be at peace among yourselves", (1 Thess. 5 v.12-13).

It is very noteworthy that the Apostle Paul quotes Luke 10 v.7, and refers to Luke's writing as Scripture. "Let the elders that rule well be counted worthy of double honour, especially they who labour in the Word and doctrine. For the Scripture saith, Thou shalt not muzzle the ox that treadeth out the corn. And, The labourer is worthy of his reward", (1 Tim. 5 v.17-18).

So the work of deacons is very important. By Christ's authority they are to remind the members of the Church of their duty to help the needy and those engaged in the service of Christ at home and abroad. The primary meaning of the Greek word from which "deacon" is derived, is "servant". The diaconate is pre-eminently the office of service. "And whosoever will be chief among you, let him be your servant: Even as the Son of Man came not to be ministered unto, but to minister, and to give His life a ransom for many", (Matt. 20 v.27-28). The whole moral law of God can be summed up in the one demand of love. "Love worketh no ill to his neighbour: therefore love is the fulfilling of the law", (Rom. 13 v.10). And Paul climaxed that great chapter on love, First Corinthians 13, with the words: "And now abideth faith, hope, charity (love), these three; but the greatest of these is charity (love)", (1 Cor. 13 v.13).

The diaconate is an office of love. In the name of Christ, the Church of God dispenses mercy and aid to God's very own, and comes to the assistance of other Churches that are in need, as well as bringing relief to the suffering saints in many lands. Significantly, Scripture tells us that of the seven deacons chosen by the Church at Jerusalem in Acts 6, two of them, namely, Stephen and Philip, were active also as evangelists. Truly, the office of deacon is spiritual as well as natural. "And the Word of God increased; and the number of the disciples multiplied in Jerusalem greatly", (Acts 6 v.7).

The Importance of proper Church Structures

The Lord Jesus Christ, the King and Head of His Church, hath therein appointed a government, in the hand of Church officers, elders and deacons, distinct from the civil magistrate. The Church is the Church of God, and its aims and functions are prescribed by its Head, its constitution is determined by its Head, and its officers are designed and appointed by its Head. The Church which is the Body of Christ is not to be ruled according to human wisdom and expediency, but only by the authority of the Word of God.

Why then does the Word of God not permit or allow women to hold the office of minister, pastor, elder or deacon, in the Church? This is a very controversial question in many parts. We shall now further proceed to study more deeply by searching the Scriptures carefully and diligently in order to answer, in a clear and Biblical fashion, this all-important question. The example of the Bereans is a very worthy one, for every child of God who is exercised about finding the truth will receive "the Word with all readiness of mind", and will follow their example who "searched the Scriptures daily, whether those things were so", (Acts 17 v.11). Many Christians today tend to be far too prone to accept that things are right, even the leadership, without searching the Scriptures for confirmation that their conduct, service, and doctrine are consistent with the teaching of the Bible or not, or whether they are in harmony with the mind and will of God or not, according to His Word.

In all matters of faith and practice, Christians have an authoritative Guide, the Bible. As we study and examine the teaching of Holy Scripture our Heavenly Father has not left us to drift, or to be in any uncertainty about Church government, the Church's leadership, and the role and function of elders and deacons who must be men, not women.

The Bible declares that the Church of the living God from past to present is glorious in His sight. There is no group, no movement, no institution of any kind in the world which can even approach to the glory, the splendour, the honour, the beauty, and the dignity of the Church of God. Our prayer is that God's children might possess a profound sense of being a people "called out" of the world, "ekklesia" (Greek), as believers into a spiritual organisation solely on the merits of the redemptive work of Christ and the renewing operations of the Holy Spirit, and be filled to overflowing with a profound joy and understanding of the glory of the Church as God sees it according to the Scriptures.

The problems about the Church would be solved if we obeyed His Word, and humbly practised the teaching of the Apostles in regard to the instructions laid down by Divine authority for the governing and maintenance of His Church. "And when they had preached the Gospel to that city, and had taught many, they returned again to Lystra, and to Iconium, and Antioch, confirming the souls of the disciples, and exhorting them to continue in the faith, and that we must through much tribulation enter into the kingdom of God. And when they had ordained them elders in every Church, and had prayed with fasting, they commended them to the Lord, on Whom they believed" (Acts 14 v.21-23). "These things write I unto thee, ... that thou mayest know how thou oughtest to behave thyself in the house of God, which is the Church of the living God, the pillar and ground of the truth", (1 Tim. 3 v.14-15). "For this cause", Paul instructs Titus, "left I thee in Crete, that thou shouldest set in order the things that are wanting, and ordain elders in every city, as I had appointed thee", (Titus 1 v.5).

The true Church of God based on Biblical principles, provides a ministry which every Christian needs. "And let us consider one another to provoke unto love and to good works: Not forsaking the assembling of ourselves together, as the manner of some is; but exhorting one another: and so much the more, as ye see the day approaching", (Heb. 10 v.24-25). Among its functions, include the following:-

(1) the opportunity for corporate worship: "Let them exalt Him also in the congregation of the people, and praise Him in the assembly of the elders", (Psalm 107 v.32);

(2) the opportunity for teaching in the Word of God by qualified men sent by God: "And He gave some, apostles; and some prophets; and some evangelists; and some pastors and teachers; For the perfecting of the saints, for the work of the ministry, for the edifying of the body of Christ", (Eph. 4 v.11-12);

(3) the opportunity to put in place the necessary structures of sound government and faithful disciplinary procedures: "Remember them which have the rule over you, who have spoken unto you the Word of God: whose faith follow, considering the end of their conversation", (Heb. 13 v.7); and

(4) the opportunity to do God's will as expressed in Scripture, whatever the cost, of all that God has revealed in His infallible Truth: "how thou oughtest to behave thyself in the Church", (1 Tim. 3 v.15).

A Church thus functioning will bring glory to God, and blessing to the people under its care who live and work in harmony of mind and heart and body according to the command of Christ as portrayed in His Word. Failure to do so is to be out of step and the will of God.

The Church in all ages should be continually modelled according to the pattern of Scripture. It is necessary to draw a distinction between the Invisible Church and the Visible Church. By this, we do not mean two Churches, but the one Church distinguished by two aspects. The Invisible Church consists of all those who have been redeemed by Christ, and is totally dependent on Him for all spiritual life, since He is its living Head and sole King. The Visible Church consists of all those who profess faith in Christ and is placed in subjection to Him as its Sovereign, and is therefore under obligation to receive from Him the doctrines and discipline as revealed in His Word. "Go ye therefore, and teach all nations, baptizing them in the name of the Father, and of the Son, and of the Holy Ghost: Teaching them to observe all things whatsoever I have commanded you: and, lo, I am with you alway, even unto the end of the world", (Matt. 28 v.19-20).

Our Lord has not left the Church to be organised and governed by the maxims of human policy, or by the whims of society, or as expediency may dictate, which are so often advocated by the liberals within the Church and the modern ecumenical movement. "In vain they do worship Me, teaching for doctrines the commandments of men", (Matt. 15 v.9); "this people honoureth Me with their lips, but their heart is far from Me", (Mark 7 v.6), "which all are to perish with the using, after the commandments and doctrines of men", (Col. 2 v.22). We are not to give heed to "fables, and commandments of men, that turn from the truth", (Titus 1 v.14).

Christ has given His Church her laws, doctrines, and committed into the hands of ministers, pastors, elders, presbyters, to maintain and see that these are acknowledged and obeyed. "Remember them which have the rule over you, who have spoken unto you the Word of God", (Heb. 13 v.7).

The true Biblical Church will be evidenced by its strong emphasis on Scriptural doctrine and the application of Bible teaching to the life of the believer and that of the Church as to how it is organised and governed. The Church should follow at all times the New Testament model of the Apostles who taught, (1) what Christians are to believe and how they are to live day by day, and (2) how its elders and deacons are to be chosen and appointed, in accordance with Scripture.

The fundamental task of the Church is clearly to obey, uphold, maintain, and defend God's Truth; and in love be zealous of God's glory and all good works of mercy and evangelism. The greatest need of our time is for living, vibrant, Biblical Churches. The pressures of ungodliness and the demeaning of the Church are weighty, and we need therefore to go forth with boldness and steadfastness as servants of God wherever Divine Providence directs us, and by the power of the Holy Ghost to declare "all the counsel of God", (Acts 20 v.27). The Church's great fundamental duty is to obey the Great Commission to go "into all the world, and preach the Gospel to every creature", (Mark 16 v.15), and to proclaim His Word until "the earth shall be full of the knowledge of the Lord, as the waters cover the sea", (Isaiah 11 v.9).

Let the Women learn

Despite the far-reaching ill effects of radical 'feminism', if we understand aright what the Bible teaches, we will be able to deal with any error that might confront us. There is perhaps no other passage of Scripture more direct and more comprehensive in addressing the role of women in the Church than that of First Timothy 2 v.9-15. That the place of women is important in the sight of God and in the Church, is deducted from the fact that so much is said about them in this one Epistle. The right kind of women can be the strength of the Church. However, the debate on the role of women in the Church has left the pages of Holy Writ to find its resolution elsewhere. The traditional Biblical doctrines are being swept away by radical 'feminism'. In the Church plagued with false doctrine and false leaders, and the so-called 'new evangelicalism', it is not surprising to find them struggling over gender roles. First Timothy 5 speaks of confronting sin in the spiritual family, the ministry of the Church to widows, the ministry of widows to the Church, and restoring Biblical eldership to effective leadership.

Timothy was pastor of the Ephesian Church, and word had reached Paul that things were not as they should be. In Acts 20, Paul says to the Ephesian elders, that he had not failed to declare the entire Word of God to the Church, but had warned them night and day for three years, that error would come in from the outside, and that evil would rise from the inside. "For I have not shunned to declare unto you all the counsel of God. Take heed therefore unto yourselves, and to all the flock, over the which the Holy Ghost hath made you overseers, to feed the Church of God, which He hath purchased with His own blood. For I know this, that after my departing shall grievous wolves enter in among you, not sparing the flock. Also of your own selves shall men arise, speaking perverse things, to draw away disciples after them. Therefore watch, and remember, that by the space of three years I ceased not to warn every one night and day with tears", (Acts 20 v.27-31).

The Church had now fallen into doctrinal error, and ungodly practice had set in. Worst of all the leadership had become corrupted and needed to be replaced. In the context here in First Timothy, Paul had dealt with two very corrupt leaders, namely, Hymenaeus and Alexander, (1 Tim. 1 v.20), and he left Timothy to straighten out the rest of the problems and encouraged him by sending this letter. "These things write I unto thee, hoping to come unto thee shortly: But if I tarry long, that thou mayest know how thou oughtest to behave thyself in the house of God, which is the Church of the living God, the pillar and ground of the truth", (1 Tim. 3 v.14-15).

Worship is central in the Church. At Ephesus there were great problems, among which some women had abandoned their faith, and abandoned the practice of good conduct and the doctrines of the New Testament Church. They became laden with lusts and an easy prey for false teachers. They were flaunting their beauty and wealth with evil intent, thus desecrating the worship service, so much so that the Apostle by Divine authority, now points out what the Biblical role of women in the Church ought to be: "let them learn", (1 Tim. 5 v.4).

In the writings of Paul to Timothy at Ephesus and to Titus at Crete, the Scriptures clearly refer to the position that women should occupy in the Church, that is in the public assembly and worship of God's people. The woman should be a learner, and she should keep silence. It is not her job to preach or teach, for by Divine authority these are the responsibility of the men. She is to be in subjection. She must not usurp authority over the man to whom God has given the responsibility of leadership and ministry. Women, as we shall see later, have their place and their ministry, but not in the public service of worship.

In the phrase "let the women learn", (1 Tim. 2 v.11), the Greek word "manthano" translated "learn", "be informed", is in the imperative mood, indicating it is a command. Scripture teaches that women be taught, and this learning is to take place when the Church meets. Of course, this goes for men too. In the early New Testament Church learning had a very high priority as we observe from Acts 2 v.42: "And they continued stedfastly in the apostles' doctrine and fellowship, and in breaking of bread, and in prayers". Women are part of the learning process, they are not to be excluded.

It clearly seems that one of the noted problems in the Church at Ephesus was that some women were teaching and exercising authority over men. In telling them to stop, the Apostle first of all settled the question of whether women have a right to learn. "Let the women learn", (1 Tim. 2 v.11), shows there is equality of the sexes in spiritual life and blessing.

Women shared spiritual equality with men, but they did not have the same role. There were no women rulers in the history of either Israel or Judah. Deborah was a judge, not a leader, which explains why she called on Barak to take military command and leadership. As far as we know, no woman wrote any portion of the Old Testament. As well as Deborah, other prominent Old Testament women, such as, Miriam, Huldah, the wife of Isaiah, and others, are mentioned, but none of them acted or spoke in an ongoing prophetic ministry or office like Elijah or Elisha, but were prophetesses used in a general way. There is no record in the New Testament of a woman apostle, pastor, teacher, evangelist, minister, elder, or deacon. The New Testament does not record any sermon or teaching ministry by a woman. There are times and places, of course, as the New Testament allows, when women can speak the Word of God and witness, but that is distinctly different from being identified as an apostle, minister, pastor, elder, or deacon.

As previously noted, Rom. 16 v.1 refers to "Phebe our sister, which is a servant of the church which is at Cenchrea". She is clearly referred to as a believer, a sister in grace, a "servant" (Greek word "diakonon") of the Church there in acts of charity and hospitality. Paul is not stressing an office here but rather the distinguished service of one who is pure and chaste, as we gather from v.2. She was "a succourer of many", relieved many that were in want and distress, and was kind to those that needed kindness and assistance. This is an area in which women likewise can exercise their functions and graces. Like Lydia, she was a woman of rank as well as being active in Christian work and would need help in connection with her visit to Rome. The Greek word "prostates" as applied in the last clause of v.2 to the service of Phebe is not the same as that used for assistance to be given her which conveys the idea of affording care and protection. Matthew Henry comments, "Christians should be helpful one to another, for we are members one of another and we know not what need of help we may have ourselves: he that watereth shall be watered also himself". Undoubtedly Phebe is one of the women memorialised in the New Testament for her devotion and dedication to the service of the Gospel whose honour is not to be tarnished or rendered iridescent by elevation to a position of role and function that is inconsistent or at variance with the teaching of Holy Scripture.

Women are not to function in the same way or role as men. Women are to learn so as to train their children as did Timothy's mother Eunice, and grandmother Lois, (2 Tim. 1 v.5), and thereby be enabled by the grace of God to point souls to Christ, and to obey God according to the Scriptures. The different roles between men and women does not in any way diminish her ability to witness or imply the spiritual inferiority of women.

There are many ways in which the prevailing views of society influenced the Church at Ephesus, and the same can be said of the Church today. The Church is often influenced by the world, instead of the Church being an influence on the world. As Christians, the elect people of God, our views and our opinions must be guided and regulated by the Scriptures, on such matters, not only of women's role in society and in the Church, but also on such subjects as abortion, homosexuality, lesbianism, creation, evolution, co-habiting, divorce and re-marriage. All of these matters, and others, are causing much havoc in the Church with detrimental effects to the faith. No matter what the pressures of the world may be, or what society may propagate, let us, as God's people, be firm and resolute in our witness to the truth of the Gospel, and pray that God will give us grace, strength, and courage to take a Biblical stand on all of these and other issues, basing our faith and belief solely on His Word, the Holy Bible.

Dr. R. C. Sproul, one time leader of the International Council on Biblical Inerrancy (1977-1987) and a prolific writer, states that "we face a crisis of authority in the Church. It is precisely our faith and practice that is in question. It is for faith and practice that we defend a fully infallible rule --- a total view of Sola Scriptura: Scripture alone . . . . . because we believe it is the truth. It is a truth we do not want to negotiate. We warmly desire . . . . . to heal the wounds that controversy so frequently brings. We know our own views are by no means inerrant. But we believe inerrancy (of the Bible) is true and is of vital importance to our common cause of the Gospel".

It is with deep conviction in the Divine plenary inspiration and supernatural inerrancy of Holy Scripture, the Old and New Testaments, originally given as the Word of God, that we believe the teaching and authority of the Bible are absolute and final as the only infallible rule in every matter of faith and life, of conduct and belief. "All Scripture is given by inspiration of God, and is profitable for doctrine, for reproof, for correction, for instruction in righteousness:

That the man of God may be perfect, throughly furnished unto all good works", (2 Tim. 3 v.16-17).

Let us therefore pray earnestly for reformation and revival in the Church, that she might be strong, firm, and steadfast for God's Truth, fearlessly testifying against all current evils in the individual, social, political, and ecclesiastical life, and thus raise up a standard for Truth, to the glory of God. "Thou hast given a banner to them that fear Thee, that it may be displayed because of the Truth", (Psalm 60 v.4).

Women keep silence in Church

The Corinthians put themselves above Scripture, either in ignoring it or interpreting it in ways that fit their predisposed notions. The problem that Paul faced in the Corinthian Church was women not accepting that Church leadership was a role for men only. He addresses the issue clearly and definitively with Divine authority so that there is no mistaking of the mind and will of God as to who should rule over whom, and who should preach and who should not.

"Let your women keep silence in the Churches", (1 Cor.14 v.34), does not mean women are not to pray publicly at other gatherings other than the Church service. The problem here within the Corinthian Church was disorderly behaviour and unbecoming conduct within the public worship services of the Church, that of preaching and teaching, and exercising an office that is not open to women. They were determined to follow their own devices regardless of God's standard. In their pride and arrogance the Corinthian Church wanted to be a law unto itself, deciding on its own volition what was right and proper. Paul challenges them, pointing out that they have no right to overrule, ignore, alter, or disobey the Word of God. To do so was putting themselves above God's Word.

Shamefully, to the detriment of truth, there are Churches today, some among them that profess to be 'evangelical', who encourage open rebellion against the Word of God by allowing women leadership in the Church, which the Bible forbids. The Bible forbids a woman to teach, that is, she is not "to usurp authority over the man, but to be in silence", (1 Tim. 2 v.11). Such portions of the Word of God must be very difficult passages for the woman 'preachers and teachers' of our day to proclaim. As a matter of fact, they most totally ignore and avoid the subject altogether. How sad, that such disobedience should prevail in Churches that profess to follow Christ . . . . . or do they?

Women are to learn in submission, the Greek word "hesuchia" translated "silence", means "silence". The Greek word "hupotasso" translated "subjection", means "to line up under". Women are not to be rebellious, refractory, or unruly, they are to be in their proper and rightful place according to Divine command. "Let the women learn in silence with all subjection", (1 Tim. 2 v.11).

Those who misinterpret this verse, do so in two ways. Those who say women are free to preach in the Church, misinterpret "silence" only to mean "a meek and quiet spirit"; "a meek and quiet demeanour". Others go to the opposite extreme and insist that women should never speak in Church under any circumstances, not even to the person sitting next to them. The Word of God clearly states in First Timothy 2 v.11-12, that women are to be silent in the sense of not teaching or exercising authority over men in the Church. "But I suffer not a woman to teach, nor to usurp authority over the man, but to be in silence", (1 Tim. 2 v.12).

The prohibition of women to preach or to teach in the Church has nothing to do with their psychological makeup or intellectual capabilities. Women are not to preach or to teach in the Church because God's Law forbids it: "Let your women keep silence in the Churches: for it is not permitted unto them to speak; but they are commanded to be under obedience, as also saith the law", (1 Cor. 14 v.34); compare this with Gen. 3 v.16, "and he shall rule over thee".

The women's Liberation movement wish to abolish, not only man's place in the home, but also in the Church. Man in his arrogance may attempt to set aside Scripture, but the Word of God can never be abrogated. Martin Luther once wrote of God's Word, "The Bible is alive, it speaks to me; it has feet, it runs after me; it has hands, it lays hold of me. The Bible is not antique or modern. It is eternal". The everlasting nature of the Bible is the theme of the Psalmist in Psalm 119 v.89; "For ever, O Lord, Thy Word is settled in heaven". The prophet Isaiah firmly declares that "the Word of our God shall stand for ever", (Isaiah 40 v.8). The only solution to man's rebellion is that the attitudes and aspirations of both men and women are transformed by the indwelling power of the Spirit of Christ, through His Word, submitting to the Lord in love and obedience, and thus fulfil the law of God. J. I. Packer makes the assertion that "the Word of God alone must rule, and no Christian man dare do other than allow it to enthrone itself in his conscience and heart".

The only source and norm of all Christian knowledge is the Holy Scriptures. "Let the women . . . . . be in silence", (1 Tim. 2 v.11-12), does not mean, however, that God does not use women, or that women can never speak God's truth. God used women such as Miriam (Exodus 15 v.20-21), Deborah (Judges 4 v.4), Huldah (2 Kings 22 v.14-22), Mary (Luke 1 v.46-55), and Anna (Luke 2 v.36-38), to speak for Him. There is a time and place for women to offer a testimony of praise to the Lord. Scripture does not say women can never do that, not at all. What the Bible clearly forbids is women teaching and preaching in the Church. They are not to take leadership roles as ministers, elders, or deacons. Women are to be in submission to men in the sense that they are not to usurp the role of leadership in the Church: "it is not permitted unto them to speak", (1 Cor. 14 v.34).

First Corinthians 11 v.5, makes reference to women praying and prophesying. In the most general sense praying is talking to God about people, including ourselves, and prophesying is talking to people about God. The Scripture firmly asserts the priesthood of all believers. Some people, for their own personal wishes, misinterpret this verse that the praying and prophesying referred to, took place during the worship service. This verse cannot be construed to permit women preachers. Paul was not speaking of Church, but rather prayer and prophecy in general. In that chapter, First Corinthians 11, it is not until verse 18, that the Apostle speaks of the formal gathering of the Church: "For first of all, when ye come together in the Church, I hear that there be divisions among you".

Prior to verse 18, as above, Paul was not speaking of the worship service, but of women who were praying and proclaiming the Word of God in the home, among the family, or amongst friends and neighbours. The point is, that when Christians get together in worship in Church, women are to maintain the decorum of submission, and veil or cover their heads attesting their womanhood and affirmation to God's Word; and men are to maintain the role of headship and leadership.

To refuse to accept the God-ordained roles in the Church, or in the family, is to undermine the foundational design of God for these institutions, and thus promote anarchy, waywardness, and the instability of society at large. Disobedience and acting contrary to God's Word, is sin. The Shorter Catechism teaches us that "Sin is any want of conformity unto, or transgression of the law of God". This speaks of two kinds of sins. The first is not doing what God commands, and the second is doing what God forbids.

Women can witness, share, pray, and proclaim the Word of God at any time and at any place, except when the Church meets and comes together for the public worship service. The responsibility of being the preacher, or teacher, or the one who leads in prayer in the worship service is a role ordained by God for men.

What the Apostle taught is not optional, and those who disregard the Word of God should themselves be disregarded and rejected as legitimate servants of God. Because it was the revelation of God as

Scripture, Paul's teaching was absolutely authoritative. Everything he taught about God, about His Gospel, and about His Church was God's own teaching, "the commandments of the Lord", (1 Cor. 14 v.37).

"Let all things be done decently and in order" (1 Cor. 14 v.40). Right revelation should be obeyed in the right way. The basic meaning of the Greek "euschemonos", "decently", is gracefully, becomingly, harmoniously, beautifully, properly. "Orderly" has the meaning of "in turn" or "one at a time". God is a God of propriety and order, and "all things" that His people do should reflect His mind and will as revealed to us in The Scripture.

For almost 2000 years the true Church of Christ has taken First Cor. 14 v.33-40, to clearly mean that women are not to be involved in the preaching and teaching of the Word, nor to holding office in the Church. Yet today many mainline Protestant denominations have fallen away from truth and are ordaining women both as teaching and ruling elders, and appointing deacons, regardless of Biblical teaching and as if it doesn't matter what The Scripture has to say on these vital matters. The argument runs that if the world is changing regarding the role of women in society, then the Church has to reflect this and change accordingly. Such reasoning is false and comes from the devil in his opposition to the Word of God. By seeking to justify their actions by making such changes they insist that the problems within the Church at Corinth and Ephesus have no relevance to the Church today. This sort of claim is absolutely false, pernicious, and an assault of Satan to supplant the Bible in his ongoing efforts to overthrow the authority and infallibility of the Divine Word.

It is extremely important to understand aright the context in which the Apostle Paul was addressing the Christians at Corinth and Ephesus. He exhorted the men to avoid angry disputes, (1 Tim. 2 v.8), and the women to dress decently, (1 Tim. 2 v.9-10). And then he calls upon the women to be silent, and to have a quiet and teachable spirit, (1 Tim. 2 v.11-12). The reference here to women is absolutely clear, "but I suffer not a woman to teach, nor to usurp authority over the man, but to be in silence", (v.12). The Apostle is speaking here with Diving authority, and his words, therefore, carry the full weight of a command of God.

The Apostle Paul is very clear in his discussion of women's duties by defining their role as learners rather than teachers during the public worship service. The verb in First Tim. 2 v.11, is an imperative form of "manthano", meaning "to learn", "to be informed", from which the Greek word translated "disciple" or "learner" derives. "Let the woman learn", is not a request, rather it is a Divine command. In this passage Paul is discussing the order of the Church to the Ephesians, how they ought to behave "in the house of God, which is the Church of the living God, the pillar and ground of the truth", (1 Tim. 3 v.15). It shows also that the learning the Apostle speaks of was to take place in that context. "And they continued stedfastly in the apostles' doctrine and fellowship, and in breaking of bread, and in prayers", (Acts 2 v.42).

It should be pointed out, however, that teaching and worship are not mutually exclusive. Rather, knowledge of God and His Word helps to stimulate worship. Worship is to be "in spirit and in truth", (John 4 v.20-24). Women should be taught God's Word, since they are spiritually equal in Christ and the commands of Holy Scripture are to all: "As newborn babes desire the sincere milk of the Word, that ye may grow thereby", (1 Peter 2 v.2).

It is abundantly clear from these passages that the public ministry of preaching and teaching is not open to women, nor to women having positions of authority in the Church. The verdict and conclusion of Scripture on the matter is clear, definite, and emphatic, and in First Tim. 2 v.13-14, the reference to the order of creation firmly indicates that the principle reaffirmed here applies to all Christians in all Churches at all times from the creation of man until the Second Coming of Christ.

I would clarify the point, however, that The Scripture has no restrictions on a woman's witnessing in public to others, even to a man. Nor does it prohibit women from taking non-leadership roles of praying with believers or for unbelievers. And there is no restriction from teaching children and other women: "teachers of good things", (Titus 2 v.3-4). "If any man or woman that believeth have widows, let them relieve them, and let not the Church be charged; that it may relieve them that are widows indeed", (1 Tim. 5 v.16).

The Scripture affirms that women have a spiritual status equal to that of men. The Mosaic Law was given to all Israel, women as well as men, (Deut. 1 v.1). Both were to teach it to their children: "thou shalt teach them diligently unto thy children", (Deut. 4 v.7). "My son, keep thy father's commandment, and forsake not the law of thy mother", (Prov. 6 v.20). Spiritual equality between the sexes did not, however, do away with the difference in their roles. "For ye are all one in Christ Jesus", (Gal. 3 v.28), teaches the absolute spiritual equality of men and women in Christ. While many use that verse to justify women assuming leadership roles in the Church, the context clearly shows that Paul is speaking of salvation.

The New Testament does not treat women as spiritual inferiors. Peter reminds us that men and women "as being heirs together of the grace of life", (1 Peter 3 v.7). The fruit of the Spirit, (Gal. 5 v.22-23), are for both men and women. All the promises, commands, and blessings of the Bible apply equally to men and women. "The fruit of the Spirit is love, joy, peace, longsuffering, gentleness, goodness, faith, meekness, temperance: against such there is no law", (Gal. 5 v.22-23).

Women and Ordination

The issue of 'women's ordination' is causing concern and major problems in the Church today, even among some 'evangelicals' with a variety of positions being taken up on the matter. Almost every denomination has had women ordained to the ministry as pastors, and to the eldership (teaching and ruling), over the past quarter of a century. While the controversy rages on it is quite amazing that there are many different opinions on this subject, mostly unBiblical, even within the two main camps "for" and "against". Those who stand on firm Scriptural platform against the ordination of women to the Christian ministry, do so for sound Biblical reasons, and therefore would not participate in any such events. But what I find disconcerting and inconsistent, is that many of these objectors, if not all of them, compromise their position by sitting and deliberating with their 'female colleagues' in the various courts of the Church, Presbytery, Synod, and General Assembly. Such practice, especially for those who are not retired, is somewhat hypocritical. Much has been written in favour of women's ordination, and obviously this is the status quo within the Church generally at large, albeit contrary to The Scripture.

As true evangelicals following in the footsteps of the Apostles of the early New Testament Church, and also following in the footsteps of the Reformers, Covenanters, Puritans, and other Heroes and Martyrs of the Faith, our sole concern should be to uphold the teaching of the Bible. The Bible is the revealed Word of God, and is the only standard of belief and conduct. The Scriptures of the Old and New Testaments were "written that ye might believe that Jesus is the Christ, the Son of God; and that believing ye might have life through His name", (John 20 v.31). As the Westminster Confession of Faith and other Historical formulae rightly affirm, the life and government of the Church must at all times and in all ages, be regulated solely according to the teaching of the Word of God.

The popular demand of the modern age in many quarters in our day for ordination of women in the Church, is diametrically opposed and contrary to the fundamental teaching of the patriarchs, prophets and apostles. Those who share and hold to Biblical orthodoxy, are often opposed, penalised, and even persecuted, by the courts of the Church, resulting in the fact that man-made laws within the Church take precedence over the Truth of Scripture. Because of this apostasy the Church generally will not easily be persuaded that it is not only a great mistake, but totally wrong, to ordain women to any office within the Church.

The authority of the Word of God must and should supersede any ruling of the courts of the Church that contravene the commands of Holy Scripture. Whenever the Church has departed from Biblical principles, it is iniquitous of any Church court to demand an implicit obedience irrespective of conscience, other than subjection "in the Lord", and according to His Word. "We have also a more sure Word of prophecy; whereunto ye do well that ye take heed, as unto a light that shineth in a dark place, until the day dawn, and the day star arise in your hearts: Knowing this first, that no prophecy of the Scripture is of any private interpretation. For the prophecy came not in old time by the will of man: but holy men of God spake as they were moved by the Holy Ghost", (2 Peter 1 v.19-21).

Scripture is sufficient to make every Christian, that is, the whole Church, complete and "throughly furnished", (2 Tim. 3 v.17), and equipped for every good work: "unto all good works". The demand for 'ordination of women', surely should raise some stirring and searching questions. The trustworthiness of God's Word continues to be attacked in various and subtle ways, with the consequence that the great doctrine of Biblical authority is relegated to accommodate the 'whims and fancies' of so-called modern thinkers.

(1) Can a woman be admitted into, appointed to, ordained to office, as a presbyter, minister, pastor, overseer, bishop, elder, or deacon?

(2) Can a woman be ordained or appointed to the regular ministry and pastorate of a Church which involves leadership and rule?

(3) By doing so, is this one of the "all good works", (2 Tim. 3 v.17)?

(4) Will the 'ordination of women' bring glory to God, and the enhancement of the Church to completion in accordance with the inspired Word?

(5) Is a woman ever "throughly furnished" and permitted by God for the position of authority, leadership, and rule, in the Church?

"All Scripture is given by inspiration of God, and is profitable for doctrine, for reproof, for correction, for instruction in righteousness: That the man of God may be perfect, throughly furnished unto all good works", (2 Tim. 3 v.16-17). God's grace is always sufficient. Those who will not only be godly, but live godly in Christ Jesus will suffer persecution. When Christians, men and women of God, are resolute in living a life of usefulness and service for the Lord, their faith and conduct will be in harmony with the teaching of Holy Scripture. A Christian principle of Biblical authority means that God is the Author of the Bible, and He has given it to direct the belief and behaviour of His people. This means of course that our ideas about God and our conduct whether in the Church, in the home, in the workplace, in society, or in the world at large, should be measured, tested, and where necessary corrected and enlarged, by reference to the Word of God.

God's written Word in its truth and wisdom is the way God has chosen to exercise His rule over us, and Scripture is the instrument of Christ's lordship over the Church. It is inspired, God-breathed, distinguishing it from all other words. As a result, the Scriptures are infallible and true in all that they affirm. They are sufficient, containing everything that is necessary to know for salvation and eternal life. They are the clear voice of God to Whose authority we must submit our thoughts and moral standards in accordance with the instruction of the Bible.

As Christian men and women, by the grace of God in His Word and Spirit, grow better and better in the building up of their "most holy faith" (Jude v.20), so bad men and women, through the subtlety of Satan and the power of their own depravity and corruption grow worse and worse. The way of sin and disobedience is always downhill, "deceiving, and being deceived" (2 Tim. 3 v.13) further into error and false doctrine. We are commanded by Scripture to continue in the things we have learned from the Sacred Writings (2 Tim. 3 v.14-15) and persevere in them unto the end. It is only by consulting in them and keeping closer to them that we find the Divine directions of how we may glorify God and be thoroughly furnished for every good work.

Because of the continuing landslide and fall in doctrine and practice, the Church today is in great need of men and women who will stand in defence of the inerrancy, inspiration, and authority of the Bible. Complete confidence in the Scriptures as the infallible Word of God is essential to the very life and witness of the evangelical Church. The authority of the Bible is a key issue for the Christian Church in this our day and generation, and in every age. To stray from the teaching of Scripture in faith or conduct is disloyalty to Jesus Christ, the King and Head of the Church, and dishonouring to God.

To the above five questions, the Church's teaching over the past two millennia (two thousand years), has said, "No"; and the Reformers of the sixteenth century fervently confirmed this position. The present day worldly, 'feminist' dispute, is over the interpretation of certain passages of Scripture, or rather the misinterpretation of them for their own purpose, and not for the glory of God. The long-held, steadfast, traditional teaching of the Church, patterned on the Word of God, throughout the ages, must not be lightly rejected.

To admit women into ministry, eldership, or the diaconate, is really to deny the authority and the sufficiency of Scripture, and also to say that the world Church throughout the centuries, including the Old Testament period, was wrong when it did not put women into office within the Church. What an affront, contempt, and insult to the Almighty, to make such a charge against the Lord, by implying that modern man in the twenty-first century knows better than God as to how to regulate and run the Church. Over and over again the tactic of Satan, as in the Garden of Eden to Eve, is casting doubt: "Yea, hath God said?", (Gen. 3 v.1).

Many 'red herrings' are brought into the debate on 'women's ordination' which do not stand up to sound Biblical reasoning and exegeses. This particular debate is not about worth and importance, nor about inferiority and superiority, because women are denied a teaching and ruling role, etc., in the Church. If that were the case, then men who are not ordained are also treated as inferior. All Christians are a holy people, a royal priesthood, to offer up spiritual sacrifices acceptable to God through Jesus Christ. "But ye are a chosen generation, a royal priesthood, an holy nation, a peculiar people; that ye should shew forth the praises of Him Who hath called you out of darkness into His marvellous light", (1 Peter 2 v.9).

The Scriptural answer to this controversy is clear and beyond doubt, and has been endorsed by the Church throughout all ages. Only men can be admitted into the ministry, eldership, and the diaconate. To deny this fundamental Biblical truth, is to deny the authority, the primacy, the supremacy, and the sufficiency of Scripture. In the light of God's clear instructions as revealed in His Word, there is no Biblical warrant that women should now be ordained in this the twenty-first century. By the very act of 'ordaining women', man is actually saying that Scripture is not sufficient to make the Church complete and throughly equipped and furnished for every good work, but that man knows better than Almighty God how to make the Church more workable, and function more correctly and properly at this present time.

There are several arguments afloat today which attempt to deny and destroy the authority and infallibility of the Word of God, among them, namely, the so-called contradictions and inconsistencies of

Scripture; the cultural ideas and customs of the early New Testament Church are not for today; the supposed prejudice of Paul against women by some far-fetched exegesis of the opening chapters of Genesis; the equality of the sexes; and the false premise that God is now 'doing a new thing' in the Church in our day. All this is far removed from the truth of the Bible.

There is nothing inconsistent in the Word of God. We should be greatly concerned of the slide away from orthodoxy that is occurring within Evangelicalism. How few there are who stand outside the camp to defend the doctrine of inerrancy. How few there are who have courage to stand up and be counted in the fight to counter the drift away from this doctrine in Churches and theological colleges. It is the duty of the Christian Church to resist all attacks on God's Word and to stand firm in defence of the Truth. "Ascribe ye greatness unto our God. He is the Rock, His work is perfect: for all His ways are judgement: a God of truth and without iniquity, just and right is He", (Deut. 32 v.3-4).

The Bible clearly teaches the equality of the sexes and the differences in roles and functions of men and women. What God has assigned as a particular role and function to men only, which He says women cannot be admitted to, and then for women to go against God's Word and take upon themselves that role, is to act against and disobey the Divine Will, and thus make themselves "an abomination unto the Lord". "For all that do such things, and all that do unrighteously, are an abomination unto the Lord thy God", (Deut. 25 v.16).

Over the past four decades in particular, there has been an increasing clamour and demand for the 'rights' of women in society, in the Church, and in the world as a whole. The Bible unequivocally asserts the equal dignity and value of both men and women. Both are made "in the image of God", (Gen. 1 v.26-27). While we welcome every effort to assert the dignity, value, and honour of womanhood, it is necessary for us to have courage to stand up against the social trends of our day when they clearly contradict the revealed Will of God in the Bible. For all believers of the Church, today, as in all ages, all issues of faith and practice are settled, not by a consensus of society and populous opinion, but by the teaching of Holy Scripture, the Word of God. "We ought to obey God rather than men", (Acts 5 v.29). "For when for the time ye ought to be teachers, ye have need that one teach you again which be the first principles of the oracles of God; and are become such as have need of milk, and not of strong meat. For every one that useth milk is unskilful in the words of righteousness: for he is a babe. But strong meat belongeth to them that are of full age, even those who by reason of use have their senses exercised to discern both good and evil", (Heb. 5 v.12-14).

Those men who have been ordained as ministers, elders, or deacons, have taken upon themselves very earnest engagements in their ordination vows, solemnly promising out of zeal for God's glory, to uphold and declare the Word of God as the only infallible rule of faith and practice. "When thou vowest a vow unto God, defer not to pay it; for He hath no pleasure in fools: pay that which thou hast vowed. Better is it that thou shouldest not vow, than that thou shouldest vow and not pay", (Eccles. 5 v.4-5). The performance of solemn vows, whether in the service of Christ, in marriage, or other occasions throughout our lives, is strictly enjoined upon us in Scripture: "Yea, they shall vow a vow unto the Lord, and perform it", (Isaiah 19 v.21).

It is a serious matter to take upon ourselves solemn vows and promises in a half-hearted manner which lack determination and resolution. When made they must be kept: "Vow, and pay unto the Lord your God", (Psalm 76 v.11). Vows are not to be lightly undertaken, and are to be promptly fulfilled. "When thou shalt vow a vow unto the Lord thy God, thou shalt not slack to pay it: for the Lord thy God will surely require it of thee; and it would be sin in thee. That which is gone out of thy lips thou shalt keep and perform", (Deut. 23 v.21 and 23). "Defer not to pay" what "thou has vowed", (Eccles. 5 v.4). Over and over again the Word of God shows how God will forgive anyone who truly repents. This is as true for a disobedient servant of God as it is for the enemies of His people. The

Book of Jonah underlines the need for those who know God to obey Him unconditionally, and a sincerity to pay what has been vowed. "But I will sacrifice unto thee with the voice of thanksgiving; I will pay that that I have vowed", (Jonah 2 v.9). Not to pay is sinful, rebellion against God, but He will forgive and restore blessing upon repentant servants. Repentance and faith always meet with His mercy and grace. In answering prayers of confession from a broken and obedient people, God achieves His plan and purpose for the Church.

To pay our vows made to God, the most important thing especially for ministers, pastors, elders, and deacons, is to perform what they have promised in their ordination vows: "but fear thou God", (Eccles. 5 v.7). To vow and not pay incurs the guilt of treachery and perjury, it is lying "unto God", (Acts 5 v.4). There is a great need today to admonish, exhort, and rebuke God's servants in the work of the Lord: "Consider your ways", (Haggai 1 v.5 and 7). The result of complacency and disobedience among God's people lead to ineffectiveness not realising that God is withholding His hand of blessing from them. We are to be alert and beware of the grave danger of admitting unspiritual men into positions of authority and allowing them to carry on unchecked. More so beware of the more subtle danger of desiring status and influence in the work of God and of wanting to be seen of others. As God's workers we need to be examples of the Christian religion, and the best evidence of our having the truth is our walking in the truth. "I have no greater joy", says the Apostle John, "than to hear that my children walk in truth. Beloved, follow not that which is evil, but that which is good. He that doeth good is of God: but he that doeth evil hath not seen God", (3 John v. 4 and 11).

The question, then, of 'ordination of women' needs, therefore, to be approached with an open Bible, and can only be settled by searching the Scriptures, not by ascertaining the prevailing whims and aspirations of society. The conclusion of Scripture, as we have already seen, is final. The Bible is our only Rule of faith, and our only Guide in life, and it is completely wrong for anyone to violate, warp, or pervert our Scripture-taught conscience. The authority of God's Word is set before us, not merely as a doctrine to subscribe to, but as a reality to live by. The controlling principle in life, is not the prevailing views of society around us, nor the current worldly opinions and fashions within Church denominations, but the Mind of God revealed in The scripture, which is the only basis of living a God-honouring life. The Westminster Confession of Faith quite rightly acknowledges the fallibility of ecclesiastical courts, and allows for liberty of conscience in matters that are contrary to Scripture.

When the Church enacts legislation that is contrary to the teaching of the Bible, acts unlawfully and contravenes the Word of God, the Christian is not bound or compelled to obey nor be bound to acquiesce in its unScriptural directives. The great tragedy is that the Church seems to be insisting that every knee should bow and tongue confess that its decisions, whether good or bad, must be obeyed. Our sole concern should always be that of diligence and faithfulness to God's revealed truth, the Bible. By calling for 'women's ordination', sadly, we are witnessing the ditching and abandonment of two thousand years of the Church's teaching on Biblical standards and practices. The authority of the Word of God is being cast overboard in favour of a present social consensus. "To the law and to the testimony: if they speak not according to this Word, it is because there is no light in them", (Isaiah 8 v.20).

Different Functions

In speaking of equality of the sexes with different roles and functions, let us take note that in the Godhead there are Three Persons, each equally infinite, eternal, and unchangeable; the same in substance; and equal in wisdom, power, holiness, justice, goodness, and truth, (Shorter Cat. No.4-6); each perfect God, but in the matter of our salvation and eternal redemption, each has a different role, and not one of the Persons in the Godhead tries to usurp the role of either of the Other Two.

Another example is that of the human body, which has different members, all equally important to the perfection and health of that body, yet all do not have the same functions.

So it is with Christ's body, the Church, there are many members, all are of equal importance to the King and Head of the Church, the Lord Jesus Christ, but Christ does not give them all the same role and function. Surely, then, He knows infinitely and sovereignly what is the best role and function of the male and female members and their usefulness to the Church.

All twelve apostles were male. Why did Jesus not choose six men and six women? Why did He lay the foundation of the Church on the male sex only? The logical Biblical answer throughout Scripture is that Christ intended the Patriarchal nature of government among the people of God from the very earliest of times should continue from the Old Covenant to the New Covenant, and nowhere in Scripture are we told that this is to change.

As in the home, it is the man who is the head and ruler, which is an order instituted by God. That order must be reflected in the family of the Church congregation, which is also an order instituted by God. The man is the one who bears rule. The local congregation is made up of several worshipping households coming together. Therefore, it is from the heads of the households that presbyters, ministers, pastors, elders, bishops, overseers, and deacons are chosen. (1 Timothy 3, Titus 1). In these chapters we read that the officers of the Church should be "the husband of one wife" and should rule their own households well.

The structure and organisation of the Christian congregation should reflect that of the family. "Wives, submit yourselves unto your own husbands as unto the Lord. For the husband is head of the wife, even as Christ is the Head of the Church: and He is the Saviour of the body", (Eph. 5 v.22-23). The family and the congregation both express God's relationship to His people, and that is why Scripture so clearly forbids women to teach or to have authority over the man in the Church. As believing members of the same body, the Church, men and women have the same privileges and the same fellowship in Christ. Women are not to assume the role of leadership or usurp authority over the man in the Church.

"Let the woman learn in silence with all subjection. But I suffer not a woman to teach, nor to usurp authority over the man, but to be in silence", (1 Tim. 2 v.11-12). The Greek word here for "suffer" is "epitrepo", meaning "permit", which is a very strong word, "do not at all allow such". The Biblical principle of submission is founded on the creation story, and not on social or other customs. Oversight of the Church should always be through men. The difference in role between men and women belongs to the Divine order as originally made. Women ministers, women elders, and women deacons are clearly forbidden by Scripture, which speaks only of male headship and male leadership.

In His Word, God has never declared His intention that women should be ministers, pastors, elders, or deacons, and for any Church to place women in these roles, has no Biblical warrant whatsoever in Scripture, and it is therefore not glorifying to God. "Nevertheless neither is the man without the woman, neither the woman without the man, in the Lord", (1 Cor. 11 v.11). Man needs the woman's help, support, and encouragement to carry out his role of leadership and teaching responsibility, and the woman needs the security that man can give her. God said to Eve, "thy desire shall be to thy husband, and he shall rule over thee", (Gen. 3 v.16). He is head of the family, and his leadership in the family is to be expressed in the Church.

The Apostle Paul wrote to the various Churches of the New Testament, including Corinth, Ephesus and Crete, as he was "moved by the Holy Ghost", (2 Peter 1 v.21), and for anyone to say that women can be appointed and ordained as ministers, elders, or deacons, is to say that Holy Scripture is not Divinely inspired, and thus showing a complete denial and rejection of the infallibility and authority of God's Word. As the Church persists in ordaining women into any of these roles, is a mockery to God and riding roughshod over the primacy and sufficiency of Scripture. By encouraging women to usurp such authority and headship which pertains only to man in the Church, or in the home, is "an abomination to the Lord": "all that do unrighteously, are an abomination unto the Lord thy God", (Deut. 25 v.16). Such flagrant apostasy is wholly unjustifiable, a gross injustice, an offence of greatest magnitude, and a glaring dishonour to God.

The Church is called by God to show forth the praises of the Lord among the nations, but ye have "made Mine heritage an abomination", (Jer. 2 v.7). "Were they ashamed when they had committed abomination? Nay, they were not at all ashamed, neither could they blush", (Jer. 6 v.15). Where there is no place for shame, there can be no place for repentance. "Thus saith the Lord, Stand ye in the ways and see, and ask for the old paths, where is the good way, and walk therein, and ye shall find rest to your souls. But they said, We will not walk therein", (Jer. 6 v.16). This is God's Word, applicable to our generation, Who commands us to turn back to the old paths. He calls us to walk in His ways with the promise we shall find rest for our souls.

"It is high time to awake out of sleep" (Rom. 13 v.11), "let us labour therefore to enter into that rest" (Heb. 4 v.11), for without this hope men have a weary pilgrimage in a world of unbelief, but "the ransomed of the Lord shall return, and come to Zion with songs and everlasting joy upon their heads" (Isaiah 35 v.10), for we know Him Who invites us to sit at His feet, thus choosing, as Mary did, "that good part" (Luke 10 v.4), and says, "Learn of Me . . . . . and ye shall find rest unto your souls" (Matt. 11 v.29).

One of the most serious problems facing the Church today, is conformity to the world and the acceptance of secular propositions with the corresponding refusal to decide issues by the criterion of

Scripture alone: Sola Scriptura. "And be not conformed to this world: but be ye transformed by the renewing of your mind, that ye may prove what is that good, and acceptable, and perfect, will of God", (Rom. 12. v.2).

How tragic, then, it is to see the Church at large in our day following the ways of the world, and allowing the world to set the agenda without hardly a voice being raised to uphold the truth. This is precisely the position in relation to the 'ordination of women'. We must vigorously oppose error and "earnestly contend for the faith which was once delivered unto the saints", (Jude v.3).

Scripture prohibits certain Roles by Women

At this juncture, let us ask the pertinent question, to what extent and in what circumstances is the woman to be subject to the man? The answer is plain and certain. The woman is to be silent in the worship and work of the Church of Christ. This is most clear from the following Scriptures.

"Let your women keep silence in the Churches: for it is not permitted unto them to speak; but they are commanded to be under obedience, as also saith the law. And if they will learn anything, let them ask their husbands at home: for it is a shame for women to speak in the Church", (1 Cor. 14 v.34-35).

"Let the woman learn in silence with all subjection. But I suffer not a woman to teach, nor to usurp authority over the man, but to be in silence", (1 Tim. 2 v.11-12).

The teaching of both passages, as above, is very similar, which debars women from exercising any spiritual role in the Church. It is completely contrary to the will of God that women should be office-bearers, whether as ministers, pastors, elders or deacons. The office of minister or elder is one of leadership and authority, and for a woman to preach and teach in public worship, or to moderate the proceedings of Church courts, is decidedly to usurp authority over the man in the life of the Church.

The role of women in the Church is a topic that is hotly debated today in many circles. The debate is not centred on Scripture and the traditional doctrines are being swept away by the flood tides of so-called 'evangelical feminism'. Many of the Churches and Seminaries are rapidly abandoning truths they have held since their inceptions. But under the pressure of modernism they have abandoned Biblical accuracy in favour of the culture. The Biblical passages on women's roles are being culturally reinterpreted and the clear teaching of God's Word is being completely ignored and passed over.

The aim of the archenemy of God, Satan, is to overthrow God's plan and corrupt His design. The devil is behind the effort to entice women away from their God-created roles in society, in the family, and in the Church. Such a satanic attack is not new; it was a serious issue in the Church at Ephesus. Writing to Timothy, Paul urges him to take action: "that thou mightest charge some that they teach no other doctrine", (1 Tim. 1 v.3). In a Church plagued with false doctrine and false leaders, it is not surprising to find them struggling over gender roles as we have noted earlier. Under the pretence of gathering for worship, women were flaunting themselves and their behaviour revealed that the intent of their hearts was evil. Since worship is central to the life of the Church, it was high on Paul's list of issues for Timothy to confront.

It is following his discussion of the role and conduct of men when the Church is called to prayer (1 Tim. 2 v.1-8), that the Apostle Paul turns to the subject of women in worship (1 Tim. 2 v.9-15). Both are connected to the same overall subject by the words "I will therefore (v.8) . . . . . In like manner also (v.9) . . . . .", the Greek verb here is from "boulomai", which has the meaning "I command", or "I purpose". The apostle is not expressing his own opinion or giving advice, he speaks with and by Divine authority. Men are the leaders when the Church meets for corporate worship. Women are permitted to pray and witness, but not "in Church", that is, when meeting for the public worship of God.

The saintly Biblical scholar, Matthew Henry, in commenting on First Cor. 14 v.34-35, says that women were not to teach, "nor so much as to debate and ask questions in the Church, but to learn in silence there; and, if difficulties occurred, ask their own husbands at home".

Again, another worthy commentator, Albert Barnes, has this to say, "No rule in the New Testament is more positive than this, and however plausible . . . . . the reasons which may be urged for disregarding it, and for allowing women to take part in conducting public worship . . . . . the authority of the Word of God is positive, and its meaning cannot be mistaken".

The great Reformer of the sixteenth century, John Calvin, in the vast legacy of his writings that have come down to us, says, "Not that this prohibition takes from women the charge of instructing their family, but only excludes them from the office of teaching, which God has committed to men only".

God's pattern for leadership in the Church is centred around elders, men who are shepherds of God's people and who have the responsibility to oversee the activities of the Church. The priesthood of all believers is a very important Biblical doctrine and every Christian, no matter how poor or uneducated, or whether they are male or female, is a priest before God, and can come directly to God through no other Person than the Lord Jesus Christ. They that worship God, "must worship Him in spirit and in truth", (John 4 v.24).

In the public ministry of the Church there are Biblical principles that all must abide by. As well as godly order and that all things should be done unto edifying (1 Cor. 14 v.26), in the order of worship there should be a clear and distinct difference between the roles of men and women. As touched upon earlier, God expects the differences between gender and headship to be clearly and visibly followed. Though there is no difference between men and women as far as salvation and the priesthood of all believers are concerned, there is a difference as far as service is concerned. That "there is neither male nor female", is true in regard to conversion. God will save all who come to Him through faith in Christ, (Gal. 3 v.28). Yet in the Church and in the home between husband and wife, God has specifically laid down the respective male and female roles to be followed.

The action of taking off or putting on of a headcovering in worship publicly acknowledges that God sees men and women as different, (1 Cor. 11 v.2-16). The wearing of hair short by men, and long by women, means in practice man should be seen to be masculine and a woman to be feminine, and all attempts by men and women to blur the distinctions between the sexes are not of God. Men are to take leadership in the public worship of God, and where this is seen in practice shows that the worshippers are content to follow God's principles of conduct, not the world's, and that the headship of God over Christ, of Christ over man, and of man over the woman is publicly acknowledged. (1 Cor. 11 v.2-5).

In many places this teaching is unpopular and frequently challenged, which thoroughly undermines the important doctrine that it is the Holy Ghost Who inspired men to write the Word of God. Some also raise the objection that it is a cultural matter in the first century, but the Apostle says in First Cor. 1 v.3 that he writes "to all that in every place call upon the name of Jesus Christ our Lord", adding that if anyone disagrees with the principle of length of hair, headcovering, and dress, as outlined in Holy Scripture, we will not recognise any other principle or follow any other pattern of behaviour. (1 Cor. 11 v.16).

Scripture prohibits Women as Deacons

Acts chapter 6, verses 1-8, deals specifically with the ministry of deacons who serve the Lord in the local Church. We must always remember the invaluable work done by womenfolk, but men have a special and a distinctive role when it comes to the matter of the spiritual oversight and administration of the Church, that is, as elders and deacons. These verses give us clear and helpful guidance as to the kind of men who should be appointed by the congregation as deacons, and placed in positions of leadership and responsibility to guide the policy and programme of the Church.

The first qualification, obviously, is that such men should have a definite experience of conversion by the grace of God, and are born again by the Spirit into God's family. "Except a man be born of water and of the Spirit, he cannot enter into the kingdom of God", (John 3 v.5). This requirement is indicated in verse 3 of the passage referred to above, where we read the words: "Wherefore, brethren, look ye out among you seven men of honest report, full of the Holy Ghost and wisdom, whom ye may appoint over this business", (Acts 6 v.3). Notice also that it says, "seven men", not women. Men are to be selected from the membership of the congregation, who are regenerate and adorn the Gospel of God in their daily walk and life. "Repent, and be baptized every one of you in the name of Jesus Christ for the remission of sins, and ye shall receive the gift of the Holy Ghost. Then they that gladly received His Word were baptized: and the same day there were added unto them about three thousand souls. Praising God, and having favour with all the people. And the Lord added unto the Church daily such as should be saved", (Acts 2 v.38,41 and 47). Membership consists of "such as should be saved", those who have repented, received the Word of God gladly, and have been added unto the Church.

One of the tragic weaknesses of many Churches today is that 'good' and 'gifted' men have been placed into office, but who have never been born again, have no clear testimony, and do not give evidence in their lives of a true change of heart.

The practice of the Early New Testament Church is clearly observed in Acts 6 v.3, "look ye out among you seven men . . . . . whom we may appoint" as deacons. The whole Church membership was invited to participate in the selection of suitable men to serve as deacons. We should remind ourselves how serious and how solemn a business it is to exercise any influence, or to cast a vote in favour of the appointment of anyone into any position of responsibility in the Church. The work of the Lord can be made or marred, advanced or retarded, by the quality of the men who are placed into office. Thus, we learn that such men should only be selected after much prayer: "Whom they set before the apostles: and when they had prayed, they laid their hands on them", (Acts 6 v.6).

The same practice and principles were emphasised in Acts 1 v.23-26, also when Matthias was chosen to be numbered with the eleven. "And they appointed two, Joseph called Barsabas, who was surnamed Justus, and Matthias. And they prayed, and said, Thou, Lord, which knowest the hearts of all men, shew whether of these two Thou hast chosen, That he may take part of this ministry and apostleship, from which Judas by transgression fell, that he might go to his own place. And they gave forth their lots; and the lot fell upon Matthias; and he was numbered with the eleven apostles", (Acts 1 v.23-26).

In Acts 6, deacons were to be "men of honest report", that is, of good reputation, which surely means that these men were not only to have a good report in the Church, but in the world as well. It is possible to have a good report or reputation in the Church and a bad one in the home, on the farm, in the office, in the shop or supermarket, at school or college, or among one's neighbours. Men who are to serve the Lord in His Church are to be utterly sincere and thoroughly honest in all their words, and in all their work and dealings with others. They must be men of consistent Christian living, God-fearing, reliable, spiritual and of moral integrity.

Furthermore, they are to be "full of the Holy Ghost and wisdom", (Acts 6 v.3), that is, Spirit-filled, in which the fruit of the Spirit will be manifestly seen in their lives. "But the fruit of the spirit is love, joy, peace, longsuffering, gentleness, goodness, faith, meekness, temperance: against such there is no law", (Gal. 5 v.22-23). What a high standard, but it is God's standard, and as true disciples and followers of Him in all the work of our Churches, do not let us lower it.

The supreme qualification required for any man, who is to be a worker in the Lord's vineyard is not popularity, seniority, nor even ability --- but spirituality. Notice too that they must also be "full of wisdom", (Acts 6 v.3), full of discernment; not tactless, lacking discernment and spiritual insight, otherwise their outlook is worldly. The serious nature of holy ministry of both elder and deacon, requires that the right men are placed in positions of leadership within the Church. "If any of you lack wisdom, let him ask of God, that giveth to all men liberally, and upbraideth not; and it shall be given him", (James 1 v.5).

"Who is a wise man and endued with knowledge among you? Let him shew out of a good conversation his works with meekness of wisdom. But if ye have bitter envying and strife in your hearts, glory not, and lie not against the truth. This wisdom descendeth not from above, but is earthly, sensual, devilish. For where envying and strife is, there is confusion and every evil work. But the wisdom that is from above is first pure, then peaceable, gentle, and easy to be entreated, full of mercy and good fruits, without partiality, and without hypocrisy. And the fruit of righteousness is sown in peace of them that make peace", (James 3 v.13-18).

Stephen was one of those chosen as a deacon, one of the "seven", "a man full of faith and of the Holy Ghost", (Acts 6 v.5). The work of God is a faith work, and the men who are appointed elders or deacons, must obviously be men of faith who know God, trust God, and believe His Word. "The people that do know their God shall be strong, and do exploits", (Daniel 11 v.32). This is God's pattern for His Church, and the kind of men upon whom the responsibility of leadership rests as His representatives in the Church, are to be channels through whom He may pour out His blessing. May all our Churches honour and obey His Word in these Divine matters for the good of His people to the glory of God.

The Place of Women in the Church

This now leads us to ask, what place and role do women really have in the life of the Church? While they cannot hold office in the Church, there is much that they can do, for which they are ideally suited. We all know how, when Jesus Christ went about preaching the Gospel and healing the sick, He was helped by women. We read in Luke 8 v.2-3, "And certain women, which had been healed of evil spirits and infirmities, Mary called Magdalene, out of whom went seven devils, and Joanna the wife of Chuza, Herod's steward, and Sus-anna, and many others, which ministered unto him of their substance".

In modern society today, equality of men and women is required to mean sameness, and therefore the Biblical teaching on submission is regarded as relegation and the fight goes on as they seek for role reversal. The problem increases when the Church adopts the thinking of the world, alters its practices, not according to Scripture, but to suit present-day 'equal sex' noisy propagators. We must learn afresh what the Bible teaches, that men and women are equal, but different, and therefore have different roles.

The Apostle Paul commends several women for the help they gave to the Church. In writing to the Romans, he says to the Christians at Rome: "I commend unto you Phebe our sister, which is a servant of the Church which is at Cenchrea: That ye receive her in the Lord, as becometh saints, and that ye assist her in whatsoever business she hath need of you: for she hath been a succourer of many, and of myself also. Greet Priscilla and Aquila my helpers in Christ Jesus: Who have for my life laid down their own necks: unto whom not only I give thanks, but also all the Churches of the Gentiles", (Rom. 16 v.1-4). There is particular reference elsewhere in Scripture to Priscilla, who along with her husband Aquila, instructed Apollos privately. "And a certain Jew named Apollos . . . . . whom when Aquila and Priscilla had heard, they took him unto them, and expounded unto him the way of God more perfectly", (Acts 18 v.24-26). Paul greeted them as his "helpers in Christ Jesus", (Rom. 16 v.3).

To a certain Philippian believer, the Apostle Paul also wrote: "And I entreat thee also, true yokefellow, help those women which laboured with me in the Gospel, with Clement also, and with other my fellowlabourers, whose names are in the Book of Life", (Phil. 4 v.3).

We have already established the Biblical principle that in the public service of the worship of God, the women are to keep silence and to take a position of quiet submission, but that does not mean that they cannot undertake any useful work for the Lord. The service that women can render can be enormous. As we look at the various ministries listed in First Timothy 5 v.10, we clearly see what scope they offer to every Christian woman who would serve the Lord.

(1) She can bring up children. If the Lord has entrusted her with children, she cannot exercise any greater ministry than to "bring them up in the nurture and admonition of the Lord", (Eph. 6 v.4);

(2) She can be given to hospitality, as in the examples (a) of Judas: "And the Lord said unto him (Ananias), Arise, and go into the street which is called Straight, and inquire in the house of Judas for one called Saul of Tarsus: for, behold, he prayeth", (Acts 9 v.11); (b) of Simon the Tanner: "And it came to pass, that he tarried many days in Joppa with one Simon a tanner", (Acts 9 v.43); and (c) of Lydia: "And they

went out of the prison (Paul and Silas), and entered into the house of Lydia: and when they had seen the brethren, they comforted them, and departed", (Acts 16 v.40):

(3) She can wash the feet of the saints. The thought surely here is of a willingness to do lowly tasks and to bring comfort to those who are in need. After supper Jesus took a towel, "poureth water into a basin, and began to wash the disciples' feet, and to wipe them with the towel wherewith He was girded. Then cometh He to Simon Peter: and Peter saith unto Him, Lord, dost Thou wash my feet?", (John 13 v.4-6);

(4) She can relieve the afflicted. "Bear ye one another's burdens, and so fulfil the law of Christ", (Gal. 6 v.2). "But we were gentle among you, even as a nurse cherisheth her children", (1 Thess. 2 v.7). "We are bound to thank God always for you, brethren, as it is meet, because that your faith growth exceedingly, and the charity of every one of you all toward each other aboundeth", (2 Thess. 1 v.3);

(5) She can follow every good work. We need such women in the Church today, and there is always room for many more: "Well reported of for good works; if she have brought up children, if she have lodged strangers, if she have washed the saints' feet, if she have relieved the afflicted, if she have diligently followed every good work", (1 Tim. 5 v.10).

This passage goes on to speak of the many dangers women must avoid. These are brought before us in words that are very solemn and full of warning: "But the younger widows refuse: for when they have begun to wax wanton against Christ, they will marry; Having damnation, because they have cast off their first faith. And withal they learn to be idle, wandering about from house to house; and not only idle, but tattlers also and busybodies, speaking things which they ought not. I will therefore that the younger women marry, bear children, guide the house, give none occasion to the adversary to speak reproachfully. For some are already turned aside after Satan", (1 Tim. 5 v.11-15). In these verses we are told (1) about women who were "wanton" (v.11) which means restless: (2) about women who had "cast off their first faith" (v.12) which means that they had grown slack spiritually; and (3) about women who had degenerated into gossips and busybodies with dangerous tongues, who went from house to house, person to person, carrying trouble and "speaking things which they ought not" (v.13). Such women lower the reputation of the Church and give an "occasion to the adversary to speak reproachfully" (v.14). Such women simply play into the hands of the Enemy (v.15).

It should be pointed out, however, that all matters the Apostle Paul wrote in reference to the ladies, so far as Christian grace and character are concerned, refer also to men.

The Labour of Women in the Gospel

The question might be asked, How did the godly women in Philippi and other places actually labour with Paul in the work of the Gospel? Most reliable commentators agree that they did not, of course, preach in the Churches, but rather supported Paul and his fellow ministers by professing the Gospel, bearing reproach and persecution for it, furthering the spread of it with their material possessions, entertaining the ministers of the Gospel, visiting the sick, instructing and exhorting other women and children in their homes.

Women are not to be downgraded as weak of will, spirit or intellect. Being "the weaker vessel", (1 Peter 3 v.7), they are not weaker in any sense beyond the physical make-up. With a Deborah rendering service to Israel, a Mary standing over against the Cross of the despised One, and a Priscilla opening the Scriptures to the mighty Apollos, are not to be thought of as inferior in rendering service to the Lord.

We read of Lydia, the first convert at Philippi, rendering useful service at the very outset by giving hospitality to the Apostle and his companions.

Euodia and Syntyche were doubtless two of the women who resorted to the "river side, where prayer was wont to be made", (Acts 16 v.13). They being converted earlier, would naturally take an active part in encouraging other women saved at a later period.

In Acts 21 v.9, we read that Philip "had four daughters, virgins, which did prophesy", but not in the gathered meetings of the Church.

There was a wonderful lady called Dorcas in Acts 9 v.36-43, who lived at Joppa, and we are told that "this woman was full of good works and almsdeeds which she did", (v.36). Being a disciple of Christ involves more than the initial act of trusting Jesus as Saviour. A disciple is one who accepts His discipline, acknowledges His authority through His Word, surrenders to His Lordship, and submits to His rule. Faith without "works, is dead", (James 2 v.17), and in her particular ministry which occupied so much of her time, she "made coats and garments" (v.39), bringing comfort and relief to those in need. Her faith was evidenced, or shown, by the works that she did, abounding in good deeds and acts of charity. There is room for all in the service of God. There are many opportunities for Christian service, and the sphere of work is just as much in the home, as in the Church. "There is one body, and one Spirit, even as ye are called in one hope of your calling; One Lord, one faith, one baptism. One God and Father of all, Who is above all, and through all, and in you all. But unto every one of us is given grace according to the measure of the gift of Christ", (Eph. 4 v.4-7).

As we combine all the relevant passages of Scripture in the study of God's Word, we get the composite truth. Women may pray and witness within the boundaries of God's revelation, and with a proper sense of submission. It is important that their deportment in so doing reflects God's order, and never at any time must they appear rebellious against God's will.

Christian women today, especially those of more mature years and Christian experience, are to give guidance to younger people. Ministers of the Gospel in the past greatly valued the advice which the older gracious women gave to younger women in their congregations about how to conduct themselves in the house of God and in their Christian profession, how to cope in a Christian manner with the responsibilities of being a wife and mother, and even about such matters as dress. "In like manner also, that women adorn themselves in modest apparel, with shamefacedness and sobriety; not with broided hair, or gold, or pearls, or costly array; But which become women professing godliness with good works", (1 Tim. 2 v.9-10).

It is important that a woman's testimony is consistent. The Greek word "epangello", translated "professing", means "to make a public announcement". Therefore, any woman who has made a public announcement about her faith and commitment to the Lord, should conduct herself in a manner consistent with such a profession. "Let us hold fast the profession of our faith without wavering; for He is faithful that promised", (Heb. 10 v.23).

"Godliness", from the Greek word "theosebeia", has the basic meaning not only of reverence to God, but also obedience to His Word. To do otherwise brings reproach on the name of Christ. This is a major problem with the 'feminist' movement pushing to be in the ministry, on the eldership, and on the diaconate in the Church. A woman who wants to serve God and desires to honour Him, cannot show disregard for what He says in His Word about the role of women. The testimony of a Christian woman professing godliness is a life of obedience and good works, for righteous deeds demonstrate her love for Truth and the genuineness of her faith. The same, of course, is true for men.

It is true from Scripture that women are also encouraged to engage in personal evangelism outside the home. All of God's people are to "shine as lights in the world", (Phil 2 v.15), and be witnesses both by life and by lip of the glorious Gospel of Christ. The ministry of reaching out to others is not to be lightly valued. Women certainly have ministries in serving, prayer, teaching, but not usurping authority, but teaching one another as portrayed in Titus Chapter 2: "That they may teach the young women to be sober, to love their husbands, to love their children, to be discreet, chaste, keepers at home, good, obedient to their own husbands, that the Word of God be not blasphemed", (Titus 2 v.4-5).

In First Peter 3 v.2-4, we read, "While they behold your chaste conversation coupled with fear. Whose adorning let it not be that outward adorning of plaiting of hair, and of wearing of gold, or of putting on of apparel; But let it be the hidden man of the heart, in that which is not corruptible, even the ornament of a meek and quiet spirit which is in the sight of God of great price".

The godly example of the older woman has a great influence on those who are younger. "The aged women", we read in Titus 2 v.3-5, are to "be in behaviour as becometh holiness, not false accusers, not given to much wine, teachers of good things; That they may teach the young women to be sober, to love their husbands, to love their children, To be discreet, chaste, keepers at home, good, obedient to their own husbands, that the Word of God be not blasphemed".

Submission, Teaching and Authority

Ephesians 5 v.22-24 requires wives to submit to their husbands, because the husband is the head of the wife, and Colossians 3 v.18 repeats this requirement.

"Wives, submit yourselves unto your own husbands, as unto the Lord. For the husband is the head of the wife, even as Christ is the Head of the Church: and He is the Saviour of the body. Therefore as the Church is subject unto Christ, so let the wives be to their own husbands in every thing", (Eph. 5 v.22-24).

"Wives, submit yourselves unto your own husbands, as it is fit in the Lord", (Col. 3 v.18).

The Bible clearly teaches the duty of the woman to submit to the man. It is implied when The Scripture says that she was created "for the man", (1 Cor. 11 v.9), and that she was created after the man. "Adam was first formed, then Eve", says the Apostle Paul in First Tim. 2 v.13, teaching that Adam was before the woman, not just in the order in which they were created, but also in their relationship with each other.

There is a mutual submission that Christians owe to one another, condescending to bear one another's burdens, but not advancing themselves one above another in a domineering fashion. We must be of a yielding and of a submissive spirit, and ready for all the duties of the respective places and stations that in providence God has allotted to us in the world.

But the submission of wives to their husbands in the Lord, is in compliance with God's authority. "The head" is a metaphor taken in resemblance of Christ's authority over the Church in that headship which God has appointed to the husband for the protection and comfort of his spouse. So let the wives be subject to their own husbands in everything, with cheerfulness, fidelity, humility and love.

Husbands are to love their wives, for without this, they would abuse their headship. The example as exhibited in Eph. 5 v.21, is the proposed pattern to both husbands and wives, so much so that much is required of each, and neither has reason to complain of the Divine injunctions. (Eph. 5 v.22-33).

If the Bible spells out that a woman should dress modestly, why do some preachers say it is unimportant? The interpretations of modesty vary but the Bible and conscience, with the Holy Spirit's guidance, will lead us aright in this matter. (1 Peter 3 v.1-6).

If the Bible spells out that "the husband is the head of the wife", (Eph. 5 v.23), why do some preachers say that women do not have to submit to their own husbands? Paul compares Christ and the Church with the relationship of husbands and wives, and plainly declares: "Therefore as the Church is subject unto Christ, so let the wives be to their own husbands in every thing", (Eph. 5 v.24).

A rejection of Biblical teaching has brought great disorder into the world, into the Church, and in the home, and reveals to the detriment of order and peace, that the Word of God has been cast aside for the whims and fancies of men and women.

The Apostle Paul states that all things must be done "with all subjection", (1 Tim. 2 v.11), not in arguing, disagreement, and self-centredness. "Let all things be done unto edifying", (1 Cor. 14 v.26). "Let all things be done decently and in order", (1 Cor. 14 v.40).

The Bible proclaims the spiritual equality of both sexes, but this does not preclude differing roles. There are no women pastors/teachers/ministers, elders, or deacons in the New Testament. A comparison of First Cor. 11 v.5 and First Cor. 14 v.34, indicates women are permitted to pray and speak the Word, but Paul makes it quite clear by Divine command that such allowance is not in the public assembly and worship of the Church. When the Church comes together, The Scripture states, "Let the woman learn in silence with all subjection", (1 Tim. 2 v.11). Women are to listen, and as the Greek text emphasises here, "to line up under" the authority of God's Word, be in complete subjection, be silent, and be content in the role of the learner.

There is no evading the plain meaning of the text of Scripture in this matter. The 'revisionist' interpretations of the present-day are a product of the devil. The context makes the meaning unmistakable to the honest reader whose constant desire and "chief end is to glorify God, and to enjoy Him for ever", (Shorter Cat. No.1).

The main words in First Timothy 2 v.11-15, concerning teaching and authority, are, "I suffer not a woman to teach, nor to usurp authority over the man".

"Let the woman learn in silence with all subjection. But I suffer not a woman to teach, nor to usurp authority over the man, but to be in silence. For Adam was first formed, then Eve. And Adam was not deceived, but the woman being deceived was in the transgression. Notwithstanding she shall be saved in childbearing, if they continue in faith and charity and holiness with sobriety", (1 Tim. 2 v.9-15).

In this passage the interpretation and meaning is clear. Women are to keep quiet in the sense of not teaching in the public worship service, and they are to demonstrate subjection by not usurping the authority of the elder or preacher. God's law commands it and is in line with His design for the weaker vessel. The argument that subordination and equality are mutually exclusive is completely wrong. First Cor. 11 v.3 states, "But I would have you know that the head of every man is Christ; and the head of the woman is the man; and the head of Christ is God".

"Suffer not", in the context really means that the role of pastor, minister, teacher, elder, is only for men. In an unqualified directive, First Tim. 3 v.2 forbids women from exercising any type of authority over men in the Church. It is the elders who "rule", (1 Tim. 5 v.17), clearly men, since they must be "the husband of one wife", (1 Tim. 3 v.2).

This of course does not mean that women cannot teach in certain circumstances. Priscilla and Aquila both instructed Apollos, whom when they had heard him speak, "took him unto them, and expounded unto him the way of God more perfectly", (Acts 18 v.26). But they taught him in private and not in the worship of the Church. And women can and must teach other women (Titus 2 v.3-5). Nor does it mean women cannot pray, merely that they are not to lead the prayers during the public worship of the Church. It does not mean that women do not have spiritual gifts in the area of public speaking and leadership. The issue is where they exercise those gifts.

God does not violate His principles for the sake of expediency. Women must stop believing the devil's lie that the only role of significance is that of leadership. Those who desire such a position is usually no more than to boost their own egos and gain power and control. For greater peace and happiness the subordinate role is a privilege, not punishment.

The subordinate role was established not in the Fall, but in the Divine order of Creation. "For Adam was first formed, then Eve", (1 Tim. 2 v.13). God made woman after man to be "an help meet for him" (Gen. 2 v.18), a suitable helper. This is not a cultural argument either at Ephesus or Corinth as some would wrongly argue, but God's intention and design for mankind.

Furthermore, Paul points out in regard to the Fall that "Adam was not deceived, but the woman being deceived was in the transgression", (1 Tim. 2 v.14). In Genesis 3 v.1-7, the details are recorded of the tragic account of what happened when Eve usurped the headship role.

"Now the serpent was more subtil than any beast of the field which the Lord God had made. And he said unto the woman, Yea, hath God said, Ye shall not eat of every tree in the garden? And the woman said unto the serpent, We may eat of the fruit of the trees of the garden: But of the fruit of the tree which is in the midst of the garden, God hath said, Ye shall not eat of it, neither shall ye touch it, lest ye die. And the serpent said unto the woman, Ye shall not surely die: For God doth know that in the day ye eat thereof, then your eyes shall be opened, and ye shall be as gods, knowing good and evil. And when the woman saw that the tree was good for food, and that it was pleasant to the eyes, and a tree to be desired to make one wise, she took of the fruit thereof, and did eat, and gave also unto her husband with her; and he did eat. And the eyes of them both were opened, and they knew that they were naked; and they sewed fig leaves together, and made themselves aprons", (Gen. 3 v.1-7).

The whole human race thus fell into total depravity and judgement. Eve was not suited by nature to assume the position of ultimate responsibility. When she stepped out from under the protection and leadership of Adam, she was highly vulnerable and fell. And when Adam violated his leadership role and followed Eve, though it was not him who was "deceived" (1 Tim. 2 v.14), the perversion of God's order was complete. The Fall of man in the Garden of Eden resulted, not just simply from disobedience to God's commands, but from violating God's appointed roles for the sexes.

This is not to say that Adam was less culpable than Eve, or that she was more defective. Although he was not deceived by Satan, as was Eve, Adam still chose to disobey God. As the head of their relationship, he bore ultimate responsibility, and that is why the New Testament relates the Fall to Adam's sin, not Eve's, (Rom. 5 v.12-21, 1 Cor. 15 v.21-22). "Wherefore, as by one man sin entered into the world, and death by sin; and so death passed upon all men, for that all have sinned . . . . . For since by man came death, by man came also the resurrection of the dead. For as in Adam all die, even so in Christ shall all be made alive". Headship by the man was part of God's plan and design from the beginning of creation.

Women are to profess godliness as well as men. Many of them down through the centuries have been eminent warriors and stalwarts of the faith, even in times of trial, great danger and persecution. How inspiring are the stories, amongst others, of the Solway Martyrs, Margaret MacLachlan, a widow of some seventy years, and young Margaret Wilson, only eighteen years of age, who died amid the swirling waters of the rising tide to win freedom to worship God. In the manner of life both were Christ like and very highly esteemed by their fellow Christians. Faith gave buoyancy to their resolution, hope was the anchor of their souls, the love of Christ shed abroad in their hearts ever spurred them on in the Cause of Christ, and before them ever loomed large "the recompense of the reward", (Heb. 11 v.26), and the gates of the city of God, the new Jerusalem.

The degree to which the Apostle Paul was used by God in producing genuine spiritual disciples of the Lord and founding Churches is astonishing. By Divine appointment, Paul's commission and orders came from God our Saviour and Christ Jesus, Who is our hope: "Christ in you, the hope of glory", (Col. 1 v.27). But in First Timothy 2, the Apostle discusses women's duties by defining their role as "learners" rather than teachers, during the public worship of God. To enjoy true Church fellowship in the Lord, knowledge of His Word and holiness of the saints are of primary importance. While women are not to be the public teachers or preachers in that context, neither are they to be shut out of the learning process. The verb "to learn", "to be informed", comes from the same Greek word in which we get "disciple" or "learner", as noted earlier. To "grow in grace, and in the knowledge of our Lord and Saviour Jesus Christ", (2 Peter 3 v.18), instruction in the Word of God is vital and helps to stimulate fervency in worship. The effect of little knowledge and lack of study of Scripture, do not enhance true discipleship, but rather greatly stunt Christian growth, behaviour and understanding. Jesus stoutly declares that "the true worshippers shall worship the Father in spirit and in truth. God is a Spirit: and they that worship Him must worship Him in spirit and in truth", (John 4 v.23-24). Worship is to be in spirit and in truth.

True worship occurs only when that part of man, his spirit, which is akin to the Divine nature, actually meets with God and in His sovereign plan and purpose finds itself praising Him for His creation, providence, redemption, wisdom, power, holiness, justice, goodness, compassion, mercy, grace and truth. We must worship and approach

God on the basis of the Biblical revelation in full accordance with the principles and admonitions of the Bible. The Word of God alone contains the way of salvation in Christ alone, and outlines the principles upon which the Church of the living God is to be governed. We must come in God's way, and not in any way of human devising. The Westminster Shorter Catechism rightly describes "man's chief end is to glorify God, and to enjoy Him for ever", (No.1).

Adornment, Meekness and a Quiet Spirit

"In like manner also, that women adorn themselves in modest apparel, with shamefacedness and sobriety; not with broided hair, or gold, or pearls, or costly array; But which becometh women professing godliness with good works", (1 Tim. 2 v.9-10).

In First Peter 3 v.1-6, women are clearly instructed as to how to "adorn" themselves and to show the Christian spirit in social relations with the exhortation: "Ye wives, be in subjection to your own husbands". The main contention of the Apostle Peter here is that the Christian life and obligations are not intended to be, and never should be, made a disturbing force in social and family relations.

"Likewise, ye wives, be in subjection to your own husbands; that, if any obey not the Word, they also may without the Word be won by the conversation of the wives; While they behold your chaste conversation coupled with fear. Whose adorning let it not be that outward adorning of plaiting the hair, and of wearing of gold, or of putting on of apparel; But let it be the hidden man of the heart, in that which is not corruptible, even the ornament of a meek and quiet spirit, which is in the sight of God of great price. For after this manner in the old time the holy women also, who trusted in God, adorned themselves, being in subjection unto their own husbands: Even as Sara obeyed Abraham, calling him lord: whose daughters ye are, as long as ye do well, and are not afraid with any amazement", (1 Peter 3 v.1-6).

The earnest desire of both man and woman should be to obey and glorify God at all times, and so enjoy all the blessings of the Covenant which is ordered in all things and sure, (2 Sam. 23 v.5). The Christian woman should dress in a distinctively feminine and modest way, not wearing make up, ear rings, trousers, and that her adornment is not outward but "the ornament of a meek and quiet spirit, which is in the sight of God of great price", (1 Peter 3 v.4).

When we observe many woman in this our present-day generation, it appears they have come a long way since the Garden of Eden. Nowadays modern women are smoking cigarettes, drinking alcohol, painting up like Jezebel, with short haircuts, and wearing trousers and other skin-tight clothing which causes men to lust. The immodest way so many women dress today is unbelievable. The Bible strictly commands God-fearing women to "adorn themselves in modest apparel, with shamefacedness and sobriety", (1 Tim. 2 v.9), so there must be few God-fearing women left, judging from their appearances. This is not just an "appearance" judgement, but a righteous" one as well. "Judge not according to the appearance, but judge righteous judgment" (John 7 v.24). The fundamental spiritual error of the human heart is to think that a person can please God by his own natural efforts. This leads to other errors, (1) concerning the Person and work of Christ, and (2) concerning the law of God. Nowhere are we taught in the Bible or encouraged to believe that the law was given to be followed as a way of salvation. Rather the law was given as a standard that is meant to condemn sinners and to drive the one who feels its condemnation to the Lord Jesus Christ. "For what the law could not do, in that it was weak through the flesh, God sending His own Son in the likeness of sinful flesh, and for sin, condemned sin in the flesh: That the righteousness of the law might be fulfilled in us, who walk not after the flesh, but after the Spirit. For they that are after the flesh do mind the things of the flesh; but they that are after the Spirit the things of the Spirit", (Rom. 8 v.3-5).

Women are mandated to adorn themselves in a manner fitting the worship of God. Part of that Divine command in making due preparation for worship, is the wearing of proper clothing. "Adorn" comes from the Greek word "kosmeo", and means "to arrange", "to put in order", or "to make ready". The word "modest" is derived from "kosmio" and means "order", or "system". Not only the clothing, but also the look, yea, the whole demeanour of women is important as they come to the corporate worship ready to face the Lord. They must not come in slovenly disarray or personal display of vulgarity or indecency by showing off an unbecoming wardrobe. There is a place for lovely clothes that reflect the humble grace of a woman. Proper adornment on the outside reflects a properly adorned heart.

The specifics of the text in First Tim. 1 v.9, also relates to "broided hair", "gold", "pearls", and "costly array". The point here is not that women should be indifferent to their hair, nor is there anything wrong with owning jewellery or having some nice clothes. When a woman dresses for Church to attract attention to herself, or by flaunting her wealth, she has violated the purpose of worship. The wearing of several rings, encircling the neck with huge tiers of pearls, eyes pencilled, eyebrows painted, and expensive perfume applied that would take away your breath, which draws attention away from the Lord are obviously inappropriate for women in the Church. They should demonstrate humble godliness, and not appear like prostitutes or some showy pagan woman. A woman should examine her motives and goals for the way she dresses. The grace and beauty of womanhood is shown by her love and devotion to her husband, and a humble heart that honours and worships God aright. By focusing on worshipping God "in spirit and in truth", (John 4 v.23-24), will dictate the woman's wardrobe and appearance.

A godly woman would be ashamed and feel guilt if she distracted someone from worshipping God. Women are to adorn themselves modestly and discreetly: "with shamefacedness and sobriety", (1 Tim. 2 v.9). The Greek word here, "aidos", refers to 'modesty mixed with humility'. As well as not to be a source of any temptation, the word also has the connotation of rejecting anything dishonourable to God. The basic sense of "sobriety" is self-control and calmness. Women are to exercise this cardinal virtue so that neither their passions nor anyone else's are excited. The testimony of "women professing godliness with good works", (1 Tim. 2 v.10), refers to works that are genuinely good, not merely good in appearance. The Greek here, "epangello", means "to make a public announcement". The Christian woman, who by virtue of her profession of love, worship, honour, and fear of the Lord, publicly commits herself to pursuing godliness. A woman cannot claim to fear God and yet disregard what His Word says about her actions and behaviour. She cannot oppose God's design for her in society and in the Church, and at the same time 'profess' to love and follow Christ as Master and Lord.

The lives of women who "obey not the Word", (1 Peter 3 v.1), cannot be exemplary or reverential, and often such influence leads to irreligion, infidelity, and arrogance in rejecting the commands of Divine Truth.

But those who are "holy women" will joyfully bow to the authority of God's Word, simply because they fear God and seek to please Him, not man. "For after this manner in the old time the holy women also, who trusted in God, adorned themselves, being in subjection unto their own husbands", (1 Peter 3 v.5). The Lord's believing people should take every care to show that the graces and virtues of their behaviour are answerable to the true profession of Christianity. Christians ought to do their duty to one another, not out of fear, nor from force, but from a willing mind, and in obedience to the command of God with the desire "to do His will . . . . . that which is wellpleasing in His sight, through Jesus Christ; to whom be glory for ever and ever", (Heb. 13 v.21).

The greatest honour of any man or woman lies in a humble, submissive, and faithful deportment of themselves in the relation or condition in which Providence has placed them. The ornaments of the body are destroyed by the moth, and perish in the using, but the grace of God, the longer and the more we wear it, the brighter and better it grows.

The Design and Role of Women

Many of the Churches today are advocating an unBiblical role for women. As we have already seen, the passage of Scripture in First Timothy 2 v.9-15, is most striking in that it sets forth the Biblical role for women in the Church. These verses speak in very clear terms what the Divine order should be. Women are to learn in silence. They are to learn in subjection. They are not to teach. They are not to usurp authority. "Let the women learn in silence with all subjection. But I suffer not a woman to teach, nor to usurp authority over the man, but to be in silence", (1 Tim. 2 v.11-12). "Suffer not", means "do not permit".

There must be order in society. The woman was created for the man, she was first in the transgression, and order in sin has an order in punishment. The woman was sentenced before the man. "Unto the woman He (God) said, I will greatly multiply thy sorrow and thy conception; in sorrow thou shalt bring forth children; and thy desire shall be to thy husband, and he shall rule over thee", (Gen. 3 v.16).

The headship of the man in marriage is not something that enters subsequent to the Fall, but it is in fact already present in the second chapter of Genesis. The woman is described as being "a help meet" made "for" the man and given "to" him, (Gen. 2 v.18 and 22). Adam's sin consists in part in being led by his wife Eve rather than leading her. "And unto Adam He (God) said, Because thou hast harkened unto the voice of thy wife, and hast eaten of the tree, of which I commanded thee, saying, Thou shalt not eat of it: cursed is the ground for thy sake; in sorrow thou shalt eat of it all the days of thy life", (Gen. 3 v.17). The woman's "desire" for her husband was willingly submitted to the leadership of the man before the Fall, but has been characterised in the Original Sin and since, by a rebellion against the rule of God.

The "desire" of Genesis 4 v.7 is strikingly parallel to that of Genesis 3 v.16. Writing on the subject, 'What is the Woman's Desire?', Sarah Foh makes this comment, "The woman has the same sort of desire for her husband that sin has for Cain, a desire to possess or control him. This desire disputes the headship of the husband. As the Lord tells Cain what he should do, that is, master or rule sin, the Lord also states what the husband should do, rule over his wife. The words of the Lord in Genesis 3 v.16[2], as in the case of the battle between sin and Cain, do not determine the victor of the conflict between husband and wife. These words mark the beginning of the battle of the sexes. As a result of the Fall, man no longer rules easily; he must fight for his headship. Sin has corrupted both the willing submission of the wife and the loving headship of the husband, to usurp his Divinely appointed headship, and he must master her, if he can. So the rule of love founded in Paradise is replaced by struggle, tyranny, and domination".

In the institution of marriage God's intention for husband and wife was that mutual attraction and love should lead to harmony and mutual support, blessing and joy, which is now distorted by the Fall.

In Ephesus women had the desire to lead the Church. Today women seek leadership roles in the Church, and part of the result of the Fall was that women would desire to control the man. The Hebrew word translated "desire" in Genesis 3 v.16, is used only one other time, in Genesis 4 v.7, as pointed out above. The conclusion therefore is that Genesis 3 v.16 is saying that women desire to take control from men. There are women in the Church at the present time who are not content with their God-given role. The Scriptures do not allow women to take an authoritative role as minister, pastor, elder, or deacon in the Church. No woman is ever presented in such offices in the New Testament.

In the phrase, "nor to usurp authority over the man" the Greek word "authentein", has the clear meaning, "not to have authority over", "but to be in silence", (1 Tim. 2 v.12). This does not mean that women can teach as long as they do not become abusive. Nor does it mean that women are not permitted to pray and witness, or that women must never teach or instruct children, or that women do not have gifts and ability, or that women cannot perform good works and serve as missionaries, or indeed that women are inferior or poorer in quality.

Women simply have a different role. The role of subordination and subjection in Church brings the greatest peace, understanding, happiness, and contentment. Submission is a privilege under Divine rule and godly practice. Subordination cannot be banned on cultural issues, because it is based on the order of Creation: "And Adam was not deceived, but the woman being deceived was in the transgression", (1 Tim. 2 v.14).

While Adam bears the responsibility for the Fall since he is the head of the human race, we must keep in mind that he did not fall first --- Eve did. When Eve got out from under the protection of Adam's leadership and attempted to deal independently with the Enemy, she was deceived. This reinforces the truth that women were designed with the need for a leader, with Adam as her head. She was thoroughly deceived as the Greek word "exapatao" in First Timothy 2 v.14, strongly implies.

The Fall resulted not only in disobeying God's command, but also of violating the Divinely appointed role of the sexes. Eve assumed the role of leadership, and Adam abdicated his leadership position to follow Eve, which proves all of us are vulnerable in different ways.

The final verse of the chapter reads: "Notwithstanding she shall be saved in childbearing, if they continue in faith and charity and holiness with sobriety", (1 Tim. 2 v.15). This verse is not referring to salvation from sin, but as the Greek word "sozo", translated "saved", refers to deliverance from other things, indicating that through childbearing all women are delivered from the stigma of a woman's originating the Fall. Through childbearing she has the opportunity to lead the race to godliness through her influence on children. The Christian mother's godliness and virtue can have a profound and lasting impact on the life of her children. The rearing of children gives her great dignity, and if she continues in faith, love, holiness, and humility, she can contribute greatly to raising a godly seed after her.

By Divine command and authority, women are to accept their God-given role, not by seeking leadership in the Church, or headship in the home, but primarily in the rearing and raising of godly children. God has given them this gift and blesses them with such a unique privilege and opportunity.

Sadly, today, Christians tend to compromise the Truth of the Bible and to relegate Biblical teaching and standards. Under pressure from the world some 'evangelical' Christians have reinterpreted the Scriptural teaching on the design and role of women in society. They have bowed especially to the philosophy of the radical 'feminist' movement.

In the Word of God, we are exhorted to "earnestly contend for the faith which was once delivered unto the saints", (Jude v.3). It is our solemn duty as believers to uphold, maintain, and defend the faith in these days of spiritual declension, religious decadence, and ecumenical barrenness in which we live. "Wolves" and "false prophets" which the Bible speaks of as cruel and evil leaders, have come in like a flood "in sheep's clothing" and are doing the work of the devil. "Beware of false prophets, which come to you in sheep's clothing, but inwardly they are ravening wolves", (Matt. 7 v.15). In the sending out of the seventy disciples, Jesus describes His followers as lambs among wolves. He warns them to "go your ways: behold, I send you forth as lambs among wolves", (Luke 10 v.3).

The revelation that God has given us begins in the Book of Genesis, chapter 1 v.1, and ends in the Book of Revelation, chapter 22 v.21. This book, the Bible, is our only Rule and sole Guide, in all matters of faith and practice. "This Book of the law shall not depart out of thy mouth; but thou shalt meditate therein day and night, that thou mayest observe to do according to all that is written therein: for then thou shalt make thy way prosperous, and then thou shalt have good success", (Joshua 1 v.8).

Our forefathers, the Reformers, the Covenanters, the Puritans, the Martyrs and Heroes of the Faith down through the centuries have suffered and died in defence of the faith. May God give us grace to pass on the Torch of Scripture Truth undimmed, undiminished, and unblemished to our children, and to our children's children. We pray that God in His sovereignty and providence will give us strength, power, and boldness to stand up for His Word, and witness to the Truth, with zeal and earnestness, and fasten a conviction of them upon our hearts, so that we may be watchful and steadfast until He comes or calls, "because the King's business required haste", (1 Sam. 21 v.8).

The Divine Pattern for the Church

In the Scriptures there is an important relationship between the home and the Church, as we see in Ephesians 5. After discussing the relationship between husband and wife, the Apostle concludes by saying: "This is a great mystery: but I speak concerning Christ and the Church. Nevertheless let every one of you in particular so love his wife even as himself: and the wife see that she reverence her husband", (Eph. 5 v.32-33). Such a relationship is to exemplify, illustrate, and demonstrate the relationship that exists between Christ and His Church. The pattern and plan that God has for the home is essentially the same for the Church.

We are told in the Word of God, that He has given gifts to every member of the Church, and it is clear that those gifts are to be used for the edifying and building up of the Church. Chapters 12-14 of First Corinthians focuses on spiritual gifts, a controversial subject today within many parts of professing Christianity. Perhaps no area of Biblical doctrine has been more misunderstood and abused, even within evangelical circles, than that of spiritual gifts. The doctrine of the Holy Spirit is most important to the spiritual health and effectiveness of the Church. Without the aid of the Holy Spirit nothing can be accomplished. Without the help and power of the Third Person of the Trinity, nothing is more vital to believers than the ministry of their spiritual gifts given by God for Christian service. "Now concerning spiritual gifts, brethren", says Paul, "I would not have you ignorant", (1 Cor. 12 v.1). The term "Lord", is used many hundreds of times in the New Testament. The lordship, deity, and sovereignty of Jesus Christ is central to the true faith, and such affirmation is the work of the Holy Spirit. What a person truly believes about Jesus Christ is the test of whether or not, what he teaches and does, is by the Holy Spirit. The Holy Spirit always leads men to ascribe lordship to Jesus Christ, to be obeyed completely. That is the testimony of the Father, "hear ye Him" (Matt. 17 v.5), "Therefore let all the house of Israel know assuredly, that God hath made that same Jesus, Whom ye have crucified, both Lord and Christ" (Acts 2 v.36); it is the testimony of the Holy Spirit, "But when the Comforter is come", says Christ, "Whom I will sent unto you from the Father, even the Spirit of truth, which proceedeth from the Father, He shall testify of Me" (John 15 v.26); and it is the testimony of the Son of God Himself, Jesus came and spake unto the disciples, saying, "All power is given unto Me in heaven and in earth", (Matt. 28 v.18).

The Apostle uses the illustration of the feet, hands, ears, and eyes as different members of the human body, each has its own function but cannot perform the function of the other members. So too in the Church, only some men are called and equipped to serve in office, but all members, male and female, have some gift that God can use, which needs to be cultivated and developed, to His glory. "There should be no schism in the body; but that the members should have the same care one for another", (1 Cor. 12 v.25). How well a Church functions and fulfils its God-given purpose depends on its leadership giving obedience to the Word of God in all matters of faith and conduct.

Leadership in the Church must not be taken lightly, nor may the qualifications that God has laid down be set aside or ignored. Church leaders, men, that is, ministers, pastors, elders, and deacons, must be called and ordained of God. According to Scripture, if you want to see whether a man is qualified to lead the Church, look at his home. He must be "one that ruleth well his own house, having his children in subjection with all gravity; For if a man know not how to rule his own house, how shall he take care of the Church of God?", (1 Tim. 3 v.4-5).

Unfortunately too many Churches have been very remiss in these matters by appointing unsuitable men into office in the Church. Some have encouraged and endorsed women into office in the Church, altogether contrary to Scripture. Women should not at all be appointed, and in many cases, some men also should not be in office. Such a call is particularly important in regard to the minister or preacher, who is to be the mouthpiece of God in declaring "the whole counsel of God", (Acts 20 v.28).

Proper Church growth must be consistent with the principles of Scripture, and in Ephesians 4 v. 12-16, we have a most concise and succinct form of God's plan by which the blessing of the Lord is assured. Since Christ has said, "I will build My Church", (Matt. 16 v.18), it is obvious that the building must be according to His plan. Attempting to build the Church by human methods and means will bring failure. Teaching elders, therefore, who should be men, are given:-

(1) "for the perfecting of the saints", (v.12), so that believers take on the likeness of their Lord and Saviour through continual obedience to His Word and by manifesting lives of godliness;

(2) "for the edifying of the body of Christ", (v.12), so that all believers are nurtured to fruitful service through the Word, continually learning and developing the Church;

(3) to bring the Church to unity, "till we all come in the unity of the faith, and of the knowledge of the Son of God, unto a perfect man, unto the measure of the fullness of Christ" (v.13), out of which flow spiritual maturity, sound doctrine, and living testimony;

(4) to make the Church stable, "no more children, tossed to and fro, and carried about with every wind of doctrine, by the sleight of men, and cunning craftiness, whereby they lie in wait to deceive", (v.14), so that they are anchored in God's truth, having a thorough knowledge of God's Word, showing spiritual knowledge and doctrinal solidarity; and

(5) to speak "the truth in love", and to "grow up into Him in all things, which is the Head, even Christ", (v.15), that is, having sufficient wisdom to understand God's truth and effectively present it to others in continual humility, grace, and power, the combination of which counteracts lack of truth and lack of compassion.

The Church receives its authority, direction, and power, as it grows "up into Him in all things, which is the Head, even Christ ..... according to the effectual working in the measure of every part, maketh increase of the body unto the edifying of itself in love", (v.15-16).

It is the responsibility of the minister to stand before his congregation and declare the Word of God in all its fullness, without fear, favour, or compromise. Too often Church members fail to attend to the means of grace, shy away from the Word of God, and stay at home from Church because of a lazy habit --- consequently the Word of

God is not important to them. Giving attendance and attention to the preaching of God's Word is enjoined upon all believers, and sometimes the proclamation of the Truth of God demands reproof and correction. "All Scripture is given by inspiration of God, and is profitable for doctrine, for reproof, for correction, for instruction in righteousness: That the man of God may be perfect, throughly furnished unto all good works", (2 Tim. 3 v.16-17).

The Word of God must not be dismissed on the basis of personal whim or fancy. When the Scriptures are faithfully proclaimed, God will hold His people responsible for what they do with it. As we practise the Biblical principles of Church leadership, God will command His blessing and benediction upon those who honour and obey His Holy Word. Jesus Christ is the sole King and Head of His Church which is composed of all those who truly believe in Him as Saviour and Lord, and not by any human merit or works whatsoever. Blessed are "the people whom He hath chosen for His own inheritance", (Psalm 33 v.12).

The Great Commission

"Go ye therefore, and teach all nations, baptising them in the name of the Father, and of the Son, and of the Holy Ghost: Teaching them to observe all things whatsoever I have commanded you: and, lo, I am with you alway, even unto the end of the world, Amen". (Matt. 28 v.19-20).

The commission to proclaim the Gospel, publish the Word, and make disciples of all nations was never confined only to the apostles, or the Church's ministers. It is a commission that rests upon the whole Church collectively, and therefore upon each Christian individually. All God's people are sent to "shine as lights in the world, holding forth the Word of life", (Phil. 2 v.15-16). Every Christian believer has a God-given obligation to make known the Good News and to teach the truth about "the unsearchable riches of Christ", (Eph. 3 v.8).

As messengers of Christ, Who is the "King of kings, and Lord of lords" (Rev. 19 v.16) our duty therefore, is to herald forth by life and by lip the glorious Gospel of grace, and to deliver the message of the Evangel with exact and studious faithfulness, adding nothing, altering nothing, and omitting nothing. "Ye shall not add unto the Word which I command you, neither shall ye diminish ought from it, that ye may keep the commandments of the Lord your God which I command you", (Deut.4 v.2).

All faithful servants of the Triune God are commanded to communicate and declare the Holy Scriptures, not in the scheme of man's bright ideas, needing to be beautified with the cosmetics and high heels of fashionable learning . . . . . but as the Word of God, spoken in Christ's name, carrying Christ's authority, and to be authenticated in the hearers by the convincing power of the Holy Ghost. "And my speech and my preaching was not with enticing words of man's wisdom", declared the Apostle Paul, "but in demonstration of the Spirit and of power", (1 Cor. 2 v.4).

The significance of being "the salt of the earth" and "the light of the world", (Matt. 5 v.13-14), does not mean that we bear witness in a harsh, bigoted or callous way, but rather to present the message of truth in a spirit of love, warm-heartedness and affection, (Eph. 4 v.15), as an expression and implementation of our earnest desire that sinners might be drawn to the Saviour by the blood of the Lamb, and the people of God built up and edified in their "most holy faith", (Jude v.20).

With unwavering conviction that the Bible is "the Word of God which liveth and abideth for ever", (1 Peter 1 v.23), the main thrust of our witness and work for the Lord is to "persuade men", (2 Cor. 5 v.11) to be "reconciled to God", (2 Cor. 5 v.20). Many Christians seem to go for weeks, even months, without apparently seeing or seizing any opportunity to witness consciously for the Saviour. The fact that we do not really care enough about people and their eternal destiny and our lack of personal Bible study and prayer, mean that our lives are not yielded to Christ for us to experience the anointing of the Holy Spirit for Christian service. "Personal witness is the work that counts most", said C. H. Spurgeon. Not every Christian is called to be a preacher as we have already seen, but every Christian is called to be a personal witness. Far too many Christians tend to shelve this responsibility while those around them at home or at work see and hear all too little of effective witness. We need to take stock and pray that God would enable us to put into practice to "be doers of the Word, and not hearers only", (James 1 v.22). It is absolutely imperative that we understand the essence of true Christianity, and one of the major evidences that the Holy Spirit has regenerated us and indwells our hearts, is that we will walk closely with the Lord and bear a faithful witness for Christ in all places.

We are called by the grace of God to witness in an unbelieving and ever-changing godless world, that The Scripture is God's Word. The Lord God Almighty still reigns, He is sovereign in creation, providence and redemption, and ultimate victory belongs to Him Who died on Calvary and rose again in the power of an endless life. All power even now is His in heaven and on earth. The Word of God firmly proclaims Jesus Christ as the sole King and Head of His Church, His Lordship over the nations, and thus over every department of life. By faith the Christian looks to Him, in faith he holds forth the Word of life to those who are perishing and bids them "look and live", (Num. 21 v.8-9). "And as Moses lifted up the serpent in the wilderness, ever so must the Son of man be lifted up: That whosoever believeth in Him should not perish, but have eternal life", (John 3 v.14-15).

All believers in Christ gladly proclaim the coming again of the Lord of glory. Testimony to Him in this present evil world is not in vain. "Light is sown for the righteous and gladness for the upright in heart", (Psalm 97 v.11). Let us pray, therefore, that the Church will yet again prosper when many "shall ask the way to Zion with their faces thitherward, saying, come and let us join ourselves to the Lord in a perpetual covenant that shall not be forgotten", (Jer. 50 v.5).

The Word of the Lord is true, says the Psalmist, (Psalm 119 v.160).
The saving knowledge of Christ, Who saves through faith alone, is given to us through the inspired Word of God. Everything that pertains to life and godliness comes through the true knowledge of Him, which is given to us in Holy Writ. "Study to shew thyself approved unto God, a workman that needeth not to be ashamed, rightly dividing the Word of Truth", (2 Tim. 2 v.15).

CHAPTER SEVEN

LEADERSHIP AND RESPONSIBILITY IN THE CHURCH

The Glory of the Visible Church

The Qualifications required of Leaders

The Responsibilities to be Undertaken

Shared Leadership: Elders and Deacons

Restoring Leadership to its Rightful Place

LEADERSHIP AND RESPONSIBILITY IN THE CHURCH

The word of God tells us that Christ's Church is glorious. Yet, today, as we look around and observe the Church, that glory is thickly veiled by advanced decadence, unwarranted leadership, wrong officers, extreme feebleness, and many of the members are only nominal 'Christians' --- a name to live, but dead. Many Churches have adulterated the Gospel of God and diluted the Bible. But the true Church is where the truth is, and sound doctrine will be its foremost mark. By and large many people do not much nowadays go to Church to learn about God from the preaching of His infallible Word, but rather they wish to be entertained and tranquillised. The glory of God and the authority of His Word are no longer central, so much so, that the Christian Church in our day is in a very sad and sorry plight.

God's rule is overthrown by evil and wicked men, and women are brazenly occupying positions in the Church that are an effrontery to God and a rebellious denial of His Word.

The world, of course, has ever opposed the Church, and always will. The struggle between the seed of the woman and the seed of the serpent is not only perennial but perpetual. If the Church was strong, active, and vibrant, as it ought to be for righteousness sake, the world would the more vehemently oppose and persecute the faithful followers of Christ. By and large, the Church of our day has lost the blessing because of its worldliness, tolerance of sin, doctrinal indifference, and relegation of the Word of God.

When the Ark of the Covenant had been taken by the Philistines, the widowed wife of the priest Phinehas give birth to a son, and she named him, "Ichabod", saying "The glory is departed from Israel", (1 Sam. 4 v.21). The question may well be asked whether today the glory has not departed from the Church. It would seem that 'Ichabod' had better be written over its gates. Yet, unbelievable though it may seem, applicable to the Church of all ages, and of this present age, is the exultation of the Psalmist: "the Lord loveth the gates of Zion more than all the dwellings of Jacob. Glorious things are spoken of thee, O city of God", (Psalm 87 v.2-3).

In the counsel of God the Church existed from eternity and comprises the communion of believers, God's elect people, of every generation throughout all time, the countless number of all the redeemed who are written in the Lamb's Book of Life from before the foundation of the world. They shall "dwell in the house of the Lord forever", (Psalm 23 v.6), in the Home of "many mansions", (John 14 v.2), for all eternity, "in the holy city, new Jerusalem . . . . . prepared as a bride adorned for her husband", (Rev. 21 v.2). Heaven has no need of the light "of the sun, neither of the moon, to shine in it: for the glory of God did lighten it, and the Lamb is the light thereof. And the nations of them which are saved shall walk in the light of it . . . . . And the gates of it shall not be shut at all by day: for there shall be no night there . . . . . And there shall in no wise enter into it any thing that defileth, neither whatsoever worketh abomination, or maketh a lie: but they which are written in the Lamb's Book of Life", (Rev. 21 v.23-27).

The Glory of the Visible Church

It follows that the glory of the visible Church of Jesus Christ on earth should be reflected in its leadership and members, by showing its loyalty to Jesus Christ, honouring and obeying His Word, and acknowledging Him as its Saviour, King, and Head: "that in all things He might have the pre-eminence", (Col. 1 v.18). There is no other institution in all the world that is comparable to the true Christian Church. Out of all the countless organisations in the world, the Great Redeemer fondly claims only the Church as His very own. "Upon this Rock I will build My Church; and the gates of hell shall not prevail against it", (Matt. 16 v.18). The Church alone "is His body, the fullness of Him that filleth all in all", (Eph. 1 v.23).

We, therefore, as disciples of Christ, must strive, without sacrifice of Truth, in obedience to The Scripture, to restore, preserve, and maintain the proper witness, Biblical structures, and Scriptural leadership of the Church today according to the pattern God has laid down in His Word. In order that it may progress in holiness and continue "stedfastly in the apostles' doctrine and fellowship", (Acts 2 v.42), the Church must delve more deeply into the truth of God's Holy Word. "Sanctify them through Thy Truth: Thy Word is truth", (John 17 v.17).

The Church is the body of Christ. "Christ is the Head of the Church: and He is the Saviour of the body", (Eph. 5 v.23). The Church's testimony and witness should be clear and distinctive. Christ is its only Redeemer, Mediator, and Head, and all who believe in Him are its members. As His people we should harken diligently unto his Word. "Buy the truth, and sell it not; also wisdom, and instruction, and understanding", (Prov. 23 v.23). "The fear of the Lord is the beginning of wisdom", and therefore the beginning of goodness, charity, love and holiness: "A good understanding have all they that do His commandments: His praise endureth for ever", (Psalm 111 v.10).

All who know the Lord should be subject to God. Those who are rebellious disturb the peace and order of the Church. To fail to obey the Word of God will bring compromise and misery. Scripture commands, "My Son, fear thou the Lord . . . . . and meddle not with them that are given to change", (Prov. 24 v.21). The prophet Zechariah bids us to "love the truth and peace", (Zech. 8 v.19).

We are commanded to seek the peace of the Church, but not at the expense of truth. Truth according to the Scriptures is an absolute prerequisite of peace that is truly peace. For that reason the Bible calls upon Church members to manifest their harmony "with all lowliness and meekness, with longsuffering, forbearing one another in love; Endeavouring to keep the unity of the Spirit in the bond of peace", (Eph. 4 v.2-3).

The sin of schism is greatly deplored amongst genuine believers which Paul denounces in 1 Cor. 12 v.25: "That there should be no schism in the body; but that the members should have the same care one for another". The evils of division, discord, dissention and self-will are too commonly found among professing Christians: "debates, envyings, wraths, strifes, backbittings, whisperings, swellings, tumults", (2 Cor. 12 v.20). Schism is a rendering of the body of Christ which damages the church and hinders edification and godly witness.

In such circumstances it is the duty of the Church leadership to exercise due and proper discipline according to the Scriptures and to be faithful in reproving sin. This gives much cause for humiliation, lamentation and repentance. The members of the body of Christ should not be schismatics whereby divisions, disunity and separate interests show their ugly heads in doubtful disputations (Rom. 14 v.1) "whereof cometh envy, strife, railings, evil, surmisings, perverse disputings of men of corrupt minds, and destitute of the truth, supposing that gain is godliness: from such withdraw thyself", (1 Tim. 6 v.4-5).

We are to follow the truth in love and be sincere in love to our fellow-believers. The members of the church should be closely united by the strongest bonds of love, peace, affection and goodwill in the Gospel: "Speaking the truth in love, may grow up into Him in all things, which is the Head, even Christ", (Eph. 4 v.15). When Christians are cold towards one another, they will be careless and unconcerned for one another. Such behaviour is the work of the flesh (Gal. 5 v.19) and a breach of Christian charity.

Schism and division then are an expression of self-will, whereas heresy tends to the setting up of sects that are built on error and false teaching, contrary to God's revealed truth. "A man that is an heretick after the first and second admonition reject; knowing that he that is such is subverted, and sinneth, being condemned of himself",

(Titus 3 v.10-11). The Church's task and responsibility, therefore, is to declare "all the counsel of God" (Acts 20 v.28) for the edification of His people, and the worldwide proclamation of the Gospel when "the earth shall be full of the knowledge of the Lord, as the waters cover the sea", (Isaiah 11 v.9).

The Church that has grown cold and indifferent to the Truth of God, is on its way out. A Church that tolerates error is sin, and because of its disobedience to the truths of the Word of God, ceases to be a true Church of Jesus Christ by virtue of its denial of The Scripture. The sole concern and mission of the Church should be to hold high the torch of Scripture Truth in the midst of "a perverse and crooked generation", (Deut. 32 v.5). "Go ye therefore, and teach all nations, baptising them in the name of the Father, and of the Son, and of the Holy Ghost: Teaching them to observe all things whatsoever I have commanded you: and, lo, I am with you alway, even unto the end of the world", (Matt. 28 v.19-20).

There is a crying need today for another spiritual awakening, another Biblical reformation and revival, within a decadent and decaying Church, that the Holy Spirit will bring us back again to honour His Word, and draw sinners nigh unto God, to serve Him, and to follow Him, as did the Bereans of old, "in that they received the Word with all readiness of mind, and searched the Scriptures daily, whether those things were so", (Acts 17 v.11).

The Qualifications required of Leaders

It is not surprising that in First Timothy, one of the important Pastoral Epistles, very specific instructions are given concerning the kind of men who should be invited to hold positions of responsibility in the Church on earth.

God's people, men and women, need to understand God's commands, which we have already emphasised demands knowing His Word of

Truth. "Study to show thyself approved unto God, a workman that needeth not to be ashamed, rightly dividing the Word of Truth", (2 Tim. 2 v.15). By so doing we shall be enabled by grace to lay His Word up in our hearts, allowing His Word to dwell in us richly, and thus practise it in our lives. "Let the Word of Christ dwell in you richly in all wisdom; teaching and admonishing one another in psalms and hymns and spiritual songs, singing with grace in your hearts to the Lord" (Col. 3 v.16). (See Appendix One).

Before looking at the qualifications of leaders in the Church, we shall briefly consider the importance of the role and the dominant thrust of the minister, who is the teaching elder to explain the Scriptures and to help to make God's Word alive to the people. "So they read in the Book in the law of God distinctly, and gave the sense, and caused them to understand the reading", (Neh. 8 v.8).

The whole objective of explaining and applying the teaching of the Bible is to illustrate the truths of God with other Scripture, so that His revelation may lodge in the minds and hearts of believers and bring greater obedience and faithfulness in life and service to the glory of our great sovereign Lord.

First Timothy, as already stated, along with Second Timothy and Titus, belongs to the group of inspired Writings known as the Pastoral Epistles. These are so named because they were addressed to two of Paul's dear sons in the faith, Timothy and Titus, who had pastoral duties. Timothy was in charge of the Church at Ephesus, and Titus of those on the island of Crete.

The Pastoral Epistles yield valuable insights into the heart of Biblical teaching concerning practical matters of Church life and organisation. The public worship of God, the selection and qualifications of Church leaders, pastoral duties, public ministry, doctrinal truths, how to confront sin in the Church, and the role of women, are among the matters discussed. In fact, that is the main purpose of the Apostle in writing First Timothy: "These things write I unto thee, hoping to come unto thee shortly: But if I tarry long, that thou mayest know how thou oughtest to behave thyself in the house of God, which is the Church of the living God, the pillar and ground of the Truth", (1 Tim. 3 v.14-15).

The Apostle Paul was writing to Timothy about Church matters and how "to behave thyself in the house of God, which is the Church of the living God, the pillar and ground of the Truth", (1Tim. 3 v.15). When Church codes and manuals do not concur, or do not agree, with the teaching of the Word of God, the Scriptures must take precedence, and the people of God must yield obedience to Divine Truth rather than obey the laws of ecclesiastical courts, which often are based on the laws of man: "which all are to perish with the using, after the commandments and doctrines of men", (Col. 2 v.22). "Howbeit in vain do they worship Me, teaching for doctrines the commandments of men", (Mark 7 v.7).

There is no matter more important in the Church than that of securing right leadership for the work of God. God's work is weak or strong according to the quality of those who are in positions of responsibility as ministers, elders, and deacons.

The ministry, effectiveness, and testimony of any Church is largely a reflection of its leaders. So important is it that those who hold office in the Church be highly qualified spiritually that the detailed list of their specific qualifications is given twice in Paul's Letters, here in First Timothy and Titus. There is an inseparable link between the character of a Church and the quality of its leadership. Leaders must set a good and godly example for the members to follow.

What then is the standard that God requires concerning the qualifications of leaders in the Church --- ministers, elders, and deacons? What kind of men are they to be? Remember, as discussed earlier, it is clear from Scripture, that women are not to be admitted into any position of leadership or teaching as elders or deacons. "This is a true saying, If a man desire the office of a bishop, he desireth a good work", (1 Tim. 3 v.1). In an earlier chapter we have discussed the Biblical meaning of "bishop", --- "overseer". Among the individual qualifications against which all Church leaders are to be measured, are the following: -

(1) He must be a man whose reputation is blameless: "a bishop must then be blameless", (1 Tim. 3 v.2). This, of course, does not mean, "perfect", for no man is perfect, otherwise there would be no ministers, elders, or deacons. Christ was the only perfect man that ever trod this earth, in Him was no sin, He "knew no sin", but God "made Him to be sin for us, that we might be made the righteousness of God in Him", (2 Cor. 5 v.21). But verse 7 carefully explains what is meant by "blameless": "Moreover he must have a good report of them which are without; lest he fall into reproach and the snare of the devil", (1 Tim. 3 v.7). This means to be "above reproach", and to have a clear testimony, not only before the Church, but also before the world: "For none of us liveth to himself, and no man dieth to himself", (Rom. 14 v.7).

(2) He must be a man of unquestioned moral integrity: "the husband of one wife", (1 Tim. 3 v.2). This does not mean that a leader must be married only once, nor that he must not be a widower. It means that he must not be a polygamist, and more than this, that he must be a man of unquestioned morality, especially in regard to his relations with the opposite sex. There must be no immoral relationships or impropriety of any kind whatsoever. No one whose marriage relationship is problematic or doubtful or questionable, or whose attitude towards the opposite sex is careless or frivolous should ever be given a position of leadership and responsibility in any part of God's work.

(3) He must be a man of Christian and spiritual discipline: "vigilant, sober, of good behaviour, given to hospitality, apt to teach; Not given to wine, no striker, not greedy of filthy lucre; but patient, not a brawler, not covetous", (1 Tim. 3 v.2-3). There are a number of things here that the Apostle specifically spells out concerning the qualities of the overseer's character.

The word "vigilant", means "circumspect", "temperate", "disciplined": "See then that ye walk circumspectly, not as fools, but as wise", (Eph. 5 v.15). He is to be one who is well-disciplined and knows how to correctly order his priorities. Such a man has a sure and steady mind, he is a person who is serious about spiritual things. His mind will be controlled by God's truth, not the whims of the flesh. Jesus Christ will be pre-eminent.

The word "sober", means "self-controlled"; and "of good behaviour", means "modest". His well-disciplined mind leads to a well-disciplined life. If he cannot order his own life and family, how can he bring order to the Church", (1 Tim. 3 v.5).

"Not given to wine", literally means "not one who lingers by the wine". The Apostle does not say a leader must be a total abstainer, because wine was extensively used in those days, and especially for health reasons: "use a little wine for thy stomach's sake and thine often infirmities", (1 Tim. 5 v.23). Paul does say that a leader must be temperate. In these days, however, it is essential for all leaders to be men of firm convictions and of God-glorifying habits with regard to all matters of behaviour and conduct.

The words "no striker", means "not quarrelsome", "not contentious", with the implication that a leader must not be a person who is very easily upset or one who easily flies into a temper. A leader in the Church must not be one who reacts to difficulty with physical violence: "not a giver of blows", "not a striker". "The servant of the Lord must not strive . . . . . in meekness instructing those that oppose themselves; if God peradventure will give them repentance to the acknowledging of the truth", (2 Tim. 2 v.24-25).

The word "patient", means "gentle", "kind", and "peaceful". A leader is one who is considerate, genial, forbearing, and gracious. He is one who easily pardons human failure, and remembers the good, and not the evil of those "that they may recover themselves out of the snare of the devil", (2 Tim. 2 v.26).

The words "not a brawler", have the meaning "not arrogant", "not overbearing", "not a stubborn controversialist". This refers to not being a quarrelsome person which only results in disunity and disharmony, seriously hindering the effectiveness of leadership in the Church.

The words "given to hospitality", mean that a leader should not only have an open house, but an open heart. "Distributing to the necessity of saints; given to hospitality", (Rom. 12 v.13). This does not refer to entertaining friends, but showing hospitality to strangers, which quite literally means "to love strangers": "Be not forgetful to entertain strangers", (Heb. 13 v.2). The door of the Christian home ought to be open to all who come in need. This is especially true of the overseer, who must be available, approachable, and open-handed to strangers, and ready to entertain them according to his ability. He is to be one who does not set his heart upon the wealth of the world and who is a true lover of his brethren with a large and generous spirit like Onesiphorus: "The Lord give mercy unto the house of Onesiphorus; for he oft refreshed me, and was not ashamed of my chain", (2 Tim. 1 v. 16).

The words "apt to teach", is the only qualification that relates specifically to the giftedness and function of an overseer. He is to be one who is able and willing to communicate to others the knowledge which God has given him, one who is fit to teach and ready to take all opportunities of giving instruction. In other words, he must have some aptitude, he must be skilled, he must have ability. One who is going to lead others must have some gift. To preach and teach God's Word is the primary task of the teaching elder: "give attendance to reading, to exhortation, to doctrine --- for in doing this thou shalt both save thyself, and them that hear thee", (1 Tim. 4 v.13, 16). The criteria of identifying a man as a skilled teacher are, (1) he must have the gift of teaching; (2) he must have deep understanding of doctrine; (3) he must have an attitude of humility; (4) he must be marked by a life of holiness; (5) he must be a diligent student of Scripture; (6) he must avoid error; and (7) he must have strong courage and consistent convictions. Ministers, pastors, and elders must be able to preach and to teach to exercise their pastoral gifts. Deacons, likewise, must be able to plan or organise or understand the temporal affairs of the Church. But the supreme qualifications for leadership are spiritual. They must be men who are "full of the Holy Ghost and wisdom – full of faith", (Acts 6 v.3-5), who must not abandon the Truth or shipwreck their faith.

The words "not greedy of filthy lucre", mean "not covetous", which denotes that a man's character can often be judged by his attitude towards money and earthly possessions. If a man has a Judas-like-attitude: "This he said, not that he cared for the poor; but because he was a thief, and had the bag, and bare what was put therein", (John 12 v.6); or if there is any suspicion of sharp practice in his business affairs, he should not be considered for any position of responsibility or leadership in the Church. It is a perverse corruption of the ministry to be in it for money. Love of money is what is at the heart of all motivation for false teachers. "Having eyes full of adultery, and that cannot cease from sin; beguiling unstable souls: an heart they have exercised with covetous practices; cursed children: Which have forsaken the right way, and are gone astray . . . . . who loved the wages of unrighteousness", (2 Peter 2 v.14-15).

(4) He must be a man who successfully manages his own household: "One that ruleth well his own house, having his children in subjection with all gravity; For if a man know not how to rule his own house, how shall he take care of the Church of God", (1 Tim. 3 v.4-5). If a man is unable to manage well his own family and domestic affairs, he cannot be expected to be a suitable leader to manage the sacred affairs of the Church. "Brethren, if a man be overtaken in a fault, ye which are spiritual, restore such an one in the spirit of meekness; considering thyself, lest thou also be tempted. Bear ye one another's burdens, and so fulfil the law of Christ", (Gal. 6 v.1-2). Integrity is living what you teach and preach. Those who would lead the congregation to Christlikeness of character must be a pattern of godly behaviour for God's people to follow.

(5) He must be a man who is spiritually taught and mature: "Not a novice, lest being lifted up with pride he fall into the condemnation of the devil . . . . . Holding the mystery of the faith in a pure conscience. And let these

also first be proved; then let them use the office", of minister, elder, or deacon, "being found blameless", (1 Tim. 3 v.6, 9-10). We learn from these verses that a young convert should never be pressed into responsible service, as this would do harm to the convert and to the work of the Church. Leaders need to be spiritually strong and have a firm grip on the truth of God. They must have discernment in spiritual matters, and be able to distinguish things that differ. As verse 10 suggests, potential leaders should serve for a probationary period, so that their gifts and qualities may be tested. Only spiritually mature men are qualified for leadership.

(6) He must be a man of obvious humility: "lest being lifted up with pride he fall into the condemnation of the devil", (1 Tim. 3 v.6). How important is this supreme requirement for a leader. The devil fell through pride, and how easy it is for any one of us to fall in the same way. "He hath shewed thee, O man, what is good; and what doth the Lord require of thee, but to do justly, and to love mercy, and to walk humbly with thy God", (Micah 6 v.8). The phrase, "lest being lifted up with pride", "conceited", derives from a Greek word meaning "smoke". Putting an immature person into a position of leadership is apt to puff him up, to put his head in the clouds, thus placing him in grave danger of sinful pride. "Pride goeth before destruction, and an haughty spirit before a fall", (Prov. 16 v.18). The opposite of pride is humility, which is the mark of a spiritually mature leader. God expects every servant's life to be a positive testimony to the watching world. "Walk in wisdom toward them that are without, redeeming the time", (Col. 4 v.5).

(7) He must be a man who has the right kind of wife: "Even so must their wives be grave, not slanderers, sober,

faithful in all things", (1 Tim. 3 v.11). The wholehearted support of a true helpmeet in the work of the ministry is most vital in the Lord's service with all the blessings of that Covenant which is "ordered in all things, and sure", (2 Sam. 23 v.5). A man's wife can make him ineligible for the ministry, the pastorate, the eldership, the diaconate, or any position of responsibility including leadership in theological education and teaching students in the training of candidates for the Christian ministry of Bible-believing Churches. When God raises up people to serve in His Vineyard, He looks for those whose hearts are right with Him. His concern is not about talents, or abilities, but spiritual virtue. The leaders' wives must "be grave", which means "serious" and "dignified", and people should hold them in awe because of their spiritual devotion. They must not be "slanderers", which means, not "malicious gossips". They must control their tongues, and be not given to false reporting or mischievous gestures or rumour. They must be "sober", which means "self-controlled", not drunkards, "but use a little wine for thy stomachs sake and thine often infirmities", (1 Tim 5 v.23). "And be not drunk with wine wherein is access; but be filled with the Spirit", (Eph. 5 v.18). Finally leaders' wives must be "faithful in all things", which means reliable and absolutely trustworthy. They must not be seekers of 'sordid gain' or lovers of 'filthy lucre', but must be faithful in every dimension of responsibility and duty in life.

These, then, as described above, are the Biblical standards and requirements concerning qualifications for leadership in the Church --- not that of man, not that of Paul, but God's. By following the Scriptural pattern what an incentive there is to faithfulness in service "for they that have used the office" of leadership well, "purchase to themselves a good degree, and great boldness in faith, which is in Christ Jesus", (1 Tim 3 v.13). Every faithful, diligent, and obedient leader of the Church will be rewarded at the Judgement Seat of Christ. Those who serve in humility will be exalted by God, and they will see His power and grace operating and emboldening them for even greater service with courage, steadfastness, and faithfulness. "Therefore, my beloved brethren, be ye steadfast, unmoveable, always abounding in the work of the Lord, forasmuch as ye know that your labour is not in vain in the Lord", (1 Cor. 15 v.58).

The Responsibilities to be Undertaken

Unfortunately, many Churches have a wrong view of ecclesiology. Being terribly delinquent in adequately articulating this doctrine, a great deal of confusion, error, and un-Biblical thinking surrounds the topic of eldership.

According to the New Testament, the elders duties and responsibilities are as follows:-

(1) to lead, direct, govern, manage, and care for the Church: "Let the elders that rule well be counted worthy of double honour", (1 Tim. 5 v.17), as good stewards and overseers of the household of God.

(2) to feed, exhort, and admonish the saints in sound doctrine. They must be "able to teach", (1 Tim.3 v.2), and preach, especially those who labour in the Word and doctrine --- the 'teaching' elder. "For the Scripture saith, Thou shalt not muzzle the ox that treadeth out the corn. And, The labourer is worthy of his reward", (1 Tim. 5 v.17-18). They must not shun to declare "all the counsel of God", (Acts 20 v.27).

(3) to protect the flock of God from false teachers, judge and correct doctrinal issues. They must have enough knowledge of the Bible to be able to refute false teaching.

> Paul instructs Titus to "set in order things that are wanting and ordain elders in every city . . . . . as the steward's of God . . . . . holding fast the faithful Word . . . . . be able by sound doctrine both to exhort and to convince the gainsayers", (Titus 1 v.5-9).

(4) to visit the sick and pray: "Is any sick among you? Let him call for the elders of the Church; and let them pray over him, anointing him with oil in the name of the Lord", (James 5 v.14). The exhortation here is to take care of the weak, infirm, and the needy of the flock --- visiting the sick, comforting the bereaved, strengthening the aged, providing counsel and attending to the inner life of the congregation.

In Biblical terminology, elders are to shepherd, to oversee, and to take care of the Church. For a Biblical eldership to function effectively, it requires men who are firmly committed to living out our Lord's principles of discipleship, obeying His commands, seeking "first the Kingdom of God, and His righteousness", (Matt. 6 v.33) --- men who have presented themselves as living sacrifices and view themselves as servants of the Lord Jesus Christ. "I beseech you therefore, brethren, by the mercies of God, that ye present your bodies a living sacrifice, holy, acceptable unto God, which is your reasonable service. And be not conformed to this world: but be ye transformed by the renewing of your mind, that ye may prove what is that good, and acceptable, and perfect, will of God", (Rom. 12 v.1-2). The only way to maintain a godly family life and employment as overseers in the Church, is by self-sacrifice, self-discipline, faith, perseverance, and hard work by the enabling power of the Holy Spirit.

Shared Leadership: Elders and Deacons

Shared leadership between Elders and Deacons is evidenced by the appointment of the Seven to take care of the widows and the material needs in the daily ministration of the Church, to allow the Twelve to give themselves continually to prayer and to the ministry of the Word. Based on all the Scriptural evidence, the deacons also, like the elders, formed a collective leadership. All such leadership is required to be patterned after the New Testament model which demands high moral and spiritual values. (Acts 6, 1 Tim. 3, 1 Tim. 5, Titus 1, etc.).

The structure of eldership in Church government is as basic as the family unit. Those who are gifted in teaching and empowered to preach are regarded as 'first among equals', (1 Tim. 5 v.17); all are labourers together as equal partners in the work of the Gospel. The same principle holds true among deacons when exercising good stewardship as "chosen men of their own company", (Acts 15 v.22).

There is much about Biblical eldership, and Biblical diaconate, that offends many Church-going people today. For some nothing is more objectionable than the Biblical concept of an all-male leadership. Jesus trained and appointed twelve men, not six men and six women, whom He called "apostles", (Luke 6 v.13). Jesus' choice of an all-male apostolate affirmed the creation order as presented in Genesis 2 v.18-25, in complete obedience and submission to His Father's will. The Biblical pattern of male leadership continued throughout the New Testament era. Regarding the marriage relationship, the apostles Paul and Peter could not have stated more pointedly the Divine order of the husband-wife relationship. (Eph. 5, 1 Peter 3).

Just as the Bible teaches male headship in the family, so too, it teaches male headship in the Church, (1 Tim. 2 and 3). A major aspect of the Church's social arrangement concerns the behaviour of women in the congregation. In the Church at Ephesus, as a result of false teaching Christian women were acting contrary to the Divine order, and so as to counter this improper female conduct in the Church, Paul restates the Christian principles of the woman's role, (1 Tim. 2 v.11-14). Immediately following this rebuke, Paul clearly describes the qualification for those who oversee the Church, (1 Tim. 3 v.1-7).

There is no warrant in Scripture for female leadership over the male. Multitudes of Churches today are in error, seemingly oblivious in the case of some, while the liberals wilfully disparage and reject the Biblical requirements for their leaders.

Restoring Leadership to its Rightful Place

The overriding concern of the New Testament in relation to Church leadership is to ensure that the right kind of men will serve as elders and deacons. The offices of God's Church are not honorary positions, nor are they to be filled with men, just because they attend Church well, senior in years, good friends, rich donors, big personalities, or indeed graduate professionals. The Church offices of elder and deacon are open to all men who meet the apostolic qualifications and Biblical requirements, as outlined in 1Timothy 3, Titus 1, and 1 Peter 5, etc.

When we speak of the elder's qualifications, most people wrongly think that these qualifications are different from those of the minister. The New Testament, however, has no separate standards for professional clergy and lay elders. The reason is simple. There are not three different offices --- pastors/ministers, elders, and deacons. There are only two offices --- elders, and deacons. A true desire to lead the Church of God is always a Spirit-generated desire. It is God's will, and God's arrangement, that matter. The only men who qualify for eldership are those whom the Holy Spirit calls according to His Word, and gives the motivation and gifts for the task.

New Testament, Christlike, elders, are to be servant leaders, not dictators. Elders are to choose a life of service on behalf of others in a humble and loving manner. The Apostle Peter warns against abusive, lordly leadership: "Neither as being lord's over God's heritage, but being ensamples to the flock", (1 Peter 5 v.3). "Yea, all of you be subject one to another, and be clothed with humility", (1 Peter 5 v.5). "God resisteth the proud", because they are like the devil, enemies to

Himself and to His Kingdom among men. He "giveth grace to the humble"; He will give more grace, more wisdom, faith, holiness, and humility. "Humble yourselves therefore under the mighty hand of God, that He may exalt you in due time", (1 Peter 5 v.6).

"Serving the Lord with all humility" implies that there is no room for "pride" or being "conceited", (1 Tim. 3 v.6). Elders must humbly relate and lovingly submit to one another, be kind and patient with their fellow colleagues, defer to one another, and speak their minds openly in truth and love, (Eph. 4 v.15). True elders do not command the consciences of their brethren but appeal to their brethren to faithfully follow God's Word. Out of love for Christ, true elders suffer and bear the brunt of difficult people and problems so that the lambs are not bruised. The elders often bear the misunderstandings and sins of other people so that the Church may live in peace.

Christians who profess the Bible to be God's infallible, inerrant and all-sufficient Word, agree that they must establish their Church practices and doctrines according to the teaching of Holy Scripture. Many contemporary scholars and present-day Church liberals, even amongst so-called 'evangelicals', say that the Bible is ambiguous or silent on matters regarding Church government and the role of women. Church government by elders is plainly and amply set forth in the Word of God. The New Testament is very clear on the doctrine of the eldership, and vividly records evidence of oversight by elders in all the Early Churches over a wide geographical and culturally diverse area --- from Jerusalem to Rome.

The Church is the people of God with a unique character, mission, and purpose, often described as the body, the bride, the temple, the flock, and the family. It is a close-knit family of brothers and sisters in the Lord. Christ is the only King and Head of His Church, and the New Testament pattern of Church government by elders enhances the loving, humble-servant character of the Christian family. Biblical eldership guards the Church and promotes the pre-eminence and position of Christ as Ruler, Head, Lord, Master, High Priest, and

King, and the form of government of the New Testament Church reflects this distinctive, fundamental, Christian truth.

The Early Church was truly Christ-centred, Christ-dependant, and Christ-honouring. There is only one flock and one Pastor (John 10 v.16), one body and one Head (Col. 1 v.18), one holy priesthood and one great High Priest (Heb. 4 v.14), one brotherhood and one Elder Brother (Rom. 8 v.29), one building and one Cornerstone (1 Peter 2 v. 5), one Mediator, one God, and one Lord (1 Tim. 2 v.5), Jesus Christ is the Chief Shepherd, all others are His undershepherds (1 Peter 5 v.4).

Lord Acton, an English historian once said, "Power tends to corrupt, and absolute power corrupts absolutely". Because of our Biblical beliefs in the reality of sin, Satan, and human depravity, we should understand well why the people in positions of power are easily corrupted. The collective leadership of a Biblical eldership provides a formal structure for genuine accountability. Church leaders can be lazy, forgetful, fearful, or too busy to fulfil their responsibilities. Thus they need colleagues in ministry to whom they are answerable for their work. We have all blind spots, eccentricities, and deficiencies. We can see the flaws so 'clearly' in others but not in ourselves. These flaws distort our judgement, deceive us, and can even destroy us.

The New Testament structure of Church government by elders is a fixed apostolic institution, (Titus 1 v.5), and Paul's instruction to Titus establishes a Divine directive that should be followed by Christians today. The Biblical teaching about elders and the pattern of Church government in the apostolic age is the norm for Churches in every age. We would do well to heed the all-sufficiency of Scripture and obey its commands in regard to the oversight and rule of the Church. All heresies and deviations in the Church spring from the abandonment of Scripture, and as the Reformers re-discovered and concluded in the sixteenth century, the Churches established by the Apostles in the New Testament era, remain the valid models for Churches of all times and places.

We have no right, then, to alter, substitute, or take anything away from the God-given mandate in Scripture for eldership. We must be convinced and committed to make eldership, and the diaconate work effectively in the Church for God's glory. If one was to ask, for example, does marriage work? --- many people would perhaps answer that it doesn't appear to be working. So should we then discard the institution of marriage and look for something better? The answer is an emphatic 'no'. The marriage institution is God's will for the human race as revealed in the Bible. So, in order to make marriage work, we must first believe it to be a Biblical teaching and then be committed to making it work. Only then will marriage work. The same conditions apply and hold true for implementing and working a Biblical eldership. We must be convinced and believe it is Scriptural, and be committed by the Holy Spirit's help in obedience to the Divine will as revealed in His Word, to making it work effectively to the glory of God. "The will of the Lord be done", (Acts 21 v.14).

CHAPTER EIGHT

WOMEN IN THE HOME

Praise of a Virtuous Woman

Childbearing and Motherhood

Homemaking, Love and Friendship

Duties and Responsibilities of Wife and Mother

Discipline, Relationships and Contentment

Building on a Firm Foundation

Family the Basic Unit of Society

Real Love is Giving

The Evils of Society

God's Design for the Home

WOMEN IN THE HOME

In coming to this aspect of the subject before us, the Word of God is most precise as to the main role of women in society.

In the Old Testament a holy woman is described as one who works at home, provides for her family and their necessities, is kind, knows nothing of idleness, appreciates her husband, and above all, fears God.

"Every wise woman buildeth her house: but the foolish plucketh it down with her hands", (Prov. 14 v.1). In Proverbs the wise woman and the foolish woman are brought before us in vivid contrast. The wise woman will guide her household in the right way by proper counsel and good example. She will direct her steps in accordance with the Word of God and will establish her house on the immovable foundation of Holy Scripture and righteousness. The foolish woman through her evil behaviour, bad temper, and unworthy instruction, lays up sorrow for herself and grief for her husband and children. The manner of life proves whether one is really sincere and walking with God or not. The testimony of the mouth and lips is worthless if contradicted by the behaviour and conduct. The one who fears the Lord with reverence and obedience will be characterised by godliness and faithfulness. "He that saith he abideth in Him ought himself also so to walk, even as He walked", (1 John 2 v.6). Perverse words and actions opposed to His revealed will in the Scriptures, prove that God is really despised and not honoured. It is a complete contradiction to talk of reverence while obeying the dictates of a selfish, carnal nature: such is absolute hypocrisy. This was Saul's great snare. The prophet Samuel summarised the issue of obedience when he said, "Behold, to obey is better than sacrifice, and to harken than the fat of rams", (1 Sam. 15 v.22).

The man or woman who loves instruction and welcomes discipline desires the truth and values true knowledge, whatever channel it may come through. The Book of Proverbs tells us that a brawling and contentious woman hates reproof and correction. An unbridled will is characteristic of one who delights in wicked devices. The face of the Lord shines on the good woman whose foot is firmly established "in all wisdom and spiritual understanding", (Col. 1 v.9). A discreet and prudent wife is a choice gift of God's providence to a man. "A virtuous woman is a crown to her husband: but she that maketh ashamed is as rottenness in his bones", (Prov. 12 v.4). It would be a mistake to limit the word "virtuous" to the thought of chastity. It is much more than that. The virtuous woman is one in whom all noble qualities shine, as fully described in Proverbs 31. Such a woman, such a wife, is indeed a crown to her husband.

Praise of a Virtuous Woman

"Who can find a virtuous woman? For her price is far above rubies. The heart of her husband doth safely trust in her, so that he shall have no need of spoil. She will do him good and not evil all the days of her life. She seeketh wool, and flax, and worketh willingly with her hands. She is like the merchants' ships; she bringeth her food from afar. She riseth also while it is yet night, and giveth meat to her household, and a portion to her maidens. She considereth a field, and buyeth it: with the fruit of her hands she planteth a vineyard. She girdeth her loins with strength, and strengtheneth her arms. She perceiveth that her merchandise is good: her candle goeth not out by night. She layeth her hands to the spindle, and her hands hold the distaff. She stretcheth out her hand to the poor; yea, she reacheth forth her hands to the needy. She is not afraid of the snow for her household: for all her household are clothed with scarlet. She maketh herself coverings of tapestry; her clothing is silk and purple. Her husband is known in the gates, when he sitteth among the elders of the land. She maketh fine linen, and selleth it; and delivereth girdles unto the merchant. Strength and honour are her clothing; and she shall rejoice in time to come. She openeth her mouth with wisdom; and in her tongue is the law of kindness. She looketh well to the ways of her household, and eateth not the bread of idleness. Her children arise up, and call her blessed; her husband also, and he praiseth her. Many daughters have done virtuously, but thou excelleth them all. Favour is deceitful, and beauty is vain: but a woman that feareth the Lord, she shall be praised. Give her of the fruit of her hands; and let her own works praise her in the gates", (Prov. 31 v.10-31).

Indeed, such a woman needs praising. The New Testament verifies that nothing has changed from the old dispensation regarding the woman's role in the home and in marriage. Clear directions are given as to how to live in this present evil world. "But speak thou the things which become sound doctrine: That the aged men be sober, grave, temperate, sound in faith, in charity, in patience. The aged women likewise, that they may be in behaviour as becometh holiness, not false accusers, not given to much wine, teachers of good things", (Titus 2 v.1-3).

In the early Church the aged women were to teach the younger women, "to be sober, to love their husbands, to love their children, to be discreet, chaste, keepers at home, good, obedient to their own husbands, that the Word of God be not blasphemed", (Titus 3 v.4-5). This is straightforward language and must not be compromised for the sake of modern society. If we desire to live unto the Lord, then we will do well to please Him. The crucial question is this, as the Shorter Catechism puts it, "What is the chief end of man? Man's chief end is to glorify God and enjoy Him, forever", (Q. & A. No.1). Who is it we are living for, ourselves or God? We are to live for God.

The whole of God's commands are summed up in one word, "LOVE". Jesus said, "Thou shalt love the Lord thy God with all thy heart, and with all thy soul, and with all thy mind. This is the first and great commandment. And the second is like unto it. Thou shalt love thy neighbour as thyself. On these two commandments hang all the law and the prophets", (Matt. 22 v.37-40).

Childbearing and Motherhood

In regard to the high calling of motherhood, it clearly states in 1 Tim. 2 v.15, that women "shall be saved in child bearing, if they continue in faith and charity and holiness with sobriety". As we have already seen, one of the greatest issues in our society today is the status and role of women. The oppression of women in many places is all too common and often held in contempt as second-rate individuals. 'Feminist' activists have greatly mistaken the root cause which subject many women to abuse and misery.

It is sin in the man which makes him thoughtless and unkind towards women, and it is sin in the woman that breeds discontentment. "And Adam was not deceived, but the woman being deceived was in the transgression", (1 Tim. 2 v.14). This by no means clears Adam, he walked into the evil rebellion against God with his eyes wide open. His was the deeper sin. But Eve was duped by Satan. The female constitution is generally a confiding simplicity which can become gullibility. This characteristic suits her in the role as a helpmeet for the man.

Drawing attention to her deception at the Fall in the Garden of Eden, reinforces the necessity of her being subject to man. The fall with all its consequences did not arise from her being subject to man. The opposite in fact is the case. When she abandoned her role of submission to Adam, and decided to take matters into her own hands, the Fall came, because she determined to lead man rather than follow. She became a temptress instead of a help. By stepping out of her God-ordained place and rebelling against the Divinely constituted social order, she brought ruin to the world, including womanhood. The influence of the devil and her defiance of man's authority as appointed by God, is at the crux of all human calamity.

The emancipation of women from man's rule by the so-called 'women's rights movement' strikes an axe at God's creation order. "Notwithstanding she shall be saved", (1 Tim. 2 v.15), is not a text on remission of sins but deliverance out of sin-related suffering and oppression. But how are women saved? By joining militant organisations? By demanding equal rights? By proving that women can make it to the top in business, politics, sport, or even the pastorate? By escaping from home and husbands? Never, Never, Never. That approach only adds to her rebellion against her God-given place, namely, motherhood. Our Maker would not allow the human race to perish. The "I will" of Genesis 3 v.15 is the message of grace. Through childbearing, deliverance comes in the birth of Christ as Saviour to break the devil's yoke.

"Notwithstanding she (women) shall be saved in childbearing, if they continue in faith and charity and holiness with sobriety", (1 Tim. 2 v.15). The word "saved" is from the Greek "sozo", from which is derived the common New Testament word for salvation. It can also mean "to rescue", "to preserve safe and unharmed", "to heal", "to set free", or "to deliver from". It appears a number of times in the New Testament without reference to spiritual salvation, in the following examples:-

(1) Matt. 8 v.25, referring to the great storm at sea "Lord, save us: we perish".

(2) Matt. 9 v.21-22, referring to the woman with the issue of blood, she was made "whole".

(3) Matt. 27 v.49, referring to the people standing at the Cross, "let us see whether Elias will come to save Him".

Women are not eternally saved from the wages of sin through "childbearing". Eternal salvation is by grace alone through faith alone in Christ alone. The pain associated with childbirth was the punishment for woman's sin, but the joy and privilege of child rearing and bringing up a righteous seed, delivers women from the stigma of that sin.

Women are far from being second-class citizens because they have the primary responsibility for rearing godly children. Mothers spend much more time with their children than do their fathers, and thus have the greater influence. Fathers cannot know the intimate relationship with their children that their mother establishes from pregnancy, birth, infancy, and early childhood. The point that Paul makes is that while a woman may have led the human race into sin, women have the privilege of leading the race out of sin to godliness.

The calling of women --- not all women (1 Cor. 7 v.25-40), is to raise a godly seed. To that end, they must "continue in faith and charity (love)", where their salvation really rests. And they must continue in "holiness with sobriety", (1 Tim. 2 v.15). "Sobriety" is the same word as in verse 9, which means "discreteness", "discernment" --- freedom from inordinate passions and unrestrained lusts. It is the very appearance, demeanour, and behaviour demanded of believing women in the Church that becomes their deliverance from any inferior status, as they live godly lives and raise godly children. The Scriptures clearly show the roles of the sexes.

It is to woman, not man, that God assigned this high calling. The central attention of Gen. 3 v.15, is upon one seed of the woman, Jesus Christ, Who has delivered the death blow to the head of the serpent on Calvary. He has purchased salvation for all who are redeemed. Childbearing prepared the way of the Lord. In the raising up of many mighty leaders, there was Jochebed, the mother of Moses; Hannah, the mother of Samuel; Manoah's wife, the mother of Samson, who are leading examples. Through their childbearing the course of history has been woven, and a godly seed carries the Gospel to all the earth to gather in God's elect and hasten Christ's return. Appreciating God's purpose, "Adam called his wife's name Eve; because she was the mother of all living", (Gen. 3 v.20).

It is obvious that true motherhood is a noble and high calling. Nothing can replace the care, love, and training of a conscientious mother, in a stable home under the leadership and headship of the husband and father. The world entices women with earthly rewards and influences, careers and fun, travel and glamour, but what a pitiful sight is the woman who perhaps 'has it all together' --- only her children have not turned out well. Sadly, many women have abandoned their highest dignity and hope for lesser things.

The glories of a mother's task and privilege is to oversee the forging of a personality in her sons and daughters. For this the establishment of Christian principles in the home are necessary for the building up of strong character in her offspring --- mentally, physically, socially, and spiritually. Talents are to be developed and trained, virtues must be instilled and encouraged, faults must be patiently corrected, and young sinners are to be evangelised. She is building men and women for the Lord. "Train up a child in the way he should go: and when he is old, he will not depart from it", (Prov. 22 v.6).

God graciously works out His purposes and Christian women in the home display the incalculable value and importance of godly, devoted childrearing and how the Gospel of Christ is the power of God unto salvation. It is a most blessed thing when the seed of the Gospel takes root early in the lives of children. The picture of a plant taking root is used in the Bible to teach us the idea of conversion. When someone's heart is turned from himself and his sinful ways to faith in Christ and devotion to God, it is like a plant which starts to shoot out roots into rich soil so that it can live and take nourishment. There is no way for a child to have life unless God turns him or her out of the way of sin and death into the way of life everlasting. It is the duty of Christian parents to relate and teach the truths of the Word of God to their offspring and prayerfully may they capture the attention of the children, and best of all their hearts to take deep root into the life-giving soil of Jesus as spiritual plants in the garden of the Lord. "Continue in prayer, and watch in the same with thanksgiving", (Col. 4 v.2).

Many women spurn this great task and mighty responsibility, preferring instead the halls of fame and government, the materialistic ranch and empire, or the busy office and prestige. There is no more important and demanding work in all the world than motherhood and the raising of a godly seed. The woman's hope, the Church's hope, the worlds hope, is joined to childbearing with continuance in faith, love, and holiness. What a calling, and when taken seriously and prayerfully, God will bless the generation to come.

By working at it spiritually, the Lord will give women the liberation they desire. "A wise son maketh a glad father: but a foolish son is the heaviness of his mother", (Prov. 10 v.1). Godly women do not live for gifts and greed, but rather to see their children, and grandchildren, and maybe, great grandchildren walking with the Lord in truth and righteousness. Husbands, to follow the Lord fully, your dear wife will need to be reminded over and over again, that you love her and share her vision for rearing a family pleasing to God, to the praise and glory of His name. This is the Biblical ideal of women's service to God which will command the seal of His approval and blessing on their work and witness in the family.

The obedience of both husband and wife (father and mother) to God would certainly be their happiness. To those that are genuine and sincere in their faith, God will give the necessary grace to persevere in it. He will abundantly bless and strengthen all who follow Him faithfully and continue in His way. "If ye will fear the Lord, and serve Him, and obey His voice, and not rebel against the commandment of the Lord, then shall . . . . . ye . . . . . continue following the Lord your God", (1 Sam. 12 v.14).

Out of thankfulness Christian parents have much cause to praise God for all His love, mercy, and grace. We gladly praise and worship Him for "His way is perfect: He is a buckler to all those that trust in Him", (Psalm 18 v.30). It is good to thank God and to praise Him continually when we are conscious of His mighty deliverance and gracious help to us. There are many reasons why we should be grateful to the Lord, for the many blessings we enjoy day by day, and His enabling power to live righteously. In the face of great opposition from the enemies of Christ and His Cause, let us fervently acknowledge with the Psalmist: "The Lord is my rock, and my fortress, and my deliverer; my God, my strength, in Whom I will trust . . . . . I will call upon the Lord, Who is worthy to be praised", (Psalm 18 v.2-3).

Homemaking, Love and Friendship

The ideal marriage is the life-long attachment of one man and one woman in love and fellowship, and it reaches its completion in parenthood when husband and wife unite in consummation and love of their child. Marriage is a union of their whole natures --- of body, soul, and spirit. In marriage the love which is in the soul's part expresses itself in bodily union, and this in turn deepens intimacy as husband and wife are knit together in harmony which is crowned by parenthood and home-making.

The happiness of married life is bound up with the children of the home, and so their interests must have our profound consideration. Sometimes a medical practitioner may have to advise against child-bearing, and this can be a hard verdict to accept. Marriage without parenthood is possible, and although adoption of children, if desired, may prove a solution to many childless couples, others nevertheless accept their inability to become parents, and live happy and fruitful lives in close companionship and usefulness.

In planning a family many considerations need to be discussed so as not to shirk responsibility nor to assume a burden past their powers to sustain. Intercourse is not just a momentary act, it is that intimacy in love-making which is expressed and responded to by both the husband and the wife, reaching a climax and leaving a sense of happiness, love, and satisfaction in each other. It is important to keep in mind that a husband and wife are responsible to each other to meet each other's sexual needs all of their lives. In the Word of God, the Apostle Paul writing to the Church at Corinth, put it this way: "Let every man have his own wife, and let every woman have her own husband. Let the husband render unto the wife due benevolence: and likewise also the wife unto the husband. The wife hath not power of her own body, but the husband: and likewise also the husband hath not power of his own body, but the wife. Defraud ye not one the other, except it be with consent for a time, that ye may give yourselves to fasting and prayer; and come together again, that Satan tempt you not for your incontinency", (1 Cor. 7 v.2-5). This concept needs to be in the forefront of every married couple's thinking, for it is then it breaks the vicious circle of self-centredness and motivates both the husband and the wife to be givers and not takers in the relationship.

The gift of sexuality has provided man and woman, within the marriage bond, with the most complete way to express and share the love God intends them to have with each other. In cultivating a good sexual relationship, we as Christians must get back to the Scriptures to see what the Bible has to say on the subject. Marriage and sex are of Divine origin, "male and female created He them", (Gen. 1 v.27). The Bible's statement, "My people are destroyed for lack of knowledge", (Hosea 4 v.6), is as true in matters of sexual understanding as it is in matters of spiritual truth. Sex exists not only for the purposes of procreation, it is also the means by which married partners can give physical pleasure to each other, as can be seen from an examination of such Scriptures as the Book of the Song of Solomon and other such passages. "Drink waters out of thine own cistern, and running waters out of thine own well. Let thy fountains be dispersed abroad, and rivers of waters in the streets. Let them be only thine own, and not strangers' with thee. Let thy fountain be blessed: and rejoice with the wife of thy youth. Let her be as the loving hind and pleasant roe: let her breasts satisfy thee at all times; and be thou ravished always with her love. And why wilt thou, my son, be ravished with a strange woman, and embrace the bosom of a stranger? For the ways of man are before the eyes of the Lord, and He pondereth all his goings", (Prov. 5 v.15-21).

A wise, loving, Christian home is a place where husband and wife are in love with each other, and should be a peaceful place where there is harmony in relationships. The Book of Proverbs has much to say about faithfulness, and speaks of the husband whose desire is focused on one woman. He rejoices in her, enraptured in her, and his energy and love are devoted solely to her and wasted elsewhere with strange women: "Let her breasts satisfy thee at all times; and be thou ravished always with her love. And why wilt thou, my son, be ravished with a strange woman, and embrace the bosom of a stranger?" (Prov. 5 v.19-20).

When conception takes place certain changes take place in the body as the woman realises that a child is developing within her. Since it is a living being from the first, the child has a right to its own life. It is therefore wrong and cruel on the part of many who seek abortion. Abortion is contrary to the teaching of the Bible. "Thou shalt not kill. Thou shalt not commit adultery", (Exodus 20 v.13-14). The Biblical arguments against abortion are very straightforward. "Whoso sheddeth man's blood, by man shall his blood be shed: for in the image of God made He man", (Gen. 9 v.6). "If men strive, and hurt a woman with child, so that her fruit depart from her, and yet no mischief follow: he shall be surely punished, according as the woman's husband will lay upon him; and he shall pay as the judges determine. And if any mischief follow, then thou shalt give life for life", (Exodus 21 v.22-23). Despite the fact that forced abortions are now legal and commonplace in almost all developed countries, they are Scripturally unlawful, and when governments justify the murder of unborn children, Christians should remember the standard raised in the Book of the Prophet Isaiah: "To the law and to the testimony: if they speak not according to this Word, it is because there is no light in them", (Isaiah 8 v.20). The Bible makes it clear it is an abomination that God hates the "hands that shed innocent blood", (Prov. 6 v.17).

The presence of the child in the womb should awaken the woman's mother-love instincts, and she with her husband's help, should attend to the duties and care that pregnancy entails. Pregnancy is not an illness but due attention must be given to health and diet throughout the nine months to ensure a safe and happy delivery at the end. As circumstances prevail medical authorities advise that intimacy should be avoided altogether during the last two months of pregnancy, and not resumed until at least six weeks after the birth of the baby.

Speaking of intimacy as an expression of the consummation of the marriage bond, of child-bearing, and the fulfilment of love, we must not be unmindful that these are just part of married life. In the whole partnership of home-making, love is continuous and is expressed in a 'thousand and one' ways in the daily routine of work and duty. The childless couple have a great thing going for them if they have created a perfect home, where, as husband and wife they share together each other's thoughts and interests, and enjoy each other's company, intimacy, companionship, and friendship, in complete trust, free from rivalry, jealousy, or animosity. With so many sides to marriage, many are the joys and sorrows that will inevitably occur. Relationships sometimes with family relatives, especially the in-laws, can be a problem and cause a drawback. It is much better for all married couples to stand on their own two feet and correct their own mistakes, without interference, but of course, they should not be above seeking consultation, guidance, or advice from their trusted friends and family that may be required from time to time.

Inviting friends and colleagues to visit the home provides occasion to welcome others into its warmth and happiness, which also gives further opportunities to learn more of each other's character and tastes. Common-sense must always prevail in that husband and wife should never neglect each other while showing the highest respects to friends and neighbours. Always be on guard and careful of tempers which often can bury themselves deep in the mind and put its ugly head up from time to time, causing squabbles about little or nothing at all. "And be ye kind one to another, tender-hearted, forgiving one another, even as God for Christ's sake has forgiven you", (Eph. 4 v.32). Sulks and grievances not only cause household friction, but hinder the act of intimacy and intercourse which is not giving due satisfaction to either partner.

As life goes on, romantic love must not be allowed to recede or to fade away, but should grow deeper and better in steadfast faithfulness and loyalty in the marriage bond. This larger, greater love, will withstand all stresses and strains, and forgiveness, when needed, is the pouring out and sharing of a difficulty by husband and wife who understand and trust each other. Such loyalty is a very beautiful thing, but the best loyalty of all which overarches all else, is loyalty to God and shown by obedience to His Royal Truth, in love, and in worship.

By the grace of God such fellowship and companionship will bind husband and wife together with strength, confidence, and courage, that will grow deeper and richer throughout their future days in the will of the Lord. It is vital that in the up-bringing and training of their children from the very first, the parents must so work and pray that they too in the providence of God will come to know and love Him through faith in Christ as Saviour and Lord in their earliest days. It is through their parents love and witness for Christ that the children form their first picture of God's love. So it behoves all Christian parents, and grandparents, by precept and example, to live and to teach the Biblical way of life and conduct. This means that personal religion and holiness must be constant, day by day, every day, together with due attendance upon the means of grace and the ordinances of public worship. In humility and grace, it means doing "all to the glory of God": "Whether therefore ye eat, or drink, or whatsoever ye do, do all to the glory of God", (1 Cor. 10 v.31).

Duties and Responsibilities of Wife and Mother

The woman is, above everything else, to be the helper of her husband in his role as head of the family. The woman is to carry out the duties and responsibilities of a wife and mother.

"The young women", as the Apostle Paul states in Titus 2, "are to be sober". In other words, they are to be modest and temperate. They are also to be wise and prudent in their conduct to their husbands, and in the management and work of family affairs. They are commanded to love their husbands, that is, they are to help and assist them all they can; to seek their honour and interest; to endeavour to please them in all things; to secure peace, harmony, and union; to conduct themselves affectionately towards them, and to sympathise with them in all their afflictions and distresses.

This love to their husbands, is not only in the sense of being faithful to them, as is covered by the requirement of the word "chaste", but also in the form of not being sullen or ill-natured. And, of course, their love to their husbands is to be shown by, among other things, obedience. "Obedient to their own husbands", (Titus 2 v.5).

Another requirement of women is "to love their children", not with an over-indulgent and ungoverned affection, but so as to seek their real good. Parents are to seek, not only their temporal good, but also their spiritual and eternal welfare. They are to bring up their children in the nurture and admonition of the Lord.

There are numerous jobs which Scripture informs us are suitable for women. Modern society again very much downplays and undervalues the craft of homemaking and child rearing, yet in the Word of God these are upheld as a very special ministry for women. In any case, when children arrive on the scene, they become the priority of mothers in ministry terms.

First Timothy 5 and Titus 2, reflect the great importance of the role of motherhood. It is most vital that children should learn the truths of Scripture at their mother's knee, and come to faith in Christ at an early age before the corrupting and evil influences of the world, of the flesh, and of the devil, can take hold on them. So here we have an evangelistic role for the mother (and fathers too) without taking a step elsewhere. The importance of this role is much neglected today.

Not one is as suitable in guiding the household practically, day by day, as the wife and mother of the home. This is a most important task, but the 'feminist' movement has been so successful in denigrating it that many, even among so-called professing Christians, think it demeaning that one should be tied to the work of being a wife and a mother. We are to note, however, that the importance of her task is shown by the word "guide", as in 1 Timothy 5 v.14, "guide the house". In the Greek, this is a very strong word, which when translated means "rule" or "rule the house", not of course, by usurping authority over the husband and father, but by managing and directing household affairs.

The housewife, who looks after the home and family, has a most privileged, high and noble calling, according to the Scripture. In this day and age this wonderful group of women is fast-disappearing. There are many records in the Bible of things that women did at home which men could not do. For example, we have the story of Miriam recruiting Moses' mother to nurse him for Pharaoh's daughter, and thereby saving a nation. We also have the account of Deborah encouraging Barak to go to war, and he won. And to take a New Testament example, we have that classic example of Eunice raising up young Timothy for God. The Christian housewife has a ready made mission field right where she is, in her own home.

Not all Christian housewives are mothers, but for those who are, there can be no higher calling than to raise children for God, and to teach and instil into their tender minds and hearts, the things of God. This kind of witnessing is an investment that will bring eternal rewards that outweigh the accumulation of riches or following a worldly career.

The understanding and vision of both husband and wife must be clear in regard to raising a family for God. Such a call demands deep sacrifice on the part of both father and mother, as mounting costs in modern society and 'keeping up with the Joneses' culture tend to push young couples more and more into materialism and greed, thus compelling both partners to be working full-time outside the home. But couples who chose to put God first in following the precepts of Scripture, by giving prayerful consideration and due attention to the primacy of family, will never regret it in this world, nor in the world to come.

In the context of the neighbourhood all around, in the street where you live, at the shopping mall, in the supermarket or other places, women meet neighbours and other people, who need Christ. This is an ideal situation for the Christian housewife to witness to the unsaved. For some reason women are much more sensitive to spiritual things than men, and given patience and perseverance for long conversations and struggles at times, the rewards are sweet.

The Scriptures abound in examples of godly wives and mothers whose work in the family, especially by teaching their children in the faith and showing them a good example, resulted in great blessing for generations to come. No doubt Hannah prepared Samuel as much as she could for serving the Lord: "For this child I prayed; and the Lord hath given me my petition which I asked of Him. Therefore also I have lent him to the Lord; as long as he liveth he shall be lent to the Lord", (1 Sam. 1 v.27-28).

The faith that dwells in real believers is unfeigned, without hypocrisy, a faith that will stand the trial, and it dwells in them as a living principle. It was the matter of the Apostle Paul's thanksgiving that Timothy inherited the faith of his mother Eunice and his grandmother Lois. "When I call to remembrance the unfeigned faith that is in thee, which dwelt first in thy grandmother Lois, and thy mother Eunice; and I am persuaded that in thee also", (2 Timothy 1 v.5). Timothy had a good mother, and grandmother, who believed. It is a good thing when children imitate the faith and holiness of their godly parents.

The whole drift of Scripture passages about family life is that the wife and mother ordinarily devotes herself to her husband, children and home. Today, many mothers go out to work and fathers look after the home, but as Anne Graham rightly says in her book, 'Womanhood revisited', "The Bible never suggests that role reversal is an option. Men and women both have important but different responsibilities, which in normal circumstances, are not interchangeable. Yet many Christians happily concur with the idea of the house-husband as a commendable alternative lifestyle. This has everything to do with 'feminist' belittling of manhood. It has nothing to do with Biblical masculinity".

Another activity in the home which some mothers engage in is home-schooling. If they are able to cope with such a tremendous responsibility, well and good, and may the Divine blessing attend their efforts and labours. But while mothers are to instruct their children in the Christian faith, we do not believe that the Scriptures lay home schooling on them as a duty.

Some mothers are very successful at home schooling, and the result of their work is to be admired. There are other mothers, however, for whom the burden of educating their children at home is just far too much, and they are forced to give it up. They should never be made to feel guilty on that account.

Discipline, Relationships and Contentment

Another very important duty of parents in training children is that they must use proper discipline, otherwise a parent may be said to hate a child. "He that spareth the rod hateth his son: but he that loveth him chasteneth him betimes ", (Prov. 13 v.24).

All women are to be "keepers at home". This does not mean that they are to be closeted up in the house, as it were, but just that they are to be homemakers. They are to be attentive to their domestic concerns, and to their duties in their families. The wife and mother of whom we read about in Proverbs 31, "looked well to the ways of her household". In other words, she was an excellent homemaker, although she was also very active outside the home.

Another verse that speaks especially to wives and mothers is found in First Timothy 5 v.14. There the Apostle Paul says, "I will therefore that the younger women marry, bear children, guide the house". It is true that this verse speaks about widows who are yet young, but at the same time it echoes the creation mandate that, through marriage, mankind is to increase and the earth be populated.

In family life especially, the woman is to be the helper of her husband. God has created man to glorify Him. Mankind is to multiply within the framework of marriage so that a godly seed may be raised up to serve and glorify God from generation to generation. Malachi 2 v.15, teaches that God made one Eve for one Adam, that Adam might never take another to vex her, nor put her away to make room for another. Designing Adam "an help meet for him", (Gen. 2 v.18), He made him one wife, not more, "that He might seek a godly seed", (Mal. 3 v.15). The word is "a godly seed" that should bear the image of God, that every man having his own wife, and but one, according to the law (1 Cor. 7 v.2) they might live in chaste and holy love, and that the children, being born in holy matrimony, which is an ordinance of God, might thus be made a seed to serve Him. "Therefore take heed to your spirit, and let none deal treacherously against the wife of his youth", (Mal. 2 v.15). God is much displeased with those who go about to put asunder what He has joined together.

Discipline and good family relationships between parents and children, who by nature are sinners, do not develop naturally. This subject is perhaps approached through the fathers, as we look at Ephesians 6 v.1-4: "Children, obey your parents in the Lord: for this is right. Honour thy father and mother; which is the first commandant with promise; That it may be well with thee, and thou mayest live long on the earth. And, ye fathers, provoke not your children to wrath: but bring them up in the nurture and admonition of the Lord". Notice that it is the fathers who are addressed in this manner. Why is it not the mothers that are addressed who spend more time with their children than fathers do?

When the Apostle speaks to the fathers, he is of course speaking to the mothers also. The reason he addresses the fathers is that what the mothers do, the fathers are responsible for. Being the head of the home, God has vested in him His authority for discipline. The husband must be "one that ruleth well his own house, having his children in subjection with all gravity", (1 Tim. 3 v.4).

The father does not always administer discipline directly, but often through his wife, his helpmeet, who spends more time with their children than he does, and therefore has to put up with their 'bad behaviour' all day long. But God still holds him responsible, he is the one as the head who is in control. Therefore Paul says, "fathers, provoke not your children to wrath", (Eph. 6 v.4). It is his duty to see that their children are properly trained.

In the exhortation to obedience, we read in Deuteronomy 6, that fathers are specially singled out as the ones who must answer any questions that their children may have about the faith. "And when thy son asketh thee in time to come, saying, What mean the testimonies, and the statutes, and the judgements, which the Lord our God hath commanded you?", (Deut. 6 v.20). Fathers are to teach their children about God, but this must not in any way prohibit the mothers from doing so too. "And thou shalt love the Lord thy God with all thine heart, and with all thy soul, and with all thy might. And these words, which I command thee this day, shall be in thine heart. And thou shalt teach them diligently unto thy children, and shalt talk of them when thou sittest in thine house, and when thou walkest by the way, and when thou liest down, and when thou risest up", (Deut. 6 v. 5-7).

Fathers must impress upon their children the laws, ordinances, and commandments of God, and explain to them the ways of the Lord in all of life's circumstances. Fathers, of course, cannot do all this personally, but he has the loyal support and assistance of his wife as his helpmeet. It must be firmly stated, that ultimately he is the one responsible to God as head of the family, for all the discipline, all the training, and all the relationships in his home.

Colossians 3 v.21, clearly states, "Fathers, provoke not your children to anger, lest they be discouraged". It is instructive to notice what the Scripture is saying here in regard to children. In other words, do not exasperate your children with such severity as to irritate rebellion and crush the spirit of any youth. In the second part of the verse, Eph. 6 v.4, there is the positive command in regard to children: "bring them up in the nurture and admonition of the Lord". Not only are we told what not to do, the Bible tells us what to do and how to do it. God commands parents to discipline their children in His way. Discipline is from God, and all real authority for training is from God, and is "of the Lord". But notice, all training and discipline must be according to the Word of God, in that it reflects the discipline He exerts over the parents who are His people. "And ye have forgotten the exhortation which speaketh unto you as unto children, My son, despise not thou the chastening of the Lord, nor faint when thou art rebuked of Him: For whom the Lord loveth He chasteneth, and scourgeth every son whom He receiveth", (Heb. 12 v.5-6). Parents must use nurture, admonition, discipline, and instruction, in God's way. "Therefore thou shalt love the Lord thy God, and keep His charge, and His statutes, and His judgements, alway", (Deut. 11 v.1).

Discipline that is firm but gracious should characterise the home. "Chasten thy son while there is hope, and let not thy soul spare for his crying", (Prov. 19 v.18). Brutal punishments are very wrong and opposed to the Spirit of God. Unloving chastisement given in rage and severity can only harden, not recover, a wayward child. "Ye fathers, provoke not your children to wrath", (Eph. 6 v.4), is a much needed admonition and warning in many families. Unreasonable demands and harsh punishments out of all proportion to the offence committed should be diligently avoided. On the other hand to leave a child to himself is to display a cruel indifference to the fate of a young life committed to our care and charge. The Word of God teaches the happy medium that produces the desired results. The child should come to realise and understand that it is his good which is sought. "The rod and reproof give wisdom: but a child left to himself bringeth his mother to shame", (Prov. 29 v.15). Parents need great wisdom for correction to be properly administered and to bring up their family in the fear and love of God. An undisciplined child will bring shame on his mother and ruin to himself. Correction and reproof, properly and justly administered, are for the child's own best interests and open his heart to wisdom. Let the father and mother exercise a firm but kindly discipline, and God has promised that their efforts will bear good fruit. "Correct thy son, and he shall give thee rest; yea, he shall give delight unto thy soul", (Prov. 29 v.17). God's Word is sure, the corrected son will give rest to the heart and delight to the soul.

God has placed before parents the immortal minds of their children, more precious than diamonds, which they are to teach and train in the Lord, not only by their instruction, but also by their spirit, example, and walk, day by day, every day, something that will remain and be exhibited for or against them at the Judgement: "For we must all appear before the Judgement Seat of Christ", (2 Cor. 5 v.10).

Building on a Firm Foundation

In the Sermon on the Mount, Jesus uses the illustration of building a house upon the rock, a sure foundation. So build your home on the Lord Jesus Christ and His teaching, and anchor your faith in His excellent Word, Christ teaches that the one who would be His disciple must build his or her entire life on the Scripture. Today there are many storms against the modern home. In true marriage love is always growing, instead of diminishing which is a firm basis to build on, and to withstand the floods of sorrow, temptation, and gales of adversity that might strike. One of the favourite benedictions of Christ was "Peace be to this house", (Luke 10 v.5). The Saviour's great love and concern is that every member of our home be a member of the household of faith. Our earthly homes ought to be a reflection of heaven. God in His sovereignty and grace "will have mercy" on whom He will have mercy, and He "will have compassion" on whom He will have compassion, (Rom. 9 v.15); (See also Exodus 33 v.19).

Nicodemus came to Jesus by night, but his religion must be openly acknowledged before men. It was not enough to think to patch up the old life, he must build on a new foundation and live a new life. "Except a man be born again, he cannot see the Kingdom of God", (John 3 v.3). By our first birth we are corrupt and shaped in iniquity and sin. We must therefore, undergo a second birth, and our souls must be "quickened together with Christ", (Eph. 2 v.5): "For by grace are ye saved through faith; and that not of yourselves: it is the gift of God", (Eph. 2 v.8). At the new birth we are given a new nature, with new principles, new affections, and new aims. Regeneration is absolutely necessary to our happiness not only here but also the hereafter. After the restored Gadarene "man with an unclean spirit", (Mark 5 v.2), from whom Christ cast out demons, and who was wonderfully converted, changed, and transformed, Jesus clearly commanded him to "go home to thy friends, and tell them how great things the Lord hath done for thee, and hath had compassion on thee", (Mark 5 v.19).

Among the things that make for a happy home with firm foundations, are the following:-

    (1)   A Divinely ordered marriage: The Bible teaches us that God performed the first marriage, (Gen. 2 v.18,22,24), and the marriage bed is honourable and undefiled (Heb. 13 v.4). God's Word gives clear instructions to husband, wife; father, mother; and children, to live according to the precepts laid down in the Scriptures concerning the home. (Eph.5 v.22-33, 6 v.1-4; Col. 3 v.18-21).

(2) Prayer and Bible reading: This is the corner-stone in the foundation of a happy home. "And these words, which I command thee this day, shall be in thine heart: And thou shalt write them upon the posts of thy house, and on thy gates", (Deut. 6 v.6,9). By setting a good example it has often been said that the family that prays together stays together.

(3) A dedicated husband and father: It is a big responsibility to be the head of the home as God commanded. It was Jacob who said to his household, "Put away the strange gods that are among you, and be clean, and change your garments: And let us arise, and go up to Bethel; and I will make there an altar unto God", (Gen. 35 v.2-3); and of Moses we are told in Hebrews 3 v.5, that he "was faithful in all his house, as a servant, for a testimony of those things which were to be spoken after". The Psalmist, a man after God's own heart, purposes in all things to behave wisely in the sight of God: "I will behave myself wisely in a perfect way . . . . . I will walk within my house with a perfect heart . . . . . I will set no wicked thing before mine eyes", (Psalm 101 v.2-3). The Bible plainly declares that sex outside of marriage is sin, fornication. "But fornication, and all uncleanness, or covetousness, let it not be once named among you, as becometh saints", (Eph. 5 v.3). Extra martial sex is adultery. The Seventh Commandment emphatically states, "Thou shalt not commit adultery", (Exodus 20 v.14). None of the commandments have ever been abrogated, and all can be summed up in this one rule --- "Love": "Thou shalt love the Lord thy God . . . . . and . . . . . Thou shalt love thy neighbour", (Matt. 22 v.37-38). The Scripture commands us to be holy: "Be ye holy, for I am holy", (1 Peter 1 v.16). (See also Lev. 11 v.44). Holiness is not some sensational periodical experience, rather, holiness

of life is manifested in those who through grace and truth obey the Lord by keeping the law of God, and thus, as believers, we lay it up in our hearts and practise it in our daily lives and everyday conduct. "Love worketh no ill to his neighbour: therefore love is the fulfilling of the law", (Rom. 13 v.10). "Having therefore these promises, dearly beloved, let us cleanse ourselves from all filthiness of the flesh and spirit, perfecting holiness in the fear of God", (2 Cor. 7 v.1).

(4) A devoted wife and mother: The call to reverence and discipline in the ways of God can only be performed by grace, and having a strong faith in the Lord, love for others, and patience amid any difficulties. Good wives are "to be discreet, chaste, keepers at home, good, obedient to their own husbands, that the Word of God be not blasphemed", (Titus 2 v.5). Good wives and wise mothers will be ready to hear and do right, but answering unreasonably, or acting in an unseemly manner, shows a lack of humility and meekness in the exercise of Christian duty. The greatest need of any nation is for Christian mothers who will rear a family to know God. The Scriptures say, "let them learn first to shew piety at home . . . . . for that is good and acceptable before God", (1 Tim. 5 v.4). Real beauty is something inside the heart, and by the grace of God, mothers can be a real blessing to others. There are many women in the Bible, Miriam, Mary, Martha, Phebe, Priscilla, Lydia, the four daughters of Philip the Evangelist, and others who have rendered wonderful service not only in the home, but also in the work of God generally. The Apostle Paul issues a stern warning against raving women who wander from house to house as busybodies and talebearers. "For we hear that there are some which walk among you disorderly, working not at all, but are busybodies", (2 Thess. 3 v.11). "And withal they learn to be idle,

wandering about from house to house; and not only idle, but tattlers also and busybodies, speaking things which they ought not", (1 Tim. 5 v.13). "But let none of you suffer as a murderer, or as a thief, or as an evildoer, or as a busybody in other men's matters", (1 Peter 4 v.15). Wives, as well as husbands, must be faithful, with chastity before marriage, and mutual love and fidelity within marriage.

(5) Disciplined and obedient children: "Train up a child in the way he should go: and when he is old, he will not depart from it", (Prov. 22 v.6). The Scripture issues a significant call to young people to think of God, and not forget their duty to Him, when they are young. "Remember now thy Creator in the days of thy youth", (Eccles. 12 v.1). And the Bible again reminds us of the exhortation: "And, ye fathers, provoke not your children to wrath: but bring them up in the nurture and admonition of the Lord", (Eph. 6 v.4). Discipline is very important and it is the duty of the child to obey. Many young people today are rebelling and the spirit of the age is to reject authority. We are to love our children, and children are to love their parents, and to honour them, and to obey them in the Lord, unless it interferes with their faith in the Lord Jesus Christ.

(6) Commitment and dedication to the Lord: We read that Hezekiah was "sick unto death" and was commanded by God: "Set thine house in order; for thou shalt die, and not live", (2 Kings 20 v.1). He was a man who had walked before the Lord with a perfect heart, God heard his prayer, and added unto his days another "fifteen years", (2 Kings 20 v.6). A happy home is based on commitment to the Lord and where Christ is acknowledged as King and Head. "Believe on the Lord Jesus Christ, and thou shalt be saved, and thy house.

And they spake unto him the Word of the Lord, and to all that were in his house", (Acts 16 v.31-32). The jailer and his family were greatly blessed when they believed and took upon themselves the profession of Christianity, submitted to the Word of God, and solemnly declaring to follow the Lord. With Christ living and reigning in our hearts, He goes with us in everything we do. "For Thou, Lord, wilt bless the righteous; with favour wilt Thou compass him as with a shield", (Psalm 5 v.12).

(7) Attendance to the outward means of grace: As committed Christians, the dedicated family will fear the Lord (Mal. 3 v.16); reverence His name (Exod. 20 v.7); submit to His authority (Phil. 2 v.9-11); observe the Christian Sabbath (Deut. 5 v.15); and will not forsake the assembling of themselves together for public worship (Heb. 10 v.25). As true servants of God we would do well to be ever thankful that by His grace we "have obeyed from the heart that form of doctrine which was delivered you", (Rom. 6 v.17); to keep humble, penitent, watchful, and quickened by the Holy Spirit to obey and adorn the Gospel of Christ: "Teaching us that, denying ungodliness and worldly lusts, we should live soberly, righteously, and godly, in this present world", (Titus 2 v.12).

Family the Basic Unit of Society

Building a strong Christian home is a great challenge whenever family values are under constant fire from the world. The erosion of home and family as the basic unit of society is accelerating at an alarming rate. From a Biblical perspective may God enable His people to evaluate, discuss, and improve the various aspects of the Christian home by applying His Word to every situation wherever in Providence He has placed us. We face the problems of a sinful world together with God "in Whom are hid all the treasures of wisdom and knowledge", (Col. 2 v.3). What makes the difference in a Christian home, is that Christ reigns there as Saviour and Lord.

The fundamental roles and relationships between husbands and wives are clearly described and outlined in Scripture. In addressing wives, the Divine command is, "Wives, submit yourselves unto your own husbands, as unto the Lord", (Eph. 5 v.22). In addressing husbands, the Divine command is, "Husbands, love your wives, even as Christ also loved the Church, and gave Himself for it", (Eph. 5 v.25). Sometimes couples allow wedges to come between, perhaps unresolved matters, between them and their parents, or with one another, or with their children. By living a lie, or acting on pretence, the marriage sadly is based on falsehood. We are commanded in Scripture to "lay aside every weight, and the sin which doth so easily beset us, and let us run with patience the race that is set before us", (Heb. 12 v.1). If you have occasion to be angry, see that it be without sin, therefore take heed of excess in your anger. If we would be angry and sin not, we must be angry at nothing but sin. Anything that is unforgiven, unsettled, uncovered, should not be carried over to the next day. "Be ye angry, and sin not: let not the sun go down upon your wrath", (Eph. 4 v.26). One common sin in anger, is to allow it to burn into wrath and a grudge. Though anger in itself is not sinful, yet there is the utmost danger of it becoming so, if it is not carefully watched. Those who persevere in sinful anger and in wrath and in grudges, clearly show that the devil is in control: "Neither give place to the devil", (Eph. 4 v.27). "He that hath no rule over his own spirit is like a city that is broken down, and without walls", (Prov. 25 v.28).

The thing that constantly saps away the witness and strength of any Church is the unreconciled state of so many believers. "Therefore if thou bring thy gift to the altar, and there rememberest that thy brother hath ought against thee; Leave there thy gift before the altar, and go thy way; first be reconciled to thy brother, and then come and offer thy gift", (Matt. 5 v.23-24).

In addition to what the Scriptures tell us what to do when we become angry or when we have done something wrong to someone else, it says in the above text that we must make the wrong right and be reconciled to our brother. We must make things right immediately, even before we worship God. The reason for this is because the sin of anger, like all sins, is ultimately against God and must be made right before Him. Reconciliation must precede worship. This is always God's requirement: "Wash you, make you clean; put away the evil of your doings from before Mine eyes; cease to do evil; Learn to do well; seek judgment (justice), relieve the oppressed, judge the fatherless, plead for the widow", (Isaiah 1 v.16-17). God demands that we be willing to forsake hatred and be made right with each other before we could be right with Him.

This could also mean, even if we hold nothing against a brother, if he is angry with or hates us, we should do everything in our power to be reconciled to him. Obviously we cannot change another person's heart or attitude, but our desire and effort should be to close the breach as much as possible from our side and to hold no anger or hatred ourselves, even if the other person does. True worship is not enhanced by better singing, better prayers, or even better preaching. True worship is enhanced by better relationships between those who come to worship. Worship may be improved by the offender staying away from Church until he has made things right with those with whom he knows his relationship is strained or broken.

When there is animosity or sin of any kind in our hearts, there cannot be integrity in our worship. The Psalmist cried out, "If I regard iniquity in my heart, the Lord will not hear me", (Psalm 66 v.18). The prophet, Samuel, asks the question, "Hath the Lord as great delight in burnt offerings and sacrifices, as in obeying the voice of the Lord?", to which he answers, "Behold, to obey is better than sacrifice, and to harken than the fat of rams. For rebellion is as the sin of witchcraft, and stubbornness is as iniquity and idolatry", (1 Sam. 15 v.22-23).

It is on record that husbands and wives frequently complain that they are having trouble with sex, but the trouble usually is not sex. Counsellors confirm that the real difficulties in bed at night come from a misguided pile up of unconfessed 'baggage' that needs to be removed. The work of the Lord cannot be done when carrying such a 'load'. "Take therefore no thought for tomorrow: for the morrow shall take thought for the things of itself. Sufficient unto the day is the evil thereof", (Matt. 6 v.34). Making reasonable provisions for tomorrow is sensible, but to be anxious for tomorrow is foolish and unfaithful. God is the God of tomorrow as well as the God of today and of eternity. "It is of the Lord's mercies that we are not consumed, because His compassions fail not. They are new every morning: great is Thy faithfulness", (Lam. 3 v.22-23). It seems some people are so committed to worrying that, if they cannot find anything in the present to worry about, they think about possible problems in the future. Tomorrow will take care of itself, Christ assures us. We cannot do anything about the future anyway. The future is in God's hands and will be managed perfectly by God whether we worry about it or not. God promises His grace for tomorrow and for every day thereafter and through eternity. But He does not give us grace for tomorrow now. He only gives His grace a day at a time as it is needed, not as it may be anticipated. "Thou wilt keep him in perfect peace, whose mind is stayed on Thee: because he trusteth in Thee. Trust ye in the Lord for ever: for in the Lord Jehovah is everlasting strength", (Isaiah 26 v.3-4).

Jesus said, "If any man will come after Me, let him deny himself, and take up his cross, and follow Me", (Matt. 16 v.24). Discipleship is on God's terms, just as coming to Him is on His terms. This verse reminds us that the key discipleship principle of winning involves self-denial, cross-bearing, and loyal obedience. It means to crucify daily the self that is within us. "Let no corrupt communication proceed out of your mouth, but that which is good to the use of edifying, that it may minister grace unto the hearers", (Eph. 4 v.29).

Scripture is very emphatic when it says, "Let all bitterness, and wrath, and anger, and clamour, and evil speaking, be put away from you, with all malice: And be ye kind one to another, tenderhearted, forgiving one another, even as God for Christ's sake hath forgiven you", (Eph. 4 v.31-32). To love we must give of ourselves, for giving is fundamental to the Biblical idea of love. And that spirit of giving brings a healthy attitude and atmosphere into any home.

We must, therefore, make every effort to preserve the institution of marriage, of the family, and of the home. The evil 'guns' of the world are pointed at their very existence, and we need to re-affirm the following two basic Biblical principles:-

(1) God ordained marriage. Marriage is honourable in all and ought to be esteemed by all. It is basic to society and described in Scripture as a covenant. In the Book of Proverbs, God warns against the adulteress, "the strange woman, even from the stranger which flattereth with her words; Which forsaketh the guide of her youth, and forgetteth the covenant of her God", (Prov. 2 v.16-17). A marriage is a covenant made in the presence of God.

(2) Marriage is ordained by God and sex is good, given to bless and to make man and wife happy and joyful. Sexual relations are holy, righteous, and undefiled unless abused and perverted by sin. Biblically, sexuality is integral to human personhood. "Male and female created He them", (Gen. 1 v.27). Scripture's creation teaching also highlights the relational value and purpose of sexuality. Woman is made as God's provision for man's need of relationship, (Gen. 2 v.18-25). "Therefore shall a man leave his father and mother, and shall cleave unto his wife: and they shall be one flesh" --- "united", which strongly describes a husband and wife's intimacy and inseparable affection for each other. Scripture is overwhelmingly positive in its treatment of sexuality, and vigorously affirms the goodness of sex. "Let

thy fountain be blessed: and rejoice with the wife of thy youth. Let her be as the loving hind and pleasant roe: let her breasts satisfy thee at all times; and be thou ravished always with her love", (Prov. 5 v.18-19). The test of love in marriage, not only finds fulfilment, but is sustained by an affirmation of body-life with a positive attitude towards sex which has no room for either abuse or withdrawal: (1 Tim. 4 v.1-5, 1 Cor. 6 v.12-15, 1 Cor. 7 v.1-17). The marriage bed must be kept undefiled: "Marriage is honourable in all, and the bed undefiled: but whoremongers and adulterers God will judge", (Heb. 13 v.4). In the Book of the Revelation, Christ speaks of His relationship to His people as that of a bridegroom to a bride --- "a bride adorned for her husband", (Rev. 21 v.2).

There are, of course, other aspects of marriage that are described elsewhere in this book, namely among them, --- the purpose of child-bearing, and the rearing and training of children. "Lo, children are an heritage of the Lord: and the fruit of the womb is his reward", (Psalm 127 v.3). Marriage is the most important basic unit in human society. The most basic family relationship is not the parent-child relationship, important as that is, but rather the husband-wife relationship: "they shall be one flesh", (Gen. 2 v.24). It is vital that the Christian husband and wife follow God's pattern for marriage, for the family, and for the home.

"Wives, submit yourselves unto your own husbands, as it is fit in the Lord. Husbands, love your wives, and be not bitter against them. Children obey your parents in all things: for this is well pleasing unto the Lord", (Col. 3 v.18-20).

Real Love is Giving

We begin this section, by asking two questions, which are very pointed, profound, heart-searching, yet practical and necessary.

They are as follows:-

(1) Husbands, do you really love your wives enough to live for them?

(2) Wives, do you really love your husbands enough to submit to them?

"Wives, submit yourselves unto your own husbands, as unto the Lord", (Eph. 5 v.22).

"Husbands, love your wives, even as Christ also loved the Church, and gave Himself for it", (Eph. 5 v.25).

"Nevertheless let every one of you in particular so love his wife even as himself; and the wife see that she reverence her husband", (Eph. 5 v.33).

An examination of these verses will show that loving and submission are relatively simple. Without love headship would be greatly abused, and, of course, by nature, submission is against the grain, the 'old man' within rebels. The woman must submit to her husband as her "head" as the Church submits to Christ as the "Head of the Church". God places this responsibility on every Christian wife, for her own good, and the good of her husband. In the role of headship, the requirement of the husband is to exemplify Christ's headship over the Church. It is one thing for wives to exemplify the Church in its relationship to Christ, but the task that God has laid on husbands is greater. As the Church's subjection to Christ is proposed as an example to wives, so the love of Christ to His Church is proposed as a pattern to husbands; and while such examples are offered to both, and so much is required of each, neither has reason to complain of the Divine injunctions.

It is only as the Spirit of God works in the life of the Christian husband that he can begin to appropriate the Lord's loving relationship over His Church. So he must aspire to nothing less in his relationship to his wife. To emulate Him and to be Christ-like in relationship to his wife is an enormous order to fulfil. The husband is to be the "head" of the home, including his wife and children, just as Christ is the head of the Church. As husband and father he is to show forth and exercise leadership that reflects this in the home.

Husbands must love their wives. The present tense of the Greek imperative, "agapate", "love", indicates continuous action, which in the New Testament is best understood to express a willing love, not the love of passion or emotion, but the love of choice, a covenant love. It could be translated, "keep on loving". The love that Paul commands sees the wife as a weaker vessel to be cared for while at the same time she is a fellow-heir to grace (1 Peter 3 v.7), a best friend, and a life-partner. Such was the love that Isaac expressed for Rebekah. "And Isaac brought her into his mother Sarah's tent, and took Rebekah, and she became his wife; and he loved her", (Gen 24 v.67).

God designed that a wife's submission operates within a context of love. In that way she is protected, for the godly husband loves his wife like Christ loves the Church. It also clearly states that husbands "be not bitter against them", (Col. 3 v. 19). They must love them with tender care and faithful affection, and not use them unkindly, harshly, or with severe treatment. The Scripture calls for a mutual concern in marriage, the husband is to seek to find "how he may please his wife", and the wife is to seek to pursue "how she may please her husband", (1 Cor. 7 v.23-24). By God's design, while the wife most pleases her husband with loving submission, and he most pleases her with loving authority, there is that spiritual equality and mutual longing for each to please the other.

Despite the straightforward clarity of the Bible on these matters, there is widespread opposition and challenge to the authority of Scripture and the teaching of the Word of God, even within certain parts of the Church. In our modern society, such people seek to usurp the role of

God and decide for themselves which parts of Scripture are inspired, and argue to reverse and confuse the duties of husband and wife, and thus destroy the blessing each is to be to the other.

All these worldly attacks on the straightforward Biblical principles for behaviour and conduct deal devastating wounds to the marriage. The Apostle's word to wives is not to submit to some detached, impersonal authority, but rather it is to an intimate, personal, vital, loving relationship, "as it is fit in the Lord", (Col. 3 v.18). The Greek New Testament form of this phrase strongly expresses an obligation, a necessary duty, and this is how God designed and commands the family to operate.

We are living in a day of corruption and compromise, moral decay and declension, and spiritual barrenness, when so much of the Church has now disregarded the full teaching of Scripture. Because the Church is engulfed and identified with worldly standards, the Word of God is deemed out-of-date, irrelevant, and offensive to the modern man.

The Biblical call to the people of God is to "walk worthy of the vocation wherewith ye are called, With all lowliness and meekness, with longsuffering, forbearing one another in love . . . . . that ye put on the new man, which after God is created in righteousness and true holiness", (Eph. 4 v.1-2,24). Few areas of modern living have been so distorted and corrupted by the devil and the world, and caused the Church so much confusion, as those of marriage and family. But in matters of role and function God has made distinctions, and He has given rulers in government certain authority over the people they rule, to Church leaders He has delegated authority over their congregations, to husbands He has given authority over their wives and children, and to employers He has given authority over employees.

In the 'feminist' movement, and even in other less extreme groups, we see women loudly and vociferously proclaiming their ideas, opinions, and rights in regard to virtually every issue. But holiness has always been the foremost concern of godly women. "For after this manner in the old time the holy women also, who trusted in God, adorned themselves, being in subjection unto their own husbands: Even as Sara obeyed Abraham, calling him lord: whose daughters ye are, as long as ye do well and are not afraid with any amazement", (1 Peter 3 v.5-6). Sara had no fear of obeying God, for He will take care of the consequences when His people are obedient to His Word. Christian women today have every opportunity for productive, helpful, and rewarding service, without sacrificing or compromising the commands of Scripture. The manner or attitude of submission and obedience is to be "as unto the Lord", (Eph. 5 v.22), to the praise and glory of God.

Life is made meaningful by relationships, the most loving and meaningful of which is that between one man and one woman in marriage: "being heirs together of the grace of life", (1 Peter 3 v.7). Today, in place of exerting consistent effort and determination to fulfil the commitment it takes to make marriage work, the solution all too readily is to bail out. Marriage was instituted to procreate mankind, to raise up children to "replenish the earth", (Gen. 1 v.28). It is also for the purpose of companionship and love, so that man would not be alone, (Gen. 2 v.18), and for the purpose of sexual fulfilment and pleasure, (1 Cor. 7 v.4-5; Heb. 13 v.4).

In the first Book of the Bible, we see the reversal of roles of husband and wife, fratricide, polygamy, perverted sexual practice, adultery, homosexuality, fornication, rape, prostitution, incest and seduction --- each of which directly attacks the sanctity and harmony of marriage and the family. For all who have eyes to see, there is no doubt that the Biblical doctrine of total depravity is found throughout Scripture. Of the many passages that teach it, hardly any are as clear, comprehensive, or compendious, as Genesis 6 v.5: "And God saw that the wickedness of man was great in the earth, and that every imagination of the thoughts of his heart was only evil continually". What a contrast this is with Genesis 1 when we think of the many earlier statements that "God saw" what He had made "that it was very good", (Gen. 1 v.4,10,12,18,21,25,31). But now five chapters later, God is "grieved" (Gen. 6 v.6) that He made man and is determined to wipe all living creatures, "both man, and beast, and the creeping thing, and the fowls of the air", (Gen. 6 v.7), from the earth by "a flood of waters", (Gen. 6 v.17, Gen. 7). In much of our modern society, these very sins as mentioned above are lauded. Sexual purity and marital fidelity are laughed at with disdain, scorn, and contempt. To follow God's standards for morality and marriage, it is immeasurably more difficult when most people nowadays mock these standards that God has laid down for mankind. The only way for the Christian to survive such a wicked, "perverse and crooked generation", (Deut. 32 v.5), is to "be filled with the Spirit", (Eph. 5 v.18). Apart from Divine grace, there is no possibility of making marriage what God intends it to be.

Because a Christian has a Christ-like nature and the Holy Spirit within him, God thereby provides for husbands to love their wives with a measure of His love for His Church, which is the husband's pattern of love for his wife. A husband is not commanded to love his wife because of what she is or is not. He is commanded to love her because it is God's will for him to love her. The husband who loves his wife only because of her physical attractiveness or pleasing temperament does not love her as Christ loved the Church. God did not love the world and send His own Son to redeem it because it was worthy of that love. Jesus Christ bled and died for sinners because of what Divine love demanded. Nowhere is our relationship to God better tested than in our relationship in marriage and family.

A young man who says he loves a young woman and wants her to compromise her sexual purity by having sexual intercourse with her before they are married, or a husband who flirts and commits adultery with another woman, does not love as God loves. True love wants only the best for the one it loves, and cannot bear for a loved one to be corrupted or harmed, (1 Peter 3 v.7).

When Christian husbands and wives constantly and continually are loving, mutually intimate, yielded to the Word of God, and walking in the power of the Spirit, they bring to each other much happiness, and enjoy the blessing of the Triune God in the home. To follow the Divine plan for marriage, family, and home, is not only pleasing to the Lord, but honours and magnifies God, to Whom be all the praise and all the glory.

There is no ambiguity concerning the different roles that God has assigned for husband and wife, as laid down in Scripture. They must not forget their obligations or be careless about their marriage vows. Both must exhibit Christ, and both must obey Christ by obedience to all His commandments. The definite distinction of the role of each partner in a marriage covenant must be clearly understood and practically applied, so as to command the blessing of God in the union of one man and one woman as "one flesh", (Gen. 2 v.25).

Authority in the home is centred in the husband, not in the wife, or in the children. Headship means leadership, not merely privilege, right, and authority --- but also to assume such responsibility in truly leading the home. The head of the home must control his home, including his wife, and his children. He must keep his whole household in subjection. The characteristics of the husband who leads, as mentioned in First Timothy 3, can be summarised as follows:-

(1) He must be an example of good behaviour;

(2) He must rule well his own household; and

(3) He must keep their children under control with all dignity.

He is the head of all who live in the house and his job is to assume good and proper leadership. He recognises that God has provided his wife as a helper suitable for him, and with a grateful and thankful heart remembers the Scripture which reads, "Whoso findeth a wife findeth a good thing, and obtaineth favour of the Lord", (Prov. 18 v.22).

Among other things, it is of vital importance that husbands be zealous to see to it that good leadership is exercised

(i) in family worship;

(ii) in family study of the Word of God;

(iii) in family prayer;

(iv) in family attendance at the means of grace and the services of the Church;

(v) in the family witness to society;

(vi) in the family's training and work for God; and

(vii) in the family's outreach activities in evangelism and mission.

The Apostle Paul speaks of husbands loving "their wives as their own bodies" (Eph. 5 v.28). He will care as much for her welfare as he does for the welfare of his own body. At no time in modern history have people more sinfully pampered, protected, painted, nourished, and indulged the body as in our own day. The amount of money spent just to decorate, protect, paint, enhance, comfort, and display the body is incalculable and sinful. The Jezebels of today with their intolerance, anti-social tendencies and evil influence, use their looks, paint, and decoration to accomplish their corrupt practices and licentious behaviour. Because, as Christians, our bodies are temples of the Holy Spirit, we should take due and proper care of them, giving them the right food, maintaining reasonable strength, getting enough rest, and so on. "For no man ever yet hated his own flesh; but nourisheth and cherisheth it, even as the Lord the Church", (Eph. 5 v.29).

In today's society, one of the greatest barriers to successful marriage is the failure of one or both partners to "leave father and mother". Once a man leaves his father and mother and cleaves unto his wife, he and his wife become "one flesh", (Gen. 2 v.24; Eph. 5 v.31). This is a very intimate relationship, so close that the husband who loves his wife receives love in return, and they "as being heirs together of the grace of life" (1 Peter 3 v.7) while they live on earth as husband and wife, there is a relationship by grace which shall never pass away.

Scripture emphasises the permanence as well as the unity of marriage. The husband and wife must love each other with an unbreakable love. God's standard for marriage has not changed from the time of Adam and Eve to the present time and will remain. In marriage a new family is begun and the relationship of the former families are to be severed as far as authority, submission, and responsibilities are concerned. Parents are no longer to control the lives of their children once they are married. The Greek word, "proskollao", translated "cleave", literally means to be glued or cemented together. Husbands and wives are to "leave" their parents and to "cleave" to each other. This is the bond God ordained for marriage, which is for life "until death us do part". "Wherefore they are no more twain, but one flesh. What therefore God hath joined together, let not man put asunder", (Matt. 19 v.6).

The husband and wife who give each other love, consideration, courtesy, and honour, contribute to the beauty and strength of their marriage and give an invaluable example and legacy to their children. Love is giving, giving, and giving of oneself to each other. It is not getting, getting, and getting as the world portrays. Love is an attitude that issues forth in something that actually happens, the giving of oneself to each other unreservedly: Love. "Nevertheless let everyone of you in particular so love his wife even as himself; and the wife see that she reverence her husband", (Eph. 5 v.33).

The Evils of Society

There are many evils in society that threaten believers which Christians must strenuously oppose. The government has from time to time imposed legislation upon the nation that morally destroys the spiritual and social values of our country and nation, not to mention the special status of marriage in law.

It is vital that Christians speak out unashamedly and boldly witness for the truth of God's Word to society. Doubtless, by opposing evil and national sins will not be popular. Many will accuse Christians of homophobia, etc., which is now an argument increasingly deployed to silence any criticism against homosexuality, lesbianism, gay marriages, civil partnerships, prostitution, sodomy, pornography, and other evils. We also need to raise our voices in opposition against abortion, euthanasia, cloning, and all other anti-Christian practices and vices that plague our land and which Parliament has legalised and promoted over the years.

The enforcement of 'equality' laws and 'gender' regulations together with the removal of copies of the Bible from public places, e.g., schools, hospitals, hotels, etc., are among the assaults of Satan upon our Christian heritage that strike deeply at the moral fabric and spiritual values of the realm. A major factor that is hastening the landslide of declension and barrenness throughout the nation, is the fact that the heart of the Christian Church at large has grown cold and indifferent. Sadly, truth is compromised in many Churches as the order of the day, and the flood-gates are now wide open to admit wave upon wave of multi-faith ideas and other Christ-rejecting efforts, in order to extinguish the light of the Gospel.

Truth is that by which the heart must be guided and governed, for without truth there is no goodness. We must heed the words of Scripture which says, "Buy the truth, and sell it not; also wisdom, and instruction, and understanding . . . . . and meddle not with them that are given to change", (Prov. 23 v.23 and 24 v.21).

All the evil things as mentioned above, are now no longer regarded as sin, and the 'ideas' of the radicals, liberals, humanists, feminists, and socialists, etc., have become the new consensus of the permissive society. There has been a surge of revolts against traditional morality and the Christian family in particular, thus corroding our civil liberties and Biblical beliefs at every level.

The Bible is clear that obedience to God's law leads to national blessing. "Righteousness exalteth a nation: but sin is a reproach to any people", (Prov. 14 v.34). Those who oppose iniquity, must understand that they are involved in a spiritual warfare and battle against the powers of evil "in high places", (Eph. 6 v.12). The battle is the Lord's. The weapon with which to slay these evils is "the Sword of the Spirit, which is the Word of God", (Eph. 6 v.17).

Today the number of people who have the heritage of a godly home and Christian Church is becoming increasingly less, and the ignorance of spiritual truth and vagueness of Biblical knowledge on every hand is truly alarming. We need to get back to the basic, life-transforming doctrines of Biblical Christianity, praying that God will awaken us to the reality of prayer, and see again the blessing of reformation and revival in these sad days of declension.

God's Design for the Home

The will of God is personal, practical, and purposeful, touching upon every area of our lives, especially in the home. The home, as we have seen, is the basic unit of society. It was established at creation before either civil government or the Church. In the home, a child receives his or her values for life, learns respect for authority and concern for others, which is the foundation of society. In order that the home might fulfil its Divine function, God has appointed the husband as the head.

According to First Corinthians 11 v.3, the principle of subordination and authority pervades the entire universe. "But I would have you know, that the head of every man is Christ; and the head of the woman is the man; and the head of Christ is God", (1 Cor. 11 v.3). This is God's order and plan. Christ is "the head of every man", the man is under authority to Christ to lead his household in a meaningful, responsible, and loving way. He is to love his wife "as Christ also loved the Church, and gave Himself for it", (Eph. 5 v.25). This means that the relationship between Christ and His Church, is the model or pattern for the home.

It is deeply significant to note that how well the "head" of the home fulfils his role, will determine how well prepared, his child is to fulfil his role in life. The child who receives proper training in the home, will be prepared for his role, in the Church, in society, and in the world. The order in which Divine wisdom has placed persons and things is best and fittest, and to endeavour to change it is to destroy all order, and introduce confusion.

The relationship between the husband/father and the wife/mother is derived from the Godhead, Who are the same in substance, and equal in power and glory. Similarly, husband and wife are the same in substance and they are equal in power. But, like the Persons of the Godhead, husband and wife have different roles. Yet, they must be in close agreement, otherwise disagreements will have a detrimental effect on the children.

Authority and submission are based on love, not tyranny. Husbands do not have authority because of greater worth, but simply because of God's sovereign design and gracious purpose. Women respond in loving submission as they are designed to do. In the home, children receive instruction in the Word of God, intercession before the Throne of Grace, and provision and discipline according to the Law of God. There is no better way than in the home, to train and prepare children for life, in society, and in the Church.

Without the beautiful adornment and gracious endowment which the wife provides, home for man would be very poor and he would miss out on the satisfaction and happiness which God intended for him. Wives are angels . . . . . well, almost . . . . . actually, they are not . . . . . but really, they are God's greatest gift to husbands. Being a wife is one of the culminations of God's plan. Wives are lovely to look at who show true beauty of character, serenity of face, and nobility of purpose. By womanly beauty we do not mean that all wives are 'ravishing beauty queens or stunning fashion models', very few in fact are, but The Scripture emphasises the modest genuine loveliness of wifehood and motherhood. Wives are priceless, their "price is far above rubies", (Prov. 31 v.10). No man, nor the yoking together as cohabitants, or of same sex couples as homosexuals or lesbians, can make a home. The blessed transformation of house to home truly comes when the wife arrives and she becomes a loving helpmeet to her husband in everything, and a dear mother to some darling children who in the providence of God may come along.

Good wives give promise of successful lives and happy homes, but bad wives are the ruin of any man. "A continual dropping in a very rainy day and a contentious woman are alike", (Prov. 27 v.15). Solomon, to whom God gave "wisdom and understanding exceedingly much, and largeness of heart, even as the sand that is on the sea shore", (1 Kings 4 v.29), became the wisest of men, once declared, "Whoso findeth a wife findeth a good thing, and obtaineth favour of the Lord", (Prov. 18 v.22). While there will be problems and perplexities by the score that may confront us in family life, the secret of success in the home is to trust in God. "Trust in the Lord with all thine heart; and lean not unto thine own understanding. In all thy ways acknowledge Him, and He shall direct thy paths", (Prov. 3 v.5-6).

Sometimes God allows disappointments, but we are to be cheerful, sincere, and not gloomy. In the world, Christians are promised tribulations, but in the warmth and love of the Christian home there is unalloyed happiness and true contentment in the Lord, which is increased and intensified as it is shared with other believers, but always measured by the approval of our ever-abiding Guest, the Lord Jesus Christ. In regard to rearing and bringing-up of children, the promise of blessing is conditional upon training. "Train up a child in the way he should go: and when he is old, he will not depart from it", (Prov. 22 v.6). Notice that the word is not merely "tell", or even "teach", but rather the deeper and more comprehensive one, "train". God's method for parents is to train, train, train; to enunciate the great principles of life over and over again to our children, and to press home at every opportunity the tenets of Christian living. In this important matter, the Biblical principle is most clear, and in addition the training is to be by right example: "Whom shall he teach knowledge? And whom shall he make to understand doctrine? Them that are weaned from the milk, and drawn from the breasts. For precept must be upon precept, precept upon precept; line upon line, line upon line; here a little, and there a little", (Isaiah 28 v.9-10).

The qualities of loving understanding, firmness, and enunciation of authority, must be shown at all times during the formative and teenage years as children progressively develop into young adults, nurtured and built up in the foundational truths of the Word of God. This is a good investment which will enable all the family through grace to shine, and will make for a happy home. After all, the home is the greatest university, and the parents are the greatest teachers. Therefore, let us prayerfully cultivate Christian principles and practice in our everyday living, so that together with our children, our homes shall be bethels of praise and honour. "Call unto Me, and I will answer thee, and shew thee great and mighty things, which thou knowest not", (Jer. 33 v.3).

CHAPTER NINE

THE SINGLE WOMAN

The Challenge of Singleness

Happiness in Singleness

Homemaking par Excellence

Godliness and Zeal

The Single Woman

In the providence and will of God there are some women who are single who have never married. If a woman who is single considers that something is wrong with her state, or is discontent with her lot, then she sins, just indeed as the one who has been given the gift of marriage fails to exercise this gift. The same principle applies also to men. We must develop and use whatever gift God has given to us that we might serve Him to His glory. God is sovereign and He distributes His gifts for His purposes and for the good of His people. "And we know that all things work together for good to them that love God, to them who are the called according to His purpose", (Rom. 8 v.28).

The single woman is sometimes made to feel guilty by thoughtless people. We can be so taken up with the value of marriage, and in promoting the traditional family, that we lose sight of the needs of single women and the valuable contribution which many of them make to society generally, and to the Church in particular.

"As Christians", says Sharon James, "we want to support family life. The danger is that we elevate the good to the position of the best, giving the impression that family life is the ultimate aim for human life". Then she rightly counsels her readers to remember that Jesus put human marriage and family in second place to following Him.

We clearly see in Scripture that it can be an advantage to be single. For example, as in the case for some women serving the Lord in a mission situation. The married Christian woman is concerned about pleasing her husband, while the unmarried Christian woman is able to devote herself more fully to the Lord. "There is a difference also between a wife and a virgin. The unmarried woman careth for the things of the Lord, that she may be holy both in body and in spirit: but she that is married careth for the things of the world, how she may please her husband", (1 Cor. 7 v.34).

It is naturally the wish of most single women to marry one day and have a family. It is not good for human beings to be alone, man has been created as a social being, but there are some Christian women whose desire before God for this blessing has not been granted. They see in the Scripture that "God setteth the solitary in families", (Psalm 68 v.6), but not in their case, as far as marriage is concerned.

So then, we ask the question, Why? Such women are enabled, sooner or later, to submit to the sovereign will of God, believing that if they delight themselves in Him, He will not fail them nor forsake them. No doubt they can testify, to an extent that others cannot, of the blessedness of being set in the family of God and having their Maker as their husband.

Scripture also shows that in certain circumstances it is not a bad thing to be single, but rather the opposite. So those who are married should not display a pitying attitude to those who are single, nor should they badger them about their singleness, but rather respect them as singles.

The Challenge of Singleness

Many Churches do not really recognise that within their ranks there are single people, especially single women, who are feeling neglected, overlooked, and missing out on their place in the Body of Christ. In the exhortation to unity, holiness, and love, we read in Ephesians 4 v.11-16: "And He gave some, apostles; and some, prophets; and some, evangelists; and some, pastors and teachers; For the perfecting of the saints, for the work of the ministry, for the edifying of the Body of Christ: Till we all come in the unity of the faith, and of the knowledge of the Son of God, unto a perfect man, unto the measure of the stature of the fullness of Christ: That we henceforth be no more children, tossed to and fro, and carried about with every wind of doctrine, by the slight of men, and cunning craftiness, whereby they lie in wait to deceive; But speaking the truth in love, may grow up into Him in all things, which is the Head, even

Christ: From Whom the whole Body fitly joined together and compacted by that which every joint supplieth, according to the effectual working in the measure of every part, maketh increase of the Body unto the edifying of itself in love".

By laying much emphasis on family, we must not project the idea that only marriage can bring true contentment and fulfilment to life, and that anything less is to be considered God's second best. This gives the devil's lie and impression that such persons are relegated in God's plan to a life of frustration, unfulfillment, false hope, confusion, and loneliness. While marriage is the usual pattern for life, it must be recognised that it is not the only pattern. Statistics clearly tell us that a large percentage of the population in our society is single. The message of the Gospel is that all of us, whatever our status and station in life, can be whole people, enjoying and knowing the rich blessing of God, Who alone brings true meaning and purpose to our lives.

The Bible presents a theology of singleness, (Matt. 19; 1 Cor. 7), as an acceptable, honourable, and normal way of life. God is interested in men and women, first of all for who they are in themselves. He works with each one of us, whatever our state or age, to bring us to discover our true identity and completeness which can only be found in Him. "And ye are complete in Him, which is the Head of all principality and power", (Col. 2 v.10).

The Bible is full of single people and many of them were significant in God's purposes in a special way, for example, Miriam in the Old testament, and Martha and Mary, the two sisters, in the New Testament. So in Scripture there is a balance, for God needs married folk as well as single people. Being single is not God's second best. Though singleness may not be a permanent calling, it needs to be accepted as the present reality. There is nothing abnormal or subnormal about being single, nor is it a question of being a failure. In God's sight, married or single, has to do with what we do with the opportunities that He has given to us in life. Let us not burden ourselves with self-pity, but rather accept the challenges that come before us. "Thou wilt keep him in perfect peace, whose mind is stayed on Thee: because he trusteth in Thee", (Isaiah 26 v.3).

It is better to face up to the fact because a woman finds herself in the single state, that it is God's will for her at present. To come to this basic acceptance and understanding of Providence is essential, and thereby be content, resting in His grace and love, knowing that we can enjoy our relationship with Him in the present, and leaving the future in His loving care and gracious will. Our dependency at all times is upon God alone, and we must be interdependent with those whom we have fellowship in the Body of Christ.

We recognise that single people have the same sexual desires and feelings as married couples, and such impulse is the same as other normal, healthy appetites, as the need for food, water, and sleep. We should thank God for our sexuality, and surrender that part of our lives to Him. "Mortify therefore your members which are upon the earth; fornication, uncleanness, inordinate affection, evil concupiscence, and covetousness, which is idolatry: For which things' sake the wrath of God cometh on the children of disobedience: In the which ye also walked some time, when ye lived in them", (Col. 3 v. 5-7). As we trust in God the Holy Spirit will produce within us the fruit of self-control, psychologically, physically, and spiritually. "And the peace of God, which passeth all understanding, shall keep your hearts and minds through Christ Jesus", (Phil. 4 v.7).

In regard to the question of loneliness, which is often misunderstood, the single person's relationship to God will determine a meaningful fulfilment of life and security in Christ. "For the Lord God is a sun and shield: the Lord will give grace and glory: no good thing will He withhold from them that walk uprightly", (Psalm 84 v.11). "Blessed is the man that feareth the Lord, that delighteth greatly in his commandments", (Psalm 112 v.1).

God made man, male and female, He does not despise or denigrate anyone. God has a purpose for every life, and whatever our lot, or the little we have, we are to be content, knowing that God will provide for us from day to day. "Not that I speak in respect of want: for I have learned, in whatsoever state I am, therewith to be content", (Phil. 4 v.11).

As well as contentment in singleness, God has created all mankind to have fellowship and meaningful relationships. The Scripture gives us the key in Proverbs 18 v.24: "A man that hath friends must show himself friendly: and there is a friend that sticketh closer than a brother". When making friends with the opposite sex, avoid flirting and being deliberately sexually attractive; such friendships will not be healthy. It is imperative to develop standards that gain respect and enhance dignity. The standard of our friendship should be the "agape" (Greek), meaning "love", and spoken of in First Corinthians 13 as "charity", which is practical, issuing from a benevolent, loving, and charitable heart that becomes a tower of strength to our lives. "Watch ye, stand fast in the faith, quit you like men, be strong. Let all your things be done with charity", (1 Cor. 16 v.13-14).

The Church should not be seen in using single ladies merely as good baby-sitters. Relationships in the congregation must not be based on status, but on people themselves, and for who they are in themselves, whether single, widowed, or fatherless. "Pure religion and undefiled before God and the Father is this, To visit the fatherless and widows in their affliction, and to keep himself unspotted from the world", (James 1 v.27). A holy life and a charitable spirit show true religion which must be our constant endeavour. A caring Church will want to show compassion and to serve one another in love. Single people can offer great potential and resources for the building up of the Church family by devoting more time and energy to the tasks suited to them that come their way as Providence allows.

Happiness in Singleness

Singleness includes people of all ages and stations. Some singles offer a multitude of gifts and talents and experiences. Yet many factors contribute to the misunderstanding of singleness today. Among them are the pressures of media misrepresentation and Church insensitivity, to name but two. The Church should be reaching out to them in a warm family acceptance, but for the most part it is not trying. Many single people are serious about knowing the Bible, walking in the Spirit, pleasing the Lord Jesus Christ in their careers, their leisure time, and their social activities. "For bodily exercise profiteth little: but godliness is profitable unto all things, having promise of the life that now is, and of that which is to come", (1 Tim. 4 v.8).

Single people need true fellowship, interaction, and encouragement that can come only from other members of the Body of Christ. The only true guarantee of happiness has little to do with marriage or singleness, but everything to do with being a follower and disciple of Christ, and being obedient to the will of God. "But godliness with contentment is great gain. For we brought nothing into the world, and it is certain we can carry nothing out. And having food and raiment let us be therewith content", (1 Tim. 6 v.6-8).

Because of sin and the ways of the world, some single persons are promiscuous and given to "vile affections: for even their women did change the natural use into that which is against nature", (Rom. 1 v.26). One of the important challenges of the Church is to help its entire congregation deal with the sexual pressures of today's world through the teaching of God's Word. Faithfulness and family solidarity are fast disappearing in our society today, and due to a compromising and lukewarm Church little impression is being made upon a lost world.

In the Old Testament story of Ruth, who showed faith, courage, and loyalty, there is a good example of an adult female single person strategically used by God to do His work. Singleness is a gift from God. Jesus said to His disciples, "All men cannot receive this saying, save they to whom it is given. For there are some eunuchs, which were so born from their mother's womb: and there are some eunuchs, which were made eunuchs of men: and there be eunuchs, which have made themselves eunuchs for the kingdom of heaven's sake. He that is able to receive it, let him receive it", (Matt. 19 v.11-12). In the New Testament, the sisters, Martha and Mary, very different to each other, yet both served Christ and were His good and loyal friends.

We need companionship and relationships, one with another, whether single or married. There is nothing in the Bible to indicate that a person who chooses not to marry has any less worth than a person who marries. It is of prime importance, whether single or married, to lean on the all-sufficient grace and work of Christ, and walk in obedience to Him. "And God is able to make all grace abound toward you; that ye, always having all sufficiency in all things, may abound to every good work", (2 Cor. 9 v.8).

It is not a sin to be single. No one is perfect, and it is only by the grace of God that we can do His will. As opportunity permits we are to serve the Lord with all our God-given gifts and talents. "Wherefore we receiving a kingdom which cannot be moved, let us have grace, whereby we may serve God acceptably with reverence and godly fear: For our God is a consuming fire", (Heb. 12 v.28-29). Though He be our God in Christ, and deals with us graciously in Him, yet He is in Himself a consuming fire, a God of strict justice, Who will avenge Himself on all despisers of His grace, and all apostates.

The Bible makes it clear that we are all to be watchful: "Take heed unto thyself, and unto the doctrine; continue in them: for in doing this thou shalt both save thyself, and them that hear thee", (1 Tim. 4 v.16). We are commanded to make good use of our time: "Redeeming the time, because the days are evil. Wherefore be ye not unwise, but understanding what the will of the Lord is", (Eph.5 v.16-17). Scripture exhorts us to use our gifts for the glory of God: "Whether therefore ye eat, or drink, or whatsoever ye do, do all to the glory of God", (1 Cor. 10 v.31). Whatever the opportunities in Divine providence that come our way, we are responsible to God. "Submit yourselves therefore to God. Resist the devil, and he will flee from you. Draw nigh to God, and He will draw nigh to you", (James 4 v.7-8).

Homemaking par Excellence

Many gracious and godly single women are homemakers par excellence, although they have neither husband nor children. Their homes are havens of hospitality and kindness to relatives and friends. They often prove to have a cementing effect on their extended family. Many of them have a warm heart and a warm home for the Lord's people, including young people, as many indeed can testify.

Think of the widow of Zarephath who fed Elijah during the famine. The Lord spoke to Elijah saying, "Arise, get thee to Zarephath, which belongeth to Zidon, and dwell there: behold, I have commanded a widow woman there to sustain thee", (1 Kings 17 v.9). God took care of them and the meal and the oil multiplied, not in hoarding, but in spending. When God blesses a little, it will go a great way, even beyond expectation.

We have the New Testament story of Martha and Mary, who entertained the Saviour. "Now it came to pass, as they went, that He (Jesus) entered into a certain village: and a certain woman named Martha received him into her house. And she had a sister called Mary, which also sat at Jesus feet, and heard His word", and to Martha, He said, "But one thing is needful: and Mary hath chosen that good part, which shall not be taken away from her", (Luke 10 v.38-42). To Martha, it was expensive to entertain Christ, for He did not come alone, but brought His disciples with Him, yet she regarded not the cost of it. How can we spend what we have better than in Christ's service. At that time, it was a dangerous thing to do, yet she cared not what hazard she ran for His name's sake.

But of Mary, we read, that she "sat at Jesus' feet, and heard His Word". Our sitting at the feet of Christ, willing to hear His Word, and giving attention to it, signifies a readiness to receive it and a resignation of ourselves to take guidance from it. Worldly business and pursuits are a snare to us when it hinders us from serving God. Worldly cares are often the occasion of disturbance in families, and of strife and contention among relatives.

This story of Jesus entering "into a certain village", (Luke 10 v.38), not far from Jerusalem, has many great lessons to teach us. It was "the town of Mary and Martha" (John 11 v.1), undoubtedly that of Bethany, and "Martha received Him into her house", (v.38). She made Jesus very welcome. He loved to visit this home: "Now Jesus loved Martha, and her sister, and Lazarus", (John 11 v.5). It is easy to picture the scene. As Jesus reached Bethany He sought out the house of His friends, and as He approached, Martha and her sister, Mary, came to greet Him. What a welcome they gave Him, and what a joy it was for Him to go into a home in which He was always a welcome Guest. A Christian home is a home in which Christ is loved and served as Lord and Master, where He reigns as Head, and is given the chief place: "that in all things He might have the pre-eminence",(Col. 1 v.18).

When Christ is Head of the house, He regulates the conduct and behaviour of the home in regard to:-

(1) Conversation: "Whoso offereth praise glorifieth Me: and to him that ordereth his conversation aright will I shew the salvation of God", (Psalm 50 v.23).

(2) Reading matter: "Let the Word of Christ dwell in you richly in all wisdom; teaching and admonishing one

another in psalms and hymns and spiritual songs, singing with grace in your hearts to the Lord", (Col. 3 v.16).

(3) Radio and television so that certain soaps and programmes are not brought into our Christian home: "I will set no wicked thing before mine eyes: I hate the work of them that turn aside; it shall not cleave to me", (Psalm 101 v.3).

(4) Questionable and doubtful things: "Know ye not that the unrighteous shall not inherit the kingdom of God? Be not deceived: neither fornicators, not idolaters, nor adulterers, nor effeminate, nor abusers of themselves with mankind, nor thieves, nor covetous, nor drunkards, nor revilers, nor extortioners, shall inherit the kingdom of God", (1 Cor. 6 v.9-10).

(5) Work and recreation: "Whether therefore ye eat, or drink, or whatsoever ye do, do all to the glory of God", (1 Cor. 10 v.31); "And whatsoever ye do in word or deed, do all in the name of the Lord Jesus, giving thanks to God and the Father by Him", (Col. 3 v.17).

How sad today it is that in many so-called Christian homes, especially among single people who seek pleasure and the ways of the world rather than the things of God, the Word of God is blasphemed and dishonoured. Furthermore, there is a great neglect of the means of grace and absence from the place of worship on the Lord's Day. God is faithful to His people, and He demands a clear and definite response from us. Joshua's personal response and choice is a challenging call to us today. "Now therefore fear the Lord, and serve Him in sincerity and in truth: and put away the gods which your fathers served . . . . . choose you this day whom ye will serve; whether the gods which your fathers served that were on the other side of the flood . . . . . but as for me and my house, we will serve the Lord", (Joshua 24 v.14-15).

May our homes, therefore, be more Christlike in which :-

(1) the common tasks are performed out of love to Christ: "and whatsoever ye do, do it heartily, as to the Lord, and not unto men", (Col. 3 v.23);

(2) troubles, perplexities, problems, burdens, sorrows, and disappointments are taken to the Lord and resolved by Him: "Now a certain man was sick, named Lazarus, of Bethany, the town of Mary and her sister Martha. It was that Mary that anointed the Lord with ointment, and wiped His feet with her hair, whose brother Lazarus was sick. Therefore his sisters sent unto Him, saying, Lord, behold, he whom Thou lovest is sick", (John 11 v.1-3); and

(3) friends of the Lord are always welcome and the grace of hospitality is extended: "Use hospitality one to another without grudging", (1 Peter 4 v.9).

The Christian witness of a godly home can be not only a great blessing to many, but one that honours and glorifies God at all times. By the grace of God we should endeavour and do our utmost by prayer and in every practical way to honour Christ, and to bring our friends and neighbours into the enjoyment of God's great salvation. To the Gadarene man, Jesus said, "Go home to thy friends, and tell them how great things the Lord hath done for thee, and hath had compassion on thee", (Mark 5 v.19).

Godliness and Zeal

In appearance and dress the Christian single woman should realise that she is not to put about to try to attract men. She should understand that it is more important that someone be attracted to her godly character rather than to her outward looks and motives. She should not be preoccupied with outward things, but with who she is in humility, living "soberly, righteously, and godly, in this present world", (Titus 2 v.12). The voice of conscience gives testimony to that which is right in the nature and manner of good conversation with corresponding good behaviour rejoicing at all times in all conditions: "For our rejoicing is this, the testimony of our conscience, that in simplicity and godly sincerity, not with fleshly wisdom, but by the grace of God, we have had our conservation in the world, and more abundantly to you-ward", (2 Cor. 1 v.12). The kingdom of God cannot be shaken, it will remain, it is eternal, unchangeable, immovable. In Christ we will never be taken from it, and it will never be taken from us. For this amazing blessing in Him, we should always show gratitude by which we may give to God the right response, that is, a worshipping life offering holy service to our worthy and awesome God. "And this word, yet once more, signifieth the removing of those things that are shaken, as of things that are made, that those things that cannot be shaken may remain. Wherefore we receiving a kingdom which cannot be moved, let us have grace, whereby we may serve God acceptably with reverence and godly fear", (Heb. 12 v.27-28).

There is nothing anywhere at any time that "shall be able to separate us from the love of God, which is in Christ Jesus our Lord", (Rom. 8 v.39). Our salvation was secured by God's decree from eternity past and will be held secure by Christ's love through all future time and throughout all eternity. We are reminded of Jesus' high priestly prayer, in which He prays on behalf of believers: "That they may all be one; as Thou, Father, art in Me, and I in Thee, that they also may be one in Us: that the world may believe that Thou hast sent Me. And the glory which Thou gavest Me I have given them; that they may be one, even as We are one: I in them, and Thou in Me, that they may be made perfect in one; and that the world may know that Thou hast sent Me, and hast loved them, as Thou hast loved Me. Father, I will that they also, whom Thou hast given Me, be with Me where I am; that they may behold My glory, which Thou hast given Me: for Thou lovedst Me before the foundation of the world", (John 17 v.21-24).

Godliness and zeal are the things most needful, for nothing without these will do us any real good in this world, and nothing but these will go with us into another world: "A new heaven and a new earth . . . . . the holy city, new Jerusalem", (Rev. 21 v.1-2), prepared for those who are God's elect people. Let us not condemn the pious zeal and godly character of any, and let us never be discouraged if we are taunted for our pious zeal, and let us ever seek to glorify God in all things.

Earnestness and enthusiasm are sometimes employed to describe zeal, which really mean putting our whole heart into whatever we are doing. There must be work or labour, in opposition to idleness; and there must be quietness in opposition to being busy-bodies in other people's affairs or meddling in the lives of others. "For we hear that there are some which walk among you disorderly, working not at all, but are busybodies. Now them that are such we command and exhort by our Lord Jesus Christ, that with quietness they work, and eat their own bread. But ye, brethren, be not weary in well doing", (2 Thess. 3 v.11-13). Paul is speaking to those who are too lazy to work, exhorting them to settle down and earn the bread they eat; and thus, order would replace the disruption caused by their idleness and meddling. The Biblical work ethic remains constant. When Christians diligently pursue the vocation to which God has called them, God is honoured.

Satan, men, and the world, cannot take eternal life away from us. Those chosen in grace to this good part have "the hope set before us: Which hope we have as an anchor of the soul, both sure and stedfast", (Heb. 6 v.18-19). Because our God is infinite in power and love, we can say with Moses, "The eternal God is thy refuge, and underneath are the everlasting arms", (Deut. 33 v.27). What God gives us from day to day we must be content with, and thankful, and future things are in the hand of God. All that men do against His people, God can turn to their good. "So that we may boldly say, The Lord is my helper, and I will not fear what man shall do unto Me", (Heb. 13 v.6).

Supremely, happiness, contentment, godliness, and zeal, come from communion with God. The more we focus on Him the less we will be concerned about anything material. When we are near to Christ, we are overwhelmed with the riches that we have in Him, and earthly possessions simply do not matter. Our treasure is in our Homeland, in heaven, and we should set our "affection on things above, not on things on the earth", (Col. 3 v.2). As Christians, our hearts are only strengthened by grace. "For the kingdom of God is not meat and drink; but righteousness, and peace, and joy in the Holy Ghost", (Rom. 14 v.17).

All in all, the contribution of many godly single women to society as a whole, in many fields and professions, cannot be calculated. By virtue of their state, they are in a position to make a commitment to various kinds of work, which married women cannot do. The faithful service of God's people will be commended at the Judgement Seat of Christ. It is not what our fellow-servants say that counts, all our work and labour of love shall be rewarded by the Master: "Well done, thou good and faithful servant . . . . . enter thou into the joy of thy Lord", (Matt. 25 v.21 and 23).

What work we do for God in this world is but so little compared with the great joy set before us, the joy of the redeemed, the joy of which Christ Himself is the fountain and centre. A crown of righteousness awaits the believer, purchased by the righteousness of Christ, and bestowed upon all who love, prepare, and long for His appearing. "Henceforth there is laid up for me a crown of righteousness, which the Lord the righteous Judge, shall give me at that day: and not to me only, but unto all them also that love His appearing", (2 Tim. 4 v.8).

CHAPTER TEN

WOMEN IN THE WORKPLACE

Social Engineering weakens the Family

Particular Circumstances may arise

Invaluable Contribution of Women to Society

Promotion of Women in the Workplace

Diligence, Integrity and Attitude

Perseverance and a Humble spirit

Witnessing as Salt and Light

WOMEN IN THE WORKPLACE

Another area of society which many women must occupy is that of the workplace. It has to be said that there are numerous women in the workplace who ought to be there. In this age of "equal rights" and "equal opportunities", there are countless openings in the world of work for women, openings that are filled by not only single women but also multitudes of married women as well.

In an article on "Worldliness" by J. P. Thackway in the 'Bible League Quarterly', says, "Too often, it is simply a higher standard of living that sends young mothers out to work, leaving small children in a day nursery. A Christian wife and mother can be blameless when judged by the evangelical taboos, that is, restrictions placed on behaviour, and yet be guilty of following the world, in her determination to 'get a life' outside the home".

In 1986 the British Government passed legislation which required that as many women as possible take up work, and that 50% of each profession should be female. One result is, as a survey by the University of Southampton revealed, that "young middle-class mums are employing childminders so that they can hold down their jobs". Then they grieve and feel guilty. Their bodies are telling them to be mums, and their minds are telling them to go out and be earners in the rat race to 'keep up with the Joneses'.

Social Engineering Weakens the Family

All the social engineering and legislation by successive governments over recent decades have caused untold damage to family life. "Many of our problems, in children's and young people's behaviour, in our morals, culture and production, are partially caused by the weakening of family ties and slack attitudes of family responsibilities. This is a paradoxical result of our sincere desire to make women equal with men in everything". The man who wrote these words in 1987 was actually President Mikhail Gorbachov of the USSR at the time, and he was speaking about the situation in his own country. Yet western governments today keep promoting their pro-feminist, anti-family, anti-marriage, and anti-Christian, programmes.

Society, fashions, and culture may change, but God's Word remains sure and relevant. Many men and women slight the gracious directions God has given us in the Bible for they prefer to take their own path in the opposite direction by following the ways of the world. The prophet Isaiah proclaims that in returning to God and reposing in Him as our rest, we shall have peace and confidence. But a lying and rebellious Israel, having rejected God's law, "would not". "For thus saith the Lord God, the Holy One of Israel; In returning and rest shall ye be saved; in quietness and in confidence shall be your strength: and ye would not", (Isaiah 30 v.15). Real repentance is the only way to return to and trust God in strength-giving "quietness and confidence". In our day this repentance is scoffed at and blatantly rejected in favour of vain self-help, which ultimately will produce defeat, fear, and death. The flaming fire of God's punishment will fall upon all who refuse His Word, and the eternality of God's judgment will remain on those who do not repent and trust Christ.

While society worldwide is changing rapidly under the influence of Satan, for the Christian there are opportunities to be grasped as well as dangers to be avoided. God is infinite, eternal, and unchangeable, as the Shorter Catechism teaches us, and this great truth is a reality that needs to be accepted. "Jesus Christ the same yesterday, and to day, and for ever", (Heb. 13 v.8). Biblical truths and the doctrines of grace need to be re-affirmed. During the last forty years or more, many false religions have arisen, and belief in the God of the Bible is considered no longer relevant. Right and wrong now depend on circumstances and popular opinion. On radio and television, soaps, dramas, and other programmes, all endorse a mixture of humanist and existentialist thought. Sadly, many Christians have been influenced and brainwashed by these thought patterns, resulting in the fact that the Bible nowadays is squeezed out, pushed aside, and is no longer regarded as the only standard of faith and conduct.

Since the beginning of time many great civilisations have come and gone, among them the Grecian and Roman empires which have risen, prospered, and then declined. They disintegrated and vanished as historians have written because of corruption, teenage rebellion, adultery, sexual permissiveness, blurring of gender differences, homosexuality practice and other sins. "Professing themselves to be wise, they became fools, and changed the glory of the incorruptible God into an image made like to corruptible man, and to birds, and four-footed beasts, and creeping things. Wherefore God also gave them up to uncleanness through the lusts of their own hearts, to dishonour their own bodies between themselves: who changed the truth of God into a lie, and worshipped and served the creature more than the Creator, Who is blessed for ever. Amen. For this cause God gave them up unto vile affections: for even their women did change the natural use into that which is against nature: And likewise also the men, leaving the natural use of the women, burned in their lust one toward another; men with men working that which is unseemly, and receiving in themselves that recompense of their error which was meet. And even as they did not like to retain God in their knowledge, God gave them over to a reprobate mind, to do those things which are not convenient; Being filled with all unrighteousness, fornication, wickedness, covetousness, maliciousness; full of envy, murder, debate, deceit, malignity; whispers, backbiters, haters of God, despiteful, proud, boasters, inventors of evil things, disobedient to parents, without understanding, covenantbreakers, without natural affection, implacable, unmerciful: Who knowing the judgment of God, that they which commit such things are worthy of death, not only do the same, but have pleasure in them that do them", (Rom. 1 v.22-32). When people reject God's rules for the family, and for living, they face the consequences of Divine wrath and judgment, and God shall give them up; punishment and hell shall be their eternal reward.

The Apostle Paul says that such people "are without excuse", (Rom. 1 v.20), because God's blueprint has been written into every human being since the time of Creation. "So God created man in His own image, in the image of God created He him; male and female created He them", (Gen. 1 v.27). The creational ordinance of marriage (Gen. 2 v.18-25) is the God-given building block of every society the world over. We are living very much in a secular society with worldliness all around us, and God's people must be firm in the faith, be alert, and not allow the world dictate to us the way in which we live out our Christian belief and witness. "For My thoughts are not your thoughts, neither are your ways My ways, saith the Lord. For as the heavens are higher than the earth, so are My ways higher than your ways, and My thoughts than your thoughts. For as the rain cometh down, and the snow from heaven, and returneth not thither, but watereth the earth, and maketh it bring forth and bud, that it may give seed to the sower, and bread to the eater: So shall My Word be that goeth forth out of My mouth: it shall not return unto Me void, but it shall accomplish that which I please, and it shall prosper in the thing whereto I send it", (Isaiah 55 v.8-11).

The Bible calls upon us to repent of our sin, to return to God, to obey His Word, to live by His standards, and not by the standards of society or of the world. By God's grace we must turn away from all that is evil, false, and corrupt, and worship "the King eternal, immortal, invisible, the only wise God", to Whom "be honour and glory for ever and ever", (1 Tim. 1 v.17). "True worshippers" are good Christians, distinguished from hypocrites, for "they that worship Him must worship Him in spirit and in truth", (John 4 v.23-24). We must get back to obeying His commandments, as our Christianity before God is evidenced by the course and tenor of our behaviour, not by our talk, but by our walk and work according to the Rule of God as laid down and revealed in the Scriptures. Of Zacharias and his wife Elisabeth, we read, that "they were both righteous before God, walking in all the commandments and ordinances of the Lord blameless", (Luke 1 v.6).

God's Word does not and never will change, it applies to all people at all times. We must base our lives firmly on God's unchanging absolutes in this so-called post-modern world. Today, the question of Truth, as it relates to the question of the inspiration, inerrancy, and authority of Scripture, is widely criticised and constantly challenged by an impotent Church and unbelieving world. The Bible is Truth unchanged, unchanging, and trustworthy. "Thy Word is true from the beginning: and every one of Thy righteous judgments endureth for ever", (Psalm 119 v.160). "And this Word, Yet once more, signifieth the removing of those things that are shaken, as of things that are made, that those things which cannot be shaken may remain. Wherefore we receiving a kingdom which cannot be moved, let us have grace, whereby we may serve God acceptably with reverence and godly fear: For our God is a consuming fire", (Heb. 12 v.27-29).

True Christianity is not founded on education, yet education may be and often is blessed to fortify young people against irreligious infection. It is a joy, nevertheless, to see children treading in good Christian parent's steps, and to rejoice in thanksgiving to God for so great a blessing. "I rejoiced greatly that I found of thy children walking in truth, as we have received a commandment from the Father. And now I beseech thee, lady, not as though I wrote a new commandment unto thee, but that which we had from the beginning, that we love one another. And this is love, that we walk after His commandments. This is the commandment, That, as ye have heard from the beginning, ye should walk in it", (2 John v.4-6).

Peculiar Circumstances may arise

The question may be asked, even at this point, 'Are there not circumstances in which it is in order for a wife and mother to work outside the home, either part-time or full-time? There are times, indeed, when circumstances are such, --- perhaps bereavement, a tragic event, having an unwell husband, or certain family financial constraints, --- which it is necessary to do so.

The wife and mother in Proverbs 31, who ran her home so well, and was called "blessed" by her husband and children, also engaged in profitable business outside the home --- buying a field, and producing and selling various articles. However, her outside activities did not result in the neglect of her family, but rather the reverse. Her working outside the home was part of her making the home.

It is a different picture if a married couple have no children, or no dependent children. There is nothing to prevent the wife taking up a job or pursuing a career, providing that by doing so she does not undermine the authority of her husband or impair his daily work, as he discharges his God-given responsibility of being the primary provider.

It has to be said, however, that there are many cases of married couples, even among professing Christians, who delay having a family so that they may become more affluent. But surely those couples who are concerned about doing the will of God will desire to raise up "a godly seed" sooner rather than later. They will be found committing their way to God as the One Who promises that those who trust in Him, and are in the path of duty, shall not lack any good thing.

There are many peculiar circumstances and situations that may arise when Christians are severely put to the test. Sometimes under pressure, and when difficulties weigh heavily upon them, they are tempted in dire situations to conform to practices and adopt relationships that are at variance and contrary to the teaching of the Word of God. There can be many trials and 'hard calls' in life, just as the believers of the Macedonian Churches experienced: "How that in a great trial of affliction the abundance of their joy and their deep poverty abounded unto the riches of their liberality", (2 Cor. 8 v.2). They were in a very low condition, and themselves in great distress, yet they contributed willingly to the relief of others.

The Apostle Peter speaks of "the trial of your faith, being much more precious than of gold that perisheth, though it be tried with fire, might be found unto praise and honour and glory at the appearing of Jesus Christ", (1 Peter 1 v.7). Even to the best of Christians there can be times of great "heaviness through manifold temptations", (1 Peter 1 v.6). The adversities, afflictions, and sorrows of God's people are but for a season. The Christian's response should always be a humble acquiescence in the wisdom and will of God.

The terms "widow" and "widower" apply respectively to a woman or man whose marriage partner has died and who has not re-married. A widow on losing her husband, the person vital to her well-being, makes it hard for her to survive alone. In such circumstances the widow and fatherless children are not to be abused, but are to be comforted and assisted where possible. "Ye shall not afflict any widow, or fatherless child", (Exod. 22 v.22).

The State, of course, nowadays provides life-long widows' pensions plus provision for dependent children. The rise of 'feminism' has radically re-shaped society, but not for the better, therefore Biblical principles must be reapplied to today's shifting cultural norms. The Christian view of death and dying is so at variance with the secular view. To the secular mind, death, on the one hand, is an ultimate terror and disaster, to be averted or postponed as far as possible. On the other hand, a life can be regarded as so broken, disabled, fading, useless, as to be not worthwhile, or of any social value, and hence it may be neglected and even extinguished by voluntary or involuntary euthanasia. The Christian view (1) is that death and dying happens to all: "Wherefore, as by one man sin entered into the world, and death by sin; and so death passed upon all men, for that all have sinned", (Rom. 5 v.12); (2) it is to be accepted where the dying process makes it inevitable: "Yea, I think it meet, as long as I am in this tabernacle, to stir you up by putting you in remembrance; Knowing that shortly I must put off this my tabernacle, even as our Lord Jesus Christ hath shewed me", (2 Peter 1 v.13-14); and (3) the Christian hope of heaven is assured for those who "die in the Lord", (Rev. 14 v.13). So, what matters most is not death, but a person's union with Christ.

"Therefore if any man be in Christ, he is a new creature: old things are passed away; behold, all things are become new", (2 Cor. 5 v.17).

It must be emphasised that life is not ours to extinguish, since it belongs to God. God, in His goodness gives life, and it is He in His sovereignty Who takes it away. But to neglect the needs of the sick, the poor, the aged, the infirm, the disabled, or the disadvantaged, is evil. This relates to all kinds of human life, whether it be the unborn child, the infant, the disabled, or the dying. To relieve the suffering of the dying is a noble and illustrious Christian aim. Christian missions have long been in the forefront of medical aid and famine relief to refugees, the under privileged, epidemic victims, prisoners, and other needy persons. As well as spiritual and ethical reasons, health care always accompanies the Gospel of Jesus Christ as a matter of Christian virtue and integrity. Jesus answered the two disciples of John and said, "Go and shew John again those things which ye do hear and see: The blind receive their sight, and the lame walk, the lepers are cleansed, and the deaf hear, the dead are raised up, and the poor have the Gospel preached to them. And blessed is he, whosoever shall not be offended in Me", (Matt. 11 v.4-6).

Death and dying are the ends of a process which begins in everyone from conception. It is inevitable that stress within the family will occur in relation to death. The sorrow of separation and the pain of bereavement must be borne with Christian fortitude and trust in the God of all grace and comfort. "Blessed be God, even the Father of our Lord Jesus Christ, the Father of mercies, and the God of all comfort; who comforteth us in all our tribulations, that we may be able to comfort them which are in any trouble, by the comfort wherewith we ourselves are comforted of God", (2 Cor. 1 v.3-4).

To dying saints it is simplest to encourage prayer who need only to be reminded and assured that by trusting in Christ who died on Calvary's Cross to bear away our sin as our Saviour and Lord, has said: "Let not your heart be troubled: ye believe in God, believe also in Me. In My Father's house are many mansions: if it were not so, I would have told you. I go to prepare a place for you. And if I go and prepare a place for you, I will come again, and receive you unto Myself; that where I am, there ye may be also", (John 14 v.1-3).

There are those facing death who have never seen or realised their need of salvation, and no one can help a dying person, or their near and dear ones, who has not come to terms with his or her own dying, for pretence is no comfort at such a time. Particular problems may arise when and if attempts are made at spiritual healing are sought, the distribution of the patient's property, the making of wills. The need for reconciliation with alienated friends or estranged members of family can also be causes of difficulty.

A time of dying evokes many reactions with relatives and friends, not all of them good or helpful. Some evince guilt about past events, or what they might or should have done to help, and often this takes the form of exaggerated blame for others even for the dying. In these peculiar circumstances the Church needs to care and to offer compassionate ministry not only to the dying, but also to the family circle, not to compete or to deny medical carers their proper place in caring. The greatest element of Christian care is love, and the parable of the Good Samaritan is the Lord's example of loving competence and compassion. "But a certain Samaritan, as he journeyed, came where he was", that is, to the place where a certain man was set upon by thieves who departed leaving him half dead, "and when he saw him, he had compassion on him, And went to him, and bound up his wounds, pouring in oil and wine, and set him on his own beast, and brought him to an inn, and took care of him. And on the morrow when he departed, he took out two pence, and gave them to the host, and said unto him, Take care of him; and whatsoever thou spendest more, when I come again, I will repay thee", (Luke 10 v.33-35).

It is an acknowledged fact that things which happen during the time when someone is seriously ill, and then dies, shape the emotions and living patterns of those about them who must live on with those memories and a conscience that confronts them in the future. "And herein do I exercise myself, to have always a conscience void of offence toward God, and toward men", (Acts 24 v.16).

Those who have lost a dear partner through death need careful pastoral care and support, and may need help in coming to terms with their sad loss themselves, and also in working it through with their bereaved children to overcome any confusion or uncertainty; and it is most necessary to provide practical assistance and encouragement toward reincorporation into the Church fellowship and the community at large. At a time when David was greatly distressed because of the mutiny of his men, we would do well to emulate his example, whatever our trials and difficulties may be, for we read that "David encouraged himself in the Lord his God", (1 Sam. 30 v.6).

Another traumatic experience is that of a wife who is pregnant when her husband dies, thus creating added difficulties and trying set of circumstances. In this case she can be expected to go through a delayed bereavement reaction some time even after giving birth. Our only help is in God says the Psalmist: "Hear me when I call, O God of my righteousness: Thou hast enlarged me when I was in distress; have mercy upon me, and hear my prayer", (Psalm 4 v.1). Believers of every age may employ this lovely form of address to God. By grace we are given a righteous standing before God and the desire and power to live righteously before men. It is all of grace, He is the God of our righteousness. God will put grace in the heart, He gives us inward joy, comfort, and sustained peace. He is our sole Protector and makes us to dwell in safety. Let us live for God today whatever the task, and tonight "the peace of God, which passeth all understanding, shall keep your hearts and minds through Christ Jesus", (Phil. 4 v.7).

Societal norms at the beginning of the twenty first century are very different from those of forty or fifty years ago. Today in the United Kingdom almost some fifty percent of marriages fail and breakdown. Over half the nation's children are reared by only one parent, and they suffer greatly by the human cost of separation and pain of divorce. As a consequence mothers and children bear stresses in many ways, sexual, emotional, and physical abuse, and often the enduring of neglect and loneliness. For their own protection many of these children are put into care, others are fostered or adopted, perhaps by couples other than those in a normal heterosexual relationship --- these certainly are hard options. In such circumstances many adults are tempted to take the easy way out, compromise, and fall into sin. Christians are reminded and they must always adhere to accept the Biblical teaching on marriage, family, and sexual continence within marriage (1 Cor. 7; Eph. 6 v.1-4). Marital infidelity, breakdown, and cohabitation are an abomination unto the Lord. Children are precious in the sight of God, and very sadly they are often the victims of irresponsible adult behaviour.

Many indeed are the perplexities and trials of life, and in the workplace a further common problem for women, is sexual harassment whether for sexual favours, or conduct of a sexual and coercive nature, directed at someone who does not welcome it. Such misconduct and vile behaviour include --- sexual jokes, offensive telephone calls, displays of obscenity, pornographic photographs, pictures, posters, sexual propositions, request for dates, persistent staring, physical contact such as patting, pinching, or touching in a sexual way, deliberately brushing against a person, or putting an arm around another person's body at work, unwelcome remarks, insinuations about a person's sex life or body, suggestive comments about a person's body, cat-calls, obscene gestures, indecent exposure, sexual assault and rape. Such vile behaviour and base conduct are more often practised by men and directed at women, which commonly occur in the workplace, in teacher-student relationships, shops, and other social situations. Sometimes sexual harassment is an issue within the Church, and far from being a sanctuary, it sometimes covers up the practice and endeavours to hide it.

The Scripture roundly condemns all forms of such vile and evil behaviour, because:-

(1) Man and woman are created by God in the Divine image, and therefore have equal value. (Gen. 1 v.26-27).

(2) Relationships, including marriage, should be characterised by mutual submission, love, and justice. (Mark 12 v.31, Eph. 5 v.21-33, Col. 3 v.18 and 4 v.1).

(3) Compassion and due care are to be shown towards the marginalised, the powerless, including women. (Isaiah 3 v.14-15, Matt. 15 v.21-28, Luke 7 v.36-50, and 8 v.43-48).

(4) Women are treated as persons in their own right and worthy of sincere human relationships that are not of a sinful nature. (Matt. 26 v.6-13, Mark 7 v.24-39, Luke 10 v.38-42, John 4 v.7-42).

(5) Women should be treated with purity. (1 Tim. 5 v.2-3).

(6) Women should not be victimised by sexual violence. (Luke 7 v.37-47, John 8 v.3-8).

(7) Sexual impurity must be avoided and is condemned in the Word of God. (Exod. 20 v.14, Deut. 27 v.20-23, Matt. 5 v.27-28, 1 Cor. 5 v.1-5, and 6 v.9-20, Col. 3 v.5, 1 Peter 4 v.3).

It is important, therefore, to be prepared to respond appropriately to the victims of sexual harassment and to the perpetrator who must be held accountable for his or her actions. When such allegations are made within a Christian organisation there is the dilemma as to what extent confidentiality should be maintained, informing the civil authorities where law-breaking has occurred, whether action should be taken to prevent further damage to the organisation, and what steps should be taken to prevent a recurrence, particularly where this impacts on families. Church authorities and Christian organisations must without hesitation do all in their power to uphold and maintain moral, ethical, and spiritual standards, and where necessary discipline those who have erred and committed transgression, according to the pattern laid down in the Word of God. Christians should be zealous for the honour of Christ, and always be on guard to maintain the Biblical teaching in respect of purity --- in thought, in word, and in deed --- repent of any complacency or self-righteousness, and seek by God's grace day by day to obey His Word and serve Him in whatsoever we do, to "do all to the glory of God", (1 Cor. 10 v.31).

Invaluable Contribution of Women to Society

It is an acknowledged fact that women are an essential part of the workforce, especially in fields of education, the caring profession, the services industries, and also that they make an invaluable contribution to the life of the Church of Christ worldwide.

In the life of the Church today, women do an important work in giving instructions in situations other than public worship. There are many Christians who have had good reason to bless God for sound teaching given to them by godly women Sabbath School teachers. In foreign mission situations, much useful work is done by Christian women who teach not only in Sabbath Schools but sow the Good Seed and also pass on Bible knowledge and truth in primary and secondary schools, or drop words of instruction "in season" to patients who attend hospitals and clinics. Women play a vital and important part by caring for the sick, educating children and young people, and exhorting the younger women to "adorn the doctrine of God our Saviour in all things", so "that the Word of God be not blasphemed", (Titus 2 v.10 and v.5).

In the secular workplace, there are tremendous opportunities for women to commend the Christian way of living by applying their Christian teaching and ethics to their every day work. It is a most valuable part Christian teachers play in building up society when they teach children even subjects other than Religious Education, and in doing so, show by their attitudes, words, and example that the Christian lifestyle is commendable and praiseworthy.

There are many very noble and worthy Christian women in strategic situations, nursing, medicine, and other caring professions who not only commend Christianity by their conscientiousness and Christlikeness of character, but also make it clear in various ways how very wrong it is to debase the sanctity of human life.

It is a deplorable fact that, in some parts of the modern workplace, there is a dire lack of respect for women, but so often this is caused by women themselves trying to be clones of men.

Women, therefore, should conduct themselves in the workplace, and in relation to men in the workplace, in such a manner as to command respect. In her book, 'God's Design for Women', Sharon James has this exhortation when she says, "It is right that there should be a reserve, a modesty, when relating to men". And how true that is both in dress and behaviour.

In one way or another all of us are in close relations to one another. As members of the same family, as members of the same Church, as members of the same workforce, as members of the same community, we are bound so closely together that what any one of us does is certain to tell upon others. It is out of this close connection with others that influence comes. "Iron sharpeneth iron; so a man sharpeneth the countenance of his friend . . . . . As in water face answereth to face, so the heart of man to man", (Prov. 27 v.17,19). The graces and conduct of good persons are sharpened by conversation and communing with those that are good; and bad persons lusts, passions, and evil habits are sharpened by communing with those that are bad. As the water is a looking-glass in which we may see our faces by reflection, so there are mirrors by which our hearts are exposed and revealed to us. Let us examine our own conscience, our thoughts, our affections, and intentions. As a looking-glass shows up the spots and defilements, so the mirror of God's Word shows us our sin, so that we can turn from our sinful ways with sorrow in repentance, looking by faith to God for grace through Christ with a sincere desire to love and serve Him unto eternal life.

Promotion of Women in the Workplace

In order to carry out her duties and responsibilities, there is nothing in The Scripture about the headship of the man over the woman preventing the woman from being promoted in the workplace to the extent that she might have to supervise men. Certainly, in the home in relation to her husband, and in the Church in relation to men, she is not "to usurp authority over the man", (1 Tim. 2 v.12), but she is at liberty to accept a supervisory position provided she does not compromise her femininity by, for example, trying to be a clone of a man, or, in the case of a married woman, that she does not undermine the leadership role of her husband as the head in the home. "A virtuous woman is a crown to her husband: but she that maketh ashamed is as rottenness in his bones", (Prov. 12 v.4).

There is no doubt that Christian women in the workplace today face and experience many anti-Christian pressures. They need our practical sympathy and prayerful support, so that they will be able to fulfil their God-appointed role and exhibit with honour and dignity something of the fragrance and beauty of the Christian life.

Everything in the practical conduct of life depends upon character, by which we mean what a man or a woman really is, in the very depth of their being, in the sight of God: 'to Whom all hearts are open, all desires known, and from Whom no secrets are hid'. (Psalm 139). The rich man of the parable was well off, probably much thought of and highly esteemed by the world, but God called him a "fool", (Luke 12 v.20). What a man or woman have they leave behind; what a man or woman are they carry with them.

The great wish that most have in beginning life is that they may be successful. Many have the idea that success consists in gaining a livelihood and wealth, but anyone may gain these things who cannot be said to have succeeded, if such are gained at the expense of health, or by means of trickery and dishonest practices. The world is full of such people who ultimately come to nothing. Essential to success in life is moral character, in its various elements of honesty, truthfulness, steadiness, temperance, and good principle. "Let us walk honestly, as in the day; not in rioting and drunkenness, not in chambering and wantonness, not in strife and envying. But put ye on the Lord Jesus Christ, and make not provision for the flesh, to fulfil the lusts thereof", (Rom. 13 v.13-14).

To "walk honestly, as in the day", is to live in a way that pleases God. It is to live honestly before our Lord and before men, to live an outward life that is consistent with our inner nature in Christ, to live a sanctified life that reflects our justified life in Him. "But let us, who are of the day, be sober, putting on the breastplate of faith and love; and for an helmet, the hope of salvation. For God hath not appointed us to wrath, but to obtain salvation by our Lord Jesus Christ, Who died for us, that, whether we wake or sleep, we should live together with Him", (1 Thess. 5 v.8-10). We are to behave properly "toward them that are without" (1 Thess. 4 v.12) and act as becomes the Gospel. By so doing we shall gain a good report from those that are without, "for we trust we have a good conscience, in all things willing to live honestly", (Heb. 13 v.18).

However, in the workforce there is often the opportunity of forming close friendships with those we admit to the inner circle of our acquaintance. For most of us there are a few persons who stand to us in a different relation from the rest. We are intimate with them, take pleasure in their company, confide in them, and in joy and in sorrow it is to them we go. The sweetness of such friendship is an important relationship of life. "A friend loveth at all times", (Prov. 17 v.17).

The highest of all examples of friendship is to be found in Christ. "Now Jesus loved Martha, and her sister, and Lazarus", (John 11 v.5). The disciples knew a friendship with Him unenjoyed by others. He offers Himself to every one of us as a "friend": "Ye are My friends, if ye do whatsoever I command you", (John 15 v.14). "A man that hath friends must shew himself friendly: and there is a Friend that sticketh closer than a brother", (Prov. 18 v.24). Christ is a Friend to all believers that sticks closer than a brother.

Fidelity is the very essence of true friendship, and once broken, it cannot be easily renewed. Quarrels between friends are the bitterest and most lasting. We should refuse to form friendships with those of a low moral tone; lack principle; whose standard of right, honesty, purity, and virtue is deficient; and those who show no reverence for God and blaspheme His sacred name. "Thou shalt love the Lord thy God with all they heart, and with all they soul, and with all thy mind", (Matt. 22 v.37). Unhealthy friendships and unsavoury companions have caused many Christians to drift away from the faith of Christ, such are deserving of our most fervent prayers and intercession, and we should do all in our power to lead them back to the Father's fold from which they have wandered. We should always choose our friends from those who have chosen the better part, so that together we become stronger and better in the service and witness of God.

With diligence and determination let us "earnestly contend for the faith" (Jude v.3), face whatever dangers and pitfalls that may confront us without flinching, and go straight on our way against all opposing forces, neither turning to the right hand or the left. "Only be thou strong and very courageous, that thou mayest observe to do according to all the law, which Moses My servant commanded thee: turn not from it to the right hand or to the left, that thou mayest prosper whithersoever thou goest. This Book of the law shall not depart out of thy mouth; but thou shalt meditate therein day and night, that thou mayest observe to do according to all that is written therein: for then thou shalt make thy way prosperous, and then thou shalt have good success", (Josh. 1 v.7-8).

Diligence, Integrity and Attitude

In the workplace women interact on a continuous basis with many people from all walks of life. There, Christian women are closely observed, and the impression they make is not so much the verbal interaction but the witness of their lives that employers and co-workers see, remember, and reflect upon. This presents a great opportunity for the Christian. Delivering exactly what they are contracted to do establishes credibility and gives weight to Christian testimony. "Servants, be obedient to them that are your masters according to the flesh, with fear and trembling, in singleness of your heart, as unto Christ", (Eph. 6 v.5).

It is important to give wholehearted commitment to perform well in doing a good job by standing firm on principles and not compromise under any circumstances. The Christian employee should be marked by integrity, consistency, truthfulness, and honesty in all his or her dealings with fellow workers and customers. It is a very poor testimony for a Christian to be known as a person who cannot get along with others. "Whatsoever ye do, do it heartily, as to the Lord, and not unto men", (Col. 3 v.23).

We do have bad days at work, but that does not prevent us from being upbeat, enthusiastic, and respectful of others. If something does go wrong when we have been involved, don't deflect blame and responsibility. First Peter 2 v.18-20 is tough medicine, "Servants, be subject to your masters with all fear; not only to the good and gentle, but also to the froward. For this is thankworthy, if a man for conscience toward God endure grief, suffering wrongfully. For what glory is it, if, when ye be buffeted for your faults, ye shall take it patiently? but if, when ye do well, and suffer for it, ye take it patiently, this is acceptable with God".

When the going gets rough, remember the verse, "A soft answer turneth away wrath: but grievous words stir up anger", (Prov. 15 v.1).

Often when words are flying and the temperature is rising it is best to use conciliatory language and diffuse the situation before saying something that one will regret. Sometimes saying very little or nothing is a better strategy during times of intense conflict.

"Blessed are the pure in heart: for they shall see God. Blessed are the peacemakers: for they shall be called the children of God", (Matt. 5 v.8-9). The character and conduct of a Christian is nothing more or less than being experientially conformed to the image of God's dear Son, the Lord Jesus Christ. May the Holy Spirit take of the things of Christ and show them to us. "Purity of heart" and being "peacemakers" do not mean sinlessness of life, as the inspired record of the history of all of God's saints makes clear. Noah got drunk; Abraham lied; Moses disobeyed God; Job cursed the day of his birth; Elijah fled in terror from Jezebel; Peter denied Christ. Paul, great servant though he was, exclaimed in his experience that "when I would do good, evil is present with me. For I delight in the law of God after the inward man: But I see another law in my members, warring against the law of my mind, and bringing me into captivity to the law of sin which is in my members", (Rom. 7 v.21-23). God desires "truth in the inward parts" (Psalm 51 v.6), but much of what we see around us today is a 'hand' religion that seeks salvation by mere human works, or a 'head' religion that rests satisfied with an orthodox creed. But God looks on the heart, an expression that includes the understanding, the affections, and the will. Real diligence, integrity, sincerity, and genuineness, with contentment, is possible only by being much in the presence of the Lord Jesus. "I have learned in whatsoever state I am, therewith to be content. I know both how to be abased, and I know how to abound: every where and in all things I am instructed both to be full and to be hungry, both to abound and to suffer need. I can do all things through Christ which strengtheneth me", (Phil. 4 v.11-13).

All good Christians make the will of God, not their own lust or desires, the rule of their lives and actions. True conversion makes a marvellous change in the heart and life of everyone drawn to the

Saviour and saved by the sovereign grace of God. It brings us out of the common ways and vices of the world, and it alters the mind, judgment, affections, and way of life of the believer, to conform to God's Word: "That ye might walk worthy of the Lord unto all pleasing, being fruitful in every good work, and increasing in the knowledge of God; Strengthened with all might, according to His glorious power, unto all patience and longsuffering with joyfulness", (Col. 1 v.10-11). We are to persevere and rejoice, even in the midst of trials and difficulties, and be counted worthy to suffer for His name, to have joy as well as patience in the troubles and problems of life.

The Christian is commanded "that he no longer should live the rest of his time in the flesh to the lusts of men, but to the will of God", (1 Peter 4 v.2). The Psalmist speaks of God's people as those whose principles are sound, keep judgment, do righteousness, are just to God and to all men. "Blessed are they that keep judgment, and he that doeth righteousness at all times", (Psalm 106 v.3). It is important, therefore, that we make the right use of time to watch over the minutes, hours, and days, and the years will take care of themselves. The great rule is, never be idle, learn to turn from one good deed to another, with due allowance of course being made for recreation and for rest.

In regard to any engagement we make either with ourselves or with others in the workplace, punctuality and promptitude should be assiduously cultivated, which bear the marks of the efficient worker whose character, order, and usefulness means that the redeemed man or woman will work and serve and labour and thus commend themselves in the Lord. They will be fruitful in every good work: "But let every man prove his own work", (Gal. 6 v.4). Such things as procrastination, putting things off to a 'convenient season', loitering, trifling, half-heartedness, etc., should be avoided, and the first requirement is that all work should be well done. "So teach us to number our days, that we may apply our hearts unto wisdom", (Psalm 90 v.12).

Diligence and punctuality also extend to meeting friends, business transactions, going to Church, reaching and leaving the place of employment, keeping promises, retiring at night, and rising in the morning. We are to examine our work and behaviour by the rule of God's law, to see whether they conform to the Word of truth in wholehearted obedience to Him. Christ must be honoured by our good works, and good words: "Comfort your hearts, and stablish you in every good word and work", (2 Thess. 2 v.17). The believer, therefore, must demonstrate by his good works the Divine grace and activity within him, which is the evidence and guarantee of sincere living faith in the Lord Jesus Christ (James 2 v.14-26). "For as the body without the spirit is dead, so faith without works is dead also", (James 2 v.26).

Perseverance and a Humble Spirit

It is not a good thing to run away from problems, solving tough issues builds character and enhances experience. Changing jobs every time a challenging situation arises weakens ability to handle stress and keep calm under pressure. Perseverance is enhanced by trials and should strengthen our resolve to do a good job. Sometimes we get an inflated sense of our own importance, and for some people it has been devastating to realise that we are not the kingpins after all whenever there are others who can do the job better. Nebuchadnezzar learned this the hard way: "The kingdom is departed from thee . . . . . until thou know that the most High ruleth in the kingdom of men, and giveth it to whomsoever he will", (Dan. 4 v.31-32). God is over all and we should keep humble and walk softly before the Lord in the workplace.

For the married mother to balance work and home life priorities is often very difficult, and erodes the foundations of family and spiritual life. This is a particular problem in today's 'feminist' environment. Due to a lack of discipline in time management, so-called urgent 'business' things crowd out important family matters. The words of the Lord God of Isaiah 30 v.15 are very appropriate --- "in quietness and in confidence shall be your strength: and ye would not". Many families are disintegrating because both spouses are giving all their time to job potential and advancement at the expense of home development and helping with the challenges of the family.

The godly woman, however, is one who is possessed with many fine qualities --- virtue, morally good, blameless, righteous, practising duty according to the moral law of God, and chaste. The important thing is for us to measure up to the full stature of God's purpose as individuals, and for us to use all the gifts and talents with which He has endowed us for His glory and for the good and blessing of others. Among the noble qualities of the virtuous woman are trustworthiness, affection, and influence: "She openeth her mouth with wisdom; and in her tongue is the law of kindness", (Prov. 31 v.26). And she shows her true neighbourliness by her charity, generosity, and involvement: "She stretcheth out her hand to the poor; yea, she reacheth forth her hands to the needy", (Prov. 31 v.20). A woman who reverently and worshipfully fears the Lord, shall be praised. Because she loves the Lord, she seeks in all things to obey, to serve, and to please Him: "She hath done what she could", (Mark 14 v.8). In a humble, faithful, and steadfast spirit, she presses "toward the mark for the prize of the high calling of God in Christ Jesus" (Phil. 3 v.14), "and watching thereunto with all perseverance and supplication for all saints", (Eph. 6 v.18). Charm is deceptive and beauty is vain, "but a woman that feareth the Lord, she shall be praised", (Prov. 31 v.30).

Witnessing as Salt and Light

All witnessing must begin where we act as "salt" and "light", (Matt. 5 v.13-16), in the world. Both of these operate silently and effectively. They influence things by simply being present. So it is with ourselves, the most effective witness we can have in the workplace, is to be seen in the way we conduct business, the quality of the work we produce, the way we handle problems, and the manner we treat people. All of these will show that we are different, as we arrest corruption, act with integrity, and manifest a genuine compassion for our workmates and colleagues. If we are not first and foremost "salt" and "light", we are disqualified for witnessing, since our lives do not match our profession.

There are many spheres of opportunity in the workplace to witness while doing one's work, without the work suffering in any way. This is where the "salt and light" principle shows best, by the very manner in which one does one's job is commendable, and therefore witnessing to one's faith.

An employer hires people to undertake certain duties for an agreed salary, and Christians in the workplace must give and apply themselves one-hundred per cent every day. It is a grave slight on the testimony when a Christian employee is slovenly, lazy, careless, idle-headed, or takes sick time off for minor ailments, and so on. For an honest day's pay, an honest day's work must be given in return. It is not a mark of spirituality to be using the employer's time standing or sitting around having lengthy discussions about spiritual things during working hours, to the neglect of the business for which one is being paid.

Our Lord Himself indicates that His people should produce good honest work. "Let your light so shine before men, that they may see your good works, and glorify your Father which is in heaven", (Matt. 5 v.16). The Apostle Peter makes the same point when he asserts that seeing Christian's good deeds causes pagans, "that, whereas they speak against you as evildoers, they may by your good works, which they shall behold, glorify God in the day of visitation", (1 Peter 2 v.12). The Bible places great emphasis on the importance of good works as evidence of God's grace in the life. A mere profession is not enough. Grace that cannot be observed and clearly seen by the outside world is no grace at all. Unbelievers are not really interested in a person's profession, though it be couched in the most eloquent theological language. Actions speak louder than words.

Profession of faith is easy. But the only way to decide whether it is genuine or not, is by its works. Quite simply, a faith without works, is bogus, empty, and of no consequence. "And why call ye Me, Lord, Lord, and do not the things which I say?" (Luke 6 v.46).

Needless to say, I haven't covered all the factors surrounding the subject of witnessing in the workplace. But all of us are aware of the Scriptural injunction: "See then that ye walk circumspectly, not as fools, but as wise, Redeeming the time, because the days are evil", (Eph. 5 v.15-16). This signifies that we are to walk accurately, exactly, in the right way. In order to do so properly, we must frequently consult our Divine Guide and Rule of Life, for only in the Sacred Oracles will we find the directions as to how best we shall be good stewards of our time to the praise of God. It is only by the grace of God we can witness "a good confession" (1 Tim. 6 v.13), be living epistles of our Lord and Master, and may the Holy Spirit enable us at all times to honour and glorify Him.

CHAPTER ELEVEN

WOMEN IN THE WORLD

Biblical Instructions to Various Groups

The Aged Men

The Aged Women

The Young Women

The Young Men

Servants

WOMEN IN THE WORLD

There is no question that the task and mission of the Church should be of inestimable blessing to humanity, including those who are hostile to God, to His Word, and to the cause of Christ. The Church's job is to maintain the truth of God and to publish it far and wide. Her great commission is clearly stated in Matthew 28 v.19-20: "Go ye therefore, and teach all nations, baptising them in the name of the Father, and of the Son, and of the Holy Ghost: teaching them to observe all things whatsoever I have commanded you: and, lo, I am with you alway, even unto the end of the world". In so doing it is impossible to enumerate or quantify the countless blessings that accrue to the world from the presence of the true Church of Christ in its midst. The Lord Jesus Christ said to His disciples, "Ye are the salt of the earth" and "Ye are the light of the world", (Matt. 5 v.13-14). As men and women believe and obey the Word of God, God regards His people who are the Body of Christ operating in the world, as preserving and seasoning salt.

"For, behold, the darkness shall cover the earth, and gross darkness the people", (Isaiah 60 v.2). So spoke the prophet Isaiah. This is a most accurate description of every period of human history since the Fall, but how applicable in particular to our own day and age. The once Christian nations are rapidly reverting to the darkness of paganism, and gross unbelief has settled down upon large swathes of Christendom in many lands. The Bible tells us that Christ, the Son of God, is "the light of the world", (John 8 v.12). By His death and resurrection He has "abolished death, and hath brought life and immortality to light through the Gospel", (2 Tim. 1 v.10).

It is the high honour of the Christian Church to consist of children of light, "For ye are all the children of God by faith in Christ Jesus", (Gal. 3 v.26): who let their light shine before the world. "Let your light so shine before men, that they may see your good works, and glorify your Father which is in heaven", (Matt. 5 v.16). As the Apostle Paul admonished the Philippian Church, we too are challenged to

Christian living and witness: "That ye may be blameless and harmless, the sons of God, without rebuke, in the midst of a crooked and perverse nation, among whom ye shine as lights in the world; Holding forth the Word of Life; that I may rejoice in the day of Christ, that I have not run in vain, neither laboured in vain", (Phil. 2 v.15-16).

Biblical Instructions to Various Groups

In the Epistle to Titus, Paul wrote to encourage him in his task of organising, instructing, and appointing leaders for the Churches of Crete. He was charged to teach sound doctrine, and instruct believers in their duties and responsibilities. He was also to impress upon the believers the necessity of maintaining godly living and manifesting good works in the fear of God, and obedience to Him, in both word and practice.

Titus chapter 2 in particular, among other Scriptures, has reference to both men and women. The Apostle exhorts Titus and furnishes him with instructions that he is to give to five classes of people. "But speak thou the things which become sound doctrine", (Titus 2 v.1). There is fullness of teaching in the Word of God to encourage, to instruct, and to enable all Christians, in all states, in all places, in whatever circumstances they find themselves, and at each stage in their lives --- to live acceptably and pleasing as unto the Lord: "That ye might walk worthy of the Lord unto all pleasing, being fruitful in every good work, and increasing in the knowledge of God", (Col. 1 v.10).

The prime purpose of the Apostle's instruction to Titus is to encourage and exhort the various groups of people mentioned, to live consistent Christian lives, harmonising their behaviour and conduct with their belief and doctrine according to the Word of God, before the eyes of the world. These instructions were very necessary for these early Christians of the New Testament Church, and they are equally necessary for us in the Church today.

This portion of Scripture, Titus 2, greatly highlights what Christians should be like, and how they should live, in the home, in the Church, in society, and in the world at large. We shall now outline in more detail these instructions --- "the things which become sound doctrine" --- with special reference to the five groups of people mentioned, which has relevance to all Christians everywhere in all generations.

(1)   The Aged Men

The first group referred to are the aged men: "That the aged men be sober, grave, temperate, sound in faith, in charity, in patience", (Titus 2 v.2). There are a number of things here that God requires of senior men.

(a)   They must be "sober", the word here means "temperate" or "vigilant", which indicates that older men must be moderate in all their habits. Old disciples of Christ must conduct themselves in everything agreeably to the Christian doctrine. Levity and frivolity are unbecoming in any, but especially in the aged. They should be composed, steadfast, and grave in habit, speech, and behaviour. Those who are full of years should be full of grace, sound in the faith, with a sincere desire of constantly adhering to the truth of the Gospel. Faith, love, and patience, are the main Christian graces, and all therefore need to be on their guard against intemperance and temptation.

(b)   They must be "grave", which means that they be "serious" and not flippant or gloomy, but rather live in the light of eternity, and to have about them a spiritual dignity.

(c) They must be "temperate", which means "prudent". The older Christian must be controlled by the Holy Spirit, which is the real meaning of Ephesians 5 v.18: "And be not drunk with wine, wherein is access; but be filled with the Spirit". The point here is that getting drunk is a mark of darkness and foolishness, and that being filled with the Spirit is the source of a believer being able to walk in light and wisdom.

(d) They must be "sound in the faith", which really means "healthy" in the faith. We are not to hold forth "any other thing that is contrary to sound doctrine", (1 Tim. 1 v.10). The Divine command to each of God's children is: "speak thou the things which become sound doctrine", (Titus 2 v.1). All other teaching, if it is not according to Scripture, is corrupt, vain, and unprofitable. It is imperative that believers must be settled and grounded in the true doctrines of the Gospel, so as to be fit vessels in the service of God.

(e) They must be "sound in charity". In other words they must be "healthy" in their love---love for God, love for His people, and love for one another. Such a love should be robust and should be the badge worn by the older generation. "Herein is our love made perfect, that we may have boldness in the day of judgement: because as He is, so are we in this world. There is no fear in love; but perfect love casteth out fear: because fear is torment. He that feareth is not made perfect in love", (1 John 4 v.17-18). The most profound and simplest description of Christian character is love.

(f) They should be "sound in patience", meaning "endurance" or "fortitude". This has particular reference to the times of trial and testing, or persecution, that come upon us in our earthly life and pilgrimage. Knowledge of

God's promises and purposes revealed in Scripture gives the strength to endure trials and suffering with steadfastness and patience. Knowledge of God's truth is necessary for a fruitful and spiritual life, and gives us the ability to endure trials and testings joyously: "Strengthened with all might, according to His glorious power, unto all patience and longsuffering with joyfulness", (Col. 1 v.11).

(2) The Aged Women

The second group of people mentioned is that of the aged women: "The aged women likewise, that they be in behaviour as becometh holiness, not false accusers, not given to much wine, teachers of good things; that they may teach the young women", (Titus 2 v.3-4). The characteristics of older women required by God are enumerated as follows.

(a) They must be "holy" in their demeanour. What a beautiful description, yet solemn challenge, to be marked out as a sound Christian in this manner. The older women must treat the whole of life as sacred. They ought to be reverent and disciplined, loving and self-controlled, spiritually sound and strong in the faith of God, showing love for others and patience amid any difficulties: "Which becometh women professing godliness with good works", (1 Tim. 2 v.10).

(b) They must not be "false accusers", which simply means that they must not spread slanderous reports or stories. What a power there is of the tongue, either for good or for evil. "Even so the tongue is a little member, and boasteth great things. Behold, how great a matter a little fire kindleth. And the tongue is a fire, a world of iniquity: so is the tongue among our members, that it defileth the whole body, and setteth on fire the course of nature; and it is set on fire of hell", (James 3 v.5-6). Like the bit in a horse's mouth and the rudder of a ship, the tongue has power to control the rest of us. It is the master of the whole body, directing every aspect of behaviour and conduct. But in order for the tongue to control us in the right way, we must resist the temptation to boast and brag, and speak only gracious words, kind words, words that build up rather than tear down; words that edify, comfort, bless, and encourage; words of humility, gratitude, peace, holiness, and wisdom. Such words can only come from a heart that is cleansed from all sin, indwelt by the Holy Spirit wholly submitted to His control, and yielded in full obedience to the Word of God. A hateful and jealous heart cannot produce loving words or works. An unrighteous and spiteful heart cannot produce righteous words or works. "A good tree cannot bring forth evil fruit, neither can a corrupt tree bring forth good fruit . . . . . Wherefore by their fruits ye shall know them", (Matt. 7 v.18 and 20). As sinners saved by grace, having been "made righteous" (Rom. 5 v.19) in Christ Jesus, "we should live soberly, righteously, and godly, in this present world" (Titus 2 v.12), according to His will and by His power.

(c) They must be "not given to much wine". We are exhorted: "to walk worthy of the vocation wherewith ye are called", (Eph. 4 v.1). Being controlled by the Holy Spirit is absolutely essential for the proper living of the Christian life by God's standards. Spirituality is determined by what we are within our hearts, of which what we do outwardly is but a manifestation of whose we are and whom we serve. Scripture always condemns drunkenness. Despite its many warnings about the dangers of alcohol, the drinking of wine is not totally forbidden in the Bible. It is in fact sometimes commended: "But use a little wine for thy stomach's sake and thine often infirmities", (1 Tim. 5 v. 23). In the light of the fact that the Bible gives many warnings about drinking wine, yet does not forbid it, and even commends it in certain circumstances, the follower of Jesus must give serious consideration to the question of Christian liberty and the obligation of strong and weak believers to accept each other in Christ without being judgmental or causing offence. In Romans 14 there are a number of principles that serve as guidelines for all Christians. By our liberty, (1) we must avoid doing anything, including what is innocent of itself, and otherwise permissible, which may occasion our brother to stumble or fall, morally or spiritually, (v.13); (2) we must be careful not to say or do anything that might grieve, sadden, or discourage one another's faith and confidence in Christ, (v.14-15a); (3) we must not act in such a way as to devastate the spiritual growth of a brother, or violate his conscience by being insensitive or unloving towards him, (v.15b); (4) we must not forget our witness for Christ by causing conflicts within the Body of believers that give the watching world reason to criticise and speak evil of the Church, (v.16-19); (5) we must not destroy the work of God for the sake of food or do anything else that is good in itself, which may injure or be a hindrance to one for whom Christ died, (v.20-21); and (6) we must exercise and show great care not to harm ourselves by belittling good gifts God has given to us, or lovelessly flaunting our liberty without caring how it might affect others, (v.22-23).

(d) They must be "teachers of good things". They must be examples of the good life, that is, of the Christian life. "Likewise, ye wives, be in subjection to your own husbands; that, if any (i.e. husbands) obey not the Word, they also may without the Word be won by the conversation of the wives; While they behold your chaste conversation coupled with fear", (1 Peter 3 v.1-2). Aged women should by their lives, by their works, and by their words, be true examples of Christlikeness.

(e) They must "teach the young women". This is a ministry that seems to have gone out of fashion. What a blessing it would be, in our homes, and in our Churches, if the older women became spiritual examples, spiritual guides, and spiritual guardians, of the younger women.

This is God's pattern and call to all older believing women, in the home, in the Church, in society, and in the world at large.

(3) The Young Women

We come now to the section dealing with young women: "That they may teach the young women to be sober, to love their husbands, to love their children, to be discreet, chaste, keepers at home, good, obedient to their own husbands, that the Word of God be not blasphemed", (Titus 2 v.4-5). Again, there are a number of things pointed out here toward the younger woman.

(a) They must be "sober". This is the same thing that is mentioned in connection with the older men, and it simply means that they must be "moderate" in all things.

(b) They are "to love their husbands". They are to be loving towards their husbands, and this rule stands and also applies in the case of Christian women who after marriage become believers even if their husbands are not yet saved. Where there is true love this will be no difficult command. God, in nature, and by His will, has made this subordination: to love their husbands and be obedient to them.

(c) They are "to love their children". It is very easy for zealous Christian women to neglect their children, but this is not the will of God. Parents are to care for their children, to give time to them, to teach them the Word of God, and to show them the love of God. Matthew Henry makes the following comment, stating that young women are "to love their children, not with a natural affection only, but a spiritual, a love springing from a holy sanctified heart and regulated by the Word; not a fond foolish love, indulging them in evil, neglecting due reproof and correction where necessary, but a regular Christian love, showing itself in their pious education, forming their life and manners aright, taking care of their souls as well as of their bodies, of their spiritual welfare as well as of their temporal, of the former chiefly and in the first place".

(d) They are to be "discreet", which simply means "sensible". Nothing is so obnoxious as a silly woman, unless it is a silly man. To be sexually virtuous, discretion and true understanding will keep young women from the evil way. Many young women expose themselves to fatal temptations, and those who do not follow and hold "fast the faithful Word" (Titus 1 v.9), are first corrupt in heart, and then become so in life.

(e) They are to be "chaste", meaning that they are to be pure in thought, word, and deed, and this is not always easy. While it is not the done thing today, the call of the Christian is to be chaste.

(f) They are to be "keepers at home". It is surely a good thing to be an earnest out-and-out Christian, but this does not mean being out at meetings all the time. Their first and primary duty is to guide the house, and they should give no occasion to the enemy to speak reproachfully. Christian married women are to find their sphere of service in the family and the home as good wives and mothers, lest the God-given Gospel be discredited for encouraging an improper freedom and disturbing domestic life.

(g) They are to be "good". This means they are to be kind, helpful, and charitable, like Dorcas of whom we read: "this woman was full of good works and almsdeeds which she did", (Acts 9 v.36). In the management of the home, they are not to be hard or mean. This is a great virtue, and while performing their tasks in the family, young women must take care that the constant strain of domestic duty does not make them veritable or cruel. They must pray for grace to remain "kind" and "good".

(h) They are to obey their husbands: "obedient to their own husbands". The husband is the head of the house and the head of the wife, as we have learned in earlier chapters, and here the younger women are told to be submissive to their own husbands. When the husband also is a believer and honours the Word, this is not a burden. But when he is not a Christian, then "as unto the Lord" makes the burden bearable, for God has promised to give grace and strength to witness "a good confession", (1 Tim. 6 v.13). This last characteristic is a climax to all the others, because any heady or high-minded behaviour here would inevitably spoil and nullify the effect of all other qualities. It would be utterly inconsistent if they should manifest any lack of love, respect, and reverence toward their husbands, for it is most important to notice why the younger women are exhorted to live in this manner: "that the Word of God be not blasphemed" (Titus 2 v.5); or to put it this way, "in order that the Word of God may be honoured", that is, that they may be a good advertisement for the Christian faith.

(4) The Young Men

The fourth group that is singled out for attention is the young men: "Young men likewise exhort to be sober minded. In all things shewing thyself a pattern of good works: in doctrine shewing incorruptness, gravity, sincerity, Sound speech, that cannot be condemned; that he that is of the contrary part may be ashamed, having no evil thing to say to you", (Titus 2 v.6-8). As in the previous sections, there are a number of characteristics that Christian young men must show forth.

(a) They are "to be sober minded", that is, to take the Christian life seriously. They are called upon and exhorted to be considerate, humble, and submissive to God's Word. They must not be rash and head-strong, for there are more young people ruined by haughtiness and pride than by any other sin. The younger men are urged to exercise self-control in every respect. The emphasis here is on morals and doctrine, young men must place themselves under the discipline of the Gospel.

(b) They are to be "a pattern of good works". In other words, they are to be an example of Christian living, and a model of noble deeds. The example is to be comprehensive, "in all things", in all actions, works that are right and honourable in the sight of God. Failure in this matter means they would lose their moral power and influence with other younger men.

(c) They are to be sound "in doctrine shewing incorruptness", that is, to be without error, which involves hard study of the Word of God. "Study to shew thyself approved unto God, a workman that needeth not to be ashamed, rightly dividing the word of truth", (2 Tim. 2 v.15). They are to teach others about the Christian life, and to demonstrate the Christian life, by their ethics and behaviour. By example and precept they must show a spirit of incorruption, that in the very mode of communicating and exhibiting Divine truth, they give not only unmistakable evidence of heart and mind freed from all deceitful tendencies, but wholly given to advance the aims of the Gospel.

(d) They are to be "grave", "shewing gravity", which means they must show all seriousness and dignity in the business of the Lord. Their attitude, manner, and form of speech, must be such that those who are the enemies of truth be put to shame.

(e) They are to be "sincere", "shewing sincerity", and not seeking for popular applause. A flippant manner and demeanour are out of character to the true follower and disciple of Jesus Christ. Jesus said, "whosoever he be of you that forsaketh not all that he hath, he cannot be My disciple", (Luke 14 v.33).

(f) They are to be characterised by "sound speech, that cannot be condemned; that he that is of the contrary part may be ashamed, having no evil thing to say to you", (Titus 2 v.8). Here again, the word "sound" means "healthy", and this refers to the kind of speech with which no one can find fault. We are to be careful about the content of the words and expressions that we use. We must avoid fanciful interpretations and anything that is contrary to the teaching of Scripture. The Apostle firmly gives the moral aim of the exhortation to young men, in order "that he that is of the contrary part may be ashamed". Those who are opposed to the truth, we must "cut off occasion from them which desire occasion" (2 Cor. 11 v.12) to blaspheme and profane the Word of God. "Having your conversation honest among the Gentiles: that, whereas they speak against you as evildoers, they may by your good works, which they shall behold, glorify God in the day of visitation", (1 Peter 2 v.12).

(5) The Servants

The fifth and final group of persons addressed in this passage is the servants: "Exhort servants to be obedient unto their own masters, and to please them well in all things; not answering again; Not purloining, but shewing all good fidelity; that they may adorn the doctrine of God our Saviour in all things", (Titus 2 v.9-10). This applies to all servants, whether men or women. In the earlier part of this chapter, Paul has been giving instructions for the aged men, the aged women, the young women, and the young men. He now turns to servants, a class which overlaps all of these groups.

(a) They are "to be obedient unto their own masters". The meaning here is to be "submissive", and what a great deal of trouble would be avoided if this injunction were heeded today. Scripture has much to say on this subject. "Servants, be obedient to them that are your masters according to the flesh, with fear and trembling, in singleness of your heart, as unto Christ; Not with eyeservice, as menpleasers; but as the servants of Christ, doing the will of God from the heart; With good will doing service, as to the Lord, and not to men: Knowing that whatsoever good thing any man doeth, the same shall he receive of the Lord, whether he be bond or free", (Eph. 6 v.5-8). (See also Col. 3 v.22-24). Paul urges servants to obey and be in subjection to their own masters as a matter of principle.

(b) They are "to please" their masters "well in all things". They are to give satisfactory service in every way, and their work is to be done gladly and willingly. This subjection is not to be rendered to masters in a reluctant and bitter manner, but actively, be well-pleasing in all things. There may be times when it is not easy to make oneself acceptable in everything, as some employers might be awkward individuals who are hard to please, but the Christian is to overcome such difficulties: "whatever ye do, do it heartily, as to the Lord, and not unto men; Knowing that of the Lord ye shall receive the reward of the inheritance: for ye serve the Lord Christ", (Col. 3 v.23-24).

(c) They are not to answer back: "not answering again". There must be no rebellion, no strife, no vindictiveness, and no resistance. Such service is to be rendered without gainsaying or contradicting. Servants are to perform well in all things, all lawful things, according to the will of God. If our Lord's commands and that of the earthly master's come into conflict or competition, we are instructed by Scripture "to obey God rather than men", (Acts 5 v.29). Good and wise masters will always be ready to hear and do right, but to answer unreasonably, or in an unseemly manner, is but to show a lack of humility and meekness of submitting to authority, of acting in good faith, and the absence of a thoroughly trustworthy spirit.

(d) They are not to steal: "not purloining". The reference here has the meaning to that form of pilfering for oneself part of something which has been entrusted to one's care. Servants are not to use or waste the firm's resources or time, because to "purloin" is to "embezzle". Adverse circumstances, no matter how dire, can never provide justification for the lowering of moral standards.

(e) They must be utterly trustworthy. They are to show "all good fidelity", be honest, and totally reliable employees. The Greek word "pistis", meaning "fidelity", conveys the idea of showing forth or providing proof; thus proving themselves faithful and trustworthy in every matter committed to their charge. The Apostle is speaking of "all good fidelity", that is, it is to be shown in everything that is good and beneficial. If being faithful to an employer means doing something dishonest or telling a lie, then the Biblical injunction is "to obey God rather than men", (Acts 5 v.29). Paul emphasises the motive for all such good conduct on the part of servants: "that they may adorn the doctrine of God our Saviour in all things", (Titus 2 v.10). "Let your light so shine before men, that they may see your good works, and glorify your Father which is in heaven", (Matt. 5 v.16). A sanctified life, which brings into clear perspective all the fruits of transforming grace, obedience, cheerfulness, integrity, showing forth the virtues of a godly character, is a precious ornament to "the doctrine of God our Saviour", namely, the Christian faith.

CHAPTER TWELVE

WOMEN OF CONVICTION, FAITH AND TRUTH

Going from Strength to Strength

The Perspicuity of the Scriptures

True Prosperity

Sins that are Offensive before God

The Final Court of Appeal

Successful Living

The Virtues Women should Possess

The Testings Women should Expect

God's Universal Dominion and Plan

Truth and Righteousness

WOMEN OF CONVICTION, FAITH AND TRUTH

In selecting chapter headings and sub-headings, it was hard to know where to stop. The leading topics presented in this treatise have been the same in all ages of the Church, and the writer's aim has been to investigate and apply the usage of the terms in which these subjects were originally communicated to the human mind by the great Author of Holy Scripture. Among God's believing people, the subject title of the book should not be a controversial one. My endeavour has been to work as a student of the Word, not as a controversialist: "Study to shew thyself approved unto God, a workman that needeth not to be ashamed, rightly dividing the Word of Truth", (2 Tim. 2 v.15).

Some readers perhaps will object to certain points of view and practice, while others will complain that the author's exposition of doctrine is not sufficiently pronounced. It is the firm belief of this writer that sound Biblical teaching and Practical theology ought to be based solely on accurate Biblical exegeses. Throughout the writing of this book it seemed best to illustrate the importance of referring a little to the study of Hebrew and Greek at certain junctures with the earnest prayer and desire that readers may gain a deepened conviction of the truth, the unity, and the authority of Holy Scripture, so that it may influence members, men, women and young people of various parties, groups and denominations to receive the Word of God with faith, meekness and love, (Rom. 5 v.5).

At the present time there is a fierce battle going on to corrupt Christianity by the flood of false teaching being peddled in regard to male and female roles, marriage, leadership, headship, equality, and justice, etc., thus undermining the authority of the Word of God. As His believing people we are charged not only to see to it that we preach and teach "no other doctrine" (1 Tim. 1 v.3), but also we must charge others that they might not add anything of their own to it or take anything from it: "that thou observe these things without preferring one before another, doing nothing by partiality",

(1 Tim. 5 v.21). It ill becomes ministers to be partial to the Truth, and discipline must be exercised in the Church and should be done without prejudice, favour, or partiality. Above everything else we must preach the pure, unadulterated, plain Word of God, at every opportunity. Writing to Timothy, Paul says, "I charge thee therefore before God, and the Lord Jesus Christ, Who shall judge the quick and the dead at His appearing and His kingdom; Preach the Word; be instant in season, out of season; reprove, rebuke, exhort with all longsuffering and doctrine", (2 Tim. 4 v.1-2).

In the Pastoral Epistles, First and Second Timothy, and Titus, we are firmly reminded of the task that lies before us. We are exhorted to conserve God's Truth by stating, vindicating, upholding, maintaining, defending, and applying the great teachings of Biblical theology and Scriptural practice. Relying on God alone for grace and strength we should earnestly pray that He may bless our efforts in promoting the Word of Truth. If we are not to betray our trust, we need to be alert to threats not only without but from within the professing Church. For, as the old Scots Covenanters used to say, "there are right hand extremes and left hand defections". While we call no man "Master", nor regard any man as infallible, yet we are thankful to God for raising up eminent Stalwarts, Heroes and Defenders of the Faith in His Church. Their faithfulness to the full-orbed Gospel of Grace is our inheritance, but we must seek to serve our generation by earnestly contending "for the Faith once delivered unto the saints" (Jude v.3), and by not relinquishing our charge till God calls us to hand it over to those coming after us who will "teach others also" (2 Tim. 2 v.2). For this task we need His constant supply of grace, for only then shall we be "faithful" (2 Tim. 2 v.2), albeit "unprofitable" (Luke 17 v.10), servants.

Going from Strength to Strength

The distinctive marks that identify women of conviction, faith and truth as true followers of the Master are manifested by devotion and fidelity in their wholehearted attachment to Christ: "For the love of Christ constraineth us", (2 Cor. 5 v.14). Many believing women want to be fashionable, who in fact know very little of the spiritual marks that brand them as belonging to Him. In order to go from strength to strength in the Christian race, the marks of the Lord Jesus Christ that should characterise the life and living of every believing woman are the following:-

(1) A cluster of fruit. Women who are Christians in sincerity and truth will make it their constant care and business to show forth the fruit of the Spirit in their lives day by day, and they will give clear evidence of good principles by their godly practice. "The fruit of the Spirit is love, joy, peace, longsuffering, gentleness, goodness, faith, meekness, temperance: against such there is no law", (Gal. 5 v.22-23).

(2) A spirit of meekness. This is such an important characteristic of the real Christian woman that she will "not be desirous of vain glory, provoking one another, envying one another", (Gal. 5 v.20). "Learn of Me", says Jesus, "for I am meek and lowly in heart", (Matt. 11 v.29).

(3) A willingness to share the burdens of others. This directive exhorts the Christian woman to sympathise with one another under the various trials, conflicts and troubles of life that may arise, and to be ready where possible to afford each other the comfort, counsel, help, and assistance as circumstances require. "Bear ye one another's burdens, and so fulfil the law of Christ", (Gal. 6 v.2).

(4) A readiness to help and support those who minister. This characteristic is shown by freely and cheerfully contributing out of our store of the good things with

which God has provided to the maintenance of those in a practical manner who labour in the Word and doctrine for the benefit of souls. The office of minister, or teaching elder, as we saw earlier, is a Divine institution, which does not lie open to all, but men only, whom God has called and qualified to teach and instruct others. By giving due "attendance to reading, to exhortation, to doctrine", (1 Tim. 4 v.13), they are to "preach the Word; be instant in season, out of season; reprove, rebuke, exhort with all long suffering and doctrine", (2 Tim. 4 v.2). "Let him that is taught in the Word communicate unto him that teacheth in all good things", (Gal. 6 v.6).

(5) A life made up of well-doing. This is a weighty exhortation to perseverance to do that which is good without fainting. Believers are to have special regard to those who profess the same faith and are members of the body of Christ, "the household of God", (Eph. 2 v.19). "And let us not be weary in well doing: for in due season we shall reap, if we faint not. As we have therefore opportunity, let us do good unto all men, especially unto them who are of the household of faith", (Gal. 6 v.9-10).

(6) A complete separation from the world. God pronounces a special blessing upon all who are in the world but not of it, that is, those who walk according to His rule, the Bible, which is the perfect law of faith, life and liberty. True Christians are not of this world: "For here have we no continuing city, but we seek one to come", (Heb. 13 v.14). The Spirit of Christ in them is opposite to the spirit of the world. We are to "worship God in the Spirit, and rejoice in Christ Jesus, and have no confidence in the flesh", (Phil. 3 v.3). "Knowing this, that our old man is crucified with Him, that the body of

sin might be destroyed, that henceforth we should not serve sin", (Rom. 6 v.6).

(7) A glorying in the Cross. "God forbid that I should glory, save in the Cross of our Lord Jesus Christ, by Whom the world is crucified unto me, and I unto the world", (Gal. 6 v.14). The more we contemplate the sufferings of our dear Saviour met with from the world and at Calvary, the glorious doctrine of eternal salvation by a crucified Redeemer becomes all the more precious. The genuine believer will earnestly pray for grace and strength to work and witness for the Lord at every opportunity.

These essential characteristics should also apply and be found in Christian men as well, for "He is the Head of the body, the Church: Who is the beginning, the firstborn from the dead; that in all things He might have the pre-eminence", (Col. 1 v.18). The word "pre-eminence" means "occupying the foremost place", and here we are not thinking of the pre-eminence of one doctrine over another, or of one creed over another, or of one denomination over another, but of Christ over the individual believer. As the Scriptures declare He alone has the right of being first in our lives because:-

(1) He made us: "For by Him were all things created, that are in heaven, and that are in the earth, visible and invisible, whether they be thrones, or dominions, or principalities, or powers: all things were created by Him, and for Him", (Col. 1 v.16).

(2) He has redeemed us: "Who hath delivered us from the power of darkness, and hath translated us into the kingdom of His dear Son: In Whom we have redemption through His blood, even the forgiveness of sins", (Col. 1 v.13-14).

(3) God has given Him the pre-eminence. According to Psalm 110 v.1, God "gave Him to be the Head over all things", (Eph. 1 v.22). All creatures are in subjection to Him, they must either yield to Him their sincere obedience, or fall under the weight of His sceptre, and receive their doom from Him. He is "the Head over all things to the Church", (Eph. 1 v.22).

May God the Holy Spirit search our hearts and show us with conviction and power that He should be "Lord of all", (Acts 10 v.36). "I am He which searcheth the reins and hearts", (Rev. 2 v.23). Only the Omniscient One could search the inward affections and thoughts that motivate the will from which the actions spring. This brings a measure of godly fear to every considering heart. As the Pre-eminent One, His absolute ownership implies unquestioning obedience, wholehearted service, and implicit trust on the part of His people to yield themselves to the claims of Christ as Lord and King over all.

The mere outward professions and observances of religious rites and ritual ceremonies do not constitute Christianity, nor will they bring us to heaven. Without a genuine conversion of the heart to Christ, the Scriptures solemnly warn against all hypocrisy. "Not every one that saith unto Me, Lord, Lord, shall enter into the kingdom of heaven; but he that doeth the will of My Father which is in heaven", (Matt. 7 v.21). It is not enough to hear the Word of Christ, we must obey Him. We mock Christ and scorn His Word if we walk in the way of our own hearts and in the sight of our own eyes. The devil is cheating us if we think that a bare profession of religion will save us, or that hearing the Word of Christ will bring us to heaven, without doing them. "Why call ye Me, Lord, Lord, and do not the things which I say", (Luke 6 v.46).

If we are to be steadfast in the Christian faith, radiant in life, effective in witness, and powerful in service, we must have the resolution and determination of Paul, and by grace be able to say with the Apostle, "this one thing I do, forgetting those things which are behind, and reaching forth unto those things which are before, I press toward the mark for the prize of the high calling of God in Christ Jesus", (Phil. 3 13-14). With God's help may we as His people offer ourselves afresh to the Lord each day:-

(1) With daily times of prayer;

(2) Daily meeting with Him to feed upon His Word;

(3) Daily dying unto sin, self, and the world;

(4) Daily endeavour to witness for Christ in the power of the Holy Ghost;

(5) Daily ministry of compassion and encouragement to others;

(6) Daily watchfulness and vigilance;

(7) Ever remembering in submission, humility and meekness the Words of Christ, "Herein is My Father glorified, that ye bear much fruit; so shall ye be My disciples", (John 15 v.8).

The fruitfulness of all Christians is for the glory of God. The more fruit we bring forth, the more we abound in every good work, the more He is exalted and glorified. "But now being made free from sin, and become servants to God, ye have your fruit unto holiness, and the end everlasting life", (Rom. 6 v.22). Only by becoming a servant of God can we truly live a life of prayer in worship, communion and intercession. Only by being a servant of God can we live by faith, walk in the Spirit, live a life of holiness and love, fulfil the Great Commission, and thereby glorify God.

Sadly, today, in the Church generally we have much by way of activities, programmes, and entertainment, but very little in the way of reality, power, and life. The Christian life is a life to be lived in the power of the Holy Spirit, a life that is directed by the will of God according to His Word to His glory. We are paying a high price for the abandonment of Scriptural Truth and Biblical practice to the exclusion of true conversion and the servant heart by the indwelling power of the Spirit. We sorely need a heaven-sent reformation to return to Biblical Christianity and a Holy Ghost revival and awakening to spirituality and practical holiness. "Ask for the old paths, where is the good way, and walk therein, and ye shall find rest to your souls", (Jer. 6 v.16).

The Perspicuity of the Scriptures

The reading, preaching and teaching of the Word of God are very important and central in worship. The witness of the Bible should be given prominence and priority at all times in the lives of Christian men and women. It is the Holy Spirit Who quickens the heart and enlightens the mind to a clear understanding of the Scriptures. God gives grace and courage to the willing, humble and obedient believer to receive and acknowledge His truth in all its fullness. The heart and mind, sad to say, are often very forgetful and slow to learn. We must, therefore, exert ourselves continually to lay the Word of God up in our hearts and practice it in our lives.

The duty exhorted to in 1Peter 2 v.2 is a strong and constant desire for the Word of God, so that we might "grow in grace, and in the knowledge of our Lord and Saviour Jesus Christ", (2 Peter 3 v.18). As mature Christians we must be able to digest the "meat". "Strong meat" is the solid food for those who are of full age. Every true Christian having received "newness of life", (Rom. 6 v.4) in Jesus Christ, stands in need of nourishment to preserve that life. "But strong meat belongeth to them that are of full age, even those who by reason of use have their senses exercised to discern both good and evil", (Heb. 5 v.14). We must saturate ourselves with God's Truth in our living until we are "no more children, tossed to and fro, and carried about with every wind of doctrine, by the sleight of men, and cunning craftiness, whereby they lie in wait to deceive", (Eph. 4 v.14).

> "Unless in Thy most perfect Law
> my soul delights had found,
>
> Thy precepts I will ne'er forget;
> they quick'ning to me brought",
> (Psalm 119 v.92-93).

True Prosperity

Everyone wants to be successful and to achieve true prosperity, whether it is a child at school, the young person in his or her first job, the business or professional entrepreneur, or the wife and mother in the home. It is God's will that we should have the right kind of success which is offered to us in the great promise of Joshua 1 v.8: "This Book of the Law shall not depart out of thy mouth; but thou shalt meditate therein day and night, that thou mayest observe to do according to all that is written therein: for then thou shalt make thy way prosperous, and then thou shalt have good success". God has a plan for every one of His children and we can only be successful as we follow His way, obey His Word, and do His will. In so doing we shall enjoy His presence and guidance with us day by day, and experience the power of God as we are enabled by the Holy Spirit to walk according to the Book of the Law, the Word of God --- the Bible.

We, therefore, must love the Bible and prize it. But more than that, we must read it and lay it up in our hearts and lives, so that it becomes our rule and guide, controlling our actions and transforming our character: adorning "the doctrine of God our Saviour in all things", (Titus 2 v.10). In the General Epistle of James we have the exhortation, "Be ye doers of the Word, and not hearers only, deceiving your own selves. For if any be a hearer of the Word, and not a doer, he is like unto a man beholding his natural face in a glass:

For he beholdeth himself, and goeth his way, and straightway forgetteth what manner of man he was. But whoso looketh into the perfect law of liberty, and continueth therein, he being not a forgetful hearer, but a doer of the work, this man shall be blessed in his deed", (James 1 v.22-25). We are to live in subjection to the Word of God. We are to bow to its authority, by day and by night. We are to bring every part of our lives and practice into submission and obedience to the teaching of God's Word. The Bible is to be the final authority for us in all matters of faith and life. We are to delight in the Law of the Lord and meditate in His Word day and night, (Psalm 1 v.2). We are commanded to lay aside "all filthiness and superfluity of naughtiness, and receive with meekness the engrafted Word, which is able to save your souls", (James 1 v.21).

Sins that are Offensive before God

Most often in our reading and studying of God's Word the tendency is to turn first to the passages of Scripture which bring comfort and encouragement. However, it is sometimes necessary to turn to those portions of the Word of God which minister reproof, correction and instruction in righteousness, (2 Tim. 3 v.16-17). The Bible emphasises and warns of the total depravity of man, the moral hideousness of the human heart, and the heinous corruption of the world in which we live. "The heart is deceitful above all things, and desperately wicked: who can know it?", (Jer. 17 v.9).

We are reminded over and over again in the Sacred Volume, the Bible, of the immaculate holiness and purity of God and of His infinite hatred of sin. The true ambition and desire of God's people, therefore, should be to please Him and to live without yielding to the offensive sins as detailed and recorded in Prov. 6 v.16-19: -

    (1)   A proud look;

    (2)   A lying tongue;

(3) Hands that shed innocent blood;

(4) An heart that deviseth wicked imaginations;

(5) Feet that be swift in running to mischief;

(6) A false witness that speaketh lies; and

(7) He that soweth discord among brethern.

In the sovereign purpose and gracious providence of God, all the inspired prophets and apostles communicated His revelation to mankind. It is His eternal and unchanging message to the world. To enjoy forgiveness of sin and freedom from those things which God hates, we can be more than conquerors, not in our own strength, but in the grace that is in Christ Jesus: "through Him that loved us", (Rom. 8 v.37). We are conquerors by virtue of Christ's victory.

We must die unto sin and "cleanse ourselves from all filthiness of the flesh and spirit" and we must endeavour by the grace of God to be holy as He is holy: "perfecting holiness in the fear of God", (2 Cor. 7 v.1). We are therefore ---

    (1) To be honest with ourselves and with God. We must let the searchlight of His Word come into our hearts and by the power of the Holy Spirit reveal to us the things which are pleasing to the Lord. We must humbly and penitently admit our wrong, confess our sin, and forsake that which grieves the Almighty. "Let the wicked forsake his way, and the unrighteous man his thoughts: and let him return to the Lord, and He will have mercy upon him; and to our God, for He will abundantly pardon", (Isaiah 55 v.7).

    (2) To seek and receive the cleansing of the precious blood of Christ: "If we walk in the light, as He is in the

light, we have fellowship one with another, and the blood of Jesus Christ His Son cleanseth us from all sin", (1 John 1 v.7). His blood applied to us discharges us from guilt of all sin so that we stand "righteous in His sight, only for the righteousness of Christ imputed to us, and received by faith alone", (S. C. No. 33). Oh, how we should thank Him that this is available for the saint and for the sinner. In Christ "we have redemption through His blood, the forgiveness of sins, according to the riches of His Grace", (Eph. 1 v.7).

(3) To rely solely upon the Word of life (Phil. 2 v.16) and by God's rich and abundant mercy (Eph. 2 v.4, 1 Peter 1 v.3) experience that liberty, joy and peace; liberty of access to God, and freedom of speech in prayer in the power of the Holy Spirit. "Now the Lord is that Spirit: and where the Spirit of the Lord is, there is liberty", (2 Cor. 3 v.17).

The Final Court of Appeal

The divisions and disputes especially those issues concerning women, that exist in the Christian Church are a source of trouble and perplexity to every thoughtful mind. It might naturally be supposed that those who profess:

(1) To follow one and the same Master, the Lord Jesus Christ; and

(2) To venerate one and the same Book, the Holy Bible, as the final court of appeal in all matters pertaining to faith and practice;

would agree on all questions of faith and behaviour. Regrettably, this is far from being the case. The Westminster Confession of Faith declares that "the infallible rule of interpretation of Scripture is the Scripture itself . . . . . all controversies of religion are to be determined, and in whose sentence we are to rest, can be no other but the Holy Spirit speaking in the Scripture", (Chap. 1 Sect. 10). "We have also a more sure Word of prophecy; whereunto ye do well that ye take heed, as unto a light that shineth in a dark place, until the day dawn, and the day star arise in your hearts: Knowing this first, that no prophecy of the Scripture is of any private interpretation", (2 Peter 1 v.19-20).

Authorised leaders of the Church, however learned, are to be regarded as fallible. It is to the Scripture alone do we reserve the authority of what we believe in faith and morals. Trusting in God the simple student may thus become a theologian in the true old sense of the word, and attain to that loving and reverential disposition toward his Maker and Redeemer that is described as "the beginning of wisdom", (Prov. 1 v.7).

The humble and devout reading of the Bible is one of the most profitable sources of growth in godliness. Augustine once said that "as the body is made lean by hunger and want of food, so is the soul that neglects to fortify itself by the Word of God rendered weak and incapable of every good work". It is recorded of the Psalmist, David, that "seven times a day do I praise Thee because of Thy righteous judgements. Great peace have they which love Thy Law: and nothing shall offend them", (Psalm 119 v.164-165).

With an appreciation and thankfulness of the Lord's greatness and goodness, we should be full of love and praise to God that:-

    (1)   He is our loving Heavenly Father (Gal. 3 v.26);

    (2)   Jesus Christ is our personal Saviour, Redeemer and Lord (John 3 v.36);

(3) The Holy Spirit is our Indwelling Comforter (John 14 v.16-17);

(4) The Bible is our Divine chart and compass (2 Tim. 3 v.16-17);

(5) God's people everywhere are all one in Christ Jesus (Eph. 3 v.15);

(6) The whole world is our parish that wherever in providence He has placed our lot we are His representatives (Matt. 28 v.19-20); and

(7) Heaven is our eternal Home (John 14 v.1-3).

In the matter of reading God's Word and prayer, many think that once a week will suffice, or once a day, but we must praise the Lord at all times, in everything giving thanks (Eph. 5 v.20, James 1 v.15). We ought always to praise God for His precepts, for His promises, and even for our afflictions when through grace in the midst of trail we are given strength and enjoy great peace within. It is best to make the best of that which is, and not quarrel with anything that God in His providence allows.

Successful Living

In the Book of Job we read, "Acquaint now thyself with Him, and be at peace: thereby good shall come unto thee", (22 v.21). This verse speaks to us of the good, the blessing, the benefits which will come to us in knowing God. There is a great difference between knowing God and simply knowing about Him. There is a theoretical and an experiential knowledge of God, and it is the experiential knowledge of Him which is so vital. "And this is life eternal, that they might know Thee the only true God, and Jesus Christ, Whom Thou hast sent", (John 17 v.3). When we really know God in Christ we share His hatred of sin and become spiritually strong and "enriched in every thing to all bountifulness, which causeth through us thanksgiving to God", (2 Cor. 9 v.11). "The people that do know their God shall be strong, and do exploits", (Dan. 11 v.32).

The earnest desire and constant aim of the committed Christian is to be well-pleasing in a life of service to the Lord. Most people today are bent on pleasing themselves with whom God is not well pleased (1 Cor. 10 v.5). In the story of David, 1 Sam. 30 v.1-6, we read of a period in his life when he was plunged into great distress and trouble. Trouble is no respecter of persons. "Man that is born of a woman is of few days, and full of trouble", (Job. 14 v.1). When trouble comes our way let us do what David did: He "encouraged himself in the Lord his God", (1 Sam. 30 v.6). This we do by reminding ourselves that we belong to Him, Who has "delivered us from the power of darkness, and has translated us into the kingdom of His dear Son", (Col. 1 v.13). We recall His loving-kindness and tender mercies toward us in past days: "Hitherto hath the Lord helped us", (1 Sam. 7 v.12). As we turn to Him in confession (1 John 1 v.9), and supplication (Psalm 34 v.6), we look in faith to Him alone for deliverance (Psalm 69 v.17). "The Lord is good, a strong hold in the day of trouble; and He knoweth them that trust in Him", (Nahum 1 v.7).

The Virtues Women should Possess

While men speak audibly to God in public worship, the question arises as to the contribution of the women. They will by the instruction of Scripture remain silent, yet nonetheless they have a vital part to play in the public congregation. This will be seen in their attitude and appearance, both of which will be in contrast to those as manifested in the society around them. There are four virtues concerning godly women particularly mentioned in First Timothy 2 v.15, which every Christian woman should display: that "they continue in faith and charity and holiness with sobriety".

(1) Faith, which means faithfulness.

(2) Charity, which means love.

(3) Holiness, which means Christlikeness.

(4) Sobriety, which means modesty.

What a blessing to any Church when there are women of this calibre in its membership. The fact that God has not given women a teaching role in Divine worship arises from the Divine order revealed in Scripture. Believing women will gladly yield to the teaching of the Word of God, when they accept, in subjection of faith, their God-given place in a Divine order.

The Greek word "meno", translated "continue", means "to remain, to abide". This is a command not to women in general, but particularly to Christian believing women. They have now entered the realm, so different from that of the world, where the dominant features are (1) faith, believing in God; (2) charity, "agape", love; (3) holiness, sanctification: "for this is the will of God, even your sanctification . . . . . God hath not called us unto uncleanness, but unto holiness", (1 Thess. 4 v.3 and 7); and (4) with sobriety, "meta", accompanied by the manifestly chaste behaviour reflecting a well-balanced mind. This, in keeping with their acceptance of the Divine order, is the evidence of subjection that speaks of spirituality. It is an acceptance by faith of a Divine order revealed in creation, but conditioned by the Fall to the vital realm of the home. Any woman grasping by faith, as Eve did, her place in the Divine order, will find in this the special preservation from the spiritual, social, and satanic evils of society.

The responsibility Christian women bear is enormous, especially those who are the wives of ministers, elders, and deacons: they are to "be grave, not slanderers, sober, faithful in all things", (1 Tim. 3 v.11). Four qualifications here are absolutely necessary.

(1) They must share the serious outlook of their husbands: "be grave"; they may greatly help or seriously hinder their husbands usefulness. "Favour is deceitful, and beauty is vain: but a woman that feareth the Lord, she shall be praised", (Prov. 31 v.30).

(2) They must be women of discretion, "not slanderers", not gossips, not carrying stories to make mischief and sow discord. "Not false accusers"(Titus 2 v.3) in the Greek, "diabolos", meaning slanderous or accusing falsely, is here employed to warn against the wrong use of the tongue. Such evil often commences with "picking holes" in other people, but it leads to spreading of criticisms and engaging in malicious gossip and false accusations. Such is the work of the devil by weakening the spiritual harmony of the Church.

(3) They must be self-controlled, "sober", showing forth the fruit of the Spirit, "love, joy, peace, longsuffering, gentleness, goodness, faith, meekness, temperance", (Gal. 5 v.22-23). The spiritual behaviour of walking by the Spirit has the effect of causing the believer to put away the habitual, ongoing evil deeds of the flesh and causing the Christian to bear the good fruit produced by the Spirit.

(4) They must be absolutely trustworthy and reliable: "fruitful in all things". They must not be given to any excess, but trustworthy in all that is committed to them.

When Christian women abide in faith, love, sanctification, exercising proper self-control and reserve, they will find their joy and delight to God's glory, in all the duties and responsibilities of Christian womanhood. It is true, that once a woman is truly saved, she remains saved forever. Yet she must persevere on the way heavenward with watchfulness, diligence, and steadfastness. The grace and strength to press on in the faith is ever from God, and from Him alone. "For by grace are ye saved through faith; and that not of yourselves: it is the gift of God: Not of works, lest any man should boast. For we are His workmanship, created in Christ Jesus unto good works, which God hath before ordained that we should walk in them", (Eph. 2 v.8-10).

In that great chapter, Proverbs 31 v.10-31, the description is given of a virtuous woman. So rare is this treasure that the challenge is given: "Who can find a virtuous woman"? (Prov. 31 v.10). The same challenge is given in regard to men when we compare Prov. 20 v.6: "but a faithful man who can find"? A virtuous woman here means a woman of strength, though the weaker vessel, yet made strong by wisdom and grace, and the fear of the Lord. She is a woman of sound resolution, who, having embraced good principles, is firm and steady in the faith. This is a gift so seldom sought perhaps, that the search is made for accomplishments, not for virtues; for external and outward recommendations, rather than for internal godly worth: "for her price is far above rubies", (Prov. 31 v.10). She is a "woman professing godliness", adorned "with good works" (1 Tim. 2 v.10), a Mary no less than a Martha. Grace and strength in the inner man gives her Christian courage and resolution that lift her up above trials and difficulties. The secret of her devoted, virtuous life, is the abiding characteristic of "a woman that feareth the Lord", (Prov. 31 v.30).

When the mists of earth have gone forever, such a virtuous woman will appear before the Judgement Seat of Christ with rejoicing, bringing her sheaves with her (Psalm 126 v.6), to hear the words of approval from the Master's lips, "Well done, thou good and faithful servant: thou hast been faithful . . . . . enter thou into the joy of thy Lord", (Matt. 25 v.21).

The Testings Women should Expect

These are referred to in First Timothy, chapter 5 v.3-16. In verse 5, there is particular reference to the "desolation" or loneliness of widowhood. "Now she that is a widow indeed, and desolate, trusteth in God, and continueth in supplications and prayers night and day".

This is not the only testing Christian women may have to face. Some are forsaken by their husbands, some are deprived of the privilege of marriage, some long to have children but they are unable to, some have children who cause them much sorrow, and some have to face all kinds of problems and perplexities that impose a heavy burden upon them. When such testings, trials, difficulties, and distresses come, their refuge is God Himself, Who never fails His people when they trust in Him, pray to Him, and obey Him. "God is our refuge and strength, a very present help in trouble", (Psalm 46 v.1).

God has always designed that women be the special objects of care and attention. They are to be under the umbrella of male protection, provision, authority, and direction. But First Timothy 5, lays particular emphasis on helping women in need, especially the widow. The Church has a duty and responsibility to care for the needy. James 1 v.27 defines true Christianity as: "Pure religion and undefiled before God and the Father is this, To visit the fatherless and widows in their affliction, and to keep himself unspotted from the world". The previous verse indicates that only someone walking with God can have his tongue tamed. That person will also practice concern and care for widows and orphans and be careful not to be soiled by worldliness. Such people are the most apt to be neglected or oppressed.

In the Early Church of the New Testament there was a distinction recognised between the different grades of widowhood, and four classes of widows are mentioned in First Timothy 5.

(1) The widow indeed, (1 Tim. 5 v.3,5,16): "Honour widows that are widows indeed", (v.3). She is desolate, quite alone in the world, having lost her husband, and without children or any other near relative to provide for her needs. The Church, in this case, must be to her in place of husband and family.

(2) The widow with a family, (1 Tim. 5 v.4,8,16): "But if any widow have children or nephews, let them learn first to shew piety at home, and to requite their parents: for that is good and acceptable before God", (v.4). It is the Christian duty of the members of the family to provide for the wants of the home. "But if any provide not for his own, and specially for those of his own house, he hath denied the faith, and is worse than an infidel", (v.8). The Church must not burden itself with responsibilities that belong to others, and which they must be taught to discharge. "If any man or woman that believeth have widows, let them relieve them, and let not the Church be charged; that it may relieve them that are widows indeed", (v.16).

The children and grandchildren, especially those in the line of male headship, are imperatively commanded to learn, as their primary responsibility, "to show piety at home", (v.4). It is good for the younger generation to put their faith into practice by providing for the needs of their older relatives. The family is the original social unit created by God, (Gen. 2 v.24), and is appointed by Him for the training of all its members through mutual caring and sharing, and by so doing, 'to put their religion into practice'. By acting in this way, the family members will be discharging a life-long obligation by repaying their parents and grandparents. Children and grandchildren are indebted to parents and grandparents for the care bestowed in earlier years, and it is right and proper this obligation should be repaid.

When the children are dependent on their parents in their formative years, it is right and proper that the parents should provide for the children, but the roles are reversed in later years when the parents become dependent on their children. In the Scriptures, grandparents are mentioned with parents, because three generations often lived together in the same house, so that grandparents took an active share in the upbringing of children. "I thank God, whom I serve", says Paul, "When I call to remembrance the unfeigned faith that is in thee, (that is, Timothy), which dwelt first in thy grandmother Lois, and thy mother Eunice; and I am persuaded that in thee also", (2 Tim. 1 v.5). But the greatest incentive for this kind of extended family care is a religious one, "for that is good and acceptable before God", (1 Tim. 5 v.4).

Failure in this very practical aspect of Christian living is no minor matter; it is, in fact, a denial of the faith (v.8). "The faith" is not just a form of words or set of theological propositions, but it involves practical fulfilment of what these teachings and doctrines set forth. Lack of such care and forethought is a clear violation of the teaching of Christ.

The way Christians treat their family members should differ markedly from that of non-Christians. In many cases aged and infirm parents are abandoned and forsaken in their time of need by their children not rendering due practical care and sacrificial deeds of love and kindness, and thus the dear old folks do not receive the quality attention and affection that they deserve however difficult the circumstances may be.

Christians who have had 'difficult' parents will find it particularly hard to respond to Paul's ethic here. But the healing mercies of God's grace in Christ Jesus can enable traumatised children who have been wronged to extend forgiveness, and to show honour to unworthy parents in their later years of infirmity, weakness, and frailty. "But there is forgiveness with Thee, that Thou mayest be feared", (Psalm 130 v.4). In the story of Ruth, we read that she loved Naomi, her mother-in-law, and therefore was better to her than seven sons. The bonds of love prove stronger than those of nature, so here was a daughter-in-law better than her own child: "for thou has shewed more kindness in the latter end than at the beginning", (Ruth 3 v.10). The same application can be fittingly made of a son-in-law. Children expect from parents care, attention, protection, love, nurture, and training. In old age parents expect the children to be restorers of life and joy. "And he shall be unto thee a restorer of thy life, and a nourisher of thine old age: for thy daughter-in-law, which loveth thee, which is better to thee than seven sons, hath born him", (Ruth 4 v.15). In old age, God's people can still be fresh and flourish spiritually under their burdens and bring forth fruit. This comes from knowing the righteous Lord as their Rock. "They shall still bring forth fruit in old age; they shall be fat and flourishing; To shew that the Lord is upright: He is my Rock, and there is no unrighteousness in Him", (Psalm 92 v.14-15).

(3) The widow living in pleasure: (1 Tim. 5 v.6,11-15): "But she that liveth in pleasure is dead while she liveth", (v.6). This describes the kind of person who leads a frivolous life, indulging in a sensual life-style, showing a wasteful and extravagant way of living, including immoral relationships, with no thought of what is right or wrong. The natural urge to marry will return to the younger widow, with the very real danger that her natural desires will overrule her religious ones, even willing to marry an unbeliever and lead her away from Christ, and so "cast off" her "first faith", (v.12). Her young, passionate nature must be restrained, and be warned not to bring discredit and disgrace upon herself and the Church.

There are other testings, perils, and dangers that may destabilise the Church: "And withal they learn to be idle, wandering about from house to house; and not only idle, but tattlers also and busybodies, speaking things which they ought not", (v.13). Because of this, Paul counsels young widows to marry, bear children, guide and manage the house, and "give none occasion to the adversary to speak reproachfully", (v.14). This is the Scriptural answer to the problems that have been discussed in the previous verses, (v.11-13). The sole qualification governing such a re-marriage is given in First Corinthians 7 v.39, "only in the Lord". Scripture is perfectly clear that there is nothing whatever wrong with a second marriage of a widow, or widower. (Rom. 7 v.1-3, 1 Cor. 7 v.39). The ultimate responsibility for rule in the home is that of the husband (1 Tim. 3 v.5), but the administration is in the hands of the wife.

(4) The enrolled widow: (1 Tim. 5 v.9-10): "Let not a widow be taken into the number under three-score years old, having been the wife of one man, Well reported of for good works; if she have brought up children, if she have lodged strangers, if she have washed the saints' feet, if she have relieved the afflicted, if she have diligently followed every good work". She must be sixty years of age; have had only one husband, that is, "a one-man woman", which does not exclude women who have been married more than once; have had experience in the bringing up of children in a godly home to follow the Lord; have given hospitality to God's servants; and is well known as devoted to good works that manifest outwardly the quality of her spiritual character.

These qualifications illustrate the sorts of caring and practical ministries expected of Christian women. Good deeds are enjoined on all Christians. "For we are His workmanship, created in Christ Jesus unto good works, which God hath before ordained that we should walk in them", (Eph. 2 v.10). Christianity is nothing if it is not practical. These good works are considered to be the visible proof of the widow's living faith in God, and evidence of her worthiness to receive the Church's support. Having served others throughout her life, the time has now come for her to receive in turn from others.

From the passage of Scripture in First Timothy 5, we would do well to heed the solemn words of warning, where we are told (1) about women who "learn to be idle" and develop harmful habits; (2) about women who were "wanton", which means "restless"; (3) about women who had "cast off their first love", which means they had grown slack spiritually; and (4) about women who had degenerated into gossips and busybodies with dangerous tongues, who went from house to house carrying trouble. Such women simply play into the hands of the devil and lower the reputation of the Church, and give "occasion to the adversary to speak reproachfully", (v.14). No one should be encouraged to attach himself or herself to the Church for the sake of personal maintenance. The Church must keep and look after her needy members, but all who can work should be encouraged and stimulated to honest and diligent industry.

Paul's warning to the Ephesian Church was timely, since, some had "already turned aside to follow Satan", (v.15). Some of the younger women had abandoned their vows to Christ. Having forsaken their true calling, they have given themselves over to various sins: "For of this sort are they which creep into houses, and lead captive silly women laden with sins, led away with divers lusts", (2 Tim. 3 v.6). Some were following false teachers, and even helping to spread false doctrine. They were no longer serving Christ, but Satan.

When families take care of their needy relatives, the Church is not burdened. It is then free to assist those who are "widows indeed", (1 Tim. 5 v.3). Only those widows with no other means of support should be cared for by the Church at large. Helping widows brings the promise of blessing from God: "the stranger, and the fatherless, and the widow, which are within thy gates, shall come, and shall eat and be satisfied; that the Lord thy God may bless thee in all the work of thine hand which thou doest", (Deut. 14 v.29). On the other hand, failing to do so brings judgment: "Cursed be he that perverteth the judgment of the stranger, fatherless, and widow", (Deut. 27 v.19). God's loving care for widows, and other needy people, must be reflected in the actions of His children.

The principle here is very clear. The "burden" for the support of widows falls first, naturally, on the children and grandchildren (1 Tim. 5 v.4); then Scripturally, upon the wider circle of believers within the extended family unit who are in a position to help. When these needs cannot be met from these private resources, it is then that the Church assumes responsibility. The Church has a moral and Scriptural responsibility to "relieve them that are widows indeed", (1 Tim. 5 v.16). These are widows in the real meaning of the word, totally bereft of resources and relatives able to help.

In the context of all this we would do well to remind ourselves that the Christian is called to witness "a good confession", (1 Tim. 6 v.13). He is commanded:-

(1) To "flee" from vice, (1 Tim. 6 v.4-11) --- pride, conceit, impurity, a discontented spirit, foolish and hurtful lusts, and the love of money. The inordinate love of money is the root of all kinds of evil. These are days in which there is a craze for getting, getting, and getting. "But thou, O man of God, flee these things", (v.11).

(2) To "follow after righteousness, godliness, faith, love, patience, meekness", (v.11). The people of God should be taken up with the things of God. It is only by the grace of God that we can bear the rebukes of Providence and the reproaches of men.

(3) To "fight the good fight of faith", (v.12). Christian believers are to be fighters, for they are engaged in a stern warfare against the flesh, the world, and the devil. We must keep going and work for the advancement of the Gospel, and the honour of the Saviour. This is not only good advice, but a duty enjoined upon us that is made possible through Christ. "I can do all things through Christ which strengtheneth me", (Phil. 4 v.13). "I press toward the mark for the prize of the high calling of God in Christ Jesus", (Phil. 3 v.14).

We must have a genuine concern for the public image of the Gospel and the Church: "that the name of God and His doctrine be not blasphemed", (1 Tim. 6 v.1); "that the Word of God be not blasphemed", (Titus 2 v.5). The great enemy is Satan, but he uses men and women as his agents to raise trouble to destroy the Church. God's people ought to be concerned for a scrupulously clean image in the eyes of the world, based on consistent Biblical practice in all departments of their corporate and individual life and work.

The Early Churches of the New Testament did not only cater for the spiritual needs of their members, but were also engaged in providing for their social, material, and personal needs as well. In the Acts of the Apostles we read not only of the Church's struggles and triumphs, but also of the administration of her affairs "in the daily ministration", that is, in the distribution of the public charity to the needy and care given to widows, (Acts 6 v.1-8). In the same way Christian families and Church congregations are encouraged to organise practical support and help for their most needy and dependent members.

In these days even where there are governmental or privately funded agencies for the relief of the poor, the aged, and the needy, the Church and their families should do all in their power to support, not only the widows and the aged, but also the same love, care, and attention can be applied quite effectively in some of its details to other vulnerable groups within the Christian community and Church fellowship, such as the unemployed, those with disabilities, the homeless, and the terminally ill. "As we have therefore opportunity, let us do good unto all men, especially unto them who are of the household of faith" (Gal. 6 v.10).

God's Universal Dominion and Plan

God has a comprehensive plan for the world and the role of the Church is an important factor in proclaiming it. The great commission of our Lord to the Church is recorded in Matthew 28 v.18-20, where we are told that Jesus came and spoke to His disciples, saying, "All power is given unto Me in heaven and in earth. Go ye therefore, and teach all nations, baptising them in the name of the Father, and of the Son, and of the Holy Ghost: Teaching them to observe all things whatsoever I have commanded you: and, lo, I am with you alway, even unto the end of the world".

We read in Ephesians 3, that "the manifold wisdom of God" is made known through the Church, "according to the eternal purpose which He purposed in Christ Jesus our Lord", (Eph. 3 v.10-11). It is also firmly stated in the Word of God that the Church is "the house of God, which is the Church of the living God, the pillar and ground of the truth", (1 Tim. 3 v.15). This means that the Church is responsible for the preservation and proclamation of the whole truth of the whole of God's inspired and inerrant Word.

The world without Christ stands under God's wrath and curse, and it awaits His judgment. It is the responsibility of the Church to warn the world "to flee from the wrath to come", (Matt. 3 v.7). The parallel passage in Luke's Gospel gives the same warning (Luke 3 v.7), and calls for repentance, a change of heart and mind, along with an outward act which manifests that change in a manner of living that demonstrates a turning from sin to serve the living God. In order to alert and arouse the world of its peril, it must be confronted by the demands of the Law of God. The people must know and realise that "all have sinned, and come short of the glory of God", (Rom. 3 v.23).

It is essential that men and women must see their spiritual predicament, plight and peril of sin, before they can understand their need of deliverance. The method God uses in calling men and women unto Himself in repentance and faith is to convict sinners by the Law, which is "our schoolmaster to bring us unto Christ, that we might be justified by faith", (Gal. 3 v.24).

Recognition of personal sin is the important first step, but by itself it is not enough, it is useless, even dangerous. A hardened Pharaoh admitted his sin (Exod. 9 v.27); a double-minded Balaam admitted his (Numb. 22 v.24); a greedy Achan acknowledged his (Joshua 7 v.20); an insincere Saul confessed his (1 Sam. 15 v.24); the rich young ruler went away sorrowful (Luke 18 v.23); and even Judas realised he betrayed innocent blood (Matt. 27 v.4). All of these men recognised their sin, yet none of them repented. True repentance will include a deep realisation of wrongdoing and of sin against God. The sinner must come like the Psalmist David in that great penitential psalm by crying out, "Have mercy upon me, O God, according to Thy lovingkindness: according unto the multitude of Thy tender mercies blot out my transgressions. Wash me throughly from mine iniquity, and cleanse me from my sin. For I acknowledge my transgressions: and my sin is ever before me. Against Thee, Thee only, have I sinned, and done this evil in thy sight", (Psalm 51 v.1-4). The Psalmist here, not only clearly saw his sin, but deeply felt his need to be rid of it. The sorrow of true repentance is sorrow for offence against a holy God. It is not simply regret over the personal consequences of our sin. Sorrow over being found out or over suffering hardship or discipline because of our sin is not godly sorrow, and has nothing to do with repentance.

Genuine repentance will result in a changed life that bears fruit: "bring forth therefore fruits meet for repentance", (Matt. 3 v.8) . . . . . "worthy of repentance", (Luke 3 v.8). The Psalmist, after confessing and expressing great remorse for his sin against a holy God, determined that, with God's grace, he would forsake his sin and turn unto righteousness. "Create in me a clean heart, O God; and renew a right spirit within me. Cast me not away from Thy presence; and take not Thy Holy Spirit from me. Restore unto me the joy of Thy salvation; and uphold me with Thy free Spirit. Then will I teach transgressors Thy ways; and sinners shall be converted unto Thee", (Psalm 51 v.10-13). "Wherefore by their fruits ye shall know them", (Matt. 7 v.20).

The Gospel has no meaning until men and women see their need to be saved from sin by the convicting and convincing power of the Holy Spirit working in their lives. To awaken them of their sin and need, the Church must declare the message of salvation through Christ the Redeemer, the only Mediator between God and man. The Church is to give clear proclamation of the Word of truth and revelation. "How then shall they call on Him in Whom they have not believed? and how shall they believe in Him of Whom they have not heard? and how shall they preach, except they be sent? as it is written, How beautiful are the feet of them that preach the Gospel of peace, and bring glad tidings of good things", (Rom. 10 v.14-15). As well as the minister, pastor, elder, and deacon being involved, the proclamation and spread of the Word of God is the responsibility of the entire Church. "But ye shall receive power, after that the Holy Ghost is come upon you: and ye shall be witnesses unto Me both in Jerusalem, and in all Judæa, and in Samaria, and unto the uttermost part of the earth", (Acts 1 v.8).

When the members of the Church have been properly taught, instructed, cared for, and disciplined, they are "throughly furnished unto all good works", (2 Tim. 3 v.17). If the Church, the body of Christ, is to speak the law of God authoritatively, teach the oracles of God distinctly, and declare the doctrines of the Gospel affirmatively, to a lost, hostile and unbelieving world, it must not be unstable, or tossed about to and fro, "with every wind of doctrine", (Eph. 4 v.14). The Church must be strong if she is to be effective: "the people that do know their God shall be strong, and do exploits", (Daniel 11 v.32).

In the wisdom and providence of God, He has placed His people in almost every walk of life, in offices, factories, farms, market places, schools, colleges, universities, court-rooms, and political chambers where they are in constant contact with ungodly people. The Lord has placed them there to challenge and to influence the unbelieving world. The life of a Christian in the world should be a rebuke to the wayward, and an example in truth, righteousness, and justice.

The guilty silence of much of the Church is testimony of her inability to voice with Biblical conviction the eternal truths and commands of God's Word. As His people, we are called to faithfulness. God never places His people in situations by chance. They may be difficult places, but His grace is all-sufficient to every situation and need. God has a work for all His children to do, and if every Christian clearly understood this, the Church would have a tremendous impact and powerful influence upon the world.

It is shameful that professing Christians spend their time in amassing the things "of this world, and the deceitfulness of riches, and the lusts of other things", (Mark 4 v.19), when men and women made in the image of God are lost. Does not the love of Christ constrain us? (2 Cor. 5 v.14). If the Church fulfils its role to its membership properly, it will produce people who will gladly follow the Master by taking the condition of the world seriously, and who will dedicate and commit themselves to sacrificial living, systematic giving, and prayerful involvement. What an impact the Church would have on the world if every professing Christian truly believed the Word of God, fervently prayed, and acted accordingly. "The effectual fervent prayer of a righteous man availeth much", (James 5 v.16).

By our prayerful concern we shall greatly lament over the sin and wickedness of the nations --- the idolatry, immorality, apostasy, anarchy, and violence that are a reproach to any people. We dishonour God when we fail to pray, abandon His service, and turn aside from following Him. The prophet Samuel reassured the people of Israel that if they will continue to repent, put away their idols and evil, and call upon the Lord and serve Him, God will not reject them. Samuel comforts the people and reassures them that he would continue his care and concern for them. "Moreover as for me, God forbid that I should sin against the Lord in ceasing to pray for you: but I will teach you the good and the right way", (1 Sam. 12 v.23). And he urges the people with an earnest exhortation to practical religion and serious godliness: "Only fear the Lord, and serve Him in truth with all your heart: for consider how great things He hath done for you", (1 Sam. 12 v.24).

Our concern, passion, and love for people are expressed in intercessory prayer. In the Church today it seems we are too busy and anxious to impress the crowds with our fine buildings, facilities, programmes, and self-image. The only way in which the world will be impressed is when it sees the genuine expression of the grace and love of God in us. "If My people, which are called by My name, shall humble themselves, and pray, and seek My face, and turn from their wicked ways; then will I hear from heaven and will forgive their sin, and will heal their land", (2 Chron. 7 v.14). The judgment of God, pestilences, and war are devouring the land, therefore national repentance, prayer, and reformation are required so that Divine mercy and blessing as promised will he poured out upon our people. The Church must not substitute 'things' of man's devising for the pure Gospel of God.

The shepherd boy facing the defiant Goliath seemed an absurd choice to challenge a duel. As David went forth, he said to the Philistine, "Thou comest to me with a sword, and with a spear, and with a shield: but I come to thee in the name of the Lord of hosts, the God of the armies of Israel, Whom thou hast defied", (1 Sam. 17 v.45). Today the Church is confronted with many giants, humanism, unbelief, ecumenism, feminism, apostasy, etc., it runs away in fear, and worse still, compromises, rejects God's truth, completely ignoring and forgetting that "the Gospel of Christ . . . . . is the power of God unto salvation to everyone that believeth; to the Jew first, and also to the Greek. For therein is the righteousness of God revealed from faith to faith: as it is written, The just shall live by faith. For the wrath of God is revealed from heaven against all ungodliness and unrighteousness of men, who hold the truth in unrighteousness; Because that which may be known of God is manifest in them; for God hath shewed it unto them", (Rom. 1 v.16-19).

The power of God is seen when "the works of the flesh" are replaced by "the fruit of the Spirit", (Gal. 5 v.16-26). Sanctification is seen as "the work of God's free grace, whereby we are renewed in the whole man after the image of God, and are enabled more and more to die unto sin, and live unto righteousness", (S.C. No.35). We must "put on the new man, which after God is created in righteousness and true holiness", (Eph. 4 v.24). This new life is only possible in Christ, "not by works of righteousness which we have done, but according to His mercy He saved us, by the washing of regeneration, and renewing of the Holy Ghost", (Titus 3 v.5). The world has no answer when it sees a Christian reigning in life in the midst of adversity. The power of God is demonstrated in godly living. "And God is able to make all grace abound toward you; that ye, always having all sufficiency in all things, may abound to every good work", (2 Cor. 9 v.8).

A major problem in the contemporary Church of today is that men and women think they can worship God without serving Him, and all the while fail to do what He says in His Word. When we worship God "in spirit and in truth" (John 4 v.23): "they that worship Him must worship Him in spirit and in truth" (John 4 v.24), the power of God will be demonstrated to an unbelieving world as we go forth to serve Him obediently and faithfully.

How we should be grieving over the fact that the Church is so impotent and having very little impact on the world in our day and generation. There is a great need for genuine reformation and revival in the Church, and not until she returns to Biblical principles and Biblical practices, will it become an effective force for good again in the world. Let us pray with the Psalmist, "God be merciful unto us, and bless us; and cause His face to shine upon us; That Thy way may be known upon earth, Thy saving health among all nations", (Psalm 67 v.1-2). Let us pray that God will give us grace and strength to fulfil our noble calling and the great purpose for which He made us and transforms our lives "as living stones" (1 Peter 2 v.5) in a world that is engulfed in a spiritual deadness which nothing but the Spirit of God can remove. "Put not your trust in princes, nor in the son of man, in whom there is no help. His breath goeth forth, he returneth to his earth; in that very day his thoughts perish. Happy is he that hath the God of Jacob for his help, whose hope is in the Lord his God: Which made heaven, and earth, the sea, and all that therein is: Which keepeth truth for ever", (Psalm 146 v.3-6).

We may think of the promise in the Book of Joel in which God pledges Himself to restore what the locust have eaten. The locust invasion was God's judgement for the people's sins and disobedience to His commands, as well as a warning of a greater final judgement yet to come; (Joel 2 v.31). Nevertheless, if the people repent, and return unto the Lord, God says "I will restore to you the years that the locust have eaten . . . . . And ye shall eat in plenty, and be satisfied, and praise the name of the Lord your God, that hath dealt wondrously with you . . . . . And ye shall know . . . . . that I am the Lord your God, and none else: and My people shall never be ashamed", (Joel 2 v.25-27).

Because of sin, rebellion against the Lord, and rejection of His Word, cause us to loose many blessings, and God's judgements can come upon the nations that turn their back on Him in many forms, by famines, pestilence's, plagues, catastrophes, wars, etc. The burden of Joel's message is revealed in the phrase "the day of the Lord", (Joel 1v.15; 2 v.1, 11, 31; 3 v.14). His warning is thought-provoking, challenging, and a cry to both Church and state, even in our day and generation, calling us to national repentance, prayer, and reformation. Only repentance will bring restoration, healing, and blessing. Let us urgently turn to the Lord now in repentance for mercy and plead for the outpouring of His grace by the Holy Spirit in these days. "Therefore also now, saith the Lord, turn ye even to Me with all your heart, and with fasting, and with weeping, and with mourning: And rend your heart, and not your garments, and turn unto the Lord your God: for He is gracious and merciful, slow to anger, and of great kindness, and repenteth Him of the evil", (Joel 2 v.12-13).

Let us pray specifically that our Churches and the nation generally will yet again show the marks of greatness and godliness by adhering to God's law, which alas can only come with the restoration of true leadership and genuine obedience on the part of the people to the Divine Word. "Wilt Thou not revive us again: that Thy people may rejoice in Thee? Shew us Thy mercy, O Lord, and grant us Thy salvation. I will hear what God the Lord will speak: for He will speak peace unto His people, and to His saints: but let them not turn again to folly", (Psalm 85 v.6-8).

May God in His sovereignty and grace lead us back in submission to Himself and sanctify our relationship one with another, realising our duty to work to the end that our land "no more may be termed Forsaken; neither shall thy land any more be termed Desolate: but thou shalt be called Hephzibah, and thy land Beulah: for the Lord delighteth in thee, and thy land shall be married" to the Lord, (Isaiah 62 v.4) . . . . . "That in all things He might have the pre-eminence", (Col. 1 v.18).

In the Hebrew of the text Isaiah 62 v.4, four names are employed: (1) "Azubah" meaning "Forsaken"; (2) "Shemamah" meaning "Desolate"; (3) "Hephzibah" meaning "my delight is in her"; and (4) "Beulah" meaning "Thou art married". The Church in relation to God is a weak but beloved bride. He calls her His spouse, married to the Lord, for she is now the object of true affection on the part of Jehovah as her Lord and Husband. "For thy Maker is thine Husband; the Lord of Hosts is His name; and thy Redeemer the Holy One of Israel; The God of the whole earth shall He be called", (Isaiah 54 v.5).

In the Church God's will for His people is that they should shine forth as bright lights to the Gentiles. Their relationship with God will be such that the Gentiles will see the love that God has for His people, and how He delights in them and rejoices over them. God's true redeemed people shall be known as those whom God has sought out and not forsaken. "For the Lord will not cast off His people, neither will He forsake His inheritance", (Psalm 94 v.14).

Truth and Righteousness

The Church today has allowed itself to be shaped and conditioned in large measure by popular opinion, modern culture, and worldly standards. In putting popularity before theology we are producing a plague of notional evangelicalism and nominal Christianity. Unless this trend is reversed by taking heed to the teaching of the Word of God, the Church is seriously heading more and more towards irrelevance and oblivion before God. The Church is not free to plot, to devise, and to plan, its success, in its own way. Our forefathers in the faith would scarcely even recognise us as their children and successors. It must be acknowledged that the Church today is in deep peril and in grave decline.

There are many matters within the Church of the present generation that are seriously amiss, among which is the anti-Biblical teaching and erroneous practice of admitting and allowing women into office as ministers, elders, and deacons. Sound theological conviction is largely absent, and firm Biblical doctrine and Scriptural teaching are greatly lacking. Sadly the weakness of the Church is seen in her willingness to lower her standards in favour of the customs and dictates of the world around us, which is having a total adverse effect on the way that the ministry and leadership of the Church is understood and practised. This is extremely dangerous and harmful to the Scriptural interests and witness of the Church, and the importance of pure Biblical theology is eclipsed by the clamour for mere entertainment and worldly enjoyment.

Modernism, ecumenism, liberalism, feminism and pluralism have adopted the church to become nothing more than a superficial veneer. In many Churches, alas, there is no place for truth, and consequently the denial and disappearance of Biblical teaching, the demise of apostolic doctrine, and the removal of New Testament Church government and practice, are all too evident.

An empty evangelical faith and belief that is not passionate about truth and righteousness, is a faith and belief that are a lost cause which no longer serve Christ. The only way the Church can recover is to re-discover the lost Word of God in our personal faith, and to re-affirm the truth of Scripture in practice. If we do not re-discover and recover the sufficiency of the Word of God in our generation; and if we do not re-learn what it means to be sustained, nourished, and disciplined by it, we will lose the right and capacity to be the people of God altogether by following headlong into the wicked paths and evil ways of liberal Christianity.

We pray that God will revive, reform, and restore the Church, yet again, and make her captive to the Truth of God as revealed in His Word regardless of the popular opinion and cultural consequences of the world. May she be given a fresh vision of God as holy, and an earnestness to serve Him with steadfastness and faithfulness. True faith in the Biblical sense of the term loses its meaning if the doctrine of the holiness of God becomes peripheral, with serious consequences following --- worship loses its awe, the truth of God's Word loses its authority, obedience loses its virtue, and the Church loses its moral compass and spiritual guide.

The Church for the most part today, has greatly fallen, greatly backslidden, and sliding more and more into compromise, darkness, and declension. Let us pray that our sovereign and gracious Lord will grant us another reformation, restore the Church unto Himself, and give to her a mighty revival of evangelical Christianity. May the Church, once again, be drawn back to God and to the truth of His Holy Word, and so be enabled by the power of the Holy Ghost to impact our world to the glory of God. May He give us the grace to repent, the willingness to honour His Word, and the fervent desire to declare "all the counsel of God", (Acts 20 v.28), without fear or favour to all mankind. May He make us, unworthy though as we are, useful instruments in His hand to uphold, maintain, and defend truth and righteousness in our day, so that the whole earth shall be filled with "the excellency of the knowledge of Christ Jesus", (Phil. 3 v.8).

"The Word of the Lord endureth forever", (1 Peter 1 v.25). God's Word never changes. "Jesus Christ the same yesterday, and to day, and for ever", (Heb. 13 v.8). We are to preach to "sinners", remembering that unless by the grace of God they accept Christ as their personal Saviour and Lord, they will be cast into outer darkness for evermore, where the lost shall be dammed and turned into hell for all eternity . . . . . and the everlasting sentence will be the Divine pronouncement: "Depart from Me, ye workers of iniquity . . . . . ye cursed, into everlasting fire, prepared for the devil and his angels", (Luke 13 v.27, Matt 25 v.41).

We are to preach also to the "saints", the called of the Lord, remembering that they will appear before the Judgement Seat of Christ to give an account of their life of service for the Master. "So then everyone of us shall give account of himself to God", (Rom. 14 v.12). There are many things relating to this great matter that should awe the most diligent of men into the utmost care and earnestness of faith and practice. "For we must all appear before the Judgement Seat of Christ; that everyone may receive the things done in his body, according to that he hath done, whether it be good or bad", (2 Cor. 5 v.10).

On that Great Day, my Christian friends, you and I will not be asked what kind of car we drove; nor the square footage of our houses; nor about the designer clothes in our wardrobes; nor what neighbourhood we lived in. The call of God to each one of us is to glorify Him in all of our lives and living. Much of our Christianity today is only play-acting, a pretence, a veneer, and hypocritical. "Be not deceived; God is not mocked: for whatsoever a man soweth, that shall he also reap", (Col. 6 v.7). May God enable us by the power of the Holy Spirit to lengthen the cords and strengthen the stakes in our service and witness of Christ, and by His grace to continue "stedfastly in the apostles' doctrine and fellowship, and in breaking of bread, and in prayers", (Acts 2 v.42).

Until it pleases the Lord in His Sovereign will and purpose, once again to pour out His Spirit upon "a dry and thirsty land", (Psalm 63 v.1, Ezek. 19 v.13), and turn its Churches away from their apostasy, rebellion, disobedience, and sin, back to Himself . . . . . our duty is to prayerfully and actively hold fast to the eternal Word, earnestly contending "for the faith which was once delivered unto the saints", (Jude v.3).

CONCLUSION

My humble prayer is that God will be pleased to use His Word as expounded in this book to speak truth, righteousness, and peace to erring souls and an afflicted Church of our day.

Much of the modern teaching of Christianity in the home, in the Church, in society and in the world at large, with its doctrinal failures and fundamental errors, is greatly dishonouring to God and a total misrepresentation by the Evil One of the teaching of the Divine Word.

Today the use of defective translations of the Scriptures and the anti-inerrancy approach to the Bible are widespread. Sadly even evangelical Churches are showing a strong reluctance to obey the Word of God in a separated stand from diabolical corruption, devilish worship, and organised apostasy.

May God raise up a willing people in our day who shall "set up a standard in the land" (Jer. 51 v.27), earnestly desiring that experience so delightfully described at the close of the Old Testament: "unto you that fear My name shall the Sun of Righteousness arise with healing in His wings", (Mal. 4 v.2). The way of righteousness is light: "the path of the just is as the shining light, that shineth more and more unto the perfect day", (Prov. 4 v.18).

With the earnest desire, yet feeble, to be a "faithful minister of Christ" (Col. 1 v.7) "and fellowservant in the Lord" (Col. 4 v.7), I have endeavoured with the help of the Holy Spirit to present this treatise, realising that as a preacher and teacher of the Word of God, one's work is many sided. It is:-

(1) to preach the Gospel to the unsaved: "For I am not ashamed of the Gospel of Christ: for it is the power of God unto salvation to every one that believeth; to the Jew first, and also to the Greek", (Rom. 1 v.16); "yea, woe is me, if I preach not the Gospel", (1 Cor. 9 v.16);

(2) to feed God's people "with knowledge and understanding", (Jer. 3 v.15); "to feed the Church of God, which He hath purchased with His Own blood", (Acts 20 v.28);

(3) to "lift up a standard for the people", (Isaiah 62 v.10); and to "take up the stumbling block out of the way of My people", (Isaiah 57 v.14); "to root out, to pull down, and to destroy, and to throw down, to build, and to plant", (Jer. 1 v.10);

(4) to be charged to "cry aloud, spare not, lift up thy voice like a trumpet, and shew My people their transgression, and the house of Jacob their sins", (Isaiah 58 v.1); to "preach the Word; be instant in season, out of season; reprove, rebuke, exhort with all longsuffering and doctrine", (2 Tim. 4 v.2); and

(5) to be commissioned and instructed to proclaim comfort to God's people: "Comfort ye, comfort ye My people, saith your God", (Isaiah 40 v.1); "For whatsoever things were written aforetime were written for our learning, that we through patience and comfort of the Scriptures might have hope", (Rom. 15 v.4).

Believers sometimes refuse to be comforted, refuse to obey God's Word, and refuse to act in accordance with Divine Truth. Because of the many temptations and vices of the flesh, the world, and the devil, often the people of God are disconsolate by their own natural corruptions, resulting in the fact that the true Cause of Christ on earth is in a very low state. The God of all grace and comfort is very tender and merciful towards such (Psalm 103), and it is His revealed will that His servants should bind up the broken-hearted and pour the balm of Gilead into their wounds. "Is there no balm in Gilead; is there no physician there? Why then is not the health of the daughter of My people recovered", (Jer. 8 v.22).

The expression, "the people refused to obey" (1 Sam. 8 v.19) strikes a chilling note, "for rebellion is as the sin of witchcraft, and stubbornness is as iniquity and idolatry", (1 Sam. 15 v.23). It is always regrettable when "the wisdom of men" and "the wisdom of the world" (1 Cor. 2 v.5-6) become the wisdom of God's people. It is to be remembered that we are not to be "conformed to this world", (Rom. 12 v.2). Today many churchmen debate and decide without even mentioning the name of God. When was the last time that the religious leaders of this country opened their Bibles, prayed for Divine guidance, took note of God's will, and thundered to the nation, "Thus saith the Scriptures"? As Christians we all should be "valiant for the truth", (Jer. 9 v.3). We all should be deeply involved in the spiritual conflict described in Eph. 6 v.10-12. We all should stand up and be counted, having our "loins girt about with truth, and having on the breastplate of righteousness", (Eph. 6 v.14).

When God forgives the sins of His people who have rebelled against His government and transgressed His Holy Law, the sins of omission, and the sins of commission, He casts them into the depth of the sea (Micah 7 v.19), never to be remembered any more against us: "Who is a God like unto Thee, that pardoneth iniquity, and passeth by the transgression of the remnant of His heritage? He retaineth not His anger for ever, because He delighteth in mercy", (Micah 7 v.18).

The Corinthian Church, as we read earlier and have noted, was in a dreadful state of error and decline. It was not spiritual, but carnal, (1 Cor. 3 v.1), with envying, strife, and divisions among them, (1 Cor. 3 v.4). The manifestation of their carnality was evident by their sinful pride, and boasting to be 'wise in their own conceits', but very ignorant of the truth. It was this very erroneous delusion that Paul sought to correct: "The Lord knoweth the thoughts of the wise, that they are vain. Therefore let no man glory in men", (1 Cor. 3 v.20-21).

Like the Corinthians of old, many today give allegiance to men: preachers, pastors, and theologians. Every denomination within Christendom has its 'big names', past and present, some with a near-celebrity status, and have a disproportionate, often very detrimental influence over large swathes of the Church. Yet the greatest of men is still nothing more than a man, unable to save a single soul by his own strength. It is God who regenerates, and gives the power to believe.

Every true Christian's testimony should be: "by the grace of God I am what I am", (1 Cor. 15 v.10). Submission to the Word of God, and acceptance of fundamental Biblical principles call for implicit obedience to Divine Truth and a responsibility to walk worthily in the way of the Lord. Sin and rebellion against the teaching of Holy Scripture dominate and blight much of the modern Church. The profane conduct of many is most alarming resulting in contempt and irreverence for that which is Divinely appointed.

We would do well, therefore, to heed the words of C. H. Spurgeon, widely referred to as the Prince of Preachers: "When you bewail the Church's iniquity, let not your emotions end in tears; mere weeping will do nothing without action. Get on your feet; ye that have voices and knowledge, go forth and preach the Word, preach it in every street and lane; ye that have wealth, go forth and spend it for the poor, and sick, and needy, and dying, the uneducated, the unenlightened; ye that have time, go forth and occupy in deeds of goodness; ye that have power in prayer, go forth and pray; ye that can handle the pen, go forth and write --- every man to his post, every one of you to your gun in this day of battle; now for God and for His Word; for God and for His Truth and for the right; let every one of us who knows the Lord seek to fight under His banner".

There are many who profess the Name of Christ today, who seek for something more than the simple, straightforward commands of God's Word. In the search for something to secure un-Scriptural tendencies, they are by their very attitude disparaging and rejecting the Word of God, doubting its authority and primacy, and doing great disservice to its Divine Author. The fact is, <u>all</u> the Word of God is for <u>all</u> the people of God in <u>every</u> generation. It is the duty of each individual Christian to personally appropriate it, believe it, obey it, and live by it.

The true saints of God will bow in glad subjection to the authority of Christ, and His Word. They will rest unquestioningly upon the truth of Scripture to the exclusion of all else in every circumstance. They will act in willing obedience to all its commands and precepts, knowing this to be the highest and best demonstration of love: "If ye love Me, keep My commandments", (John 14 v.15). Diligent obedience, resting implicitly upon all that God has said in His Word, following after the Master, and living accordingly, are ever the hallmarks of genuine discipleship.

In the Church today the role of women has far-reaching consequences, and several of the issues involved have been given due and proper consideration in a Biblical context in the foregoing pages. Many Churches are simply ignoring Biblical principles, being disobedient and neglectful of God's commands, and consequently are engaging in un-Scriptural practices. Some, indeed, may heed the call to reconsider, and those women who are in positions as 'teaching' or 'ruling' elders should be encouraged to give serious thought to what the Holy Scripture says on these important matters. In obedience, therefore, to the Word of God, they should resign their positions of 'headship', knowing that God will bless them as they find other appropriate avenues of usefulness and areas of work within the Church of serving the Lord in a faithful manner.

Sharon James, writes in her book, 'God's Design for Women', great words of advice and comfort, "The Bible has a most high and exalted view of women, but her dignity does not lie in grasping the role of headship. If she truly desires to glorify God, she will not listen to those who equate submission with relegation but will go back to Scripture. There she will see women, joyfully, energetically, willingly serving Christ to the utmost. They are labourers for the Gospel, and servants of the Gospel".

In the Western world, the Christian religion is not what it once was. While many people would identify themselves as 'Christian', there is an increasing secularisation of society. The professed allegiance of the majority to Christianity is largely ignored in their general approach to moral and social issues. Much of the decline in the Church's influence can be traced to the adoption of attitudes to these and other issues which are formulated on humanistic considerations rather than Gospel principles. The basic cause of the loss of influence by the Church, and failure of the Church, is its general abandonment of the message and mission which was entrusted to her by the Lord, and regrettably by her refusal to recognise His authority as that which is communicated to us in His Word.

In this moment of darkness at the present time 'the spirit of the age' prevails rather than the Spirit of God. Toward the end of the nineteenth century, General William Booth rightly predicted when he wrote: "The chief danger that confronts the coming century will be religion without the Holy Ghost, Christianity without Christ, forgiveness without repentance, salvation without regeneration, politics without God, heaven without hell". As an antidote to this spirit of the present age, a missionary Bible teacher to Jamaica, Harold Wildish, had the following written in the flyleaf of his Bible: "As you leave the whole burden of your sin, and rest upon the finished work of Christ, so leave the whole burden of your life and service, and rest upon the present inworking of the Holy Spirit. Give yourself up, morning by morning, to be led by the Holy Spirit and go forward praising and at rest, leaving Him to manage you and your day. Cultivate the habit, all through the day, of joyfully depending on, and obeying, Him, expecting Him to guide, to enlighten, to reprove, to teach, to use, and to do in and with you what He wills. Count on His working as a fact, entirely apart from sight or feeling. Only let us believe in and obey the Word of God as the Rule of our lives, and cease from the burden of trying to manage ourselves; then shall the fruit of the Spirit appear in us to the glory of God".

Sadly the road to destruction is broad, and people go along it at all sorts of speed. No one should presume that all is well just because they are not guilty of gross, flagrant and immoral sins. Neglecting the teaching of the Bible is a great sin, and brings great catastrophe, great danger, and great peril. The only remedy for recovery is that the professing Church of Christ returns to the proclamation of the certainties and primacy of God's Word, accompanied by the gracious outpouring of the Holy Spirit in reformation and revival. "Wilt Thou not revive us again: that Thy people may rejoice in Thee?" (Psalm 85 v.6).

Grace can overcome the strongest prejudices, and root out the deepest unbelief, against God's holy religion. Grace can restore the erring conscience and put an end to the Church's hardness and blindness. Let us pray that God will grant forgiveness and restoration so that His "people shall be willing in the day" (Psalm 110 v.3) of His power, make confession and obey His Word . . . . . and thus set about personal reformation, family reformation, and Church reformation against the defections and apostasy of our day.

The major objective of women in society, whether in the home, in the Church, or in the workplace, must be the same as that of everyone else, namely, to glorify God. "Whether therefore ye eat, or drink, or whatsoever ye do, do all to the glory of God", (1 Cor. 10 v.31).

May we all, male and female, attend to the roles which God has appointed us, and may we conduct ourselves in relation to one another in such a way that God would indeed be glorified.

"Thou art worthy, O Lord, to receive glory and honour and power: for Thou hast created all things, and for Thy pleasure they are and were created", (Rev. 4 v.11).

"Unto the Lord the glory give
    that to His name is due;
And in the beauty of holiness
    unto Jehovah bow", (Psalm 29 v.2).

"In the beauty of His holiness,
    O do the Lord adore;
Likewise let all the earth throughout
    tremble His face before", (Psalm 96 v.9).

EPILOGUE

In appending some verses from the Scottish Metrical Psalms, the Psalmist in a life of principled obedience, highlights the essential elements of faithful Christian living . . . . . explaining the major ingredients of such a life, the foundation on which it is built, the context in which it develops, and the blessing to which it leads. The heart of true godliness and the essence of true discipleship to Jesus Christ in the Christian life, is a life of conscientious obedience to the will of God as revealed in the Holy Scriptures.

When God created Adam and Eve and placed them in the Garden of Eden, He plainly revealed to them that all the joy and blessedness which they had known would remain only as long as they adhered to a path of obedience to His Word. Tragically, our first parents disobeyed and rebelled against the command of God. When Adam fell from the path of obedience, and as the representative head of the human race, he took all his descendants with him in his first transgression. Apart from the grace of God in Christ, every member of the human race is by nature numbered amongst "the children of disobedience", (Eph. 2 v.2). All of mankind by nature is committed to a course of disobedience to the revealed will of God in the Bible. "For all have sinned, and come short of the glory of God", (Rom. 3 v.23).

The Word of God affirms that when the Lord Jesus Christ came into the world to redeem His people, He delivered them to a path of obedience to His Father. "For as by one man's disobedience many were made sinners, so by the obedience of One shall many be made righteous", (Rom. 5 v.19). "Though He were a Son, yet learned He obedience by the things which He suffered; And being made perfect, He became the Author of eternal salvation unto all them that obey Him", (Heb. 5 v.8-9).

When the salvation which Jesus purchased is Divinely applied by the power of the Holy Spirit, it produces in all who are saved by the grace of God in Christ, that desire to obey and to walk with the Lord according to His Word.

The Scriptures describe the people of God as those "that keep the commandments of God, and the faith of Jesus", (Rev. 14 v.12). The marvel of God's regenerating grace, the wonder of the New Birth, is that God changes the disposition of "the stony heart" to "give them an heart of flesh", (Ezek. 11 v.19). "A new heart also will I give you, and a new spirit will I put within you: and I will take away the stony heart out of your flesh, and I will give you an heart of flesh. And I will put My Spirit within you, and cause you to walk in My statutes, and ye shall keep My judgements, and do them", (Ezek. 36 v.26-27). Every man or woman, boy or girl, that is born again by the Spirit of God, becomes a new creation: "Therefore if any man be in Christ, he is a new creature: old things are passed away: behold, all things are become new", (2 Cor. 5 v.17).

The Bible promises many precious blessings in this life to those who live a life of obedience, enjoying communion with God and assurance of His love. "If ye keep My commandments, ye shall abide in My love; even as I have kept My Father's commandments, and abide in His love. These things have I spoken unto you, that My joy might remain in you, and that your joy might be full", (John 15 v.10-11). The only religion which is true and saving is the one which the Bible sanctions and which produces a life of obedience according to the standards of the Word of God in society and in the Church. In His great Priestly prayer, Christ prayed: "Sanctify them through Thy truth: Thy Word is truth", (John 17 v.17).

The universal goal of men and women is blessedness or happiness. There is no happiness or joy while walking in disobedience to the will of God. In Psalm 119, Scripture's longest chapter, the Psalmist praises God for the gift of His Word, and exhorts us to get to know and live by the whole of God's revelation, which is what we call the Bible. We must learn to love, trust, and obey The Scripture.

We are living in a day when people, even in evangelical Churches, do not much value God's Word. We may say we value and cherish the Bible, but our neglect of large swathes of its teaching and contents, greatly belies our confession. Many modern-day ministers, pastors, and elders have abandoned Biblical authority in the government and ruling of the Church, and as a result have turned to worldly methods and devices, humour, drama, and other forms of entertainment. Biblical worship, practice, and discipline are almost non-existent. The expository preaching of the true Evangel in "holding forth the Word of life", (Phil. 2 v.16), with fervency, passion and blessing, is notably absent in many of the local Churches at the present time.

In many ways Psalm 119 is a very remarkable chapter, and tells us that if we grow in grace and increase in the knowledge of God through the Scriptures, we shall be directed in a right path, and be enabled by the Holy Spirit to honour and glorify Him. This Psalm is divided into 22 parts or sections, totalling 176 verses, and with only a few exceptions, each verse refers to the Word of God, which is a great testimony not only of the value of the Holy Scriptures, but also contains very clear evidence of the Divine inspiration of the Bible.

The synonyms (a word having the same meaning with another) for "Scripture" in the original Hebrew text, dominate the entire Psalm, for example:-

"law" (torah) occurs 25 times;

"word" (dabar) occurs 24 times;

"rulings" or "ordinances" (mishpatim) occurs 23 times;

"testimonies" ('edot) occurs 23 times;

"commandments" (miswot) occurs 22 times;

"decrees" or "statutes" (huggim) occurs 21 times;

"precepts" or "charges" (piqqudim) occurs 21 times;

"sayings", "promise", or "word" ('imrah) occurs 19 times.

It was the Hebrew language that God chose to convey the writings of the Old Testament to mankind. The New Testament revelation was given in the Greek language, and it is significant that He Who is the Living Word said, "I am Alpha and Omega, the beginning and the end, the first and the last. Blessed are they that do His commandments", (Rev. 22 v.13-14).

The path to a happy life . . . . . blessedness . . . . . is conforming to the law of God, that is, to know the Bible, study it, keep it, and obey it. There is something that rings true and is commendably honest about the heartfelt cry of the Psalmist in this portion of the Hebrew Psalter. To make a better or more obedient way of life that pleases God . . . . . the question is, do we really desire to seek the Lord, know the Bible, and actually obey its instructions and walk by God's commands?

The whole Psalter, and this Psalm in particular, has been a delight and blessing to the people of God in every generation. "It is better to trust in the Lord than to put confidence in man", (Psalm 118 v.8). The beauty of the Psalms is brought out most effectively in the Authorised Version, which is the best and most trustworthy version of the Bible in the English language. This is the translation followed throughout the study as presented in this book. "I will worship toward Thy holy temple, and praise Thy name for Thy lovingkindness and for Thy Truth: for Thou hast magnified Thy Word above all Thy name", (Psalm 138 v.2).

The book of Psalms is unique in the Bible. It was "The Hallal Book" . . . . . "The Book of Praises" . . . . . of Israel, and the Divine pattern for all God's people throughout the ages. The Hebrew word for "Psalms" is "Mizmer", which means "songs". It is trust in God and obedience to His Word that enables the believer to be joyful in the Lord . . . . . in spite of all the troubles, conflicts, and opposition of modern-day society to the doctrines and teaching of the Bible.

In the midst of the continuing war of the enemies of God that is waging most strongly against His revealed Truth, the Bible, the promise is, "The Lord preserveth all them that love Him: but all the wicked will He destroy", (Psalm 145 v.20). God gives grace, comfort, and assurance to His people who love Him and follow Him even in a crooked, hostile, and sinful world. God will continue to have a witness on earth, and the satanic rebellion against the Church of Christ shall ultimately fail. The battle of the sexes still rages on, primarily between "the counsel of the ungodly" and "the law of the Lord". May God give us grace, wisdom, and the strength to fulfil our purpose, calling, and various roles in society by proclaiming the law of God clearly, by expressing the love of God fervently, and by demonstrating the power of God authoritatively. Let us show the effect and outworking of God's Word in our homes, Churches, society, and in the world in general; and humbly pray that we might practice the Truth in all of life and living to the glory of God.

The following are some selected verses from Psalm 119.

> V.1 Blessed are they that undefil'd,
> and straight are in the way;
> Who in the Lord's most holy law
> do walk, do not stray.
>
> V.2 Blessed are they who to observe
> His statutes are inclin'd;
> And who do seek the living God
> with their whole heart and mind.
>
> V.3 Such in His ways do walk, and they
> do no iniquity.
> V.4 Thou hast commanded us to keep
> Thy precepts carefully.
>
> V.5 O that Thy statutes to observe
> Thou would'st my ways direct.

V.6 Then shall I not be sham'd, when I
    Thy precepts all respect.

V.7 Then with integrity of heart
    Thee will I praise and bless,
    When I the judgments all have learn'd
    of Thy pure righteousness.

V.8 That I will keep Thy statutes all
    firmly resolv'd have I:
    O do not then, most gracious God,
    forsake me utterly.

V.9 By what means shall a young man learn
    his way to purify?
    If he according to Thy word
    thereto attentive be.

V.10 Unfeignedly Thee have I sought
    with all my soul and heart:
    O let me not from the right path
    of Thy commands depart.

V.11 Thy word I in my heart have hid,
    that I offend not Thee.
V.12 O Lord, thou ever blessed art,
    Thy statutes teach thou me.

V.13 The judgments of Thy mouth each one
    my lips declared have:
V.14 More joy Thy testimonies' way
    than riches all me gave.

V.15 I will Thy holy precepts make
    my meditation;
    And carefully I'll have respect
    unto Thy ways each one.

V.16 Upon Thy statutes my delight
   shall constantly be set:
  And, by Thy grace, I never will
   Thy holy word forget.

V.33 Teach me, O Lord, the perfect way
   of Thy precepts divine,
  And to observe it to the end
   I shall my heart incline.

V.34 Give understanding unto me,
   so keep Thy law shall I;
  Yea, ev'n with my whole heart I shall
   observe it carefully.

V.38 Confirm to me Thy gracious word,
   which I did gladly hear,
  Ev'n to Thy servant, Lord, who is
   devoted to Thy fear.

V.57 Thou my sure portion art alone,
   which I did choose, O Lord:
  I have resolv'd, and said, that I
   would keep Thy holy word.

V.58 With my whole heart I did entreat
   Thy face and favour free:
  According to Thy gracious word
   be merciful to me.

V.65 Well hast Thou with Thy servant dealt,
   as Thou didst promise give.
V.66 Good judgment me, and knowledge teach,
   for I Thy word believe.

V.67 Ere I afflicted was I stray'd;
    but now I keep Thy word.
V.68 Both good Thou art, and good Thou do'st:
    teach me Thy statutes, Lord.

V.89 Thy word for ever is, O Lord,
    in heaven settled fast;
V.90 Unto all generations
    Thy faithfulness doth last.

V.97 O how love I Thy law. It is
    my study all the day:
V.98 It makes me wiser than my foes;
    for it doth with me stay.

V.103 How sweet unto my taste, O Lord,
    are all Thy words of truth.
Yea, I do find them sweeter far
    than honey to my mouth.

V.104 I through Thy precepts, that are pure,
    do understanding get;
I therefore ev'ry way that's false
    with all my heart do hate.

V.105 Thy word is to my feet a lamp,
    and to my path a light.
V.106 I sworn have, and I will perform,
    to keep Thy judgments right.

V.116 According to Thy faithful word
    uphold and stablish me.
That I may live, and of my hope
    ashamed never be.

V.117	Hold Thou me up, so shall I be
	    in peace and safety still;
	And to Thy statutes have respect
	    continually I will.

V.124	In mercy with Thy servant deal, Thy laws me teach and show.
V.125	I am Thy servant, wisdom give, that I Thy laws may know.

V.133	O let my footsteps in Thy word
	    aright still order'd be:
	Let no iniquity obtain
	    dominion over me.

V.140	Thy word's most pure, therefore on it Thy servant's love is set.
V.141	Small, and despis'd I am, yet I Thy precepts not forget.

V.142	Thy righteousness is righteousness
	    which ever doth endure:
	Thy holy law, Lord, also is
	    the very truth most pure.

V.169	O let my earnest pray'r and cry
	    come near before Thee, Lord:
	Give understanding unto me,
	    according to Thy word.

V.176	I, like a lost sheep, went astray;
	    Thy servant seek, and find:
	For Thy commands I suffer'd not
	    to slip out of my mind.

APPENDIX ONE

WORSHIP

Psalms and Hymns and Spiritual Songs unaccompanied

Worship is right conceptions of the character and works of God suitably expressed. It is an act of the soul. We are called upon to pour out our hearts to the Lord. "God is a Spirit: and they that worship Him must worship Him in spirit and in truth", (John 4 v.24).

Worship is to be directed and presented to God in His presence, and addressed to Him personally. That cannot be until the one who would worship has been accepted of Him. As sinners we must come by the way of the Cross when we approach God to worship Him. It is only through the Blood of Christ that we can know the joy of sins forgiven, the peace of heart, and reconciliation towards God, (Col. 1 v.20).

Christ is the Author and Finisher of our faith, (Heb. 12 v.2), and it is only by the working of the Holy Spirit in our hearts through faith in the Substitutionary Death of the Lord Jesus Christ and His Resurrection as the only way of salvation, that we can be called the children of God, (Rom. 8 v.16). Unbelievers, who know not Christ as Saviour and Lord, cannot offer true worship to God. "The secret of the Lord is with them that fear Him; and He will shew them His Covenant", (Psalm 25 v.14).

Worship is to be directed to the Triune God alone. Prayer, the reading of Scripture, preaching, the hearing of the Word, praise, the observance of Baptism and the Lord's Supper, are all part of true worship. With due preparation of heart and mind, as Christians we should attend thereunto with diligence, and apply the teaching of the Bible to our hearts and lives day by day.

In the Scriptures of God's revealed Truth, He has prescribed how we may worship Him acceptably. "What thing soever I command you, observe to do it: thou shalt not add thereto, nor diminish from it", (Deut. 12 v.32). It is a clear Biblical principle, that whatever is not commanded in the worship of God is forbidden. Worship is to be rendered to God through the only Mediator, Jesus Christ our Saviour and Redeemer. A very significant fact in Scripture, is the care with which God guarded the purity of His worship. To embrace many of the so-called modern styles of 'praise', hymnody, and 'prayer' modes, is to lose sight of the true character and nature of the Divine Persons within the Triune Godhead and a misrepresentation of the infallible Word of God.

Today, sadly, there is much 'dead wood' within the Church at large not only in this land, but further afield as well. The rejection of the absolute authority of Holy Scripture is widespread in many quarters. Not only are the doctrines of grace fast disappearing, the relegation of the singing of the Psalms of the Bible is almost universal, a Biblical practice that virtually remained intact in the history of the Church until the beginning of the twentieth century. The Book of Psalms, as with all Scripture, composed under the inspiration of the Holy Spirit (2 Tim 3 v.16-17), is the common possession of the whole family of God, its ordained manual of praise. Having a connected record through thousands of years down to our own times, it is consecrated forever as having been the hymnary of our Saviour and of the Apostolic Church.

During the past century, one of the most significant trends in religious worship, has been the drift and departure from the Psalms of the Bible to songs of mere human composition. Indeed, the 'modernism' in the Church today can be directly traced to the departure from the Divine to the human . . . . . the infallible to the fallible. The use of uninspired songs, which today is usually designated 'hymns', has no warrant whatsoever in Scripture. The Divine appointment of the Psalms inspired by God (2 Tim. 3 v.16), establishes the exclusive adaptation of them to the service of praise. (1 Chron. 16 v.4, 7; 2 Chron. 29 v.36; Neh. 12 v. 24; Matt. 26 v.30).

Much confusion is caused by the modern popular habit of distinguishing Psalms from hymns. The word 'hymn' is most erroneously used to distinguish humanly composed songs of praise from the Songs in the Book of Psalms. Consequently, those who use the humanly composed songs very often rely on Ephesians 5 v.19 and Colossians 3 v.16, for their Divine authorisation, whereas in fact this is not true.

The two passages are as follows:-

(1) "Speaking to yourselves in psalms and hymns and spiritual songs, singing and making melody in your heart to the Lord", (Eph. 5 v.19).

(2) "Let the Word of Christ dwell in you richly in all wisdom; teaching and admonishing one another in psalms and hymns and spiritual songs, singing with grace in your hearts to the Lord", (Col. 3 v.16).

From the Greek, which is the original language of the New Testament, the word "songs" might be translated "odes". The notion that finds in these terms, "psalms and hymns and spiritual songs", a warrant for an uninspired hymnology in the matter of the Church's praise, does not bear Biblical truth.

The three Greek words used in both instances by Paul are "psalmois", "humnois", and "ordais". That the Apostle uses precisely the same three words in both instances shows that he was referring to what would be perfectly well understood by those to whom he wrote these two Epistles, Ephesians and Colossians, without a moment's hesitation of the need of explanation. He was writing in both cases to a Greek-speaking people, to whom the Septuagint Version was the Bible, just as the Authorised Version is the Bible to English-speaking people. Turning up the Book of Psalms in the Greek Septuagint, we find that every one of the Psalms except the first two, have a separate title prefixed.

In the Septuagint, the Greek translation of the Old Testament, which was commonly used by the Jews and early Christians, we find that the word "hymn" is used in the title of six of the Psalms in the Bible. This is the exact identical word in Ephesians 5 v.19 and Colossians 3 v.16.

In 67 of the Psalms the word "psalm" appears, although this is the title given to the whole book.

We also find that the word "song" or "ode", found in the above-mentioned New Testament passages, is used in the title of 34 of the Psalms of the Bible.

Together the words "psalms and "song" are used in the title of 12 of them.

In two of them "psalms" and "hymns" are used together.

Psalm 76 has got all three terms in its title.

Also, at the close of the 72nd Psalm, the Greek Septuagint reads, "the hymns of David, the son of Jesse, are ended".

The translation of the Old Testament into Greek, which was the common language of the early New Testament Church, comprehended many of the Psalms under the name "hymns".

Quoting again from the Septuagint Version, Psalm 137 v.3, the Greek reads, "There they who took us captive demanded of us words of 'songs', and they who led us away said, chant us a 'hymn' out of the 'songs' of Zion".

In the Greek Septuagint Bible, the Psalms are frequently called "hymns" and "songs", especially in 2 Samuel, 1 and 2 Chronicles, and Nehemiah.

The "psalms and hymns and spiritual songs", referred to in the Ephesians and Colossians passages, are simply the inspired Songs of Scripture, under the titles commonly used for these Psalms in New Testament times.

These different words do not describe three different collections of songs, but one and the same collection, namely, the 150 Psalms of the Bible. All those titles were in current use in the Apostolic Church, and there would be no misunderstanding whatsoever as to what the Apostle Paul meant, when he instructed the Churches at Ephesus and Colosse to sing "psalms and hymns and spiritual songs".

Let us note and emphasise the significance of the word "spiritual". The Greek word "pneumatikais", translated "spiritual", signifies composed under the guidance of the Holy Spirit. It is an adjective, and qualifies all three nouns, "psalms", "hymns", and "songs".

Instead of prefixing "spiritual" to songs, as it would naturally do if meant to qualify it alone, but follows the whole three in the original Greek New Testament, the proper translation should run as follows . . . . . "in psalms and hymns and songs, inspired by the Spirit".

There is extra Biblical evidence that the Psalter was the only manual of the Church's praise. In the Jewish Talmud literature consisting of the Mishnah and the Gemara, the Psalms are referred to as "songs and praises and hymns", and in the Apostolic canons they are called "the hymns of David". David is called "the sweet psalmist of Israel", because he penned many of the Psalms under Divine guidance for the use of the Church.

The Evangelists Matthew and Mark, with regard to the use of the Psalms, have recorded of our Saviour and His disciples . . . . . "And when they had sung an hymn, they went out into the mount of Olives", (Matt. 26 v.30, Mark 14 v.26). In the Greek New Testament it will be noticed that the fact is expressed, not by a noun but by the participle of a verb, "Kai humnesautes" . . . . . "and having sung praises they went out into the mount of Olives". The Authorised Version has for "an hymn" very rightly put in the margin, "or Psalm". Reputable Biblical scholars and commentators are agreed that this was part of the "Great Hallel", which consisted of Psalms 113 to 118 inclusive, always sung in connection with the observance of the Passover. Here we see the Saviour linking the Psalms with the sacrament of the Lord's Supper.

Among the diversities of gifts mentioned in the New Testament, it is significant to note that there is no reference to the gift of composing sacred songs, (1 Cor. 12). If that had been so, then there would have been a poetical book added to the New Testament by Divine inspiration.

One main objection urged against the exclusive use of the Psalms in worship is that there is not enough about the Saviour in them. This objection is absolutely false, and founded on insufficient knowledge of the book. The Book of Psalms is more often quoted in the New Testament as referring to Christ, than is any other Old Testament book.

Our Saviour Himself said, "These are the words which I spake unto you, while I was yet with you, that all things must be fulfilled, which were written in the law of Moses, and in the prophets, and in the psalms, concerning Me. Then opened He their understanding, that they might understand the Scriptures", (Luke 24 v.44-45).

Christ is the Perfect Man of the 1st Psalm, the Shepherd of the 23rd, the Bridegroom of the 45th, the Rock of the 40th, and the King of Glory of the 24th. These are but a few examples for the Psalms continually speak of the Person and the Work of Christ. The Psalms are Messianic in character, Christ-centred, and all things relating to Him from His incarnation to His Second Coming are spoken of and celebrated therein.

'Hymns' of mere human composition were never appointed by God, neither is there in the New Testament any warrant for the use of musical instruments accompanying the praise. Here it is objected that music was used in Old Testament times. Instrumental music, in the Old Testament period, was inseparably connected with the sacrificial service, but unknown in the tabernacle services. (2 Chron. 29 v.26-30). The instruments when used in worship were part of the gorgeous ceremonial ritual of the Temple service. But the Temple services were fulfilled in Jesus Christ Himself. He was the true Temple, the great High Priest, the One offering for sin.

The New Testament Church was patterned after the Synagogue, and not after the Temple, from which she took her institutions and her forms of worship. The names, "presbyter", "elder", and "deacon", which were given to office-bearers in the New Testament Church, are all derived from the Synagogue. Never once are they called "priest", the title of those who officiated in the Temple. (Acts 13 v.15).

Musical instruments were not used in the Synagogue, and to this very day still remain unused by orthodox Jews. It was never commanded for any worship except that which pertained to the Temple ritual in the old dispensation. It is an acknowledged fact beyond all doubt that instrumental music was unknown in the Christian Church for many centuries, and it wasn't until the Dark Ages, the period prior to the Reformation, that much corruption and error crept into the Church. But even then the matter of instrumental music was looked upon with suspicion as savouring too much of the old Jewish ritual. To Christians the Spiritual injunction is, to "offer the sacrifice of praise to God continually, that is, the fruit of our lips giving thanks to His name", (Heb.13 v.15).

New Testament worship is pre-eminently spiritual in character. We cannot worship God through a machine. "God is a Spirit: and they that worship Him must worship Him in spirit and in truth", (John 4 v.24). "Ye shall seek Me, and find Me, when ye shall search for Me with all your heart", (Jer. 29 v.13).

The Psalms were written for the Church of God, and for the Church of all ages. These Songs of the Bible by their Divine origin are exalted far above any earthly human hymn book, being the very oracles of God. In every age they have been the great source of uplifting and unfailing comfort and inspiration to God's people in every land where the Bible is known.

"Ye shall not add unto the Word which I command you, neither shall ye diminish ought from it, that ye may keep the commandments of the Lord your God which I command you", (Deut. 4 v.2).

"What thing soever I command you, observe to do it: thou shalt not add thereto, nor diminish from it", (Deut. 12 v.32).

In the matter of praise and worship we have a sure guide. God's own Word is the chief instrument that God uses in guiding us in every aspect of life, religious or otherwise. All must be tested by the Scripture. "To the law and to the testimony, if they speak not according to this Word, it is because there is no light in them", (Isaiah 8 v.20).

In the New Testament, in the great evangelistic campaigns carried on by the Apostles, they sang as well as preached, and the Psalms of the Psalter was the manual of praise. Paul exhorts his converts to speak "to yourselves in psalms and hymns and spiritual songs, singing and making melody in your heart to the Lord", (Eph. 5 v.19); and "Let the Word of Christ dwell in you richly in all wisdom; teaching and admonishing one another in psalms and hymns and spiritual songs, singing with grace in your hearts to the Lord", (Col. 3 v.16).

The Psalms only, as already seen, were the material of song in the evangelistic movement of the Early Christian Church.

It is significant to note that God in His sovereignty and providence during the great spiritual awakening of the sixteenth century Reformation, never allowed the witness for Psalmody to die out. The witness for purity of worship and doctrine were restored to their rightful place. The Waldenses, Huguenots, Calvinists, Reformers, Covenanters, Heroes and Martyns of the faith throughout Europe and the British Isles, adhered very strictly to the Psalms, their influence being very powerful and far-reaching in the promotion of pure Christianity.

In Scotland, these songs in all their richness were heard on the mountains, in the glens, over the moors, as well as on the scaffold and at the stake. Vast crowds attended the preaching of the Covenanters, and as many as 500 were converted to God under a single sermon. Would to God there was more of that sort of preaching today. Let us pray, pray, pray. Reformation is needed! Revival is needed!

The Divine will and eternal purpose of God for this world is the missionary challenge of establishing and perfecting in the whole earth the Kingdom of Righteousness. This stupendous achievement can only be accomplished by the power of the Holy Spirit wrought through "the Church of God, which He hath purchased with His own Blood", (Acts 20 v.28).

> "All nations whom Thou mads't shall come
> and worship reverently
> Before Thy face; and they, O Lord,
> Thy name shall glorify", (Psalm 86 v.9).

APPENDIX TWO

FAIRVIEW REFORMED PRESBYTERIAN CHURCH
(COVENANTER)
COUNTY MONAGHAN

Where Rev. Prof. Dr. R.H. Creane attended Sabbath School and Church

It was here also under the influence and preaching of Hugh William Stewart, Irish Mission Colporteur, that Robert was converted to Christ as a teenage boy; and where he worshipped God in his early years.

THE OLD MEETING HOUSE spanned some three centuries

(partly demolished to make way for car park at the new Church)

FAIRVIEW NEW MEETING HOUSE 2005

Service of Thanksgiving to mark its completion was held on
Saturday 18th March 2006

"It was a great privilege and joy", says Prof. Creane, "to be associated with the minister, elders and members on such a special occasion", recalling many happy days and joyful memories during his boyhood years at Fairview. A message of Christian Greeting was conveyed by him to the congregation with the prayer that the Lord will greatly bless the ministry of His holy and inspired Word "in demonstration of the Spirit and of power" (1 Cor. 2 v.4) to the salvation of souls, and His people built up and edified in their "most holy faith" (Jude v.20). In the providence of God there remains a people of the Reformed Biblical Faith adhering steadfastly to the Church of the Covenants in the Castleblayney area that desire to fear the name of the Lord.

> "And yet a banner Thou hast giv'n
> To them who Thee do fear;
> That it by them, because of truth
> displayed may appear",
> (Psalm 60 v.4)

INTERIOR OF THE NEW CHURCH

Part of the interior of the new Church with solid mahogany Communion Table and five matching chairs donated in memory of their parents, Wallace and Suzanna (Anna) Creane, by their family and spouses, namely, Robert & Rhoda, James & Georgina, Wallace & Lily, Myrtle & John, David & Jennifer, Dorothy, and William & Mary.

>   "How lovely is Thy dwelling place,
>   O Lord of hosts, to me!
>   The tabernacles of Thy grace
>   how pleasant, Lord, they be.
>
>   My thirsty soul longs veh'mently,
>   yea faints, Thy courts to see:
>   My very heart and flesh cry out,
>   O living God, for Thee",
>   (Psalm 84 v.1-2)

APPENDIX THREE

The Bible Christian Mission

Founded 1970

Founder and Director: Rev. Prof. Dr. Robert H. Creane

OBJECTS AND AIMS

(1) To win the lost to Christ by means of Gospel preaching and Gospel literature.

(2) To foster Biblical teaching and to promote closer fellowship among the people of God by prayer, Bible study, encouragement and service, and to expose the dangers involved in compromise with unsound doctrine and practice.

(3) To provide opportunities for meetings and conference, and to stimulate action and co-operation in the extension of the Kingdom of God through evangelism and outreach.

(4) To promote truth and righteousness upon all areas of life, whether personal, social, national or religious, that Biblical standards be upheld and error and ungodliness resisted.

(5) To teach and promote Bible Christian Unity, inclusive of all who by free sovereign grace, believe in Christ Jesus as Saviour and Lord, and thus show their determination to preserve the Evangelical Protestant Faith.

(6) To pray and work for the revival and renewal of the Work of God in our land and to co-operate with those who seek to uphold the Word of Life.

DOCTRINAL BASIS OF FAITH

1. The Divine Plenary Inspiration of Holy Scripture, the Old and New Testaments originally given as the Word of God, and their Absolute Sufficiency and Sole Authority in all matters of Faith and Practice both for the Church and the individual believer.

2. The Trinity in Unity of the Godhead—one God, eternally existing in three persons—Father, Son and Holy Spirit, Who are the same in substance, equal in power and glory.

3. The Sovereignty of God, revealed in the Lordship of Jesus Christ, over the world and thus over every department of life.

4. The Essential, Absolute and Eternal Deity and Perfect Humanity of our Lord Jesus Christ—His Conception by the Holy Spirit, His Birth of the Virgin Mary and His real but sinless life.

5. The Substitutionary and Atoning Death of Jesus Christ as the one Sacrifice for sin, His triumphant Bodily Resurrection from the dead on the third day, His glorious Ascension into Heaven, His Mediatorial Reign and continual Intercession at the Throne of God, and His visible and personal Return in power and glory to receive His people unto Himself.

6. The Deity and Personality of The Holy Spirit, and His essential work in conviction, regeneration and sanctification; His infilling of the indwelt believer for grace and power to live and witness for Christ.

7. The Total Depravity and Utter Ruin of man through the Fall, the necessity of the New Birth of the sinner and his acceptance with God only on the ground of the Imputed Righteousness of the Lord Jesus Christ.

8. Full salvation solely by the Grace of God in repentance and faith through Christ alone, and the eternal security of the believer.

9. The Personality of the Devil, his opposition to God and His purposes, and the corruption and enslavement of man by Satan.

10. The Covenant relationship between God and those redeemed through Christ as their Mediator, in which, believers, solemnly bind themselves, by His grace, to be loyal to the Saviour.

11. The Purity of Doctrine, Worship, Church Government and Life.

12. The due observance of the Sabbath as a day sacred to rest and worship.

13. Expository, evangelical preaching with a service conforming to the New Testament pattern in its simplicity and dependence upon the Word of God.

14. The Divinely appointed and binding character of the ordinances of Believer's Baptism and the Lord's Supper.

15. The Bodily Resurrection of the just and the unjust, the judgment of the world by our Lord Jesus Christ at the last day, the everlasting blessedness of the saved in Heaven, and the conscious eternal punishment of the unpenitent who will be damned in Hell without hope for evermore.

16. The one holy, universal Church which is the Body and Bride of Christ and to which all true believers belong.

17. The spiritual unity of all redeemed by the precious Blood of the Lord Jesus Christ and their duty to uphold in themselves and in the Church standards of doctrine and life that are in conformity with the teaching of the Infallible Word of God—"to live soberly, righteously, and godly in this present age", (Titus 2 v. 12).

"For the Word of God, and for the Testimony of Jesus Christ", (Rev. 1 v.9)

THE BIBLE CHRISTIAN MISSION

A Series of Talks and Addresses

on the

Leaders, Martyrs and Heroes of the Faith

by

Rev. Prof. Dr. R. H. Creane

"Earnestly contend for the faith which was once delivered unto the saints", (Jude v.3)

Let us hold forth the Banner of Biblical Truth, maintain and defend our Protestant Christian heritage, and unashamedly seek to witness and pray for the advancement of Christ's Cause on earth.

JOHN WYCLIFFE
1324-1384, renowned Englishman, . . . Died aged 60 years
A NATIONAL HERO – 'THE MORNING STAR OF THE REFORMATION'
The Doctrine of Transubstantiation without Biblical Warrant
"Dominion is founded in grace".

JOHN HUSS
1373-1415, a Czech Reformer, . . . Martyred aged 42 years
THE FORERUNNER OF THE REFORMATION
The Antichrist in Scripture
"The Papacy is an institution of Satan".

JEROME OF PRAGUE
1380-1416, the Messenger who paved the way, . . . Martyred aged 36 years
THE DIPLOMAT OF REFORMATION
The Romish Priesthood a reproach to the Name and Profession of Christianity
"Our Lord Jesus Christ, when He suffered death for me, a most miserable sinner, did wear a crown of thorns upon His head, and for His sake will I wear this cap".

GIROLAMO SAVONAROLA
1452-1498, an Impassioned Campaigner, . . . Martyred aged 46 years
THE PROPHET OF THE REFORMATION
Signs of Renewal and the Near Approach of a Momentous Spiritual Upheaval
"It is Satan, that would prevent, by these terrors, the confession of the Truth in the assembly of princes, for he foresees the blow it would inflict upon his kingdom".

MARTIN LUTHER
1483-1546, 'The Monk who Shook the World', . . . Died aged 63 years
THE PIONEER OF THE REFORMATION
Justification by Faith Alone
"Unless I be convinced, by Scripture, I neither can nor dare retract anything . . . My conscience is captive to the Word of God. There I take my stand, I can do no other. So help me, God".

PHILLIPP MELANCHTHON
1497-1560, Luther's chief Associate, . . . Died aged 63 years
THE COMPANION OF THE REFORMATION
The Principal Author and Architect of the Augsburg Confession of Faith
"We cannot yield, nor can we desert the Truth . . . we are determined to preserve purity of doctrine and the true worship of God in the churches committed to our Faith".

HULREICH ZWINGLI
1484-1531, a Forceful Advocate, . . . Died in Battle aged 47 years
THE PREACHER OF THE REFORMATION
The Priesthood of all Believers and the Abolition of Religious Idolatry
"The renaissance of True Christendom is founded on the Scriptures".

MARTIN BUCER
1491-1551, a Ceaseless Missioner, . . . Died aged 60 years
THE PEACEMAKER OF THE REFORMATION
The Renewal of the Whole of Society resulting from the Preaching of the True Gospel
"This reform, through conversion, piety, and discipline, finds its fullest expression in the teaching of the Word of God . . . Christ suffered and taught for no other purpose but that we should be one and embrace each other with the same love with which He embraced us".

HEINRICH BULLINGER
1504-1575, noble Successor of Zwingli, . . . Died aged 71 years
THE MODEL PASTOR OF THE REFORMATION
The Word of God brings Salvation and Grace to the Human Soul
"I there found all that is necessary for man's salvation, and from that time I adhered to this principle, that we must follow the sacred Scripture alone, and reject all human additions".

WILLIAM TYNDALE
1484-1536, 'Father of the English Bible', . . . Martyred aged 52 years
HEROIC TRANSLATOR AND ESSAYIST OF THE REFORMATION
The Authority and Supremacy of the Holy Scriptures
"Lord, open the King of England's eyes".

HUGH LATIMER
1491-1555, a Warrior for Truth, . . . Martyred aged 64 years
THE POPULAR EXPONENT OF THE REFORMATION
The Meaning, Mission and Marks of a True Church
"Be of good cheer, Master Ridley, and play the man. We shall this day, by god's grace, light up such a candle in England, as I trust, shall never be put out".

NICHOLAS RIDLEY
1500-1555, a Fearless Stalwart, . . . Martyred aged 55 years
THE MASTER SPIRIT OF THE REFORMATION IN ENGLAND
The Establishment of the Thirty-Nine Articles of Religion
"In defence and confirmation of the Gospel", (Phil. 1 v.7)

JOHN HOOPER
1500-1555, a Zealous Adherent,, . . . Martyred aged 55 years
THE DISCIPLINARIAN OF THE REFORMATION
A Godly Confession and Protestation of the Christian Faith
"The wise men of the world can find shifts to avoid the Cross . . . but the simple servant of Christ doth look for no other but oppression in the world".

THOMAS CRANMER
1489-1556, a Courageous Counsellor, . . . Martyred aged 67 years
THE FIRST PROTESTANT ARCHBISHOP OF THE REFORMATION AT CANTERBURY
Protestantism and Romanism must for ever Remain Apart
"This hand hath offended; Oh, this unworthy right hand".

PETER MARTYR
1500-1562, esteemed Colleague and true Delegate, . . . Died aged 62 years
THE DEFENDER OF THE REFORMATION
The Defender of the Orthodox Faith in the Sacred Trinity
"To kill a man is not to defend a doctrine; it is simply to kill a man".

WILLIAM FAREL
1489-1565, an Evangelical of Stature, . . . Died aged 76 years
THE DISPUTATIONIST OF THE REFORMATION
The Biblical Theology of Apostolic Preaching essential to True Religion and Worship
"You may speak here as boldly as you please; our arguments are neither faggot, fire, nor sword, prison nor torture; public executioners are not our doctors of divinity, Truth is strong enough to outweigh falsehood; if you have it, bring it forward".

JOHN CALVIN
1509-1564, an International Figure, . . . Died aged 55 years
THE MOST PRE-EMINENT THEOLOGIAN OF THE REFORMATION
The Sovereignty of God and Human Responsibility
"Whatever is not commanded in the Word of God, is forbidden".

THEODORE BEZA
1519-1605, worthy Successor to Calvin, . . . Died aged 86 years,
THE CHAMPION OF THE REFORMATION
The Church and it's Head
"Do not shudder at the sight of this adversary, if the liberty promised to us in the Edict lasts, the papacy will fall to the ground of itself".

JOHN KNOX
1505-1572, a Fearless Contender, . . . Died aged 67 years
THE MOST POWERFUL LEADER OF THE REFORMATION IN SCOTLAND
The Merits and Satisfaction of Christ's Redemption
"Go, read, where I first cast anchor".

RICHARD CAMERON
1648-1680, a most uncompromising Field-Preacher, . . . Killed in Battle aged 32 years
THE LION OF THE COVENANT
The Scriptural Attainments of the Covenanted Reformation.
The National Covenant of 1638. The solemn League and Covenant of 1643.
"Lord, spare the green, and take the ripe".

THE BIBLE CHRISTIAN MISSION

Searching for Absolutes in a Postmodern World

A Special Series of Conference Subjects

by

Rev. Prof. Dr. R. H. Creane

"For the Word of God, and for the testimony of Jesus Christ",
(Rev. 1 v.9)

Today, the question of Truth, as it relates to the question of the inspiration, inerrancy, and authority of Scripture, is widely criticised and constantly challenged.

These addresses are to encourage all who are concerned about the true meaning of the term "Evangelical" in this present age.

"Thy Word is true", (Psalm 119 v.160)

Truth Unchanged, Unchanging and Trustworthy

Present day rationalism and humanism discrediting the Bible

Widespread evils and corruption have infested the Church

Testimony to the Truth the Christian's Responsibility

"And this Word, Yet one more, signifieth the removing of those things that are shaken, as of things that are made, that those things which cannot be shaken may remain. Wherefore we receiving a kingdom which cannot be moved, let us have grace, whereby we may serve God acceptably with reverence and godly fear: For our God is a consuming fire", (Heb. 12 v.27-29).

The Case for the Authorised Version of the Bible

The modern English versions --- perversions !!

Commitment to the belief in God-given word for word Scripture

The King James Version is superior

"All Scripture is given by inspiration of God, and is profitable for doctrine, for reproof, for correction, for instruction in righteousness: That the man of God may be perfect, thoroughly furnished unto all good works", (2 Tim. 3 v.16-17).
"The Lord gave the Word: great was the company of those that publish it", (Psalm 68 v.11).

The Compromise of the Modern Ecumenical Movement

The threat of its pernicious claims and recent rise world-wide eroding the faithful proclamation of the Apostolic Faith

Evangelical Churches fast losing their vision of what Truth is and faltering in their fidelity to it

The urgent need to guard against any substitution of the age-long beliefs of New Testament Christianity

"To the law and to the testimony: if they speak not according to this Word, it is because there is no light in them", (Isaiah 8 v.20)
"Therefore we ought to give the more earnest heed to the things which we have heard, lest at any time we should let them slip", (Heb. 2 v.1).

The Confusion of the Charismatic Phenomenon

Modernistic teaching on revival gravely at variance with the Scriptural view of the work of the Holy Spirit of Truth

Continuance of 'revelation' through 'charismatic gifts' irrelevant and contrary to Scripture

Unwavering zeal and undiminishing faithfulness to the Gospel of Christ most necessary

"God sending His Own Son in the likeness of sinful flesh, and for sin, condemned sin in the flesh: That the righteousness of the law might be fulfilled in us, who walk not after the flesh, but after the Spirit", (Rom. 8 v.3-4)
"If we live in the Spirit, let us also walk in the Spirit", (Gal. 5 v.25).

The Communion of Saints --- a foretaste of Heaven

Departure from Biblical doctrine, precept and practice, means loss of blessing

The urgency to preserve the integrity of true Biblical doctrine and Christian belief in a permissive age

The Christian's responsibility to bear witness and demonstrate the saving power of godliness and holiness

"For where your treasure is, there will your heart be also", (Matt. 6 v.21)
"Set your affection on things above, not on the things on the earth", (Col. 3 v.2)
"Be thou faithful unto death, and I will give thee a crown of life", (Rev. 2 v.10)

The Command to Worship and Glorify God

Departure from ancient Christian standards greatly accelerated in today's society

'Decay' invariably follows 'change': all too evident in many Churches

The will and guidance of the Lord discernible in every matter of faith and practice

"Lead me in Thy truth, and teach me: for Thou art the God of my salvation; on Thee do I wait all the day", (Psalm 25 v.5)
"If I regard iniquity in my heart, the Lord will not hear me", (Psalm 66 v.18)
"Give unto the Lord the glory due unto His name: worship the Lord in the beauty of holiness", (Psalm 29 v.2)

The Call to Repentance and earnest Contention for the Faith

The Church today guided by secular culture thereby losing its Biblical fidelity, moral compass and missionary zeal

Reluctance to obey God's commands in a separated stand from organised apostasy

A more vigorous defence of the 'whole counsel of God' urgently required

"Repent ye, and believe the Gospel", (Mark 1 v.15)
"When the enemy shall come in like a flood, the Spirit of the Lord shall lift up a standard against him", (Isaiah 59 v.19)
"Earnestly content for the faith which was once delivered unto the saints", (Jude v.3)

The Challenge of the Christian Message --- "Christ in you, the hope and Glory".

The concept of Truth in contemporary theology not conducive to Evangelical distinctives

Satan waging an all-out attack on the Biblical fundamentals of the Christian faith

Hold fast to the declaration that Christ is "the way, the truth, and the life: no man cometh unto the Father, but by Me", (John 14 v.6)

"To whom God would make known what is the riches of the glory of this mystery among the Gentiles; which is Christ in you, the hope of glory: Whom we preach, warning every man, and teaching every man in all wisdom: that we may present every man perfect in Christ Jesus: Whereunto I also labour, striving according to His working, which worketh in me mightily", (Col. 1 v.27-29).

APPENDIX FOUR

Urban Divinity Unit UK Limited

Affiliated to Canada Christian College and School of Graduate Theological Studies

Urban Divinity Ministries

11-13 Oughton Road, Highgate, Birmingham, B12 0DF
Telephone: 0121 440 3103

Introduction and Welcome

Board of Directors

Aims and Objectives

Doctrinal Basis

The Alone Principles

Effective Service

Associated Colleges

Introduction and Welcome

Urban Divinity Unit UK, Birmingham, is the collective name of the combined ministries of Urban Divinity Ministries and other affiliated Seminaries and Colleges. Originally established as an independent body, it is non-denominational, interdenominational and international, founded primarily to serve the needs of those who desire to continue their training and study while engaged in the ministry of preaching, teaching, evangelism, pastoral care, religious education, missionary work, and other spheres of service in the Lord's work worldwide.

Candidates who have received the call of God to serve Him in whatever capacity and field of service, are accepted and welcomed regardless of race, colour, or denominational allegiance from all over the world. "In the defence and confirmation of the Gospel, ye all are partakers of My grace", (Phil. 1 v.7). It is imperative, therefore, "to stand fast in the Lord" (Phil. 4 v.1), so that the labours of both teacher and student redound to the praise, honour, and glory of God.

Education that is distinctively Christian is based on the Bible, and the Christian philosophy of life cannot be embraced apart from the experience of the new birth which involves a real encounter with God through repentance from sin and faith in the Lord Jesus Christ. Christian education, therefore, in the true sense of the term, is structured on the Protestant Reformation viewpoint that the Bible is the infallible and inerrant Word of God. UDM Birmingham is not a secular group of colleges, but is unashamedly evangelical and conservative, and should not be confused with professional colleges of liberal arts. Our vision is "to make known the mystery of the Gospel" (Eph. 6 v.19) by promoting a high level of theological education, training and scholarship in the preparation of candidates for ministry and mission in the twenty-first century.

The superficiality of much of the modern teaching of Christianity with its doctrinal failures and errors lead only to impoverished service and a serious decline in true worship. This is due in no small measure to a misrepresentation and distorted view of the Bible and of the true character and nature of the Divine persons within the Triune Godhead. "The Word of the Lord endureth for ever. And this is the Word which by the Gospel is preached unto you", (1 Peter 1 v.25).

There is a great need in the Church today for men who are called to preach and are able to preach the everlasting Word. Jesus proclaimed, "Upon this Rock I will build My Church; and the gates of hell shall not prevail against it", (Matt. 16 v.18). God's spokesmen will be strong Biblical preachers and firm ambassadors in the line of the great leaders of the early New Testament Church, the Reformation age, the Covenanting period, the Puritan era, the Great Evangelical Awakening, and other Revival times, including the Martyrs and Heroes of the Faith who in every age have faithfully sought to hold "forth the Word of Life" (Phil. 2 v.16) in the most difficult and trying of circumstances. In order to fulfil such a need, UDM Birmingham was established and called into existence some two decades or more ago. "This is the Lord's doing, and it is marvellous in our eyes", (Psalm 118 v.23).

Students are encouraged to "live soberly, righteously, and godly, in this present world", (Titus 2 v.12). The Bible is the sole authority in all matters of doctrine and practice. All our courses and programmes major on the content, exegesis, application and communication of the Holy Scriptures. "Thy Word is true from the beginning: and every one of Thy righteous judgments endureth for ever", (Psalm 119 v.160).

We warmly welcome you to join us in an in-depth study of the Word of God. With UDM Birmingham you will discover "the unsearchable riches of Christ" (Eph. 3 v.8) that are to be found in the Bible.

President:	Rev. Prof. Dr. C. L Ryan
Vice-President:	Rev. Prof. Dr. R. H. Creane

Urban Divinity Unit UK Limited

Affiliated to Canada Christian College and School of Graduate Theological Studies

THE BOARD OF DIRECTORS

Clinton L. Ryan
Robert H. Creane
Patrick G. Powell
Joseph E. Badu
Joseph Roberts

Urban Divinity Ministries

MISSION STATEMENT

By the Word of God (2 Tim. 3 v.16-17) and guidance of the Holy Spirit (John 16 v.13), we are committed to training and equipping candidates called of the Lord (Acts 26 v.16), for a powerful and effective ministry (Acts 6 v.4; 1 Cor. 9 v.14) as servants of Christ (Eph. 6 v.6), the only Head and Lord of the Church (Col. 1 v.18), communicating the Gospel of God (Rom. 1 v.1; Gal. 6 v.6) around the world (Matt. 28 v.19-20) to men and women for their salvation (Acts 4 v.12; Rom. 1 v.16), and for the edifying of the Body of Christ (Eph. 4 v.12), preaching the Word (Acts 11 v.19), motivated by devotion and love to the Lord Jesus Christ (John 21 v.15-17; Col. 1 v.10), and compassion for souls (Matt. 9 v.36-38), to the glory of God (Rev. 7 v.12).

"Go ye therefore, and teach all nations, baptizing them in the name of the Father, and of the Son, and of the Holy Ghost: Teaching them to observe all things whatsoever I have commanded you: and, lo, I am with you alway, even unto the end of the world. Amen",
(Matt. 28 v.19-20)

Aims and Objectives

(1) To uphold and promote the ministry of God's Word, to encourage men called to the Lord to preach His Gospel and to pastor churches, and to further the proclamation and defence of the doctrines of Free and Sovereign Grace, by offering residential and 'open distance' learning and programmes that are spiritually useful, intellectually stimulating and practically relevant.

(2) To provide education and training for men and women called to serve God in other areas of Christian work at home and abroad, by offering specialised 'core' study courses and programmes tailored to their particular needs for future service in Christ's Church.

(3) To promote relevant and rigorous Christian scholarship, to offer a solidly Biblical alternative to secular theology by helping in some measure to develop those gifts which only the Lord can give to make a man a preacher "to reprove the world of sin, and of righteousness, and of judgment", (John 16 v.8).

(4) To organise in-service training for church ministers, pastors, missionaries and other Christian professionals, and to hold conferences and other services to re-affirm the old Biblical truths in these days of apostasy and declension.

(5) To raise a testimony against the evils of rationalism, liberalism, higher criticism, and all other such matters of doctrine and practice that are contrary to sound Biblical teaching and at variance with Holy Scripture.

(6) To serve the Church of Christ universal by providing effective theological education worldwide, to share divinity programmes inter-denominationally, and to extend its courses to private students aspiring to be professionals in religious education and other spheres of service believing there is no dichotomy between being deeply spiritual and unashamedly academic and work to encourage growth in both these vital areas of life.

(7) To work with all who share these beliefs; to affirm and display the centrality of the Bible in worship, preaching, teaching, church life and mission; to defend the Truth; to voice the evangelical perspective on theology and ethics; and to declare "all the counsel of God", (Acts 20 v.27), without fear of favour.

"Set for the defence of the Gospel", (Phil. 1 v.17)

"Now the God of peace, that brought again from the dead our Lord Jesus, that great Shepherd of the sheep, through the blood of the everlasting covenant, make you perfect in every good work to do His will, working in you that which is well pleasing in His sight, through Jesus Christ; to Whom be glory for ever and ever", (Hebrews 13 v.20-21).

The Doctrinal Basis of Faith

Affiliation and candidature is open to all who ascribe to the following Articles of Faith and Practice.

(1) The Divine plenary inspiration and supernatural inerrancy of Holy Scripture, the Old and New Testaments, originally given as the Word of God, and that its teaching and authority are absolute, supreme and final as the only infallible rule in every matter of faith and life.

(2) The Trinity in unity of the Godhead --- one living and true God, eternally existing in Three Persons --- the Father, the Son and the Holy Spirit, the same in substance, equal in power and glory.

(3) The Sovereignty of God in creation, providence and redemption, revealed in the Lordship of Jesus Christ, the only Mediator between God and men.

(4) The God and Father of the Lord Jesus Christ, holy, righteous, full of grace, Who in His infinite love has sent forth His Son, that the world through Him might be saved.

(5) The Personality and Deity of the Lord Jesus Christ, the only incarnate Son of God, begotten of the Holy Spirit, His virgin birth, His perfect and sinless humanity, truly God and truly man, in two distinct natures, and one Person for ever.

(6) The Personality and Deity of the Holy Spirit, the source and power of all acceptable worship and service, the infallible interpreter of the infallible Word, and His essential work in conviction, regeneration and sanctification, Who indwells every true believer with grace and strength to live and witness as unto the Lord.

(7) The creation of man in the image of God, his subsequent total depravity and utter ruin through the Fall, the fallen state and lost condition of the whole human race, the subjection of all men to God's wrath and condemnation, the necessity of the new birth of the sinner and his acceptance with God only on the ground of the imputed righteousness of the Lord Jesus Christ.

(8) The substitutionary and redemptive nature of the atonement in the life and death of Christ as the one propitiatory and expiatory sacrifice for sin, His triumphant bodily resurrection, His glorious ascension, His mediatorial reign, His continual intercession at the Throne of God as the believer's Great High Priest and Advocate, and His visible and personal return for His Church in glory and future judgement.

(9) Salvation from the penalty of sin only by the grace of God in repentance unto life and justification of the sinner through faith in Jesus Christ alone, Who is the sole King and Head of His Church which is composed of all those who truly believe in Him as Saviour and Lord, and not by any human merit or works whatsoever.

(10) The personality of the Devil, his evil opposition to God and the Divine purposes, the corruption and enslavement of man by Satan, and his final doom.

(11) The resurrection and eternal blessedness of the redeemed in heaven, and the conscious everlasting punishment of the impenitent in hell.

(12) The spiritual unity and eternal security of all believers in the Lord Jesus Christ, and the responsibility of all saved souls to "live soberly, righteously and godly in this present world", (Titus 2 v.12).

(13) The expository, evangelical preaching of the Word of God; the preservation and purity of doctrine, worship and life, avoiding schism and heresy; and the encouragement of the exercise of all true gifts for the edification of the saints to the glory of God.

"To the law and to the testimony: if they speak not according to this Word, it is because there is no light in them", (Isaiah 8 v.20).

"Now therefore ye are no more strangers and foreigners, but fellow citizens with the saints, and of the household of God; And are built upon the foundation of the apostles and prophets, Jesus Christ Himself being the chief corner stone", (Eph. 2 v.19-20).

The Alone Principles of Historic Christianity

Sola Scriptura	:	the Scriptures are the sole authority in all matters of doctrine and practice
Christo Solum	:	the certain salvation by Christ alone of all that the Father has given to Him, having put away sin by the sacrifice of Himself
Cruce Solum	:	the efficacy of the atoning work and death of Christ on the Cross alone for the remission of sins
Sola Gratia	:	the invincibility of God's grace alone in saving His people from their sins and drawing them unto Jesus Christ
Sola Fide	:	the justification of sinners through faith alone in the person and work of the Lord Jesus Christ
Soli Deo gloria	:	The ultimate purpose of creation, providence, and redemption, is the glory of God

"And He is the Head of the body, the church: Who is the beginning, the firstborn from the dead; that in all things He might have the pre-eminence", (Col. 1 v.18).

Effective Service

The seeds of Urban Divinity Ministries were planted in 1984 and soon thereafter established with the sole aim of promoting the ministry of God's infallible and inerrant Word around the world to the glory of His great and holy name.

We give thanks and praise to Almighty God for the many achievements by Divine grace over the years. "The Lord hath done great things for us; whereof we are glad", (Psalm 126 v.3). Under His Providential care, guidance and blessing, much noble work is being done for the extension and furtherance of Christ's Kingdom on earth. "Thou art worthy, O Lord, to receive glory and honour and power: for Thou hast created all things, and for Thy pleasure they are and were created". (Rev. 4 v.11).

In bearing witness for the Truth of God's Word, whether by staff or student, the Biblical exhortation to steadfastness is imperative by showing an unflinching maintenance to Apostolic Doctrine, which must be clearly apprehended, earnestly embraced, firmly held, and stoutly defended. "Therefore, brethren, stand fast, and hold the traditions which ye have been taught, whether by word, or our epistle", (2 Thess. 2 v.15).

The Word of God firmly declares that it is "Not by might, nor by power, but by My Spirit, saith the Lord of Hosts", (Zech. 4 v.6). As God's servants we are charged with the solemn task and awesome responsibility of preaching the righteous demands of a Holy God. "For we preach not ourselves, but Christ Jesus the Lord; and ourselves your servants for Jesus' sake", (2 Cor. 4 v.5).

By the grace of God, wherever our lot shall be cast in future days, let us endeavour by the help of the Holy Spirit to be steadfast in the faith, faithful in ministry, devoted in pastoral duties, with the unceasing burden of a preacher's heart to proclaim and uphold the truth of God's inspired Word by maintaining a proper relationship between sound doctrine and sincere heavenly zeal in evangelism. "Upon this Rock I will build My Church; and the gates of hell shall not prevail against it", (Matt. 16 v.18). So may the time come when "the earth shall be full of the knowledge of the Lord, as the waters cover the sea", (Isaiah 11 v.9).

Anyone wishing to join us in an in-depth study of the Word of God is very welcome to write for information, and you will find that 'open distance' learning programmes provide an incredibly flexible way to achieving your aims.

Urban Divinity Unit UK and Associated Colleges
Affiliated to Canada Christian College and School of Graduate Theological Studies

Highgate UDU Theological Seminary, Birmingham

Calvary Theological College, London

Urban Divinity Unit, St. Vincent

International Theological College, London

South Florida International College, U.S.A.

First Born Theological College, Birmingham

City Theological College, Leicester

The Grenadines Divinity Unit, West Indies

Reformed Bible Seminary UDU Scotland

Covenant School of Theology UDU Ireland

FOR THE GLORY OF GOD

AND

THE INCREASE OF HIS KINGDOM

THROUGH

THE PROCLAMATION OF THE DIVINE WORD

AND

DEFENCE OF THE DOCTRINES OF FREE AND

SOVERIGN GRACE

"For the Word of God, and for the testimony of Jesus Christ",
(Rev. 1 v.9)

URBAN DIVINITY MINISTRIES

PROVIDING THEOLOGICAL EDUCATION BY

EXTENSION WORLDWIDE

"Study to show thyself approved unto God, a workman that needeth
not to be ashamed, rightly dividing the Word of truth",
(2 Timothy 2 v.15)

APPENDIX FIVE

Brief Personal Profile on Rev. Prof. Dr. R. H. Creane with Interview, by Rev. Dr. Wm. J. Malcolmson

(1) Family

Robert Harold Creane was born the eldest of five sons and two daughters to Wallace and Suzanna (Anna) Creane --- (both called Home to Glory to higher service on 14th January 2003 and 21st August 2002 respectively): "absent from the body, and present with the Lord", 2 Cor. 5 v.8) --- in the townland of Tullycaghney, Drumacrib, Castleblayney, Co. Monaghan, Republic of Ireland. He is married to Rhoda (née Adamson), a school teacher, of Dundalk Street, Newtownhamilton, Co. Armagh, Northern Ireland. They have a very fine Christian family of four daughters, three sons-in-law, and six grandchildren.

(2) Education

McKelvey's Grove National School, Drollagh, Castleblayney, Co. Monaghan. (Presbyterian).

Dundalk Grammer School, Dundalk, Co. Louth. (Church of Ireland).

College of Technology, College Square, Belfast; accountancy.

The University of Dublin, Trinity College, Dublin; Honours Hebrew and Oriental Languages; additional Studies in Greek and Latin.

The Theological Hall, Reformed Presbyterian Church of Ireland, Grosvenor Road, Belfast.

(3) Research Work

Believing that true scholarship is of the highest value in Biblical ministry, Prof. Creane's post-graduate studies and academic achievements have shown that such research programmes are spiritually useful, intellectually stimulating and practically relevant. There is no dichotomy between education that is distinctively Christian and unashamedly academic, provided it is structured on the Reformed Protestant viewpoint embracing Reformation principles that the Bible is the inerrant and infallible Word of God as manifested in his preaching, teaching and writing. He is fully committed to the truthfulness and veracity of Holy Scripture, and to the necessity of the Holy Spirit's ministry to give understanding and spiritual power that will regenerate, reform and revive at a time when many, especially in modern western society, feel that Christianity has run its course.

"The Word of the Lord endureth for ever. And this is the Word which by the Gospel is preached unto you", (1 Peter 1 v.25)".

(4) **Accountancy**

Articled Clerk and Trainee Accountant to Sir Thomas Desmond Lorimer, K.B., F.C.A., D.Sc.(QUB), D.Sc.(NUU), Hugh Smylie & Sons, Chartered Accountants, Donegal Square North, Belfast.

Having successfully finished Grammar School, Prof. Creane often fondly reminisces about his earlier days as a young boy and teenage innocent country youth. He says, "I found living away from home for the first time, which seemed at the time quite a major traumatic 'culture' shock and the unnerving experience of leaving the special affections of the family homestead and farm in the beautiful and peaceful rural setting of County Monaghan to come to the City of Belfast to live and work, had a big effect and impact upon my life. During those early days, I was profoundly thankful, and will always appreciate, not only to have had a gracious, fair, and kind boss at work who was both a friend and fatherlike-figure to me, but also to have the benefit and companionableness in the 'big city' of my Uncle Robert and Aunt Nancy Armstrong, and also Auntie Rita (née Armstrong) Smith, with whom I visited and frequented often, and was made most welcome at their Church where I was glad to join the fellowship and worship of Cregagh Road Reformed Presbyterian Church, Belfast".

Assistant Accountant with Harmood Banner Smylie & Co., Chartered Accountants, Belfast.

(5) Consultancy Services

Principal and Proprietor: R H C Consultancy Services, incorporating (1) accountancy practice of Robert Harold Creane, 40 High Street, Portadown, established in 1974, registered on 20th September 1974, Registration No. N.I. 18091, and (2) R. H. Creane & Company, 68 Church Street, Portadown, marketing and management services, established in 1977, Registration No. N.I. 19780.

(6) Minister, Teacher, and Lecturer

Divinity Student under the care of the Southern Presbytery and later Pastor of Dervock Reformed Presbyterian Church, Co. Antrim, under the care of the Northern Presbytery as a Minister of the Reformed Presbyterian Church of Ireland, 1958-1970.

Director: Bible Christian Mission.

R. E. Teacher 1966-1974:	The High School, Ballycastle
	Ashfield High School, Belfast
	The Royal School, Dungannon

Elected in 1982 an Elder of the Presbyterian Church in Ireland.

Over the past two decades Prof. Creane has been deeply involved in Bible teaching, Theological training and Christian education. In his exposition of the Word, he endeavours by the grace and help of God to labour valiantly, firmly declaring the infallibility and inerrancy of THE SCRIPTURE as the sole authority in all matters of faith and practice. He exhibits a freshness of exegesis whereby the great doctrines of sovereign grace are unashamedly expounded and warmly enforced with singular clarity, Biblical fidelity, and evangelical zeal.

In my interview with Prof. Creane, I asked him,

How would you sum up your experiences in ministry, mission and theological teaching, over the past fifty years or so?

Throughout our meeting he quoted and referred to many Scripture passages while talking passionately about service in the Master's vineyard, and among them his first quotation readily came to mind of the verse found in 1 Cor. 9 v.14: "Even so hath the Lord ordained, that they which preach the Gospel should live of the Gospel".

Commenting on this text, Dr. Creane reflected with a deep sense of purpose, as follows, "To have the assurance of the Master's call, with His seal of approval and blessing on my ministry as a poor servant of the Lord in communicating the Word of Life to theological students and research candidates all around the world, is a humbling privilege and weighty responsibility. The preaching of the Gospel to the souls of men and women, boys and girls, with heavenly influence from on High in the saving of sinners, opening 'blind' (Luke 4 v.18) eyes in repentance and forgiveness of their sin and quickening the spiritually 'dead' (Eph. 2 v.1) unto 'faith' in Christ (Rom. 5 v.1) ----- cannot but bring simple dependence on Divine grace and patient hope in a sovereign God. Such results that attend the fervent preaching of the Good News of the 'everlasting Gospel' (Rev. 14 v.6) cause great rejoicing in heaven ----- for 'there is joy in the presence of the angels of God over one sinner that repenteth', (Luke 15 v.10). We rejoice with adoration, praise and thanksgiving to God, for the spiritual benefits and permanent fruit of grace in life that are manifested by the power of the Holy Spirit in the conversion of sinners and their subsequent walk as 'children of God' (Gal. 3 v.26) in the faith, hope, and love of the Gospel ----- 'walking in truth' (2 John v.4) 'through sanctification of the Spirit' (2 Thess.2 v.13) 'as instruments of righteousness unto God' (Rom 6 v.13)".

What has been the greatest disappointments you have encountered during your ministry as a preacher in the service of Christ over the past half-century?

"The preaching of the Word of God", Prof. Creane fervently confirms, "is fundamental and central to the public worship of God. In the verse, 1 Cor. 9 v.14, we are told that Christ has ordained that those who are called to preach 'the Gospel of God' (Rom. 1 v.1) are to derive their income and stipends from that all important task. 'The labourer is worthy of his reward', (1 Tim. 5 v.18). To withhold such payments and the due maintenance of the pastor is to transgress an appointment of Christ and deny the Biblical principle of support toward the preacher ----- 'for the labourer is worthy of his hire', (Luke 10 v.7). However, for posterity I would place on record to preserve my good cause in regard to the Dervock issue, that the right to such maintenance and stipends as duly covenanted were unlawfully withheld and wilfully denied to me during 1966/67 for a very long period, extending to almost one year with no salary or allowances whatsoever, and the failure of this monthly responsibility for such a long duration, was part of a cruel plot and underhand malpractice conspired by 'some few' with the design to push by forcing one to leave the pastorate in North Antrim to seek spheres of labour and service in Christ's vineyard elsewhere. Under the pressures of life, the most effectual motive to diligence and perseverance in Christian service, is a good understanding and firm belief of the eternal truths of the glorious Gospel of Christ, which encourages us to keep labouring abundantly for the Lord in the salvation of the lost. We are commanded to stand firm and our hope is built upon the sure foundation of the Word of Scripture, the guarantee 'of our inheritance until the redemption of the purchased possession' (Eph. 1 v.14) by the power of the risen Saviour, and the promise of God. 'Therefore, my beloved brethren, be ye stedfast, unmoveable, always abounding in the work of the Lord, forasmuch as ye know that your labour is not in vain in the Lord', (1 Cor. 15 v.58)".

How were the difficulties you mention remedied and overcome, and what steps did you take to restore harmony, reconciliation and goodwill?

With inmost thought and consciousness, Dr. Creane continued, "God calls His children always to 'be kind one to another, tender-hearted, forgiving one another, even as God for Christ's sake hath forgiven you', (Eph. 4 v.32). Every sin by a believer stains the entire fellowship of believers. Love that winks at sin, turns a blind eye to skulduggery, and smiles at shenanigans, or that is more concerned for superficial calm in the Church, is but worldly and selfish sentimentality. Surface righteousness does not come from faith and the renewing power of the work of the Holy Spirit, but from religious pride and conditional conformity to tradition --- such religion is counterfeit. When a Presbytery of the Church fails to do everything to remedy problems or do things in the wrong way, or in the wrong spirit, it can do great damage by fostering self-righteousness and legalism. As the Church gathers in the name of the Lord and for His Cause, it must always be engaged in actions that are pure under His authority, to the glory of God. It is important that we do not show resentment or bitterness, whatever may befall or happen to us, and in my voluminous correspondence of several dates regarding the whole Dervock affair, I simply pointed out and emphasised among many other things, for a fair and proper hearing, as follows:-

(1) efforts seeking due payments of long overdue and outstanding stipends, which eventually 'came' with a shortfall after much delay, distress, abuse, and hurt;

(2) earnest pleas seeking due redress, justice, genuine Christian conciliation and unity;

(3) appeals for natural justice, mutual understanding, honesty and peace according to the Scriptures;

(4) quests for the restoration of harmony, reconciliation, integrity and goodwill among all concerned, so that together 'speaking the truth in love, (all) may grow up into Him in all things, which is the Head, even Christ: From Whom the whole body fitly joined together and compacted by that which every joint supplieth, according to the effectual working in the measure of every part, maketh increase of the body unto the edifying of itself in love', (Eph. 4 v.15-16); and

(5) calls for earnest prayer and meditation with a sincere desire for the glory of God, 'that in all things He might have the preeminence', (Col. 1 v.18), the Covenanters motto.

These endeavours largely went unanswered with a wall of silence and a compromise of the truth that fell far short of the honour of our great Redeemer and only Mediator (1 Tim. 2 v.5) between God and men, Christ Jesus our Lord and Saviour, the sole King and Head of His Church".

In the face of such opposition and problems, how were you enabled to exercise benevolence in showing the forgiving spirit, peace of mind and patience in service?

Prof. Creane poignantly points out, "On foot of QCs' Opinion, many of my supporters strongly urged me to pursue justice through the Civil Courts, but for the sake of the Cause of Christ it was decided not to proceed to press matters in legal or worldly circles. Having done all in my power to uphold truth, restore order and avoid schism, I encountered an unwillingness and refusal among my fellow-presbyters to deal with the situation fairly, factually and amicably in the spirit of genuine trust and brotherly love. Despite the trauma and miscarriage of justice, I sought by the grace of God not to be rebellious or contemptuous but to show the forgiving spirit, appropriate peace of mind and relief from the burden of pain and hurt caused by 'those' who wrongfully injured and conspired against me, ever resting in the assurance that the afflictions and sorrows of God's people are but for a season. 'Many are the afflictions of the righteous: but the Lord delivereth him out of them all', (Psalm 34 v.19). We have need of patience to stay in the race by a humble acquiescence in the wisdom and will of God, and go forward in obedience to His Word, and in hope, for 'the Lord is my helper, and I will not fear what man shall do unto me', (Heb. 13 v.6)".

How would you summarise these various trials and afflictions in relation to the text 'all things work together for good' and holding on to the assurance of the keeping power of God?

Dr. Creane emphasises, "We all need constant grace and help day by day, and in the mercy of God let us rejoice with gladness and joyfulness in this world in the Lord's service with all the blessings and provision of that 'everlasting covenant, ordered in all things and sure', (2 Sam. 23 v.5). Thank God, no ecclesiastical forum or ruling can take that away from us or snatch us from the sheepfold, 'neither shall any man pluck them out of My hand', (John 10 v.28), for 'we are more than conquerors through Him that loved us', (Rom. 8 v.37). Saved by grace, nothing at all in the past, present or future, and nothing on this earth or anywhere else, is 'able to separate us from the love of God, which is in Christ Jesus our Lord', (Rom. 8 v.39). What a comfort and joy to rest in the knowledge and assurance that no man, nor the devil, can prevent any of God's dear believing people, whatever the trials and difficulties, from having communion with Him and the hope of entering into future glory. We conquer because we have the Conqueror living within and working for us. Our standing before God in Christ is absolutely sure, and those whom He has called can be absolutely certain that in His sovereign purpose 'all things work together for good to them that love God', (Rom. 8 v.28)".

Dr. Creane further relates, "By trying to brush the matters at issue re-Dervock under the carpet, it was banefully destructive and very painful to find that the barriers of ambiguity, ambivalence, dishonesty, misrepresentation, bullyism and lying which I encountered in the process, continually increased, even fourfold. The evidence of this I furnished and distributed to the Reformed Presbyterian Church in printed form, went unheeded, and to which the Northern Presbytery did not reply. My supporters and I were greatly astonished and heavily disappointed at the extreme lack of due consideration, support or thought, practically and morally, shown towards myself, my wife and young family with the arrival of newly born twin girls. There was an absolute absence of deeds of kindness and mercy, and a complete failure to administer any pastoral care whatsoever. None of my Northern Presbytery colleagues ever paid us a visit to pray with us, convey words of encouragement or to wish us well. Yet through it all, difficult as it was, in the providence of God we are reminded of the all-sufficiency of His grace (2 Cor. 12 v.9), and of His all-caring, keeping and preserving power, 'For in Him we live, and move, and have our being', (Acts 17 v.28). God has given us strength and courage to battle onward in His goodness and grace pressing 'toward the mark for the prize of the high calling of God in Christ Jesus', (Phil. 3 v.14)".

In the context of your own personal experience how would you explain the connection between God's love and forgiveness of us and our love and forgiveness of others?

With earnest appeal, Prof. Creane pleads when he says, "It remains my fervent prayer that in humility measures be taken that are restorative, not retributive, and may this yet be a reminder and call to the Reformed Presbyterian Church of Ireland to labour more consciously in love to the Redeemer, in love to one another, with purity and integrity before God, in obedience to the Word. There is an unbreakable connection between God's love and forgiveness of us and our love and forgiveness of other people. We need grace to snap out of our lethargy and rejoice in the liberty of the life-changing power of the Gospel. As servants of the Lord may we in full and glad surrender to the service of Christ, perform all our labour for the Master, as from the heart. With piety and devotion we are commanded to testify our joy by putting on the garments of praise instead of the spirit of heaviness: 'for the joy of the Lord is your strength', (Neh. 8 v.10). By the grace of God nothing should hinder our obedience and cheerfulness in the performance of our duties in His service as we draw upon His bountiful goodness and provision day by day. By standing before the Holy God and seeing ourselves as the sinners we are ----- guilty, vile, helpless, and yet redeemed, pardoned and forgiven through the life and death of Christ, solely because of the undeserved favour and mercy of

God. May that awareness humble us and enable us to rejoice in the everlasting deliverance and blessing of Almighty God so that in all our work and witness ----- harmony, peace and prosperity shall prevail among believers to the glory of God. May acts of selfish expediency, contrivance and divisiveness, either in theory or in practice, therefore, be no more. In the light of eternity as fellow-sojourners and travellers on the way heavenward, may there yet be that firm evidence and deeper cultivation of true reconciliation, restoration and goodwill shown by all to the glory of our great Jehovah, 'forbearing one another in love; Endeavouring to keep the unity of the Spirit in the bond of peace', (Eph. 4 v.2-3)".

With thankfulness and joyfulness you have acknowledged the goodness and grace of God throughout all of life, a busy and highly distinguished career if I may say so, what further service of usefulness do you envisage as you reach the senior years of life?

"As stated in the Prologue of this book", says the Rev. R. H. Creane, "service for the Lord will continue while health and strength allow me, and as God may lead and guide in future days, continuing to lecture and teach with Urban Divinity Ministries, and perhaps concluding in a pastoral position under a light charge. As time permits, I am working presently on a number of projects, editing some manuscripts for print and distribution, in the will of God as the Lord provides, by setting up a Special Book Fund, calling for a return to Biblical truth and worship, reform of the Church, and revival of true religion throughout the land. Satan always causes controversy and mockers to arise whenever spiritual reformation takes place which inspires renewed confidence and faith in the infallibility of the Bible as the Word of God. During my early days as a young minister, as well as in missions, and on other occasions over the years, I have encountered much scepticism and deep opposition when our great 'adversary the devil' (1 Peter 5 v.8) through his willing agents, even using Church 'officers and presbyters', shamefully, to disrupt and oppose the preaching of the Gospel, as, for example, was the case during the six weeks Evangelistic Mission Campaign at Dervock Orange Hall. The disruption there was organised by certain persons but ceased after the first week, due to the fact that one of the ringleaders involved, became seriously ill and was admitted to hospital whom I visited and prayed with daily, but sadly died within a few days. This came as a warning to the culprits, two of whom started to attend the mission regularly and were converted. The Hall Management Committee and Trustees were most gracious and extremely helpful throughout, and provided the full on going use of the hall and its facilities free of charge. But despite enemy opposition during its opening days, the mission continued under Divine guidance, when thirteen souls were gloriously saved by the grace of God. Subsequently there followed the establishment of weekly follow-up classes for the new converts and monthly outreach meetings. For all such seasons of blessing, we are always careful to render all the praise, honour, and glory to God for the in-gathering of precious lost 'souls' (Heb. 13 v.17) and spiritual edification in the building up of believers on their 'most holy faith' (Jude v.20). Whatever future service in the Master's Vineyard falls to my charge, I shall endeavour with earnest prayer and commitment by God's grace to further advance the work and witness of the Cause of Christ where Providence directs. As well as being evangelistic, I trust that God's people will be edified by the teaching gleaned from the exposition of God's Word, and that the Book Club will prove to be a means of bringing much comfort and encouragement of how Christians can speak by life and lip of the grace of God in Christ to a generation that has largely rejected the teaching of the Word of God and which has little or no time for the claims of Bible truth. 'God is able to make all grace abound toward you; that ye, always having all sufficiency in all things, may abound to every good work', (2 Cor. 9 v.8). By His enabling grace and strength, may He graciously grant us that continuing desire and courage to uphold, maintain and defend the principles of Holy Scripture, which alone is the inspired and inerrant Word of God, the only infallible rule in all matters of faith and conduct ----- 'for the Word of God, and for the testimony of Jesus Christ', (Rev. 1 v.9)".

During your remaining days of sojourn upon earth, God-willing, what is your prayer and desire for the Church and the advancement of the kingdom of God amongst men?

With a passion for preaching, Prof. Creane ardently declares in the words of the Apostle Paul, "My hearts desire and prayer to God for Israel is, that they might be saved", (Rom. 10 v.1). In professing his good affection for the souls of men and women, boys and girls, Dr. Creane clearly states, "The principle of salvation is by grace alone through faith alone in the Lord Jesus Christ alone. 'Faith in Jesus Christ is a saving grace, whereby we receive and rest upon Him alone for salvation, as He is offered to us in the Gospel', (Shorter Catechism No.86). 'Neither is there salvation in any other: for there is none other name under heaven given among men, whereby we must be saved', (Acts 4 v.12). Men and women everywhere are trying to establish their own righteousness, which they can never do, and merely shows their ignorance of God's righteousness. That can only be found in Christ, Who 'is the end of the law of righteousness to every one that believeth', (Rom. 10 v.4). In other words they must come to faith in Christ to be saved. Our God 'is worthy to be praised' (2 Sam. 22 v.4 and Psalm 18 v.3), let us 'worship Him in spirit and in truth' (John 4 v.24) and pray that it may please the Father to pour out His Spirit upon us to behold His wondrous love and grace in abundant measure, undeserving though we are, so that the benefits and blessings of reformation and revival of the Church, even at large, will be increasingly evident, when people shall call upon the Lord for mercy in repentance and faith to worship Him, exhibiting the marks of the fruit of the Spirit with cheerfulness and a constant delight in God, showing soundness of growth 'in grace' (2 Peter 3 v.18), and piety (1 Tim. 5 v.4), in accordance with 'the Word of Life', (Phil. 2 v.16). Only then shall we truly know Divine instruction, heavenly guidance and a deep-searching knowledge of Scripture in every purpose of conviction, conversion and sanctification. With godly zeal in evangelism and the demonstration of holy boldness for the witness of Biblical truth, may we go forth in the power of the Holy Ghost, proclaiming the Word of the Lord for the establishment, comfort, and eternal salvation of all who are willing to receive it. 'Grace be with all them that love our Lord Jesus Christ in sincerity', (Eph. 6 v.24). Let us pray that God will thrust us forth with the message of the Gospel of Glad Tidings in the name of Christ, so that by the help of the Holy Spirit we may raise high the banner of the Captain of our salvation (Heb. 2 v.10) to a lost world, and may men and women, boys and girls, be drawn unto the Saviour. 'And I', says Jesus, 'if I be lifted up from the earth, will draw all men unto Me', (John 12 v.32). No suffering we endure for Him, or for His Cause or teaching, can compare with His suffering for sin on our behalf. He suffered 'that He might bring us to God', (1 Peter 3 v.18), why then should not we submit to difficulties since they are of so much use to quicken us in the performance of our duty and service to Him? As servants in the Master's vineyard, wherever Providence allows, may we declare 'all the counsel of God' (Acts 20 v.27), 'preaching the Word' (Acts 8 v.4) without fear or favour to saint and sinner, until He comes or calls".

> "And yet a banner Thou has't given
> to them who Thee do fear;
> That it by them, because of truth,
> displayed may appear",
> (Psalm 60 v.4).

"To God be the glory and dominion for ever and ever. Amen", (Rev. 1 v.6).

(7) Preacher, Pastor, and Chaplain

The life and work of Prof. Creane can best be summed up as a Covenanter by birth and persuasion; Undenominational by temperament; Biblical by conviction; Reformed in doctrine; Presbyterian in Church government; Saved by the sovereign grace of God; Serving the Lord.

The source of his strength is demonstrated by his humility, prayerfulness, commitment, and dedication to duty which has remained steadfast and fervent for more than fifty years, bearing unambiguous and unflinching testimony in the teaching of Biblical Truth, faithfulness in the preaching of the Word of God, and perseverance in various ministries and missions at home and overseas, manifesting a constancy of love, reverence, and devotion to Him Who is the King and Head of the Church, the Lord Jesus Christ.

In the role of chaplaincy and other official offices held by Prof. Creane over the years, he has always shown a pastoral heart and caring role when requested to visit the sick and infirm, attend to the dying and bereaved, and performed many other calls laid upon him by the Lord.

Being greatly concerned that many Churches today, especially in Western Christendom, continue to come up with conclusions that move them further away from Biblical Truth and Reformation Principles, Prof. Creane's great desire and prayer is to "earnestly contend for the faith" (Jude v.3) holding "fast the faithful Word" (Titus 1 v.9), and by putting "on the whole armour of God" (Eph. 6 v.11) be enabled by the Holy Spirit "to withstand in the evil day, and having done all, to stand" (Eph. 6 v.13).

"Now unto Him that is able to keep you from falling, and to present you faultless before the presence of His glory with exceeding joy, to the only wise God our Saviour, be glory and majesty, dominion and power, both now and ever. Amen", (Jude v.24-25).

WHAT THEY SAY ..... REVIEWS

Dr. S. J. McCammick (1)

I count it a great privilege and high honour to be asked to comment on this book. I would describe it as a masterpiece. The doctrines and related subjects as expounded herein have been thoroughly researched, displaying sound Biblical theology and reaffirmed by Scriptural Truth.

Christians of our generation need such a book more so than the generation before us. The permissive culture has ruined and destroyed our society, and alas, also, has crept into the foundations of the Church itself. As the standards of the Church crumble, faith and works are becoming very far apart. We profess faith in Christ, but trust in materialism. We say we love our wives as Christ loved the Church, but the number of divorces among Christian people is rapidly rising. In a world which no longer seems capable of distinguishing free speech from character assassination, we need to be reminded from James, as he writes in his Epistle, that "the tongue is a fire . . . . . and it is set on fire of hell", (James 3 v.6). So we need again to note that faith without works is dead.

Rev. Prof. Dr. R. H. Creane is a practical man and pulls no punches in dealing with the various doctrines and subject matter in this enlightening and informative book. He has always been nearer to the ordinary Christian than to the institutional Church and has always kept to his deeply held convictions that Biblical truth does not change, never changes. The man and his message could not be better matched.

The author speaks of today's society, 'its immorality, its dishonesty, its greed, its selfishness, its violence, its envy, its arrogance, its blasphemy, its cruelty, its materialism, its obsession with pleasure, and above all its careless and calculated rejection of God'. That is not the way our sycophantic press agents and media personnel reflect our society. It is not the way our intellectual leaders like to see the society that they have created, but the corruption and rottenness all around is now showing through the façade that can no longer be denied. Those with responsible positions who have to deal with the world as it is, trade union leaders, managers, police, politicians, etc., are increasingly pessimistic and despondent. They know something has gone badly and terribly wrong, but they cannot put their finger on it. This book puts the finger on it very precisely.

The manner and conduct of our lives as professing Christians, and what we believe, as the author emphasises, must be founded on the clear principles and teaching of the Bible. There must be that absolute reverence for the Word of God, and that earnest desire to regulate and to adhere to it, as the only infallible Rule and Guide for godly living. Biblical standards in behaviour and lifestyle must be based on sound doctrine. Scriptural revelation must illuminate, challenge, and transform cultures, structures, and civilisations.

We dare not submit to the wisdom of men, be they never so wise and holy. Men are subject to error, susceptible to sin, and prone to partiality. Only the unchanging authority of God's Word can provide the sure foundation on which to build a God-honouring home, and a Christ-serving Church.

Prof. Creane urgently calls for a return to Biblical standards, and for Christians everywhere to raise their voices in support of Biblical authority and Biblical morality. What great blessings would flow nationally and internationally if believers were to dedicate themselves to a closer walk with God by a renewed adherence to His Word. The usefulness and worth of any work for the Lord is dependent on the spiritual calibre of His people. There is no substitute for personal faith in the Lord Jesus Christ, of real conversion of the soul as manifested by a changed life and transformed nature. All matters of faith and practice in every sphere of life must be in accordance with the Word of God.

This book is practical, relevant, soundly based on Christian theology, loyal to the Scriptures, and I heartily commend it to the reader.

S. James McCammick

Killiecomaine Baptist Church
Portadown
Co. Armagh

Rev. Canon B. T. Blacoe (2)

In commending this Book for study I would first of all thank Rev. Prof. Dr. R. H. Creane for his invitation to make this contribution to his challenging Bible based assessment of the ministry of women in the Church, Home, Workplace, Society and in the World at large.

The primary concern of the author is to highlight the central place of God's Word in the affairs of mankind, both male and female, who under God's authority should complement each other's God given gifts, style and characteristics, in their relationships one with the other, which are designed to help them reach their full potential as human beings, as those created in the image of God. Prof. Creane states "male and female roles are complimentary not interchangeable" which observation based on the Biblical revelation, leads to his affirmation of male headship especially within the Home and Church. He goes on to say, "that God's all wise design is that men and women are equal in value but different in roles" so emphasising his argument that male headship fits God's perfect plan and purpose for men and women in the outworking of His will for their lives.

Attention is drawn to the role of women in our modern society that has become increasingly secularised and driven by consumerism. The effect has been to damage family life by driving women into the work place to keep pace with the cost of living so undermining the essential role of mothers within the home where children are meant to be brought up in 'the fear and nurture of the Lord'. The author acknowledges that while particular circumstances do arise to undermine the Biblical ideal of home care, the social climate now is to encourage state care for children funded by benefit schemes, whose effect is to undermine the authority of parents, a contributing factor to the social ills of today.

In conclusion, any reading of this exhaustive treatise, whether it be critical or commendatory, whether it inspires or infuriates, the central characteristic of the author's concern is the place of God's Word, the

Bible, in the affairs of men and his passion to uphold its authority to the Glory of God and for the good of all men and women.

The reality is that the Bible is not man's view about God conditioned by time and culture but rather it is God's view of man unaffected by time and culture, for as the central Character of Scripture, Our Lord Jesus Christ says:- "Heaven and earth shall pass away: but My Words shall not pass away", (Luke 21 v.33).

Prof. Creane argues that if the ills of our society are to be overcome we must restore the Authority of God's Word, proclaim the Gospel of Jesus Christ and "live soberly, righteously, and godly, in this present world" (Titus 2 v.12) in faith and obedience.

May all who read this book be renewed in their faith.

                                                    Brian T. Blacoe

Tandragee
Parish Minister Knocknamuckley 1995-2008 Diocese of Dromore; formerly Annalong, Desertcreat, Drumcree and Dundonald

SYNOD HALL AND CHRIST CHURCH CATHEDRAL, DUBLIN

Rev. Dr. S. Barnes (3)

This is a comprehensive book packed with practical detail and instruction on the important role of women in the home, Church and society. The author sets forth clearly the Biblical principles and imperatives in a positive manner. Sadly we live in an age when these Scriptural standards are largely ignored and disregarded by many Churches.

The chapter headings of this work provide an insight into the wide variety of subjects dealt with by Prof. Creane. For example:-

- The Basic Principle of Headship
- Headship, Head Covering and Dress
- Women in the Church
- Women in the Home, etc.

The author bases his arguments upon the great Protestant Reformation principle of 'Sola Scriptura' as the 'only rule of faith and practice' for the Christian. This is a timely and necessary book of insights, guidance and practical help that will enable the reader to unapologetically hold firm to a Biblical position in an age of such confusion within many branches of professed Christendom.

I hope that this volume will have a wide readership and prove to be a valuable resource for believers that will equip them to stand firm in a day when many are blown about by the winds of false doctrine.

This book deals with an important subject. Only by implementing God's Divine order for men and women can we expect His blessing upon the individual, the home, the Church and society.

Stanley Barnes

Hillsborough Free Presbyterian Church 1973-2008
Co. Down

Dr. V. Maxwell (4)

This volume entitled 'The Place, Role and Function of Women' is a work of distinction. The impressive chapter titles, layout and presentation with numerous sub-headings make for compelling reading. In these pages the author has shown great clarity and depth of conviction. His careful exegeses of the Biblical text clearly upholds the authority of Scripture throughout.

Someone once said, "When a man climbs to success, some woman is probably holding the ladder". Moses was one of Israel's greatest leaders but the Lord used his godly mother Jochebed and sister Miriam to form his early life. Later his wife Zipporah helped him face the pressures of his immense ministry. Several ladies, as pointed out by the author, were highly involved in the ministry of our Lord as well as the ministry of the Apostles in the Early Church. Mark reminds us of "certain women" who travelled with the Saviour ministered to Him from their substance. When it came to standing by the Cross at Calvary only one of the disciples turned up, but several ladies defied the ire of religious bigots and the might of Roman soldiers to show their devotion to the Saviour they loved. One of those ladies was first at His tomb on the resurrection morning where she met the Risen Christ. In various letters Paul greeted women as co-workers and helpers in the Gospel. These faithful ladies wholeheartedly dedicated their lives to the work and witness of the Gospel and received extravagant accolades from several New Testament writers.

These commendations of the weaker sex came in spite of the rabbinical traditions in ancient Israel. One of the three routine praises Jewish men uttered during morning prayers was, "Thank God I am not a woman". We say, as the author of this book emphasises: "Thank God for the valuable and influential role Christian women play in our homes, in the Church, in the workplace and in society today".

I commend this book of my good friend Prof. R. H. Creane. "Thanks be to God", (2 Cor. 8 v.16).

Victor Maxwell

Banbridge Baptist Church
Co. Down

Rev. Dr. W. W. Porter (5)

The Bible, the textbook of Christianity, stands alone among books. The core fundamental principle of the Sixteenth Century Reformation was 'Sola Scriptura' --- Scripture alone. Martin Luther claimed, "It is impossible that Scripture should contradict itself". In the same manner, John Calvin spoke of Scripture, "Moses and the prophets did not utter at random what we have from their hand, but, since they spoke by Divine impulse, they confidently and fearlessly testified, as was actually the case, that it was the mouth of the Lord that spoke --- it has proceeded from Him alone, and has nothing of man mixed with it".

In this book, 'The Place, Role and Function of Women', Rev. Prof. Dr. R. H. Creane has clearly devoted much effort, time and research into this massive, wide-ranging study which covers many related topics and issues, with the aim, as he clearly states, "to advance in some little measure the Biblical teaching thereon, and to cultivate an obedience of the Word and a joyful spirit among the people of God".

Undoubtedly there will be controversial skirmishes from opponents in many quarters, but these will almost certainly be on the fringes and outworks of this thorough-going thesis. Its main thrust and its central core of argument will remain unshaken (Heb. 12 v.27), based firmly and solely on the authority of the Bible. The rich and relevant body of Scripture quotation which the author cites will ensure that.

As well as being lucidly written and clearly expressed, Prof. Creane's language weds firmness of conviction with a gracious courtesy of expression. Not every controversial publication achieves this.

"Thou art worthy, O Lord, to receive glory and honour and power: for Thou hast created all things, and for Thy pleasure they are and were created", (Rev. 4 v.11).

W. Warren Porter

Senior Presbyterian Minister
Moneydig Church
Co. Londonderry

Dr. J. Hughes (6)

I heartily commend this book, 'The Place, Role and Function of Women'. This is a timely work. When the apostle Paul wrote the words of Galatians 3 v.28, "There is neither Jew nor Greek, there is neither bond nor free, there is neither male nor female: for ye are all one in Christ Jesus", did He mean that the role of men and women in the church was the same?

One of the most contentious issues we have to face today concerns the role of the woman in the Church. Some of the questions that arise are: Do the Scriptures show us that a woman can occupy the role of the teaching elder in the Church? Or, Is there an office of deaconess to be filled by the woman? The society we live in is one that keeps reminding us of equal rights, if that is the case how can we then say that in the Church the woman is to be in subjection?

These and many other issues surrounding the place of the woman in the Church are dealt with in a very scholarly and theological way by Prof. Creane in this in-depth study of the woman's role in the Church. There is no doubt that women have a part to play in the life of the Church but the part played must be within the confines of the Scriptures.

I believe as you read this book you will be given much food for thought. May God bless its ministry to a wide circulation of readers. To Him be the glory.

Jackie Hughes

Ballykeel Baptist Church
Dromara Road
Hillsborough
Co. Down

Dr. A. R. Passmore (7)

I read the contents of this courageous book, 'The Place, Role and Function of Women' by Rev. Prof. Dr. R. H. Creane, with ever increasing admiration and thankfulness that such a subject should be treated so fully and ably by the author. As a statement of Biblical record, it is long overdue. It cuts across, and explodes the myths of modern humanistic social doctrines which have wreaked division and despair on our culture. I found the able scholarship of the writer refreshingly Biblical and clear-cut.

The contentious issues of gender and human sexuality are dealt with from a deeply devotional and Scriptural standpoint and call us to bow to the will and order of God and His Word, in the church, in the home, and modern secular culture.

I thank God for this courageous and weighty work on some of the most contentious and pressing issues of our day. May it be widely read.

"Blessed are they that do His commandments", (Rev. 22 v.14).

Alex R. Passmore

Omega Ministries International
Incorporating Balkan Vision Eastern Europe
Great Eccleston
Preston

Rev. Dr. T. Boyle (8)

In this book, "The Place, Role and Function of women", Rev. Prof. Dr. R. H. Creane has given to us a true Biblical picture of the place of women as mentioned in the Scripture.

Today we are faced with widespread opposition to the authority of Scripture. There are Churches in our society who seem to interpret the Scriptures to suit themselves. Movements like that of the 'Feminist' who over the last few years, even since the sixties, have pushed their opinions on society very strongly. As Prof. Creane says "The enforcement of equality laws and gender regulations together with the removal of copies of the Bible from public places are among the assaults of Satan upon our Christian heritage and strike deeply at the moral fabric and spiritual values of the realm". Because of the lack of attendance at Church many have fallen away from, not only knowing the Bible but also Biblical principles. For these reasons, and others, some Churches have lost their backbone and this has led them to compromise.

The author has taken time not only to look at the place of women in Scripture which in turn looks at their role in Church, family, and society, but backs everything up with Bible doctrine and Biblical principles to show us the real truth.

Today the common statement is "There are no absolutes". We need to state clearly where we stand and on Whom we stand. We do not depend upon the wisdom of man, nor on his philosophies or ideals, we rely upon the revelation of God, and often this will come into conflict with what people think. What has been delivered to us, e.g. by the Apostle Paul is of Divine revelation and will conflict with man, for his reasoning is tainted by sin.

Prof. Creane has made a determined and faithful effort to relate these truths to us and I would recommend a close examination of this thesis.

Tom Boyle

Donegall Street Congregational Church, Belfast
Chaplain: Queen's University, Belfast and
          University College, Stranmillis

Rev. Dr. F. F. Greenfield (9)

The great Bible commentator Matthew Henry said "The woman was made of a rib out of the side of Adam; not made out of his head to rule over him, nor out of his feet to be trampled on by him; but out of his side to be equal to him, under his arm to be protected, and near his heart to be loved".

How refreshing it is to have this instructive and incisive book by Rev. Prof. Dr. Robert H. Creane to expound the Scriptural Place, Role and Function of Women in the church, the Home, the Workplace, in Society and the World at large.

Living in the day of the increasing secularisation of society and rapidly falling spiritual standards, this book is like a spring of pure clear water in the midst of the muddy streams of Liberalism and Secular Humanism of this age.

Dr. Creane in a scholarly manner sets forth in a Scriptural and systematic fashion "Precept upon precept, line upon line" (Isaiah 28 v.13) appealing to the authority of the Word of God as he unfolds the subject in hand.

I trust that this book will be of great blessing to the believing people of God and that they will be enriched and enabled to live for Christ standing firm in the day of adversity set for the defence of the Gospel and the whole counsel of God.

Fred F. Greenfield

Dunmurry Free Presbyterian Church
Belfast

FOUR CLOSING SCRIPTS

Rev. Prof. Dr. C. L. Ryan (1)

The author of this book, Rev. Prof. Dr. Robert H. Creane, has dealt with some of the contentious and controversial subjects with which the Christian church is faced today. His strong belief in the fundamental interpretation of Holy Scripture, will not make him popular in some parts of Christendom, but he does not seek to be popular, rather he seeks to be prophetic and he is calling the Christian Church back to its original mandate.

This book cites ethical dilemmas in Church leadership and the author argues that those dilemmas have arisen because the Biblical Model of leadership has been changed and there is Gender Confusion. God made the male very different from the female and while one should compliment the other, He blessed the male with Headship and the female with a different kind of leadership skill.

Prof. Creane has challenged us to an insightful consideration of leadership and to repent of our compromising attitudes, to turn away from the lure of being congratulation experts and hype-artists, to be honest enough with ourselves and deal with the causes of leadership confusion and not the symptoms. The carefully documented principles give it textbook authority and quality, while its freshness of style and invigorating word choice, crisp illustrations and tangible examples make it a thinking person's manual. No one aspiring to be a leader should leave home without it. "The fear of the Lord is the beginning of knowledge", (Prov. 1 v.7).

Clinton L. Ryan

New Testament Church of God
Highgate
Birmingham

Rev. Dr. S. N. Morgan (2)

This is a most worthy and weighty work containing twelve chapters with several sub-headings which make it easy to read, and for good measure there are five appendices.

Thoughtful Christian women who desire to please and honour the Lord and want positive Biblical teaching on womanhood and a clear understanding of the Biblical perspective on true feminism, including a wide range of issues such as marriage, submission, headship, sex, motherhood, singleness, work and the workplace, etc., should read this book. In these pages they are passionately exhorted to live under Scripture's authority which will bring help and blessing to all who desire to know and follow God's design and order for their lives.

This work by Rev. Prof. Dr. R. H. Creane clearly upholds the Divine order of Creation in a most thorough, dignified and balanced fashion, showing God's equal value in men and women, and that their roles are complementary, not interchangeable. In this extensive study of the subject, he sets forth in clear and unmistakeable terms the Biblical authority showing God's design and purpose for mankind in all matters of faith and life. All who truly love the Truth will find this book an invaluable tool, easy to comprehend, yet profoundly deep and sincere in knowledge of the Scriptures on what, sadly, has become acutely controversial in a pluralist, politically-correct society.

In the opening chapter the author sets the scene by laying a firm foundation and stresses the importance of the Holy Scriptures, since here we stand on safe ground it is hoped that those who read this book will be drawn to fully appreciate the inspired teaching of the infallible and inerrant Word of God, bearing in mind that it contains all that is needed for faith and practice.

It is encouraging that the writer has expounded the principle of headship in some depth, firmly acknowledging that the Creation order remains unchanged since we have a never changing God. He points out that the basic principle undergirding the role of women in society and in the Church, is that God has appointed a certain order between the man and the woman (1 Cor. 11 v.3). He states that today, the role of women has become a battleground having escalated to a place of imbalance in society that perverts the male and the female roles and relationships.

The author courageously expounds the position of women in the Church and details the significance of head covering as outlined in 1 Cor. 11 v.1-16. The considerable coverage touching upon several issues that are considered controversial will undoubtedly raise many eyebrows, but as the writer maintains the Biblical standpoint this is a work that is very soul searching and much needed to challenge the false teaching and corruption that abound on every hand. Prof. Creane is well equipped and able to produce such a book at a time when there is so much declension, barrenness, breakdown and weakness of witness "for the Word of God, and for the testimony of Jesus Christ", (Rev. 1 v.9).

It is always heartening to know that there are still those who refuse to compromise the Faith (Jude v.3), and we are deeply indebted to Prof. Creane for an outstanding work on matters of such profound gravity and importance.

"Put not your trust in princes, nor in the son of man, in whom there is no help. His breath goeth forth, he returneth to his earth; in that very day his thoughts perish. Happy is he that hath the God of Jacob for his help, whose hope is in the Lord his God: Which made heaven and earth, the sea, and all that therein is: which keepeth truth for ever", (Psalm 146 v.3-6).

Samuel N. Morgan

New Testament Church of God
Walsall
West Midlands

James A. Dickson (3)

We are living in an age of tremendous opportunity. At the present time we have comparative freedom in this country to preach and teach the Gospel of our Lord Jesus Christ. Today there are more Bibles, Christian books, ministers, missionaries, Christian workers, seminars, workshops, conferences, conventions, deeper-life programmes, evangelical efforts, radio and television ministries, etc., than ever before, yet there is less vital, enthusiastic, real Christianity, godly expression and holy living than there has been since the Reformation.

Throughout our nation both Church and State seem to be swamped in moral chaos and darkness. Even in 'evangelical' circles unBiblical beliefs and practices are rampant. Why is the church in such a malaise and disarray? How has it come to such a state where His will for us is so completely cast off and worldly living has become the norm for so many who claim to be 'believers'? What epitomizes our day and generation more than anything else is the great preoccupation with self. Rather than being disciples and followers of Christ and His Word, many come merely as spectators and customers, and there is a noticeable absence of humility, shame, guilt, remorse and repentance. We need to be taught the precious truths of the Bible and learn about sin and salvation by faith alone in Christ alone. We need to learn about love, honesty, and justice, so that Biblical principles are brought to bear on the affairs of life in society.

I have read this most enlightening and instructive book with a mixture of pain and pleasure. Pain and sorrow because I have been reminded of a frightful, sinful departure by believers in our day from the stated will and order of God. The declension and apathy all around us is most apparent. The pleasure I experienced was in realising afresh that we have a great, loving and forgiving Father Who pleads with us to renounce our waywardness, sin, and disobedience by walking in the light of His Word. Pleased because in these vital pages we are reminded again of God's way for us.

The Church is impotent and sick, and we need to pray and cry to God for revival, reformation and a return to His Word. We now live in a land steeped in atheistic, humanistic and godless philosophies with no regard for God. Our law-makers legalise heinous sin that God has clearly forbidden --- sodomy, adultery, abortion, etc., and furthermore, theft, rape, cursing, blasphemy, lying, murder, greed, drunkenness and every sort of iniquity abounds. Churches are emptying and the Bible is a closed Book to millions in THIS country who have no absolute standards of morality or regard for the Gospel. Many who call themselves 'evangelical' are so far removed from Bible doctrine and practice, and as a consequence of disobedience, our nation has completely lost its way, morally and spiritually.

The answer to this dire situation as Dr. Creane ably points out, is to reassert again the great doctrine of the Lordship and Kingship of our Lord Jesus Christ. Christ reigns, He has not abdicated His throne, nor delegated His authority to another. We are commanded to preach the Gospel in all its fullness, and the priority of all Christians is to live for Christ now. (Eph. 1 v.21). In this excellent book, Dr. Creane has drawn us back to "What saith the Lord" and to our duty and privilege of lovingly obeying and applying the teaching and principles of God's Word to every area of our lives.

In dealing with God's order concerning the role of woman in her relation with man, her role in the church, in the home, in the workplace and in society, Dr. Creane has grasped a thistle. Controversy may surround this subject but as the author rightly maintains, the Bible is abundantly clear. God's order is perfect. His order regarding leadership is perfect. His order regarding the role of women in the Church and in the home is perfect. He gave us His Word in order that we may avoid confusion and obey His rule. From a Biblical perspective the author expounds the various issues involved in the role of women, leadership in the Church, and much more, in a straightforward and honest fashion, emphasising that the Scriptures must always be our guide.

This is not a negative book about the role of women but rather the opposite. It shouts loud and clear for the dignity, femininity, Biblical equality of personhood and worth, and of the importance of her role in the church and in society. When God's Word is honoured and Christ reigning in the individual life and in the home, then shall we see churches reformed and reforming according to the Bible. May we as a people turn away from doing those things which are right in our own eyes, and as Dr. Creane proclaims, 'pray for revival and reformation in the Church, that she might be strong, firm and steadfast for God's truth, fearlessly testifying against all current evils in the individual, social, political, and ecclesiastical life, and thus raise up a standard for truth, to the glory of God'.

James A. Dickson

Congregational Church of Scotland
Kilsyth
Glasgow

COVENANTERS WORSHIPPING IN THE OPEN FIELD

Maurice Grant (4)

I am honoured to be invited by Professor Creane to provide a summary conclusion to his book *The Place, Role and Function of Women*. I believe this work is both timely and important. It offers a very comprehensive treatment of a subject which is vital to the well-being of our modern society. For the Christian, its main attraction must be the emphasis which it places throughout on the authority of Scripture. This is all the more notable in a day when Scripture teaching is so much at a discount. The infallible Word of God does not change, and the principles enunciated there are as relevant for our society as they ever were. As the Creator of the human race --- He who made them male and female --- God has the sovereign right to prescribe the distinctive role of each, and how these are to be fulfilled to His own glory and for the good of His creation. It is my own firm belief that the perversion of the Scriptural role of women is at the root of many of the disorders we see in society today --- the failed marriages, the single-parent families, the broken homes --- all of which tell a tragic story of failure to follow the Scriptural pattern.

The Church itself, sadly, is not free from blame. For fear of giving offence, it has obscured the position of Scripture on this vital subject. The plain teaching of God's Word has been set aside and subjected to spurious interpretations dictated essentially by a humanist agenda. Within the Church, women have been placed in positions of authority to which they have no Scriptural calling. In other times it was so different. In conforming to their God-given role, women were given an honourable place in the outworking of God's covenant purposes. Over the years it has been my privilege to make a particular study of how the people of God in Scotland conducted themselves in the period of bitter persecution towards the end of the seventeenth century. A striking feature of that period was the role played by godly women. This is graphically portrayed in Rev. James Anderson's work *The Ladies of the Covenant*, a classic in its own right. That role consisted not only in supporting their menfolk --- important though that was --- but in their own personal testimony for the Crown Rights of Christ, sometimes even to death. And, be it noted, this was not achieved by aspiring to positions to which they had no Scriptural warrant, but by manifesting that character which is the particular glory of the woman of scripture, "the ornament of a meek and quiet spirit, which is in the sight of God of great price", (1 Peter 3 v.4).

A pleasing feature of the book is the way in which the author does not avoid the more difficult areas, such as the headship of the man, the role of women in the workplace, and the challenges facing the single woman in society. He shows a particular skill in relating these to the circumstances of the modern world. These issues, too, are handled with transparent faithfulness to Scripture.

I congratulate Professor Creane on his very able work. It is clearly and cogently written, free from technical jargon, well researched and informed, and, above all, honouring to the Word of God. It deserves every success.

Maurice Grant

Free Church of Scotland (Continuing)
Edinburgh

COVENANTER WORSHIPPING BY THE BANKS
OF THE WHITADDER RIVER

SCRIPTURE INDEX

Old Testament

	Page Number	Reader's Notes
Genesis		
1	72,142,314	
1 : 1	72,249	
1 : 4,10,12,18,21, 25,31	315	
1 : 26-27	215,351	
1 : 27	55,56,96,102,112,115,177,289, 309,343	
1 : 28	103,139,314	
1 : 31	65	
1 - 2	57	
1 - 3	97	
2	56,87,127,128,142	
2 : 7	56,87,142	
2 : 18	58,87,115,117,124,125,128,129, 137,154,155,156,238,297,314	
2 : 18,22	245	
2 : 18,22, 24	129,301	
2 : 18,23-24	139	
2 : 18-20	124	
2 : 18-25	124,162,274,309,343	
2 : 20	126,142	
2 : 21	125,142	
2 : 21-22	87	
2 : 21-23	125	
2 : 21-24	152	
2 : 22-23	56	
2 : 23	57,126	
2 : 24	60,61,113,116,128,133,143,145, 310,318,400	
2 : 25	316	
2 : 30	164	
3 : 1	58,213	
3 : 1,6	58	
3 : 6	57	
3 : 1-7	238,239	
3 : 9	57	
3 : 15	59,284,285	
3 : 16	59,60,88,130,133,204,220,245,

			246
3	:	16-17	163
3	:	17	246
3	:	20	285
4	:	7	59,246
4	:	19	130
5	:	1-2	57
6	:	1-8	131
6	:	5	314
6	:	6	315
6	:	7	315
6	:	17	315
7			315
9	:	6	290
24	:	67	312
35	:	2-3	302
39			141
39	:	9	141

Exodus

3	:	16-18	89
4	:	29	89
9	:	27	408
15	:	20-21	204
17	:	5	89
20	:	3	80
20	:	7	305
20	:	13-14	290
20	:	14	136,302,351
21	:	22-23	290
22	:	22	346
24	:	1	89
33	:	19	301

Leviticus

11	:	44	302
18			149
18	:	6	149

Numbers

11	:	16	89
11	:	16-30	89
21	:	8-9	255
22	:	24	408

Deuteronomy

1	:	1	208
2	:	7	9
4	:	2	66,254,443
4	:	7	208
5	:	15	305

6			298
6		5-7	298
6	:	6, 9	302
6	:	16	80
6	:	20	298
8	:	3	80
10	:	20	80
11	:	1	299
12	:	32	67,437,443
14	:	29	405
18	:	18	22
22	:	5	176,177,178,179
23		21,23	216
25	:	16	214,220
27	:	19	405
27	:	20-23	351
32	:	3-4	214
32	:	5	262,315
33	:	19	301
33	:	27	337

Joshua

1	:	7-8	356
1	:	8	249,389
7	:	20	408
24	:	14-15	334
24	:	24	41

Judges

4	:	4	204

Ruth

3	:	10	402
4	:	15	402

1 Samuel

1	:	27-28	295
2	:	30	117
4	:	21	258
7	:	12	395
8		4	89
8	:	19	421
12	:	14	287
12	:	23	411
12	:	24	411
15	:	22	280
15	:	22-23	307
15	:	23	421
15	:	24	408
17	:	45	411

21 : 8	249	
30 : 1-6	395	
30 : 6	27,349,395	

2 Samuel

3 : 17	89
22 : 2-4,33	74
22 : 4	478
23 : 1	73
23 : 5	24,63,242,271,475

1 Kings

4 : 29	322
17 : 9	332
21 : 8	89

2 Kings

20 : 1	304
20 : 6	304
22 : 14-22	204

1 Chronicles

16 : 4,7	438
28 : 9	71

2 Chronicles

7 : 14	411
29 : 26-30	442
29 : 36	438

Ezra

5 : 9-11	89
6 : 7	89

Nehemiah

8 : 8	48,263
8 : 10	477
12 : 24	438
13 : 27	148

Job

14 : 1	395
22 : 21	394
31 : 1	173

Psalms

1	441
1 : 1-2	131
1 : 2	390
3 : 8	105
4 : 1	349
5 : 12	305
15 : 2	152
15 : 3	152
15 : 4	152

15	:	5	152
16	:	5-6	20
18			74
18	:	2-3	288
18	:	3	478
18	:	30	287
23			441
23	:	3	107
23	:	4	108
23	:	6	19,108,259
24			441
25	:	5	456
25	:	14	436
27	:	11	33,112
27	:	11,14	25
29	:	2	426,456
32	:	5	104
33	:	4	47
33	:	12	253
34	:	6	395
34	:	8	74
34	:	19	475
40			441
45			441
46	:	1	399
46	:	11	122
50	:	23	333
51	:	1-4	408
51	:	4	71
51	:	6	358
51	:	10-13	409
60	:	4	122,202,446,479
63	:	1	418
66	:	18	307,456
67	:	1-2	413
68	:	6	326
68	:	11	455
69	:	17	395
72	:	17	100
72	:	17-19	49
76	:	11	215
78	:	5-6	99
78	:	5-7	75
84	:	1-2	447
84	:	11	328
85	:	4,6-7	36
85	:	6	425
85	:	6-8	414

86	:	9	444
87	:	2-3	259
90	:	12	359
90	:	17	66
92	:	14-15	402
94	:	14	415
96	:	9	426
97	:	11	256
101	:	1-3	173
101	:	2-3	302
101	:	3	334
103			420
106	:	3	359
107	:	32	195
110	:	1	386
110	:	3	425
111	:	10	260
112	:	1	328
113	-	118	441
118	:	8	430
118	:	23	460
119			428,429,431
119	:	1	431
119	:	2	431
119	:	3	431
119	:	4	431
119	:	5	431
119	:	6	432
119	:	7	432
119	:	8	432
119	:	9	432
119	:	10	432
119	:	11	432
119	:	12	432
119	:	13	432
119	:	14	432
119	:	15	432
119	:	16	433
119	:	33	433
119	:	34	433
119	:	38	433
119	:	57	433
119	:	58	433
119	:	65	433
119	:	66	433
119	:	67	434
119	:	68	434
119	:	89	51,80,204,434

119	:	90	434
119	:	92-93	389
119	:	97	79,434
119	:	98	434
119	:	103	434
119	:	104	434
119	:	105	119,434
119	:	106	434
119	:	116	434
119	:	117	435
119	:	124	435
119	:	125	435
119	:	130	119
119	:	133	435
119	:	140	435
119	:	141	435
119	:	142	435
119	:	160	52,120,256,344,454,460
119		164-165	393
119	:	169	435
119	:	176	435
126	:	3	466
126	:	6	398
127	:	1	1,32
127	:	3	138,310
130	:	4	402
137	:	3	439
138	:	2	20,80,430
139			354
145	:	17	71
145	:	20	431
146	:	3-6	413,494

Proverbs

1	:	7	393,492
2	:	16-17	309
3	:	5-6	322
3	:	5-7	119
4	:	18	419
5	:	15-19	159
5	:	15-21	289
5	:	18-19	310
5	:	19-20	290
6	:	16-19	390
6	:	17	290
6	:	20	208
9	:	10	190
10	:	1	287
12	:	4	281,354

12	:	28	76
13	:	24	296
14	:	1	280
14	:	12	38
14	:	34	320
15	:	1	357
16	:	18	270
16	:	25	38
17	:	17	355
18	:	22	116,316,322
18	:	24	329,356
19	:	2	102
19	:	14	155
19	:	18	299
20	:	6	398
22	:	6	286,304,323
23	:	23	41,180,260,319
24	:	21	180,260,319
25	:	28	306
27	:	15	322
27	:	17,19	353
29	:	15	300
29	:	17	300
29	:	18	122
31			281,296,345
31	:	1	173
31	:	10	322,398
31	:	10-12	174
31	:	10-31	151,282,398
31	:	11	151
31	:	12	115
31	:	13	151
31	:	20	151,361
31	:	26	151,361
31	:	27	151
31	:	30	141,361,397,398

Ecclesiastes

3	:	1-5	135
5	:	4	216
5	:	4-5	215
5	:	6	167
5	:	7	216
12	:	1	304

Song of Solomon

8	:	7	150

Isaiah

1	:	16-17	307
3	:	12	176

3	:	14-15	351
5	:	24	169
8	:	20	21,72,217,290,443,455,464
11	:	9	197,262,466
19	:	21	215
26	:	3	328
26	:	3-4	308
28	:	9-10	323
28	:	13	491
30	:	15	341,361
30	:	17	40
34	:	16	21
35	:	10	221
40	:	1	420
40	:	8	204
40	:	9	185
42	:	21	80
54	:	5	414
55	:	7	391
55	:	8-11	343
55	:	11	27,122
57	:	14	420
58	:	1	420
59	:	14-15	42
59	:	19	71,457
60	:	2	365
62	:	4	414
62	:	10	420
64	:	6-8	109

Jeremiah

1	:	10	420
2	:	2	46
2	:	7	220
3	:	1	36
3	:	3	70
3	:	15	420
6	:	15	220
6	:	16	40,117,220,388
8	:	22	420
9	:	3	421
10	:	2	184
17	:	7	122
17	:	9	390
29	:	1	89
29	:	13	443
33	:	3	323
50	:	5	256
51	:	27	419

Lamentations
  3 : 22-23   308
Ezekiel
  11 : 19   428
  19 : 13   418
  20 : 1   89
  36 : 26-27   428
Daniel
  4 : 31-32   360
  11 : 32   46,228,395,409
Hosea
  4 : 6   21,46,289
Joel
  1 : 15   413
  2 : 1   413
  2 : 11   413
  2 : 12-13   414
  2 : 25-27   413
  2 : 31   413
  3 : 14   413
Amos
  3 : 3   118
  6 : 1   122
Jonah
  2 : 9   216
Micah
  6 : 8   270
  7 : 18   421
  7 : 19   421
Nahum
  1 : 7   45,395
Haggai
  1 : 5,7   216
Zechariah
  3 : 2   26
  4 : 6   466
  8 : 19   260
Malachi
  2 : 14   148
  2 : 15   130,297
  3 : 15   297
  3 : 16   305
  4 : 2   419

New Testament

	Page Number	Reader's Notes

Matthew

3 : 7	407	
3 : 8	408	
4 : 4	120	
4 : 4,7,10	51,80	
5 : 8-9	358	
5 : 13-14	254,365	
5 : 13-16	120,361	
5 : 15	120	
5 : 16	362,365,379	
5 : 18	51	
5 : 23-24	306	
5 : 27-28	351	
5 : 27-30	139,140	
5 : 28	139	
5 : 31-32	129	
6 : 21	456	
6 : 33	118,273	
6 : 34	308	
7 : 15	249	
7 : 18,20	370	
7 : 20	409	
7 : 21	386	
8 : 25	284	
9 : 13	108	
9 : 21-22	284	
11 : 4-6	379	
11 : 29	221,383	
13	188	
13 : 30	188	
15 : 9	32,196	
15 : 21-28	351	
16 : 18	251,259,460,466	
16 : 24	308	
17 : 5	105,250	
19	327	
19 : 3,6,9	129	
19 : 4	90	
19 : 4-5	129	
19 : 5	129	
19 : 5-6	118	
19 : 6	96,149,156,158,318	
19 : 11-12	331	

19 : 12	132	
20 : 27-28	192	
21 : 42	79	
22 : 29	51,53	
22 : 37	356	
22 : 37-38	302	
22 : 37-40	282	
24 : 24	44	
25 : 21	398	
25 : 21,23	338	
25 : 41	417	
26 : 6-13	351	
26 : 30	438,441	
27 : 4	408	
27 : 49	284	
28 : 18	84,250	
28 : 18-20	407	
28 : 19-20	35,196,253,262,365,394,461	

Mark

1 : 15	457
2 : 2	80
4 : 19	410
5 : 2	301
5 : 19	301,335
7 : 6	196
7 : 7	264
7 : 24-39	351
10 : 6-9	97
10 : 8-9	143
11 : 17	79
12 : 26	79
12 : 31	351
14 : 8	361
14 : 26	441
16 : 15	197

Luke

1 : 6	343
1 : 46-55	204
2 : 36-38	204
3 : 7	407
3 : 8	408
4 : 4,8	51
4 : 16	79
4 : 18	472
6 : 13	274
6 : 46	363,386
7	90
7 : 36-50	351

7	:	37-47	351
8	:	2-3	228
8	:	43-48	351
10	:	3	249
10	:	4	221
10	:	5	300
10	:	7	191,192,473
10	:	26	79
10	:	33-35	348
10	:	38	333
10	:	38-42	332,351
12	:	20	354
13	:	27	417
14	:	33	376
15	:	10	472
17	:	10	382
18	:	23	408
20	:	17	79
21	:	33	80,484
22	:	31	26
24	:	27	80
24	:	44	51
24	:	44-45	441

John

1	:	14	109
3	:	3	225,301
3	:	5	225
3	:	5-7	111
3	:	14-15	255
3	:	16	158
3	:	30	187
3	:	36	393
4			90
4	:	7-42	351
4	:	20-24	207
4	:	23	412
4	:	23-24	240,243,343
4	:	24	224,412,436,443,478
4	:	34	85
5	:	39	79
6	:	37	110
6	:	44	106
7	:	24	242
8	:	3-8	351
8	:	12	365
8	:	31-32	78
10	:	16	277
10	:	28	475

10	:	34	79
10	:	35	51
11	:	1	333
11	:	1-3	335
11	:	5	333,356
12	:	6	269
12	:	26	141
12	:	32	479
12	:	49	23
13	:	4-6	230
14	:	1-3	348,394
14	:	2	259
14	:	6	106,457
14	:	15	423
14	:	15,21,23-24	118
14	:	16-17	394
14	:	21	22
14	:	21, 23	107
15	:	4	170
15	:	8	387
15	:	10-11	428
15	:	14	356
15	:	26	250
16	:	8	185,462
16	:	13	111
17	:	3	394
17	:	4-5	110
17	:	17	260,428
17	:	21-24	337
18	:	37	80
20	:	31	209
21	:	15	157
21	:	15-17	157
21	:	16	157
21	:	17	157

Acts

1	:	8	409
1	:	23-26	226
2	:	36	250
2	:	38,41,47	226
2	:	42	199,207,260,418
4	:	12	478
5	:	4	216
5	:	29	180,215,378,379
6			90,191,192,227,274
6	:	1-2	191
6	:	1-8	91,225,406
6	:	3	225,225,227

6	:	3-5	268
6	:	5	228
6	:	6	226,227
6	:	7	193
6	-	7	186
7	:	38	80
8	:	4	479
9	:	11	230
9	:	36	232,374
9	:	36-43	232
9	:	39	232
9	:	43	230
10	:	36	386
11	:	30	89
13	:	15	442
14	:	21-23	194
15	:	2, 6, 23	89
15	:	22	274
16	:	4	89
16	:	13	232
16	:	31-32	305
16	:	40	230
17	:	11	121,193,262
17	:	28	476
18	:	24-26	229
18	:	25	40
18	:	26	238
20			198
20	:	17	187
20	:	17, 28	89
20	:	17-35	89
20	:	27	28,168,170,185,186,197,272, 462,479
20	:	27-31	198
20	:	28	88,89,186,187,251,262,417, 420,444
20	:	35	143
21	:	9	232
21	:	14	278
21	:	18	89
24	:	16	349
27	:	23	187

Romans

1	:	1	473
1	:	16	24,419
1	:	16-19	412
1	:	17	77
1	:	20	343

1	:	22-32	342
1	:	24-27	144
1	:	26	330
1	:	26-27	149
3	:	4	71
3	:	9-12	109
3	:	23	93,105,407,427
3	:	23-26	108
5	:	1	472
5	:	5	74,381
5	:	12	104,346
5	:	12-21	239
5	:	19	370,427
6	:	4	388
6	:	6	385
6	:	13	472
6	:	14	106
6	:	17	305
6	:	22	387
6	:	23	104
7	:	1-3	403
7	:	2-3	129
7	:	14	109
7	:	21-23	358
8	:	3-4	456
8	:	3-5	243
8	:	16	436
8	:	21	93
8	:	28	325,476
8	:	28-30	107
8	:	29	277
8	:	29-30	111
8	:	37	391,475
8	:	37,39	107
8	:	39	336,475
9	:	15	301
10	:	1	478
10	:	4	478
10	:	13	447
10	:	14-15	409
10	:	17	24
12	:	1-2	112,273
12	:	2	221,421
12	:	13	267
13	:	10	192,303
13	:	11	220
13	:	13-14	355
14			371

14	:	1	261
14	:	5	28
14	:	7	265
14	:	12	417
14	:	13	371
14	:	14-15	371
14	:	15	371
14		16-19	371
14	:	17	338
14	:	20-21	371
14	:	22-23	371
15	:	4	420
16	:	1	86,200
16	:	2	200
16	:	1-4	229
16	:	3	229

1 Corinthians

1	:	3	225
2	:	4	29,254,446
2	:	4-5	77
2	:	5	29,30
2	:	5-6	421
2	:	7	130
2	:	13	23
3	:	1	421
3	:	4	421
3	:	20-21	421
4	:	5	76
5	:	1-5	351
6	-	7	117
6	:	9-10	136,334
6	:	9-11	144
6	:	9-20	351
6	:	12-15	310
6	:	13	136
6	:	16	129
6	:	18-20	136
7			135,327,350
7	:	1-17	310
7	:	2	297
7	:	2-5	289
7	:	3	159
7	:	3-5	116
7	:	4-5	146,314
7	:	5	146
7	:	12-17	146
7	:	15	129
7	:	23-24	312

7	:	25-40	285
7	:	34	325
7	:	39	117,129,131,133,148,150,403
9	:	14	472
9	:	16	419
9	:	24-25	141
10	:	5	395
10	:	13	65
10	:	31	118,292,332,334,352,425,
11			64,86,163,165,166,175,181,205
11	:	1-16	161,163,168,169,494
11	:	1-19	177
11	:	2-5	224
11	:	2-16	224
11	:	3	60,61,83,84,162,166,175,179, 237,321,494
11	:	4	166
11	:	4-7	164
11	:	5	163,166,205,236
11	:	7	162,166,167,175
11	:	8	167,175
11	:	8-9	85,87,129,161
11	:	9	115,175,235
11	:	10	164,175
11	:	11	167,219
11	:	11-12	164
11	:	13-15	175
11	:	14	168
11	:	14-15	171,178
11	:	15	167
11	:	16	168,170,175,225
11	:	18	205
11	:	29	181
11	:	32	181
12			441
12	-	14	250
12	:	1	250
12	:	25	251,261
13			148,159,192,329
13	:	4-7,13	148
13	:	13	192
14			64,86,154
14	:	26	224,236
14	:	26,40	73,181
14	:	29	181
14	:	33-34	72
14	:	33-35	183
14	:	33-40	206

14	:	34	90,130,183,202,204,236
14	:	34-35	154,221,223
14	:	35	90
14	:	37	206
14	:	40	206,236
15	:	10	422
15	:	21-22	239
15	:	22	57
15	:	57-58	45
15	:	58	272,473
16	:	13-14	329

2 Corinthians

1	:	3-4	347
1	:	12	336
1	:	20	28
2	:	16	189
3	:	17	392
4	:	5	466
4	:	5-6	111
5	:	8	469
5	:	10	300,417
5	:	11	255
5	:	14	383,410
5	:	17	111,347,428
5	:	17-21	119
5	:	20	255
5	:	21	105,265
6	:	1	74
6	:	14	134
6	:	14-16	151
7	:	1	303,391
8	:	2	345
8	:	16	486
9	:	8	19,331,412,478
9	:	11	395
11	:	12	377
12	:	9	476
12	:	20	261

Galatians

1	:	6-10	111
2	:	20	74,111
3	:	24	408
3	:	26	365,393,472
3	:	28	181,208,224,488
5	:	16-26	412
5	:	19	261
5	:	19-21	137
5	:	20	383

5	:	22	158
5	:	22-23	208,227,383,397
5	:	25	456
6	:	1-2	269
6	:	2	230,383
6	:	4	359
6	:	6	384
6	:	9-10	384
6	:	10	407
6	:	14	385

Ephesians

1	:	7	392
1	:	14	473
1	:	21	496
1	:	22	386
1	:	23	259
2	:	1	472
2	:	2	93,427
2	:	4	392
2	:	4-5	111
2	:	5	301
2	:	8	301
2	:	8-9	94,110
2	:	8-10	398
2	:	10	404
2	:	19	384
2	:	19-20	464
2	:	20	53
3			407
3	:	7-8	19
3	:	8	254,460
3	:	10	167
3	:	10-11	407
3	:	15	394
4	:	1	35,370
4	:	1-2,24	313
4	:	2-3	260,477
4	:	3	76
4	:	4-7	233
4	:	11	89
4	:	11-12	195
4	:	11-16	326
4	:	12	252
4	:	12-16	251
4	:	13	252
4	:	14	43,252,388,409
4	:	15	252,254,261,276
4	:	15-16	252,474

4	:	18	93
4	:	23	105
4	:	24	102,412
4	:	24-25	112
4	:	26	306
4	:	27	306
4	:	29	308
4	:	31-32	309
4	:	32	291,473
5			86,135,153,154,155,156,249,274
5	:	1	98
5	:	3	302
5	:	15	266
5	:	15-16	363
5	:	16-17	331
5	:	18	158,271,315,368
5	:	19	438,439,443
5	:	20	394
5	:	20-21	159
5	:	21	113,114,236
5	:	21-33	351
5	:	22	88,154,155,156,306,311,314
5	:	22-23	117,130,176,219
5	:	22-24	235
5	:	22-25	63
5	:	22-33	138,153,236,301
5	:	23	60,155,236,260
5	:	24	156,236
5	:	25	61,156,158,306,311,321
5	:	25,33	88
5	:	25-33	113
5	:	28	317
5	:	29	317
5	:	31	318
5	:	31-32	60
5	:	32-33	249
5	:	33	62,150,311,318
6	:	1-4	297,301,350
6	:	4	230,298,299,304
6	:	5	357
6	:	5-8	377
6	:	10-12	421
6	:	11	480
6	:	12	320
6	:	13	480
6	:	14	421
6	:	16-17	26
6	:	17	81,320

6 : 18	361	
6 : 19	459	
6 : 24	479	

Philippians
1 : 6	66
1 : 7	452,459
1 : 17	462
2 : 9-11	305
2 : 10-11	84
2 : 11	166
2 : 15	28,77,234
2 : 15-16	254,366
2 : 16	24,77,392,429,460,479
3 : 3	108,384
3 : 8	187,417
3 : 13	20
3 : 13-14	387
3 : 14	361,406,476
4 : 1	459
4 : 3	229
4 : 7	328,349
4 : 11	329
4 : 11-13	358
4 : 13	406

Colossians
1 : 7	419
1 : 9	281
1 : 10	366
1 : 10-11	359
1 : 11	369
1 : 13	395
1 : 13-14	385
1 : 16	385
1 : 18	84,147,259,277,333,385,414,465, 474
1 : 20	436
1 : 23	53
1 : 27	240
1 : 27-29	457
2 : 3	306
2 : 10	327
2 : 16-23	132
2 : 22	196,264
3 : 2	338,456
3 : 5	351
3 : 5-7	328
3 : 10	102
3 : 15	115

3	:	16	48,263,334,438,439,443
3	:	17	334
3	:	18	235,313,351
3	:	18-19	60
3	:	18-20	310
3	:	18-21	301
3	:	19	312
3	:	21	299
3	:	22-24	377
3	:	23	335,357
3	:	23-24	378
4	:	1	351
4	:	2	286
4	:	5	270
4	:	7	419
6	:	7	418

1 Thessalonians

2	:	7	230
2	:	13	43,51,55,77
4	:	3,7	396
4	:	3-4	137
4	:	4	113
4	:	12	355
5	:	8-10	355
5	:	12-13	192

2 Thessalonians

1	:	3	230
2	:	13	472
2	:	15	83,466
2	:	17	360
3	:	11	303
3	:	11-13	337

1 Timothy

1	:	3	222,381
1	:	9	243
1	:	10	368
1	:	17	343
1	:	20	198
2			29,64,154,240
2	:	1-8	223
2	:	5	277,474
2	:	8	172,207,223
2	:	8-10	172
2	:	9	172,223,242,244,285
2	:	9-10	171,207,233,241
2	:	9-15	197,223,237,245
2	:	10	167,244,369,398
2	:	11	199,203,207,236,237

2	:	11-12	203,204,207,219,222,245
2	:	11-14	274
2	:	11-15	154,237
2	:	12	130,203,207,247,354
2	:	13	56,129,167,235,238
2	:	13-14	207
2	:	14	238,239,247,283
2	:	15	86,248,283,284,285,395
2	-	3	274
3			91,219,274,275,316
3	:	1	89,264
3	:	1-7	274
3	:	1-13	92
3	:	2	237,238,265,272
3	:	2-3	266
3	:	2-6	189
3	:	2,12	133
3	:	4	154,298
3	:	4-5	251,269
3	:	4-5,7	190
3	:	5	266,403
3	:	6	189,270,276
3	:	6,9-10	270
3	:	7	265
3	:	9	133
3	:	10	270
3	:	11	90,271,397
3	:	13	271
3	:	14-15	194,198,264
3	:	15	79,195,207,264,407
4			135
4	:	1-3	132
4	:	1-5	310
4	:	3	133
4	:	7	46
4	:	8	135,330
4	:	13	384
4	:	13,16	268
4	:	16	331
5			197,274,293,399,404
5	:	2-3	351
5	:	3	400,404
5	:	3-16	399
5	:	3,5,16	400
5	:	4	198,303,400,401,405
5	:	4,8,16	400
5	:	5	399
5	:	6	402

5	:	6,11-15	402
5	:	8	400,401
5	:	9-10	403
5	:	10	229,230
5	:	11	231,405
5	:	11-13	403
5	:	11-15	231
5	:	12	231,402,406
5	:	13	231,304,403
5	:	14	231,294,297,403,404
5	:	15	231,404
5	:	16	208,400,405
5	:	17	89,186,238,272,274
5	:	17-18	192,272
5	:	18	473
5	:	21	382
5	:	23	266,271,371
6	:	1	406
6	:	4-5	261
6	:	4-11	405
6	:	6-8	330
6	:	11	174,405
6	:	12	406
6	:	13	363,374,405

2 Timothy

1	:	5	200,295,401
1	:	7	156
1	:	10	365
1	:	13	22,169
1	:	16	268
2	:	2	382
2	:	2,14	169
2	:	15	5,48,81,121,256,263,376,381,468
2	:	19	54
2	:	22	137,173,174
2	:	24-25	267
2	:	24-26	65
2	:	26	267
3	:	6	404
3	:	13	169,212
3	:	14-15	212
3	:	16	437
3	:	16-17	52,202,211,253,390,394,437,455
3	:	17	210,211,409
4	:	1-2	382
4	:	1-4	185
4	:	2	79,384,420
4	:	3-4	169

4 : 8		338
Titus		
1		91,219,274,275
1 : 5		194,277
1 : 5-9		89,92,273
1 : 7-9		88
1 : 9		92,189,190,373,480
1 : 14		196
1 : 15-16		139
2		26,293,366,367
2 : 1		366,368
2 : 1-3		282
2 : 2		367
2 : 3		397
2 : 3-4		208,369
2 : 3-5		234,238
2 : 4-5		234,372
2 : 5		66,293,303,352,374,406
2 : 5,10		352
2 : 6-8		375
2 : 8		376
2 : 9-10		377
2 : 10		352,379,389
2 : 12		305,336,370,448,460,464,484
2 : 15		174
3 : 4-5		282
3 : 5		412
3 : 10-11		262
Hebrews		
2 : 1		455
2 : 8		84
2 : 10		479
2 : 17		110
3 : 5		302
4 : 11		220
4 : 12		80
4 : 14		277
5 : 8-9		427
5 : 12-14		215
5 : 14		388
6 : 18-19		337
7 : 25		106
9 : 11-12		110
10 : 14-17		110
10 : 23		233
10 : 24-25		195
10 : 25		21,305
11 : 6		106,120

11	:	26	240
12	:	1	306
12	:	2	436
12	:	5-6	299
12	:	27	487
12	:	27-28	336
12	:	27-29	344,455
12	:	28-29	331
13	:	2	267
13	:	4	143,149,301,310,314
13	:	6	338,475
13	:	7	195,196
13	:	8	341,417
13	:	9	78
13	:	14	384
13	:	15	442
13	:	17	180,477
13	:	18	355
13	:	20-21	462
13	:	21	245

James

1	:	5	190,227
1	:	15	394
1	:	21	390
1	:	22	255
1	:	22-25	390
1	:	27	329,399
2	:	14-26	360
2	:	17	232
2	:	26	360
3	:	1	180
3	:	5-6	370
3	:	6	481
3	:	9	103,166
3	:	13-18	73,228
4	:	7-8	332
5	:	14	273
5	:	16	410

1 Peter

1	:	3	120,392
1	:	4	120
1	:	6	346
1	:	7	346
1	:	8,10	121
1	:	16	302
1	:	18-19	84
1	:	23	80,254
1	:	25	71,417,460,470

2	:	2	207,388
2	:	5	277,413
2	:	9	213
2	:	9-10	184
2	:	12	362,377
2	:	18-20	357
2	:	23	71
3			274
3	:	1	244
3	:	1-2	372
3	:	1-6	236,241,242
3	:	1-7	118
3	:	2-4	234
3	:	4	119,242,499
3	:	4-6	179
3	:	5	244
3	:	5-6	314
3	:	7	113,114,119,152,208,232,312, 314,315,318
3	:	18	94,105,479
4	:	2	359
4	:	3	351
4	:	9	335
4	:	15	304
4	:	19	24
5			275
5	:	1	89
5	:	1-3	181
5	:	1-4	89
5	:	3	275
5	:	4	277
5	:	5	275
5	:	6	276
5	:	8-11	98,140

2 Peter

1	:	10	106
1	:	13-14	346
1	:	16	46
1	:	19-20	393
1	:	19-21	210
1	:	20	100
1		21	72,220
2	:	9	65
2	:	14-15	269
3	:	18	22,107,121,240,388,479

1 John

1	:	7	120,392
1	:	7-10	109

1	:	9	66,395
2	:	6	280
2	:	16-17	174
3	:	1	24
3	:	4	94
4	:	8	148
4	:	17-18	368
5	:	3	118
5	:	4	35

2 John	4	472
	4-6	344
3 John	4,11	217
Jude	3	105,176,185,221,248,356,382, 418,449,457,480,494
	20	176,212,254,446,477
	24-25	480

Revelation

1	:	3	68
1	:	5-6	108
1	:	6	22,479
1	:	9	49,448,454,478,494,
1	:	10	21
2	:	10	456
2	:	23	71,386
4	:	11	49,425,466
9			168
14	:	6	472
14	:	12	428
14	:	13	346
19	:	1	468
19	:	13	22
19	:	16	254
21	:	1-2	337
21	:	2	259,310
21	:	23-27	259
22	:	13-14	430
22	:	14	489
22	:	18-19	67,68
22	:	21	72,249

WORD INDEX

Abomination(s)	149,160,176,177,179,214,220,259,290,350
abortion	201,290,319,496
abstain	132,137,146
abstainer	266
abstinence	131,132,146,147
abuse	164,235,283,310,350
abused	250,309,311,346
abusers	136,144,334
abusive	188,247,275
accountability	58,277
accountable	59,64,168,351
administration	90,225,403,406
admonition(s)	174,229,241,261,293,297,299,304
adoration	74
adulterers	136,143,144,149,310,334
adultery	64,70,129,136,137,139,141,148,149,171,269,290,302,314,315, 342,496
adversary	98,140,168,230,231,403,404,453
advertisement	375
affection(s)	68,104,125,128,137,143,145,149,254,261,293,301,309,312,328, 330,338,342,352,353,358,359,361,373,386,401,414,456,470,478
affectionately	293
affinity	149
affirmation(s)	81,205,250,310,483
affliction(s)	140,293,329,345,346,394,399
agape	116,123,148,155,157,158,159,329,396
agenda	37,66,98,221,498,548
AIDS	142
Alexander	198,549
almsdeeds	232,374
anarchy	205,410
Anna	204,447,469
apathy	32,35,40,495
apology	22,78
apostasy	67,185,210,220,410,411,418,419,425,457,462
application	40,68,80,121,164,196,402,460
appointment	89,90,92,97,180,226,240,273,437
arrogance	177,189,202,204,244,481
asceticism	131
assurance	52,77,106,107,121,167,428,431
atonement	108,110,464,564
attention	25,38,41,44,47,120,139,173,243,253,283,285,286,291,295,333, 375,399,401,402,406,483

attitude(s)	68,140,154,155,168,169,172,173,186,190,204,265,268,269,307, 309,310,314,318,326,339,340,353,357,376,395,422,424,492
authoritative	31,51,53,69,72,75,90,99,155,175,193,206,246
authoritatively	409,431
authority	20,26,27,28,31,32,41,42,44,46,50,51,52,54,57,63,67,68,69,70,73, 75,76,77,78,79,81,84,85,86,87,88,91,99,112,130,131,134,135,136, 146,155,163,164,165,166,167,169,172,174,176,179,180,182,183, 184,187,192,193,194,198,199,201,202,203,206,207,210,211,212, 213,216,217,219,220,221,222,223,232,234,235,236,237,244,245, 247,248,252,254,258,283,294,298,299,304,305,312,313,316,318, 320,321,323,344,345,354,378,381,390,393,399,416,422,423,424, 429,437,451,454,460,463,465,471,474,482,483,484,486,487,490, 491,492,493,496,498,552,565
Bastion	43
battleground	83,494
behaviour	30,43,91,105,130,162,171,175,189,202,211,222,224,234,240,244, 261,266,269,274,280,282,285,298,313,316,317,333,336,340,343, 350,353,360,367,369,370,374,376,392,396,397,482
behavioural	135
benchmark	83
bereavement	344,347,349
birth	31,150,258,284,285,291,301,349,358,428,459,463
bisexual	96
breasts	289,290,310,323
Career success	42
career(s)	286,294,330,345
carnal	157,280,421
carnality	421
celibacy	131,146
ceremonies	386
challenge(s)	26,30,35,40,47,54,79,202,305,312,324,326,327,330,361,369,398, 410,411,444,457,482,494,499
challenged	27,30,98,224,344,365,454,492
challenging	27,34,36,334,360,413,483
channel(s)	228,280
character	46,73,76,86,105,121,152,156,173,231,264,266,268,269,276,286, 291,322,335,337,353,354,355,358,359,360,368,376,379,389,403, 436,437,442,443,459,481,484,499
characterise(d)	37,152,246,280,299,351,376,383
characteristic(s)	96,134,140,165,174,175,281,283,316,369,374,375,383,385,398, 483,484
charity	86,137,148,174,191,192,200,230,232,237,247,260,261,282,283, 284,285,329,361,367,368,395,396,406
chaste(n)	200,234,241,282,293,296,297,299,303,361,372,373,396

chastened	181
chastening	299
chastity	99,136,141,178,281,304
child birth	59,88,284
citadels of error	100
civil	143,147,162,193,320,351
civil partnerships	319
civilisations	342
cloning	319
codes	264
cohabitants	322
cohabitation	64,96,136,350
cohabiting	137
commandment(s)	21,23,58,66,75,107,118,132,136,149,196,206,208,254,260,264, 282,287,298,302,316,328,343,344,423,428,429,430,443,489,562
commission	35,182,197,240,253,365,387,407,421
commissioned	86,420
commitment	31,53,70,117,118,138,139,233,304,314,338,357,455,478,480
committed	22,62,64,119,139,173,175,196,220,223,273,278,299,305,308,352, 379,395,397,427,451,470
companion(s)	58,62,115,123,124,125,126,127,128,133,148,151,162,180,232, 356,451
companionship	115,137,138,159,162,288,291,292,314,331
compassion(s)	95,240,252,301,308,329,335,348,351,362,387
compassionate	348
complacency	35,216,352
compromise(s)	21,40,78,117,122,170,209,248,252,260,313,315,350,354,357,411, 416,455,474,490,494
compromised	163,282,319
compromising	314,330,492
conduct	45,54,73,76,112,168,177,178,188,193,198,201,202,209,211,212, 222,224,233,251,266,274,280,292,293,303,313,333,342,350,353, 354,358,361,366,367,370,379,422,425,478,482
conducted	498
conducting	223
confession(s)	52,53,69,75,76,149,209,216,217,363,374,392,395,405,425,429, 450,451,452,549,554,555,562
confidence	28,41,46,47,54,74,90,108,115,212,292,341,361,371,384,430
confident	66,122
confidentiality	351
confidently	26,129
conflict(s)	59,122,135,246,358,371,378,383,421,430,490
conflicting	29
confusion	50,64,69,71,72,73,162,175,178,183,227,272,313,321,327,349,438, 456,485,492,496
congregation(s)	47,48,85,90,167,168,170,173,185,186,195,218,225,233,252,269, 273,274,313,329,330,395,406,446
congregational	36,490,497

consanguinity	149
conscience(s)	91,106,107,132,133,139,141,188,204,210,217,236,269,276,336, 348,349,353,355,357,371,425,450
consensus	215,217,320
constitution	193,283
consummation	288,291
contention	168,241,333,457
contentment	162,247,279,296,322,327,329,330,338,358
controversialist	267,381
controversies	53,393
controversy	37,38,44,53,54,65,184,201,209,213,496
contumacy	188
conversation(s)	73,157,195,227,234,241,295,333,336,353,372,377
conviction(s)	20,27,29,34,44,46,47,54,74,76,78,81,99,201,249,254,266,268,380, 381,382,386,410,415,463,479,481,486,487
convinced	67,278,450
counsel(s)	28,131,168,170,185,186,197,198,251,259,262,272,273,280,325, 383,403,417,431,457,479,491
counsellor(s)	308,452
courtesy	113,318,487
covenant	24,63,73,90,110,133,139,144,147,148,150,173,191,218,242,256, 258,271,309,312,316,436,446,453,462,467,473,475,498,549,562
covenantbreakers	342
covenanters	28,76,104,209,249,382,444,474,565
covenanting	460
creation	42,55,56,58,64,66,70,82,85,87,96,97,98,102,115,125,126,128,133, 142,153,154,155,158,161,163,164,175,178,179,183,191,201,207, 219,238,239,240,247,255,274,283,297,309,320,343,396,428,463, 465,493,498
creational	61,343
cultural	44,79,183,214,224,238,247,346,416
culturally	40,222,276
culture(s)	91,93,135,154,222,294,340,341,415,457,470,482,484,489
Dangers	37,230,341,356,370,403
death	69,88,97,104,108,116,132,142,147,148,149,150,239,285,286,304, 318,341,342,346,347,348,349,365,436,450,456,464,465,477,499
Deborah	199,204,231,294
declaration	75,80,184,457
declension	34,40,69,168,184,248,313,319,320,416,462,494,495
defence	48,78,80,212,214,249,452,457,459,462,468,491
definition	94,143,148,156
defraud	116,146,289
delinquent	142,272
delusion(s)	32,183,421
demeanour	172,173,203,243,285,369,376
democracy	185

denominations	45,185,206,217,381
dependence	56
deportment	232,244
depraved	109
depravity	64,104,212,239,277,314,390,463
desertion	129,148
design	42,44,47,60,63,65,66,85,94,95,116,138,139,164,175,176,179,182, 205,222,237,238,239,244,245,248,279,312,320,321,353,423,473, 483,493,556
designed	58,60,65,86,96,113,116,139,177,193,247,312,313,321,399,483
despot	156
devices	47,69,82,92,202,281,429
devotion	20,22,173,200,243,271,286,382,477,480,486
devotional	489
dictator(s)	156,275
dictatorship	88
dignity	40,42,55,63,102,103,160,162,194,214,248,286,316,329,354,367, 376,423,497
discernment	94,227,270,285
discipleship	26,76,240,273,308,423,427
disciplinary	195
discipline(s)	21,26,70,131,135,140,188,196,232,261,266,273,279,280,296,297, 298,299,300,303,304,321,352,360,375,382,408,429,451
disciplined	90,141,188,266,304,369,409,416
discrimination	32,94
disobedience	59,73,122,127,134,203,205,212,216,239,262,328,413,418,427, 428,495,496
disobedient	65,139,171,215,342,423
dispensation	282,442
dispute(s)	32,71,206,212,246,392
dissention	261
distinction(s)	54,55,61,82,87,90,91,96,98,177,178,179,195,224,313,316,399,486
distinctive	26,44,88,96,98,128,142,160,165,174,225,260,277,382,457,498, 560
distinctively	57,242,459,470
distortion	55,59,68
distribution	348,406
divorce	141,146,148,201,349,481,549,553
domination	55,64,97,246
duties	119,129,147,156,207,235,240,263,272,279,290,292,296,313,354, 362,366,397,466
duty	76,81,92,100,131,132,133,168,188,191,192,197,214,235,244,248, 254,261,271,286,291,296,298,303,304,313,345,361,374,388,399, 400,406,414,418,423,479,496
Ecclesiology	272
ecstasy	116

ecumenical	26,31,93,185,196,248,455
ecumenism	50,69,70,411,416
edification	72,261,262,464
education	19,48,94,111,162,271,344,352,353,373,459,462,468,469,470,471
effeminacy	171,178
emancipation	179,283
embrace(s)	44,106,134,135,137,147,289,290,437,451,
embraced	398,451,459,466
employee(s)	313,357,362,379
employer(s)	313,357,362,378,379
encourage(d)	28,30,32,42,48,54,68,78,96,122,170,198,202,234,242,251,286, 347,349,366,370,395,404,406,423,454,460,462,473,483
encouragement	24,25,26,27,28,47,191,219,330,349,387,390,464,476,478
endeavour(s)	46,162,163,293,321,329,335,350,381,387,391,466,471,478
endeavoured	47,177,419
endeavouring	83,260,477
entertainment	78,185,387,415,429
enthusiasm	27,28,47,337
equal(s)	40,55,58,63,64,65,66,86,87,90,94,96,126,127,144,152,207,208, 214,217,218,274,284,321,340,351,463,483,488,491,493
'equal sex'	228
equally	63,64,164,208,217,218,366
eros	123,155,157,158,159
erotic	158
erotic love	116,139,157,158
error(s)	25,32,51,75,78,100,144,149,167,184,197,198,212,221,242,261, 262,268,272,275,342,375,419,421,442,459,482
ethics	352,376,462,560
Eunice	200,294,295,401
Euodia	232
euthanasia	319,346
evangelical(s)	21,29,40,41,43,44,75,188,202,208,209,212,222,248,250,276,340, 416,419,429,453,454,455,457,459,460,462,471,495,496,552, 554
evangelicalism	197,214,415
evangelism	19,44,86,196,234,317,459,466,556
evangelist(s)	192,195,199,293,303,326,441,443,,564
evangelistic	293,443,444
evolution	37,201
examination	75,289,311,490
exegeses	27,31,34,213,381,486,556
exegesis	214,460,471
exegetical	35
exhortation	27,65,168,187,191,241,268,273,298,299,304,326,353,376,384, 389,411,466
exhorted	79,113,206,248,370,374,375,382,388,493
expediency	193,196,238
exploitation	64

exposition	25,26,27,381,471,478,554,558,559,560
expositor	26,553,558
expository	21,44,78,429,464,556,560,561
expounding	78
Federation	185
fellowship	19,24,26,28,31,48,102,103,109,114,134,151,199,207,219,240,260, 288,292,328,329,330,349,392,406,418,470,473
feminine	26,55,175,224,242
feminism	37,38,64,82,92,94,95,97,155,160,171,197,222,346,411,416,493
feminist(s)	26,31,41,43,54,64,71,83,91,93,94,95,96,97,98,99,126,171,179, 180,212,233, 248,283,294,296,313,320,341,360,490
fidelity	37,61,147,235,304,315,356,377,379,383,455,457,471
flirtation	140
flirting	329
fornication	64,136,137,139,302,314,328,342
fornicators	136,144,334
foundation(s)	29,53,54,69,70,74,81,145,218,259,279,280,300,301,302,320,337, 360,427,464,473,481,482,493,550
foundational	47,83,142,169,205,323
four daughters	232,303,469
freedom	93,96,119,135,155,240,285,374,391,392,495
friend(s)	27,28,41,47,86,115,170,205,267,275,291,301,312,329,331,332, 333,335,348,353,355,356,360,417,470,486
friendly	329
friendship(s)	25,31,116,137,138,140,151,152,279,288,291,329,355,356
fundamental	37,54,83,84,156,196,197,209,213,242,277,306,309,419,422,457, 472,487,492
Gay marriages	143,319
gay partners	96
Gemara	440
gender	37,96,179,181,197,222,224,319,342,489,490,492
genealogy	97
generation(s)	21,25,40,41,46,54,57,66,67,74,75,99,113,168,176,184,212,213, 220,242,259,262,287,295,297,315,367,368,382,400,401,412,413, 415,416,423,430,434,478,481,495,
gifts	55,61,66,103,113,114,126,135,154,183,191,238,247,249,250,268, 270,275,287,325,330,331,361,371,441,456,462,464,483,
glamour	173,286
godliness	46,120,135,172,174,189,190,233,239,241,243,244,248,251,256, 261,280,285,324,330,335,337,338,369,393,398,405,411,414,427, 456
government(s)	21,35,62,89,96,184,186,193,195,209,218,274,276,277,286,290, 313,319,320,340,341,416,421,429
governmental	406

grandparents	292,400,401
guidance	19,26,27,81,117,120,145,190,225,233,236,291,333,389,421,440, 456,466,477,478,485
guidelines	89,117,136,371
Hannah	285,295
happiness	38,93,94,128,139,152,238,247,287,288,291,301,316,322,324,330, 338,428
harmonies	145
harmonious	113
harmoniously	206
harmonising	366
harmony	58,62,113,145,148,156,159,180,193,195,211,246,260,288,290, 293,314,397,474,477,554
Hebrew(s)	110,191,302,462,469,550,553,562
help meet	24,87,115,117,124,125,126,128,129,142,154,164,238,245,297
helper(s)	58,62,66,115,124,126,127,154,155,229,238,292,297,316,338
helpmeet	58,60,62,63,87,115,117,123,124,125,127,133,136,137,152,155, 156,271,283,298,299,322
heritage	20,112,138,181,186,220,275,310,319,320,421,449
hermeneutics	27,556,561
heterosexual(s)	61,96,350
humankind	86
hierarchy	185
hindrance	87,127,189,371
holiness	86,102,105,112,131,217,234,237,240,247,248,260,268,276,282, 283,284,285,287,292,295,302,303,313,326,369,370,387,388,390, 391,395,396,412,416,426,456
homophobia	319
homosexual(s)	96,143,322
homosexualism	64
homosexuality	143,149,201,314,319,342
hospitality	86,88,91,92,189,200,229,232,266,267,332,335,403
household salvation	25
Huldah	199,204
humanism	411,455,491
humanist(s)	320,341,498
humanistic	41,424,489,496
humanity	86,96,148,365,463
humility	20,65,132,160,172,173,189,235,243,248,252,268,270,272,275, 276,292,303,336,370,378,387,476,495
Hymenaeus	198
Illuminating	34,120
illumination	106,120,
illustration	250,300,492

immoral	96,141,142,171,173,265,402,425
immorality	98,410,481
immortal(ity)	300,343,365
impropriety	265
incest	143,314
incestuous	149
inconsequential	165
indifference	68,243,262,319
inequality	126,167,170,181
inerrancy	28,67,69,81,201,212,214,344,419,454,463,471
inerrant	19,20,27,31,41,43,52,79,99,154,201,276,407,459,466,470,478,493
infallibility	67,206,213,220,471
infallible	20,22,27,28,41,43,50,52,53,55,67,72,76,79,81,99,100,112,188, 195,201,211,212,215,258,276,382,393,437,459,463,466,470,478, 482,498
inferior(s)	21,55,58,78,87,164,170,208,213,231,247,285
inferiority	98,102,115,200,213
infidelity	148,149,244,350
influence(s)	26,75,95,155,201,216,226,234,244,248,283,285,286,293,317,341, 353,361,375,381,410,422,424,444,445
influenced	95,201,341
inheritance	20,114,253,378,382,415
injunction(s)	156,235,311,363,377,379,442
innocence	103
inspiration	27,28,52,53,55,67,69,76,77,201,211,212,253,344,429,437,441, 443,454,455,463
inspired	19,20,31,35,4352,72,79,81,99,154,168,184,211,219,224,256,263, 313,358,391,407,437,440,446,466,478,493
institution(s)	62,69,70,79,95,96,97,98,125,128,136,147,194,205,246,259,277, 278,309,384,442,450
instructing	48,65,172,231,267,366
instruction(s)	31,41,52,72,102,103,117,126,136,166,168,180,194,201,211,213, 240,253,260,262,268,277,280,299,300,301,319,321,352,364,366, 367,377,390,395,430,455,479,485
instructive	34,299,491,495
integrity	152,226,265,269,307,339,347,357,358,362,379,432,456
intellectual pride	93,183
intercession	106,321,356,387,464
intercourse	133,136,138,145,288,292,315
interpretation	27,30,40,72,100,210,212,236,237,376,393,492,498
intimacy	115,139,147,288,291,292,309
investment	294,323
issues	37,41,42,46,47,65,71,81,201,215,220,222,247,272,283,303,304, 318,360,392,423,424,487,488,489,493,494,496,499
'Jack of all trades'	186
Joanna	228

Jochebed	285,486
judgement(s)	120,173,176,181,190,214,239,242,277,298,299,300,338,368,393, 398,413,417,428,464
Knowledge	21,22,24,27,46,65,70,73,79,102,104,105,106,107,111,113,120, 121,158,187,190,197,204,207,227,240,252,256,262,268,272,280, 289,306,320,323,326,342,352,359,366,368,369,388,394,417,420, 422,429,433,441,466
Lecturer(s)	19,471
lecturing	24,48
legacy	223,318
legislation	96,217,319,340
lesbian(s)	96,143,322
lesbianism	64,143,149,201,319
liberal	37,43,69,94,196,275,276,320,416,459
liberalism	37,41,50,69,70,416,462,491
liberality	345
liberally	190,227
liberation	41,43,93,154,165,171,180,204,287
liberty	50,66,77,131,132,150,160,168,217,354,371,384,390,392,453
Lois	200,295,401
loyalty	22,75,116,145,259,292,330
lusts	143,169,184,198,285,305,342,353,355,359,404,405,410
Lydia	200,229,230,232,303
MacLachlan, Margaret	239
maintenance	194,384,404,466
manhood	54,55,96,296,558
mankind	43,54,55,75,77,84,85,93,99,102,104,105,129,136,144,177,238, 297,314,315,329,334,391,417,427,430,483,493
manual(s)	264,437,440,443,492,564
marital fidelity	315
marital love	117
marital sex	136
Martha	303,327,331,332,333,335,356,398
Mary	127,204,220,228,231,303,327,331,332,333,335,398,447
masculine	55,175,224
matrimony	133,297
messengers	164,254
minister(s)	19,25,27,45,46,48,70,86,90,168,175,181,184,186,187,188,189, 191,192,193,196,199,200,204,210,215,216,218,219,221,231,233, 236,237,246,251,252,253,263,264,265,268,270,275,308,382,383, 384,390,396,409,415,419,429,446,462,471,495
ministered	132,228,486
ministration(s)	191,274,406

538

ministries	55,63,86,183,229,234,403,458,459,460,461,466,468,489,495
ministry	19,20,24,26,34,45,48,69,72,78,86,88,89,90,91,119,184,194,195, 197,199,207,209,210,212,213,223,225,226,227,229,232,233,234, 250,263,264,269,271,274,277,293,326,248,348,372,387,415,446, 459,462,466,469,470,472,483,486,549,554,563
Miriam	199,204,294,303,327,486
misconduct	163,171,177,350
Mishnah	440
misogyny	38
missionary	48,127,424,444,457,459
modesty	99,160,173,177,191,236,243,353,396
monachism	132
monarchy	89,185
monasticism	132
monogamy	129
morality	43,96,99,123,130,134,135,140,265,315,320,482,496
movement(s)	26,30,31,41,54,83,93,95,97,154,165,171,185,193,196,204,233, 248,283,294,313,444,455,490
Multi-faith	319
mutual attraction	158,246
mutual love	125,140,145,147,153,304

N.T. Greek Bible:	
Textus Receptus	21,549
novice	91,189,269

O.T. Hebrew Bible:	
Masoretic Text	20,549
obedience	31,34,35,41,44,47,49,51,53,69,72,74,85,87,106,112,118,135,183, 203,204,210,221,233,244,251,260,263,264,274,278,280,287,292, 293,298,308,314,316,320,331,360,366,370,379,386,390,414,416, 422,423,427,428,430,475,476,484,487
obedient	68,112,121,126,175,216,234,271,282,293,303,304,314,330,357, 372,373,374,377,388,430
obediently	412
obey	26,35,41,44,48,62,64,72,107,149,154,168,173,174,180,196,197, 200,215,216,217,228,241,242,244,253,260,264,277,280,287,297, 303,304,305,307,310,316,343,352,361,365,371,374,378,379,386, 389,399,419,420,421,423,424,425,427,428,430,457,496
obeyed	36,52,72,179,194,196,206,217,241,250,305,314
obeying	76,134,170,259,273,280,307,314,343,424,496
objection	224,441
objectionable	274
obligation(s)	21,98,100,160,168,196,241,253,313,316,371,400
observance	21,112,386,436,441
omission	421

opposition	19,206,288,312,319,337,430,464,474,477,490
oppression	283,284,452
oracles	80,215,363,409,443
ordained	55,61,128,129,133,136,146,147,149,155,162,171,183,194,205, 209,210,213,215,219,251,283,309,318,398,404,437,472,564
ordinance(s)	32,83,98,128,132,153,155,156,161,292,297,298,343,429
organisation(s)	37,79,155,176,194,218,259,263,284,351,
origin	69,142,179,190,289,443,557
original	30,53,102,105,129,133,146,150,156,178,246,400,429,438,440,492
originally	20,201,219,381,459,463
originated	130
originating	248
ornament(s)	162,174,179,234,241,242,244,379,499
orthodoxy	209,214
oversight	89,181,189,219,225,276,277
Parents	25,58,105,117,142,143,149,153,286,287,288,292,293,295,296, 297,299,300,304,306,310,318,323,342,373,400,401,402,427,447, 483
parliament	319
partner(s)	96,101,116,117,118,134,139,142,144,146,147,150,158,274,289, 292,295,312,316,318,346,349
partnership	57,58,64,117,291,319
passion(s)	150,244,285,353
pastoral care	349,459
pattern(s)	40,54,61,62,70,98,99,117,127,135,142,155,169,175,182,195,223, 224,228,235,249,260,269,271,274,276,277,310,311,315,321,327, 341,348,352,372,375,430,498
patterned	212,274,442
paucity	190
penalty	94,464
perfection	128,131,152,218
permissive	95,320,456,481
permissiveness	342
persecution	211,231,239,368,498,561
perseverance	19,107,273,295,339,360,361,384,473
persevere	20,35,212,287,306,359,398
personhood	56,102,309,497
persuasion	20,52
perverse	28,198,261,262,269,280,315,366
perversity	64,67
Phebe	86,200,228
phileo	123,155,157,159
philosophy	43,95,99,248,459
physical love	147,158
physical pleasure	289
piety	174,303,400,451,477,479,555

pilgrimage	20,220,368
plenary	67,201,463
pluralism	70,416
plurality	88
political	31,38,79,94,202,410,497
political correctness	31
political society	79
politics	185,284,424
polygamy	130,143,314
pornography	64,319
possession	107,231,269,338,437
posterity	128,136
practical	25,26,27,34,35,47,76,78,121,135,136,140,190,263,294,310,316, 320,329,335,349,354,381,384,388,401,403,404,406,411,462,482, 485,558
practice(s)	20,21,27,29,30,35,36,40,44,45,47,50,51,52,53,54,55,62,68,70,71, 72,76,79,81,83,120,121,131,135,140,145,147,168,170,175,177, 179,180,183,185,193,198,201,209,212,215,217,224,226,228,247, 249,255,269,276,314,317,319,323,342,345,350,355,366,381,382, 383,388,390,392,399,400,406,412,415,416,417,423,429,431,437, 456,460,462,463,465,471,477,482,485,493,496
preach	19,48,72,78,79,109,110,111,184,197,198,202,203,222,231,268, 269,272,274,381,382,384,409,417,419,420,422,457,460,462,466, 472,473,495,496
preached	44,51,80,110,165,194,347,443,460,470
preacher(s)	19,46,78,186,203,205,236,237,240,251,255,419,422,451,453,460, 462,466,472,473,479,555
preaches	120,186
preaching	21,24,29,44,48,69,77,78,90,111,185,188,190,202,204,206,207, 228,253,254,258,307,388,429,436,444,445,451,453,459,462,464, 466,470,472,478,479
precedence	167,210,264
pregnancy	285,290,291
principle(s)	22,26,27,34,41,47,53,56,58,69,71,72,78,81,82,83,84,85,93,97,100, 102,114,118,129,131,138,154,161,163,164,171,172,175,176,179, 183,194,207,210,211,215,217,219,223,224,226,229,238,241,251, 253,273,274,286,295,301,308,309,313,321,323,325,346,355,356, 357,359,362,371,378,383,398,405,412,422,423,424,427,437,451, 458,465,470,473,478,480,482,485,487,490,492,493,494,495,496, 498,561,565
Priscilla	229,231,237,303
proclaim(s)	31,76,81,180,186,197,203,205,236,253,255,341,420,466,484,497
proclaimed	253,460
proclaiming	19,21,45,205,313,407,431
proclamation	48,253,262,407,409,425,455,462,468
procreate	146,314
procreation	129,139,162,289
profession(s)	94,174,233,244,305,338,340,352,353,362,363,386,450

professional(s)	275,389,459,462
prohibition	132,178,179,203,223
promiscuity	98
prophesying	161,204,205
propitiation	108
prostitutes	243
prostitution	64,138,145,171,314,319
protection	113,124,125,164,200,235,239,247,350,399,402,465
providence	19,20,22,24,36,48,67,125,145,197,235,240,244,249,255,281,292, 305,322,325,328,329,332,391,394,405,410,444,446,463,465
providential	48,74,466
providentially	20,79
provision	84,152,308,309,321,346,355,399
prudent	155,281,293,368
pseudo-spirituality	112
punishment(s)	88,133,238,245,284,299,341,342,464
Qualification(s)	89,91,100,117,127,133,189,225,227,251,257,262,263,264,265, 268,271,274,275,397,403,564
Radical(s)	38,41,82,87,95,96,97,98,99,126,165,197,248,320,346
rape	64,314,350,496
Rebekah	312
rebellion	59,93,105,168,171,203,204,216,246,283,284,299,307,342,378, 413,418,421,422,431
rebellious	84,171,203,233,258,260,341
reconciled	104,119,254,306,307
reconciliation	105,106,110,119,307,348,436
recreation	334,359
redemption	24,63,84,105,107,108,110,121,217,240,255,385,392,453,463,465
reformation	21,27,33,34,36,44,67,69,77,111,202,262,320,388,411,412,413, 416,425,442,444,450,451,452,453,459,460,470,479,480,485,487, 495,496,497,556,563,565
regeneration	108,301,412,424,463
relation(s)	58,59,124,128,130,136,145,146,147,149,163,189,221,241,244, 265,275,309,347,353,354,355,414,425,496
relationship(s)	19,47,54,55,56,58,59,60,61,62,65,70,74,83,98,103,114,115,116, 117,118,126,127,128,134,137,138,140,145,146,149,154,155,156, 157,158,163,165,170,175,176,181,219,235,236,239,249,265,274, 279,285,289,290,291,296,297,299,306,307,309,310,311,312,313, 314,315,318,321,328,329,331,345,350,351,355,402,414,466,483, 494
relegation	70,228,258,423,437
religion(s)	29,36,43,53,73,97,130,174,176,216,292,301,329,341,358,386,393, 399,400,411,424,425,428,452,453,564,567
remission	108,225,284,465

repentance	34,35,65,106,107,108,185,216,220,261,267,341,354,407,408,411, 413,424,457,459,464,472,479,495
reputation	226,231,265,404
resolution	74,197,215,240,386,398
responsibility	25,55,56,57,58,60,61,64,66,127,138,143,168,180,185,186,188, 189,199,205,219,223,225,226,228,239,247,252,255,257,258,262, 264,265,269,271,285,286,288,296,302,311,316,345,357,396,399, 400,403,405,407,409,422,453,455,456,464,466
responsible	58,155,189,253,270,288,298,299,321,332,407,481,
restoration	59,105,106,413,414,425
restriction(s)	171,208,340
revelation	28,29,35,38,43,47,49,52,67,72,75,99,106,108,111,155,168,205, 206,232,241,249,263,310,391,409,428,430,456,482,490
reverence	22,62,72,88,138,150,162,233,249,280,303,305,311,318,331,336, 344,356,374,422,455,482
revisionist	29,237
revival	21,34,36,44,67,202,262,320,388,412,416,425,444,456,460,496, 497,564
revolutionary period	95
righteousness	19,35,40,52,71,73,76,83,102,105,107,108,109,112,118,119,134, 137,151,152,174,185,188,201,211,215,227,242,253,258,265,273, 280,287,313,320,338,349,359,380,390,392,405,408,410,411,412, 415,416,417,419,421,432,435,444,455,456,462,463
role(s)	26,29,30,32,34,37,40,41,42,43,44,45,46,53,54,55,56,57,59,60,61, 62,63,64,65,66,71,81,82,83,85,86,87,90,91,92,93,95,96,98,99,100, 115,153,154,155,163,164,165,170,175,176,180,182,183,188,193, 197,198,199,200,201,202,204,205,206,207,208,213,214,217,218, 219,220,221,222,224,225,228,233,236,237,238,239,240,245,246, 247,248,263,274,276,280,282,283,285,292,293,296,306,311,312, 313,314,316,321,354,381,396,401,407,410,423,425,431,480,483, 485,488,489,490,491,493,494,496,498,499
romance	157
romantic love	292
Ruth	402
Sabbath	21,79,132,305,352,445
sacrifice	105,112,213,216,260,273,280,294,307,442,464,465
sanctification	107,113,137,396,397,412,463
sanctity	133,157,179,314,353
Sara	179,241,314
Sarah	246,312
satisfaction	74,103,104,144,162,288,292,322,453
scandal	66
schism	250,261,464
seductions	141,183
selection	91,226,263
self-discipline	131,273

sensual	73,140,227,402
sensualism	183
separation	143,347,349,384,565
servant(s)	19,28,65,86,111,121,127,133,141,187,191,192,197,200,205,215, 216,228,254,267,270,273,275,276,302,305,338,356,357,358,364, 377,378,379,382,387,388,398,403,419,420,423,433,435,452,466
service(s)	19,20,24,26,37,66,69,74,90,112,127,173,183,185,192,193,198, 199,200,202,205,207,211,215,224,229,231,232,237,250,252,255, 263,270,271,272,273,275,287,303,314,317,333,336,338,352,356, 368,374,377,378,386,395,410,417,418,422,424,438,442,446,458, 459,462,463,466,469,471,472,473,475,477,479
sex relations	145
sexual abstinence	147
sexual attraction	138
sexual attractiveness	158
sexual desires	328
sexual expression	146
sexual fulfilment	314
sexual harassment	350,351
sexual immorality	98
sexual intercourse	315
sexual intimacy	139
sexual love	116,138,159
sexual permissiveness	342
sexual purity	315
sexual relations	136,146,147,149,309
sexual violence	351
sexuality	64,96,127,289,309,328,489
sexually attractive	329
social climate	30,475
social institution	70
social organisation	79
social problems	155
socialists	320
societal change	94
society	26,29,30,31,32,33,34,37,41,42,43,44,46,54,62,64,66,71,79,81,83, 84,85,92,95,97,98,99,100,121,135,137,140,141,143,145,147,148, 149,165,173,178,183,196,201,205,206,211,214,215,216,217,222, 228,244,245,248,279,280,282,283,293,294,305,309,310,312,315, 317,318,319,320,321,325,327,330,338,339,340,341,343,346,352, 367,372,395,396,419,424,425,428,430,431,451,456,470,481,483, 484,485,486,488,490,491,493,494,495,496,497,498,499
sodomy	319,496
solemnity	180
sorrow(s)	59,88,164,245,280,291,300,335,346,347,354,355,399,408,475,495
spiritual battle	26
spouse(s)	25,134,136,143,146,147,149,150,235,361,414,447

standard(s)	34,42,43,45,53,54,63,70,83,98,99,112,122,134,135,137,138,168, 177,185,189,202,209,211,217,227,242,248,264,271,275,290,313, 315,318,329,340,342,343,352,356,370,379,415,419,420,428,456, 457,481,482,485,491,496,497,554
status	65,90,127,208,209,216,283,285,319,327,329,422
stewardship	274
stigma	248,284
strategies	99
strategy	62,82,96,98,358
strong delusion	32
struggle(s)	24,47,124,295,406
subjection	81,84,86,88,91,130,133,162,179,189,190,195,199,203,210,219, 221,236,237,241,244,245,247,251,269,298,311,314,316,371,378, 386,390,396,423,463,488
submission	38,47,55,61,62,63,64,81,86,87,88,115,154,167,182,203,204,205, 219,228,229,232,234,235,246,247,274,283,311,312,314,318,321, 351,387,390,414,422,423,493
submissive	60,85,90,155,164,170,174,175,176,235,244,374,375,377
submissiveness	164,175
submit(s)	52,60,62,63,66,72,84,85,88,113,117,137,146,150,154,156,167, 175,176,180,211,218,232,234,235,236,276,305,306,310,311,313, 326,332,479,482
submitted	84,85,86,245,305,370
submitting	114,155,156,159,204,378
subordinate	70,127,154,170,238
subordination	84,85,115,129,130,133,164,165,176,237,247,321,373
sufficiency	19,24,28,212,213,220,277,331,412,416,476,478
superior	20,55,56,96,455
superiority	85,98,102,147,162,213
suppression	97
Sus-anna	228
sustenance	191
Suzanna	447,469
synagogues of Satan	100
syntyche	232
Talmud	440
teacher(s)	19,26,28,35,48,165169,181,183,184,195,198,199,203,205,207, 208,215,234,236,237,240,268,269,272,282,323,326,350,352,369, 371,404,419,424,459,469,471,564
teaches	32,41,42,48,68,94,103,118,178,188,191,197,199,205,208,214,228, 235,250,274,297,299,300,301,341

teaching(s)	20,21,24,25,26,30,32,34,35,38,40,41,42,46,47,48,52,54,63,64,65, 66,67,70,72,78,79,83,86,89,90,92,93,96,98,99,104,112,115,116, 117,118,121,137,140,154,155,156,159,165,166,168,169,170,177, 180,182,184,185,186,187,189,190,193,194,195,196,199,200,201, 202,203,204,206,207,208,209,211,212,213,215,217,219,221,222, 223,224,228,234,235,236,237,248,251,253,261,262,263,264,268, 271,272,274,276,277,278,290,295,300,305,309,312,313,330,333, 345,350,352,365,366,368,376,381,382,384,388,390,396,401,407, 415,416,419,422,423,425,429,430,436,438,443,451,456,457,459, 461,462,463,470,471,477,478,479,482,487,488,493,494,496, 498
temptation	65,103,112,139,141,147,168,173,178,243,300,346,367,370,373, 420
temptress	283
testimony	21,49,52,71,74,77,81,99,163,173,204,217,226,233,244,250,252, 255,260,264,265,270,280,290,302,336,357,362,410,422,429,443, 448,454,455,462,464,468,478,494
tolerance	44,70,258
tradition(s)	81,83,165,466,473,486
traditional family	95,98,99,325
traditional(ly)	29,43,70,95,99,171,197,212,222,320,
training	19,25,48,271,285,292,296,299,310,317,321,323,400,402,459,462
transgression(s)	94,103,104,105,205,226,237,238,245,247,283,352,408,420,421, 427
translated	53,59,90,157,158,172,179,199,203,207,233,246,247,294,312,318, 385,395,396,438,440,549
translations	20,70,78,419
transvestism	178
trustworthiness	76,78,210,361
trustworthy	75,78,151,271,344,378,379,397,430,455
tyranny	85,156,246,321
Unbelief	59,104,220,365,411,425
unbreakable love	318
uncompromising	20,79,185,453
uncompromisingly	185
undermine(s)	26,62,155,205,224,345,354,483
undermining	58,69,96,381,483
understand(s)	31,42,48,62,65,66,104,114,121,127,156,163,170,197,206,252,255, 262,263,268,277,292,300,320,323,335,408,441
understandable	46
understandeth	71,109
understanding(s)	27,28,30,31,38,41,42,46,47,48,53,54,55,64,66,68,76,80,81,93,102, 116,119,121,180,190,194,240,247,260,268,276,281,289,294,319, 322,323,328,331,342,349,358,373,388,420,433,434,435,440,441, 470,474,493
unequal yoke	151

unhappiness	134
uninspired	437,438
union	61,65,97,113,117,118,123,125,133,134,139,142,143,150,156,288, 293,316,346,481
unity	47,60,61,70,76,88,93,114,129,130,148,156,159,252,260,318,326, 381,463,464
usurp	59,86,130,176,183,199,203,204,207,217,219,220,221,222,237, 245,246,247,312,354
usurpation(s)	55,78
usurped	238
usurping	155,234,237,294
Veracity	58,68,80,470
vessel(s)	26,65,101,112113,114,137,174,231,237,312,368,398
vigilance	28,387
violence	74,155,267,351,410,481
virgins	141,232
virtues	26,61,148,244,286,379,380,395,398
virtuous	153,174,279,281,354,361,373,398
virtuously	282
vocation	24,35,54,313,337,370
vows	117,149,150,157,215,216,316,404
Watchword	28,122
wedding	24,128,147
wedlock	118,133,142,147,153
well-being	21,152,156,346,498
whoremongers	143,149,310
widow(s)	90,135,191,197,208,230,239,273,297,307,329,332,346,399,400, 402,403,404,405,406
widowed	258,329
widower	265,346,403
widowhood	399
wifehood	322
Wilson, Margaret	239
wisdom	23,29,30,37,38,41,48,62,65,73,77,81,91,97,120,132,151,152,162, 167,180,190,193,211,217,225,227,240,252,254,260,263,268,270, 276,281,300,306,319,321,322,333,336,346,359,361,368,370,393, 398,407,410,421,431,435,438,443,457,475,482,490
witnessed	45
witness(es)	20,24,25,26,40,44,47,48,52,79,80,81,100,110,118,127,164,174, 178,181,188,200,201,205,212,223,232,234,247,249,254,255,260, 261,287,292,295,306,317,319,335,343,356,357,361,362,363,366, 371,374,385,386,387,388,391,405,409,415,418,431,444,449,456, 463,466,477,478,479,486,494
witnessing	208,217,294,339,361,362,363

womanhood	42,54,55,94,96,162,165,205,214,243,283,296,398,493,554,558
Women's Lib	95
Women's Liberation	43,93,154,165,171,204
women's movement	30
workforce	352,353,355
workplace	26,34,41,42,44,46,66,81,121,211,339,340,350,352,353,354,357, 359,360,361,362,363,425,483,486,491,493,496,499
worship(s)	21,34,73,78,80,87,90,100,103,132,138,161,162,163,164,167,170, 171,172,173,177,188,195,196,198,199,202,205,207,221,222,223, 224,229,236,237,238,240,243,244,263,264,287,292,305,307,317, 334,343,352,384,387,388,395,396,412,416,419,429,430,436,437, 441,442,443,444,451,453,456,459,462,463,464,470,472,478,564
worshipers	177,240,343
worshipped	143,342,445
worshipping	132,218,243,336
Youthful lusts	137
Zeal	19,28,215,249,317,324,335,337,338,456,457,466,471,479
zealous(ly)	79,196,317,352,373,452

BIBLIOGRAPHY

J. E. Adams — *Christian Living in the Home*
Presbyterian & Reformed, Phillipsburg, 1972

Marriage, Divorce and Re-Marriage in the Bible
Presbyterian & Reformed, Phillipsburg, 1980

J. A. Alexander — *The Psalms Translated and Explained*
Evangelical Press. Welwyn, 1975

O. T. Allis — *The Five Books of Moses*
Presbyterian & Reformed, Philadelphia, 1942

J. Anderson — *The Ladies of the Covenant*
Blackie & Son, Glasgow, 1850

Arudt & Gingrich — *Greek Lexicon of the New Testament*
Cambridge, 1957

Augustine — *The Confessions*
Liveright, New York, 1943

S. Bagster — *Analytical Greek Lexicon*
Bagster, London, 1870

J. Bannerman — *The Church of Christ*
Banner of Truth, Edinburgh, 1960

A. Barnes — *Barnes Notes*
Baker, Grand Rapids, 1998

J. Barr — *The Semantics of Biblical Languages*
University Press, Oxford, 1961

R. Baxter — *The Reformed Pastor*
Banner of Truth, Edinburgh, 1974

L. Berkhof — *Systematic Theology*
Banner of Truth, Edinburgh, 1958

The Bible League — *Truth Unchanged, Unchanging*
The Bible League, Abingdon, 1984

Bibles	Hebrew:	*The Hebrew & Chaldee Old Testament*, Masoretic Text
	Greek:	*The Greek New Testament*, Textus Receptus
	English:	*The King James Authorised Version*, 1611

Black & Rowley
Peake's Commentary on the Bible
Nelson, London, 1962

H. Blamires
The Christian Mind: How Should a Christian Think?
Servant Books, Michigan, 1963

H. Blocker
In the Beginning
I.V.P., Leicester, 1984

L. Boettner
Studies in Theology
Presbyterian & Reformed, Philadelphia, 1967

J. M. Boice
Foundations of the Christian Faith
Inter Varsity, Leicester, 1986

Standing on the Rock
Kregel, Grand Rapids, 1994

A Bonar
Christ and His Church in the Book of Psalms
Tentmaker, Stoke-on-Trent, 2001

H. Bonar
Words to Winners of Souls
Chapel Library, Pensacola

T. Boston
Complete Works
Tentmaker, Stoke-on-Trent, 2002

C. Briggs
The Christian Ministry
Banner of Truth, London, 1959

J. D. Brooke
Major Doctrines of the Christian Faith
Brooke, Newburg, 1982

Brown Driver & Briggs
Hebrew Lexicon of the Old Testament
Clerendon, Oxford, 1959

F. F. Bruce
Paul: Apostle of the Heart Set Free
Eerdmans, Grand Rapids, 1999

H. Bullinger
Works
Reformation Heritage, Grand Rapids, 2004

A. Cairns	*Dictionary of Theological Terms* Ambassador, Belfast, 1998
	A Sure Foundation Ambassador, Belfast, 1996
J. Calvin	*The Institutes of the Christian Religion* Eerdmans, Grand Rapids, 1948
	Commentaries Baker, Grand Rapids, 1998
Capper & Williams	*Towards Christian Marriage* I.V.F., London, 1960
	Heirs Together I.V.F., London, 1956
Carson Moo & Morris	*An Introduction to the New Testament* Apollos, Leicester, 1992
L. S. Chafer	*Systematic Theology* Victor, Wheaton, 1998
A. C. Cheyne	*Studies in Scottish Church History* Clark, Edinburgh, 1999
G. H. Clark	*What Presbyterians Believe* Presbyterian & Reformed, Phillipsburg, 1965
A. Cruden	*Complete Concordance of the Old and New Testaments* Lutterworth, London, 1955
R. D. Culver	*Systematic Theology* Mentor, Fearn, 2005
W. Cunningham	*Historical Theology* Banner of Truth, Edinburgh, 1960
	The Reformers and the Theology of the Reformation Banner of Truth, Edinburgh, 1967
R. L. Dabney	*Systematic and Polemic Theology* Zondervan, Grand Rapids, 1972
A. B. Davidson	*The Analytical Hebrew and Chaldee Lexicon and Syntax* Edinburgh, 1932

Davidson Stibbs & Kevan	*The New Bible Commentary* I.V.F., London, 1958
J. H. M. d'Aubigne	*History of the Reformation of the Sixteenth Century* Sprinkle Publications, Harrisonburg, 2000
	The Authority of God Carter, New York, 1851
Day One	*The Bible Panorama* One Day Publications, Leominister, 2005
J. Denney	*Studies in Theology* Hodder and Stoughton, London, 1895
J. Dickinson	*The True Scripture Doctrine* Presbyterian Board, Philadelphia, 1853
D. Dickson	*The Psalms* Banner of Truth, Edinburgh, 1959
J. D. Douglas (Ed.)	*The New Bible Dictionary* Inter Varsity Press, London, 1962
J. M. Dryerre	*Heroes and Heroines of the Scottish Covenanters* John Ritchie Limited, Kilmarnock, Scotland
B. H. Edwards	*Nothing But The Truth* Evangelical Press, Darlington, 1993
	Men, Women and Authority Day One, Kent, 1996
J. Edwards	*Works* Banner of Truth, Edinburgh, 1986
W. A. Elwell (Ed.)	*Evangelical Dictionary of Theology* Baker, Grand Rapids, 1991
	Baker Encyclopaedia of the Bible Baker, Grand Rapids, 1988
P. Erb	*The Alpha and the Omega* Herald Press, 1956

M. J. Erickson	*Concise Dictionary of Christian Theology* Baker, Grand Rapids, 1985
L. R. Eyres	*The Elders of the Church* Presbyterian and Reformed, Phillipsburg, 1980
P. Fairbairn	*The Pastoral Epistles* Banner of Truth, Edinburgh, 2002
Ferguson & Wright	*New Dictionary of Theology* I.V.P., Leicester, 1988
R. A. Finlayson	*A Just God and a Saviour* Knox, Edinburgh, 2002
Free Church of Scotland	*Report on Marriage and Divorce*, 1988
The Free Presbyterian Church of Scotland	*The Free Presbyterian Magazine*, Various Numbers *The Young People's Magazine*, Various Numbers *History of The Free Presbyterian Church of Scotland*, Free Presbyterian Publications, Glasgow, 1933 and 1973
S. Foh	*What is the Woman's Desire?* Westminster Theological Journal, 1975 *Women and the Word of God* Presbyterian and Reformed, Phillipsburg, 1980
F. E. Gaebelein	*The Expositor's Bible Commentary* Zondervan, Grand Rapids, 1990
J. L. Garrett	*Systematic Theology* Eerdmans, Grand Rapids, 1990
N. L. Geisler	*Baker Encyclopaedia of Christian Apologetics* Baker, Grand Rapids, 1999
W. Gesenius	*Hebrew-Chaldee Lexicon of the Old Testament* Bagster, London, 1846
J. Gill	*The Cause of God and Truth* Baker, Grand Rapids, 1981

R. B. Girdlestone	*Synonyms of the Old Testament* Baker, Grand Rapids, 1983
T. Goodwin	*Works* Tanski, U S A., 1996
R. Gordon	*Christ in the Old Testament* Free Presbyterian Church of Scotland, Glasgow, 2002
A. Graham	*Womanhood Revisited* Christian Focus, Fearn, 2002
A. Green	*Lectures on the shorter Catechism* Presbyterian Board, Philadelphia, 1841
J. B. Green	*Harmony of the Westminster Presbyterian Standards* Reformation Heritage, Grand Rapids
C. L. W. Grimm	*Greek Lexicon of the New Testament* Clark, Edinburgh, 1914
H. J. Grimm	*The Reformation Era* Macmillan, New York, 1973
W. Grudem	*Systemic Theology* Zondervan, Grand Rapids, 1994 *Countering Claims of Evangelical Feminism* Multnomah, Publishers, Colorado, 2006
R. Haldane	*Exposition of the Epistle to the Romans* Banner of Truth, London, 1960
P. Hall	*The Harmony of the Protestant Confessions* Still Waters Revival Books, Edmonton, 1992
H. H. Halley	*Bible Handbook* Oliphants, London, 1960
Harrison (Ed.)	*Baker's Dictionary of Theology* Baker, Grand Rapids
Hatch & Redpath	*Concordance to the Septuagint* Oxford, 1897

W. Hendriksen	*Survey of the Bible* Evangelical Press, Welwyn, 1976
	New Testament Commentaries *1 and 2 Thess., 1 and 2 Tim. and Titus* Banner of Truth, Edinburgh, 1991
M. Henry	*Commentary on the Whole Bible* Hendrickson, Peabody, 1992
	Complete Works Baker, Grand Rapids, 1979
H. Heppe	*Reformed Dogmatics* Wakeman, London, 1950
D. Hilliard	*Britain Awake* Abbey, Belfast, 1995
A. A. Hodge	*Outlines of Theology* Nelson, Edinburgh, 1891
	The Confession of Faith Banner of Truth, London, 1958
C. W. Hodge	*Systematic Theology* Eerdmans, Grand Rapids, 1970
	Commentary on the Epistle to the Romans Banner of Truth, London, 1972
	The Church and its Polity Nelson, London, 1879
A. A. Hoekema	*Created in God's Image* Paternoster, Carlisle, 1994
	Saved by Grace Paternoster, Carlisle, 1994
J. A. James	*An Earnest Ministry* Banner of Truth, Edinburgh, 1993
	Female Piety Soli Deo Gloria, Morgan, 1994

S. James	*God's Design for Women* Evangelical Press, Darlington, 2002
H. Jahn	*Exegeses of the Bible* World Bible Publishers, Iowa Falls, 1993
Jamison Fausset & Brown	*Commentary on the Whole Bible* Oliphants, London, 1961
E. E. Johnston	*Expository Hermeneutics* Academie, Grand Rapids, 1990
O. Jones	*Some of the Great Preachers of Wales* Tentmaker, Stoke-on-Trent, 1995
R. Jones	*Does Christianity Squash Women?* Broadman & Holman, Nashville, 2005
R. T. Jones	*The Great Reformation* Inter Varsity, Downers, 1985
Keil & Delitzsch	*Commentary on the Old Testament* Hendrickson, Peabody, 2001
Kircher	*Greek Concordance* Augsburg, 1602
John Knox	*The Church and the Reality of Christ* Collins, London, 1963
R. B. Kuiper	*The Glorious Body of Christ* Eerdmans, Grand Rapids, 1958
	God-Centered Evangelism Banner of Truth, Edinburgh, 1966
E. W. Lane	*Arabic Lexicon* London, 1863-77
D. M. Lloyd-Jones	*Studies in the Sermon on the Mount* I. V. P., London, 1960
	The Epistle to the Romans Banner of Truth, Edinburgh, 1985

	The Epistle to the Ephesians Banner of Truth, Edinburgh, 1978
M. Luther	*The Bondage of the Will* Clarke, London, 1957
J. MacArthur	*Different by Design* Chariot Victor Publishing, Eastbourne, 1994
R. M. McCheyne	*New Testament Sermons* Banner of Truth, Edinburgh, 2004
McClintock & Strong	*Cyclopaedia of Biblical, Theological and Ecclesiastical Literature* Baker, Grand Rapids, 1981
A. T. B. McGowan	*Women Elders in the Kirk* Christian Focus, Fearn, Scotland
J. G. Machen	*What is Christianity?* Hodder & Stroughton, London, 1925
	The Origin of Paul's Religion Macmillan, New York, 1925
D. Macleod	*A Faith to Live by* Mentor, Fearn, 1998
	Behold Your God Christian Focus, Fearn, 1995
J. Macleod	*Scottish Theology in Relation to Church History since the Reformation* Banner of Truth, Edinburgh, 1974
J. Magill	*The Englishman's Hebrew Concordance* Zondervan, Grand Rapids, 1974
T. Manton	*Works* Nesbitt, London, 1874
W. Metzger	*Tell the Truth* I.V.P. Downers Grove, Illinois, 2002
D. M. Miller	*The Topical Bible Concordance* Lutterworth, London, 1947

	Topical Concordance of Vital Doctrines Lutterworth, London, 1955
B. Milne	*Know the Truth* Inter Varsity, Leicester, 1982
E. N. Moore	*Our Covenant Heritage* Christian Focus, Ross-Shire, 2000
Moulton Geden & Moulton	*A Concordance of the Greek Testament* Clarke, Edinburgh, 1978
C. F. D. Moule	*An Idiom Book of New Testament Greek* Cambridge, 1959
J. Murray	*Collected Writings* Banner of Truth, Edinburgh, 1982
W. R. Nicoll	*The Expositor's Greek Testament* Hodder & Stroughton, London, 1912
E. M. Osterhaven	*The Faith of the Church* Eerdmans, Grand Rapids, 1982
John Owen	*Works* Banner of Truth, Edinburgh, 1965-68
I. R. K. Paisley	*An Exposition of the Epistle to the Romans* Marshall, Morgan & Scott, London, 1968
W. Pannenberg	*Systematic Theology* Eerdmans, Grand Rapids, 1991
D. Pawson	*Leadership is Male* Highland Books, Guildford, 1988
R. A. Penney	*A Faith for the Times* Puritan, Proprint, Peterborough, 2002
A. W. Pink	*Practical Christianity* Baker, Grand Rapids, 1974
J. Piper & W. Grudem	*Recovering Biblical Manhood and Womanhood* Crossway Books, Wheaton, 1991

M. Poole	*A Commentary on the Holy Bible* Banner of Truth, Edinburgh, 1974
R. P. Church	*Testimony of the Reformed Presbyterian Church of Ireland*, 1912
	Testimony of the Reformed Presbyterian Church of Scotland, 1932
D. A. Reid	*The New Topical Text Book* Oliphants, London, 1964
R. L. Reymond	*A New Systematic Theology of the Christian Faith* Nelson, Nashville, 1998
H. Ridderbos	*Paul: An Outline of His Theology* Eerdmans, Grand Rapids, 1975
L. J. Roberts	*Let Us Make Man* Banner of Truth, Edinburgh, 1988
S. Rutherford	*The Trial and Triumph of Faith* Banner of Truth, Edinburgh, 2001
J.C. Ryle	*Churches Beware!* Evangelical Press, Darlington, 1998
	Home Truths Triangle Press, Conrad
Sabbath School Society of Ireland	*Child's Catechism* Strule Press, Omagh
G. Salmon	*Introduction to the New Testament* Murray, London, 1889
S.A.R. of China	*The Story of Robert Moffat* Achieve Printing, Hong Kong, 2006
P. Schaff	*The Creeds of Christendom* Baker, Grand Rapids, 1998
	History of the Christian Church Hendrickson, Peabody, 2002

S. Scott	*The Exemplary Husband* Focus, Bemidji, 2000
R. Shaw	*The Exposition of the Confession of Faith* Christian Focus, Lochcarron, 1973
W. G. T. Shedd	*Dogmatic Theology* Klock & Klock, Minneapolis, 1979
	Homelitics and Pastoral Theology Banner of Truth, London, 1965
R. Shelly	*Written in Stone: Ethics for the Heart* Howard, West Monroe, 1994
A. Smellie	*Men of the Covenant* Banner of Truth, Edinburgh, 1960
J. Smith & M. Smith	*Concise Bible Concordance* Hodder & Stroughton, London, 1970
N. H. Snaith	*The Distinctive Ideas of the Old Testament* London, 1994
R. C. Sproul	*The Intimate Marriage* Living Books, Wheaton, 1986
	Scripture Alone Presbyterian & Reformed, Phillipsburg, 2005
	The Invisible Hand Word Publishing, Dallas, 1996
C. H. Spurgeon	*Expository Encyclopaedia* Baker, Grand Rapids, 1996
	The Treasury of David Hendrickson, Peabody, U S A
A. H. Strong	*Systematic Theology* Judson Press, Valley Forge, 1907
J. Strong	*Extensive Concordance of the Bible* Zondervan, Grand Rapids, 2001
	Greek Dictionary of the New Testament Abingdon & Cokesbury, New York, 1890

F. A. Tatford (Ed.)	*The Faith* Ritchie, Kilmarnock, 1999
M. C. Tenney (Ed.)	*The Zondervan Pictorial Encyclopaedia of the Bible* Zondervan, Grand Rapids, 1975
Tentmaker Publications	*Sermons in times of Persecution in Scotland* Tentmaker, Stoke-on-Trent, 2003
M. S. Terry	*Biblical Hermeneutics* Academie, Grand Rapids, 1988
J. P. Thackway	*Worldliness* Quarterly Record, Trinitarian Bible Society, 2006
J. H. Thayer	*Greek Lexicon of the New Testament,* 1886
G. Thomas	*Philip and the Revival in Samaria* Banner of Truth, Edinburgh, 2005
R. C. Trench	*Synonyms of the New testament* MacMillan, London, 1880
Trueman Gray & Blomberg	*Solid Ground* Apollos, Leicester, 2000
S. Ullmann	*The Principles of Semantics* Oxford, 1957
M. F. Unger	*Bible Dictionary* Moody, Chicago, 1988
A. Vale (Ed.)	*Our National Life* Monarch, London, 1998
W. A. VanGemeren	*Dictionary of Old Testament Theology and Exegesis* Paternoster Press, Carlisle, 1997
M. R. Vincent	*Word Studies in the New Testament* Hendrickson, Peabody, U S A.
T. Vincent	*The Shorter Catechism* Banner of Truth, Edinburgh, 1980

W. E. Vine	*Expository Dictionary* Nelson, Nashville, 1997
G. Vos	*Biblical Theology* Banner of Truth, Edinburgh, 1975
J. G. Vos	*A Commentary on the Larger Catechism* Presbyterian & Reformed, Phillipsburg, 2002
	The Scottish Covenanters Crown & Covenant, Pennsylvania, 1940
B. B. Warfield	*Biblical and Theological Studies* Presbyterian & Reformed, Philadelphia, 1976
T. Watson	*A Body of Divinity* Banner of Truth, London, 1958
	The Beatitudes Banner of Truth, Edinburgh, 1971
	The Ten Commandments Banner of Truth, London, 1965
N. Weeks	*The Sufficiency of Scripture* Banner of Truth, Edinburgh, 1988
D. F. Wells	*No Place for Truth* Eerdmans, Grand Rapids, 1993
Westminster Divines	*The Confession of Faith*, 1643-47
	The Larger Catechism, 1648
	The Shorter Catechism, 1648
Wigram	*The New Englishman's Hebrew Concordance* Hendrickson, Peabody, 1984
G. I. Williamson	*The Shorter Catechism* Presbyterian & Reformed, Phillipsburg, 1970
	The Westminster Confession of Faith Presbyterian & Reformed, Philadelphia, 1964
W. Wilson	*Hebrew Concordance* Mackintosh, London, 1866

T. Witherow	*The Apostolic Church* Adshead, Glasgow, 1955
C. H. H. Wright	*Pocket Concordance and Bible Guide* Pickering & Inglis, London
E. J. Young	*Thy Word is Truth* Eerdmans, Grand Rapids, 1957
	An Introduction to the New Testament Tyndale Press, London, 1960
R. Young	*Analytical Concordance to the Bible* Lutterworth Press, London, 1939
Zondervan	*Expanded Concordance* Oliphants, London, 1968
R. B. Zuck	*Rightly Divided* Kregel, Grand Rapids, 1996

Other Published Works by the Author

1. **The Power, Passion and Purpose of Prayer**
   "Pray without ceasing",
   (1 Thess. 5 v.17)

2. **Reformation Today**
   Does the Evangelical Church need Revival?

3. **The Crisis in Contemporary Preaching**
   What Lessons can we Learn?

4. **An Appreciation of John Calvin**
   500th Anniversary

5. **The Eighteen Fifty-Nine Revival**
   A Brief Overview

While stocks last, copies available from:

P.O. Box 55
57 Parkmore
Townland of Balteagh
Craigavon
County Armagh
BT64 2AE
Northern Ireland
United Kingdom

Other Theses and Dissertations by the Author

The Call, Qualifications and Work of the Christian Ministry
Apostles, Prophets, Evangelists, Pastors and Teachers

The Atonement of Christ
The Biblical Theology of Apostolic Preaching Essential to True Religion and Worship

The Biblical Basis and Practice of Worship
The Substance, Structure, Style and Setting of Worship

The Present Crises in Protestantism
A Return to New Testament Christianity and the Simplicity of the Apostolic Church

The Psalter: The Book of Praises
The Inspired and Ordained Manual of Praise

Biblical Protestantism and Roman Catholicism Forever Apart
Evangelical Christianity and the Divine Principle of Separation

The Covenanters and the Revolution Settlement
The Crown Rights and Royal Prerogatives of Christ Jesus over Church and Nation

The Bible and the Reformation
Sola Scriptura: The Sole Authority in all matters of Doctrine and Practice

The Life and Times of Oliver Cromwell
The Man, and the Task that lay before him

Samuel Rutherford: The Saint of the Covenant
A Man of Spiritual Stature and Valiant in Leadership

Patrick: The Apostle of Ireland
The Man, His Message and Mission

The Church and the Means of Grace
Ekklesia --- called out --- the Body of Christ

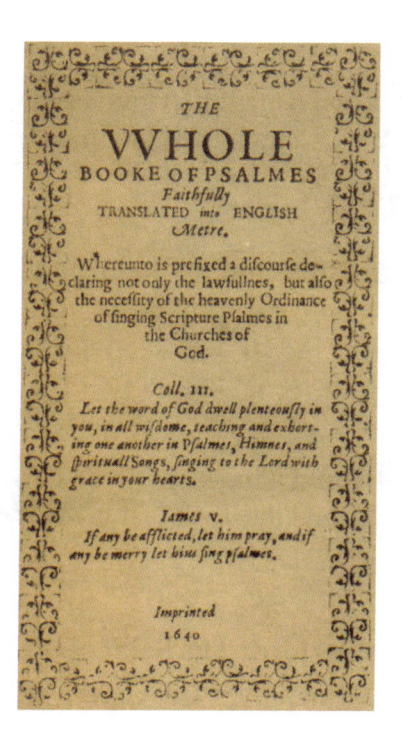

The Book of Psalms in Metre, Bodleian Library, Oxford
(Printed in Great Britain at the Oxford University Press)

Transcript of above inscription

THE WHOLE BOOK OF PSALMS
Faithfully TRANSLATED into ENGLISH Metre.

Whereunto is prefixed a discourse declaring not only the lawfulness, but also the necessity of the heavenly ordinance of singing Scripture Psalms in the Churches of God.

Col. 3 v.16
"Let the Word of Christ dwell in you richly in all wisdom; teaching and admonishing one another in psalms and hymns and spiritual songs, singing with grace in your hearts to the Lord".

James 5 v.13
"Is any among you afflicted? let him pray. Is any merry? let him sing psalms".

Imprinted

1640

John Calvin, William Farel, Theodore Beza and John Knox

with other Reformers, Geneva

Calvin College, Geneva

John Calvin 1509-1564
The Geneva Reformer

Calvin's Chair

Martin Luther (1483-1546) studying the Scriptures
'The Monk who shook the World'

"Unless I be convinced, by Scripture, I neither can nor dare retract anything ..... My conscience is captive to the Word of God. There I take my stand, I can do no other. So help me, God".

John Knox 1505-1572
Scottish Protestant Reformer

John Knox's house, Edinburgh

The Martyrs' Memorial, Oxford

HUGH LATIMER 1491-1555
The Uncompromising Warrior of the Reformation

NICHOLAS RIDLEY 1500-1555
The Fearless Stalwart of the Reformation

THOMAS CRANMER 1489-1556
The Courageous Counsellor of the Reformation

Burned at the stake on the orders of 'Bloody' Queen Mary

Bunyan Meeting House, Bedford

John Bunyan's Statue, Bedford

John Bunyan, 1628-1688
Author of 'The Pilgrim's Progress'

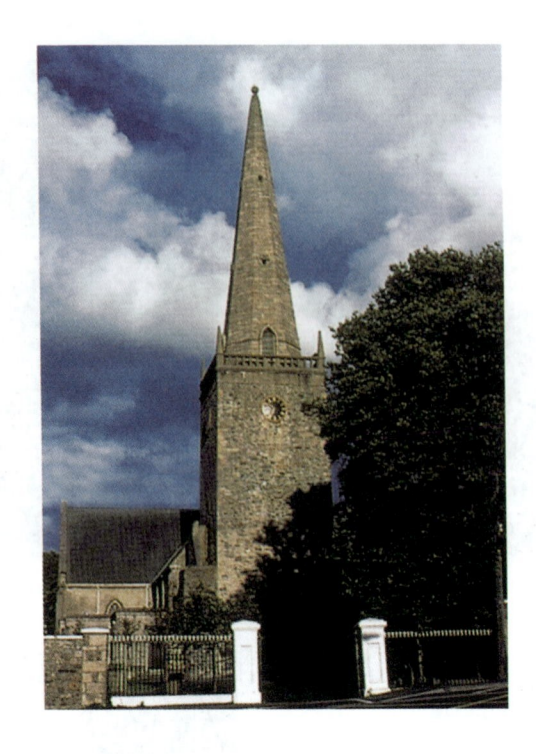

BANGOR ABBEY CHURCH
Scots Covenanter, ROBERT BLAIR (1593 - 1666)
ministered here for many years.

At the beginning of the seventeenth century a great number of Scots ministers were driven out of Scotland because of their loyalty to Covenant Engagements. Seeking immunity from persecution, they crossed over to Ulster, and with magnaimous courage and single-hearted devotion to the Lord Jesus Christ, unfurled the banner, "For Christ's Crown and Covenant".

For the clear propagation and witness of the Gospel, a succession of many gifted ministers from Scotland, settled in Ireland, who were not ashamed to "earnestly contend for the faith which was once delivered unto the saints", (Jude v.3). Among them was one Robert Blair, who ministered at the above Church in Bangor, County Down. He faithfully visited the twelve hundred souls under his care, and with other ministers established a witness for truth and righteousness, of which the National Covenant was a declaration to defend the "true religion" as revealed in Holy Scripture.

In the midst of fiery opposition many Covenanters were martyred for the faith, others survived the days of persecutuion, perpetuated the Covenanting testimony, and consolidated the basis from which the Covenanter Church grew. What Blair did at Bangor, Brice at Ballycarry, Cunningham at Hollywood and Donegal, Livingstone at Killinchy, Dunbar at Carrickfergus and Larne, Hamilton at Ballywalter, Welsh (grandson of John Knox) at Templepatrick, Stewart at Donegore, Glendenning at Carnmoney, Crookshanks at Raphoe, McCormac at Magherally, Pedden at Kells, Houston at Armoy and Dervock, and many others, for the cause of Christ, only the last great Day shall fully declare.

The Church's mission in every age is to preach the Gospel of sovereign grace, proclaim the truth of God's Word, and to publish the doctrines of the Christian Faith as revealed in Scripture far and wide. Nothing less is adequate to revive the Church that has largely lost its way, or to meet the need of a sin-sick world. (1 cor. 1v 17-21).

As servants of Christ we are to go "and teach all nations .... teaching them to observe all things whatsoever I have commanded you", says Christ, (Matt. 28 v19-20). The implications of the Gospel for family, social, and community life will be manifested in purity, sobriety and humility, "that ye walk worthy of the vocation wherewith ye are called" (Eph. 4 v.1), submitting to the Lordship of Christ in every part of life, according to the pattern set forth in the Word of God, the Bible.

Let us pray that the Spirit of God will awaken His people in our generation to a new reformation and revival. May the torch of Scripture truth be rekindled among us to bear clear and uncompromising testimony for Christ against all apostasy and defection from God's Holy Word.

Our forefathers paid an enormous price in sacrifice, privations, and persecutions, even martyrdom, to secure and perserve for us the benefits of civil and religious libert, so that we might enjoy the freedom and privileges of the glorious Gospel. We need to be aroused from on High, to perform our duty in the positions of life to which Providence has called and placed us. With renewed devotion and dedication to the Saviour, may we love, follow, and serve Christ with all our heart, and soul, and strength, and mind, to the glory of God.

MANORHAMILTON CASTLE, COUNTY LEITRIM

The above castle was built by Sir Frederick Hamilton around 1630. He was the major leading figure in the Scottish settler community of County Leitrim. He signed the Covenant, and later died in Scotland in 1647 where he was serving in the Covenanter army. In April 1644, William Guthrie of Fenwick in Ayrshire (pictured above) wrote, "....There was a brave day in Ireland .... at the swearing of the Covenant in Belffast ....".

For Readers Notes

For Readers Notes